Benedict, Me and the Cardinals Three

William Martin Morris, DD

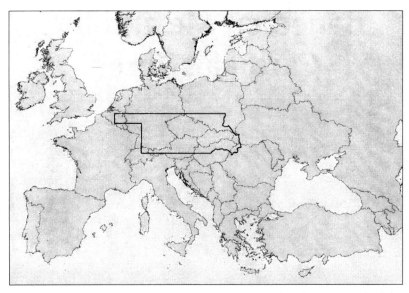

The Toowoomba Diocese covers 188,280 square miles, (488.000 sq km) an area larger than the state of California, over twice the area of Great Britain and over one a half times the area of Italy.

Benedict, Me and the Cardinals Three

The Story of the Dismissal of Bishop
Bill Morris by Pope Benedict XVI

William Martin Morris, DD

ATF Press

2014

National Library of Australia Cataloguing-in-Publication entry (pbk)

Author: Morris, William Martin, author.

Title: Benedict XVI me and the cardinals three : the story of
             the dismissal of Bishop Bill Morris by Pope
             Benedict XVI / William Martin Morris.

ISBN: 9781921511417 (paperback)
             9781921511424 (hardback)
             9781921511431 (ebook)

Notes: Includes bibliographical references and index.

Subjects: Morris, William Martin.
             Benedict XVI, Pope, 1927-
             Papacy–Vatican city–Relations–Australia.
             Catholic Church–Doctrines–Criticism, interpretation, etc.
             Catholic Church–Bishops–Dismissal of.

Dewey Number: 262.122

Reprinted 2014
Fourt Reprint 2014

Cover artwork by Fiona McLaren
Cover design by Astrid Sengkey
Layout/Artwork by Anna Dimasi

Text Minion Pro Size 11

Published by:

An imprint of the ATF Ltd.
PO Box 504
Hindmarsh, SA 5007
ABN 90 116 359 963
www.atfpress.com

The Church is at its best when it is most transparent, when the eyes of justice and the eyes of the Gospel are so clear that all rights are respected for individuals, no matter who they are in the community.
William M Morris

CONTENTS

Appendices

Index

Acknowledgments

The writing of this book would not have been possible without the support and encouragement of the Priests, Pastoral Leaders, Parishioners of the Toowoomba Diocese, my family and the many friends and supporters throughout Australia and the World. I would like in particular to thank the College of Consultors who journeyed with me in the formidable years before my retirement. I am grateful to members of the Council of Priests and the Diocesan Pastoral Council, the Heads of all Diocesan Bodies for their generosity of spirit, their commitment to all projects undertaken by the Diocese and for their friendship. The Heads of Churches and members of the Ecumenical Pastoral Care Team have always been an inspiration and encouragement to me. I gratefully acknowledge the guidance and assistance of the publishers, editors and all who have contributed to the completion of this book. This project could not have been completed without the selfless service of Josephine Rice, whose dedication and hard work made the task of researching and typing of this book possible.

I dedicate this book to my Toowoomba diocesan family who loved me in ministry and continue to love me in life, empowering me to continue to serve.

William M Morris
May 2014

Photo taken during Vatican II
from left to right
1. Archbishop Guilford Young
2. Bishop Francis Rush
3. Fr Salgado OMI
4. Archbishop Owen McCann, Capetown South Africa,
   who was later Cardinal

Foreword

Hans Küng

No one who cares about the well being of the Church and about justice for its members will remain indifferent toward the book by Bishop William Morris, in which he explains the history of his conflict with the Vatican. I am sincerely grateful to Bishop Morris for initially resisting all pressure and for now revealing in a detailed report the actions of the Roman bureaucracy against human rights.

When one recalls the order of events, one has the following impressions:

- From the very beginning, the bishop had to deal with a small group of opponents and whistle blowers who had no backing to speak of in the diocese, but found a willing ear in Rome at the Holy See.
- When the bishop was not intimidated, the Vatican nominated an Apostolic Visitator who consulted the various groups, but obviously later gave a report which the bishop in question never saw.
- Soon, the invitation for a voluntary resignation arrived which the bishop rejected for reasons related to his conscience.
- The entire procedure of Vatican activities which lacked any transparency for the accused bishop, would be unthinkable in any law abiding government.
- An unbiased discussion of the bishop's pastoral issues were never on the agenda, instead pressure to voluntarily resign from his office was constantly increased.
- In each phase of this development Bishop Morris responded with calm and reason and fortunately resisted all attempts to pressure him. Without a doubt, he was supported in all steps by formidable advisers.

- The Roman officers of the Curia were clearly not interested in taking seriously the views of the vast majority and the clerics of the diocese.
- The highest court of the Apostolic Signatura refused to take a legal stance and relegated the responsibility back to the conference of bishops.
- Pope Benedict seemed decided in his view from the very beginning and he pointed out to the bishop that he would be unable to appeal his judgment.
- He refused to discuss the ordination of women and the recognition of Anglican orders and awaited the resignation of the bishop which he had not promised.

I note my personal impressions of these sad events from the personal trajectory of being a recipient of a similar Roman process. This looks all too familiar: It stands in contradiction to the most fundamanetal rules of 'due process' and Human Rights as laid down in the General Declaration of Human Rights from 1948. The breaking of these rules is, among others, the reason why the Vatican cannot join the European Convention of Human Rights.

The Vatican law like the bank of the Vatican urgently requires radical reform. Countless men and women, priests, theologians, religious and bishops had to endure similar things. Many did not have the strength to resist to the end, but they bowed to force and remained unhappy. It is clearly a tragedy that the wellbeing of one bishop and one diocese was sacrificed on the altar of the doctrinal-legal Roman system.

If Pope Francis wants to help the poor, he should also show mercy and justice to those that have suffered under the constraints of the Roman system.

Tübingen, Germany, 20 January 2014

Preface

This is the story of my dismissal as the Catholic Bishop of the Diocese of Toowoomba, in Queensland, Australia. It relates, from my perspective, the dealings I had with various Congregations (Dicasteries) of the Vatican's Curia in Rome and with certain cardinals and officials in those Congregations, as well as with Pope Benedict XVI, regarding pastoral activities and a letter I wrote to the diocese in Advent of 2006 while the Bishop of Toowoomba.

The book details the background and events which led to my being asked by Pope Benedict XVI to resign as Bishop of Toowoomba when I had a meeting with him in Rome at the Holy See on the 4th of June 2009.

I did not agree to resign, but negotiated with Pope Benedict to take early retirement which was announced on 2 May 2011.

The book is accompanied by various Appendices of documents and letters from this period, including several letters from cardinals at the Holy See and the pope. Some of the documents and the Appendices have already been published in various places or are in the public domain in some way. They are published here again so that these documents are all in one place.

The book has been written to give the story from my perspective of what happened in the lead up to my taking early retirement after refusing to resign. In the view of a number of civil lawyers, canon lawyers and theologians, both here in Australia and overseas, I was deprived of natural justice as I was in no way able to appeal the judgments or decisions that were made in these circumstances. This was made clear to me by the three cardinals at the Holy See with whom I had most contact over the time and by Pope Benedict XVI himself when we met in June 2009 and he said: 'It is God's will that you resign'. Then in a letter to me of 22 December 2009 he wrote: 'Canon Law does not make provision for a process regarding bishops, whom the Successor of Peter nominates and may remove from office.'[1]

I was denied natural justice and my reputation as a bishop of the Catholic Church was called into question and yet I could do nothing.

While now there is a new and different papacy under Pope Francis, the processes that culminated in my being asked to resign are still the same.

The events related in this book occurred some years ago. While for some this is all ancient history from which I should move on, it is important to stress that the book has not been written out of spite, or to restore my reputation. Nor has the book been delayed by anything other than my need for time to gather my thoughts together, to have the space and the energy to put pen to paper, and to gather the various documents into one collection. I have written the book so that people in the Diocese of Toowoomba and those many others who are keen to know the background to my dismissal should know the story, which I believe needs to be told, and that they should know it from me.

I wish to acknowledge, and thank, a number of my brother bishops in this country who wrote to the Vatican and to the papal nuncio in Australia appealing on my behalf at various stages during the years leading up to my dismissal and after it occurred. Others were in the background supporting me as best they felt they could or should, while there were others who did not. Then there are the many priests and religious, individuals and groups from Australia, and also from around the world, who came out in various ways to support me. I wish to acknowledge and thank them. Finally, I wish to acknowledge and thank all those people who have assisted me in putting together the writing of this book. I am indebted to them all.

---

1. For the full text of this letter see Appendix 16.

Chronology

The following is an overview of the history between Bishop Morris and the Roman Dicasteries prepared by Fathers Peter Dorfield, at the time the Vicar General and Peter Schultz, Diocesan Canonical Advisor. The full story is found in the following chapters.

- October 8, 1943: Born in Brisbane only son of William and Sylvia Morris. One sister Janice.
- June 28, 1969: Ordained Priest for the Archdiocese of Brisbane in St Stephen's Cathedral, Brisbane.
- January 1970 – 1973 appointed Associate Pastor, Our Lady of Lourdes Parish, Sunnybank, Brisbane.
- 1973 – January 1975 appointed Associate Pastor, St Joseph's Parish, Nambour, Queensland.
- January 1975 – January 1979 appointed Associate Pastor, St Agnes's Parish, Mt Gravatt, Brisbane.
- January 1979 – January 1985 appointed Secretary to Archbishop Francis Rush and Archdiocesan Vocation Director.
- January 1985 – July 1986 appointed Parish Priest of St Francis Xavier Parish, Goodna.
- August 1986 – January 1993 appointed Parish Priest of Sacred Heart Parish, Surfers Paradise, Queensland.
- November 1992: Announced as the new Bishop of Toowoomba. Succeeded Bishop Edward Kelly MSC, DD, who had retired in accord with canon 401 § 1 having completed his seventy-fifth year.
- 9 February 1993: Presented the Apostolic Letter of Appointment to the clergy of the diocese in a para-liturgy held at the James Byrne Centre, Highfields. All clergy signed a copy of the letter

to indicate their acceptance of William Morris as Bishop of
Toowoomba.

- 10 February 1993: Ordained bishop in St Patrick's Cathedral,
Toowoomba.
- Bishop Morris, immediately, proved to have a very different style
of leadership from previous bishops. The bishop encouraged
dialogue and collaboration. Among differences of approach
were:

> The creation of a Personnel Board to deal with
> appointments of clergy. This body consulted with the
> people of the parishes concerned and interviewed
> applicants before recommending the most suitable
> person for the position. In the past, appointments,
> apart from a few exceptions, were made on seniority of
> ordination.

> The bishop established a Diocesan Liturgical Commission
> to facilitate education and formation of priests and
> people in matters of liturgy.

> A Policy was established for initiation of children that
> returned the sacraments of confirmation and first
> eucharist to their ancient order.

> Guidelines for the use of General Absolution within
> the celebration of Communal Rites of Reconciliation
> were developed. These celebrations were generally well
> received and the prayerful participation of the laity was
> evident to all who presided at them.

> A Diocesan Assembly was called that resulted in the
> formation of a Diocesan Pastoral Council and the
> development of a Diocesan Pastoral Plan. There have
> now been several of these Assemblies, each designed to
> invigorate the pastoral life of the diocese and review and
> refine the Diocesan Pastoral Plan.

The bishop broke with tradition and wore a tie, embroidered with his coat of arms, rather than the Roman collar. The bishop offered each priest a black tie with the Diocese of Toowoomba 'Coat of Arms' and indicated that the wearing of the tie was to be considered clerical dress, along with the collar and the white shirt with crosses, the choice being left to the individual cleric.

- The bishop's relaxed and open style was welcomed by most of the diocese. However, there was a small but vocal minority who found fault with nearly every action he took and decision he made.

When a parish in Toowoomba was given to the junior applicant, and one considered by a small group of clergy to be radical, there were meetings of some clergy to consider action against the bishop.

Over time there was a growing campaign of letters of complaint from the minority of dissatisfied people. Most of these letters were sent directly to Congregations at the Holy See. Many of the letters concerned the use of General Absolution as one of the few areas where there might have been divergence between the practice of the diocese and the liturgical regulations.

- The issue of the use of General Absolution led to a dispute between the bishop and Cardinal Francis Arinze, Prefect of the Congregation for the Sacraments and Divine Worship. Some of this dispute took on a personal aspect.

- Despite all attempts to explain how the practice of the diocese fulfilled the requirements of canon and liturgical law and how it was becoming more and more necessary as clergy numbers decreased, and that the ordinary means of reconciliation was still the first rite of penance, the Congregation insisted that the practice cease. This demand was complied with in a gradual way so as not to distress people.

- 22 May 1994: Pope John Paul II promulgates the Apostolic Letter *Ordinatio Sacerdotalis* concerning the ordination of women and declares the conversation ended.

- 18 May 1998: Pope John Paul II makes additions to two canons of the Code of Canon Law in a *motu proprio: Ad Tuendam Fidem*. The additions to canons 750 & 1371 effectively make it an offence punishable in canon law for any of the faithful to discuss the possibility of the ordination of women. In the normal course of events the punishment would be decided by a tribunal and depending on the severity of the case could range from a censure to removal from office to excommunication; in the case of a cleric other penalties might include suspension or removal from the clerical state.

- The Synod of Oceania – 22 November-12 December, 1998.

- 2 May 2002: Pope John Paul II promulgates the *motu proprio Misericordia Dei* concerning the celebration of the Sacrament of Penance. The *motu proprio* essentially limited the use of General Absolution to extreme circumstances, for example, war and imminent threat of attack.

- Advent 2006: the bishop's Pastoral Letter made reference to the various discussions going on around the world as a result of the crisis in priestly vocations in the western world. The letter referred to discussions concerning: orders (deacons, priests and bishops) of other faith communities, and the ordination of married men and of women.

- In December 2006 the bishop received a letter, via fax, demanding that he attend a meeting with three Cardinals, Re, Levada, and Arinze, in the Congregation for Bishops at the Holy See. The letter was dated 21 December 2006. The meeting was to be held in February 2007 and possible dates were given. The bishop replied by letter, dated 22 December 2006, that he would be willing to meet but stated there were serious pastoral reasons why he could not be absent from the diocese at that time. He indicated that he would be in Rome in May 2007, representing the Australian bishops at an international Church meeting on professional standards and would be willing to meet the three cardinals at that time.

- In a letter dated 4 January 2007 Cardinal Arinze insisted that the issue was important enough that the bishop present himself in February as previously demanded.

- In a letter dated 17 January 2007 the bishop repeated his previous position.

- In March 2007 the bishop received notification that an 'Apostolic Visitor' had been appointed by the Congregation for Bishops and would undertake a Visitation in the near future. Archbishop Charles Chaput OFM Cap, from the Archdiocese of Denver in the United States, arrived for the Visitation on 23 April 2007. He spent the night with Archbishop Bathersby in Brisbane.

- On Tuesday 24 April 2007 the Apostolic Visitor arrived in Toowoomba, met informally with Bishop Morris, then met with the Council of Priests. He then began a series of meetings with various diocesan bodies, officials, priests, directors of agencies and people of the diocese. Prior to his arrival Archbishop Chaput had named various people, clergy, officials and groups, he wished to meet. Others were nominated by the bishop. There was a cross section of people and clergy of the diocese representing all levels of support and opposition to the bishop. On Wednesday and Thursday he travelled around the diocese and conducted interviews. The interviews resumed in Toowoomba on Friday and Saturday morning. After lunch with the bishop on Saturday midday the Visitor departed and prepared his Report, which was presented to the Congregation for Bishops by early May 2007, prior to the bishop's scheduled journey to Rome.

- After the Apostolic Visitor left the majority of the clergy and Pastoral Leaders of the diocese gathered to discuss what had happened. All except three priests signed a letter of support for Bishop Morris and these individual letters along with letters of support from the Pastoral Leaders and the Diocesan Pastoral Council were sent to the Congregation for Bishops.

- While Bishop Morris was at the Holy See in May 2007, no meeting with the cardinals took place, despite the fact that he had previously been summoned to meet with them and that the report of the Apostolic Visitor had been presented to the cardinals.

- The Report of the Apostolic Visitor has never been shown to the bishop.

- In September 2007 an unsigned memorandum, dated 28 June 2007, from the Congregation for Bishops was received by Bishop Morris. It concluded with a request for the bishop to resign.

- On 17 September 2007, the bishop indicated by letter, that he would reflect on the memorandum and reply after his October 2007 holidays.

- 3 October 2007: a letter from the Congregation for Bishops stated that the request for the bishop's resignation was being made in the name of the Holy Father.

- 6 November 2007: a letter from the bishop to Cardinal Re suggested collaboration and dialogue. The bishop stated he would provide a detailed answer to the memorandum as far as that was possible. The bishop stated he would be prepared to meet with the cardinals in January 2008 with Archbishop Philip Wilson, President of the Australian Episcopal Conference (ACBC) and with Archbishop Bathersby, Metropolitan of the Queensland Province, present with him at the meeting.

- In a letter dated 30 November 2007 Cardinal Re set 19 January 2008 for a meeting with the bishop and Archbishop Wilson. In this letter the Cardinal said he saw no reason for Archbishop Bathersby to accompany the bishop.

- On 27 and 28 December 2007, the bishop convened a meeting of several canon lawyers and bishops to advise him on how he could best respond to the memorandum and the Letter requesting his resignation. This Advisory Group consulted international canonists.

- In mid-January 2008, the bishop travelled to Rome. On 19 January 2008, the bishop met with Cardinals Re, Levada and Arinze in Rome at the Vatican. Archbishop Wilson was with him. The bishop had previously suggested he bring a canonical advisor with him to the meeting as well but was discouraged from doing so by Cardinal Arinze. The bishop also asked to speak with the Holy Father but was told this would only be permitted after he had resigned. His resignation was still being demanded by the cardinals.

- In a letter dated 24 January 2008 the bishop informed Cardinal Re that in conscience he felt unable to resign.

- On 8 February 2008 the Diocesan College of Consultors was convened and briefed by the bishop on the details of all that had happened since the Apostolic Visitation in April 2007 and in particular on the January 2008 meeting with the cardinals in Rome. Only those priests of the diocese in the Advisory Group had previously been aware of the bishop's meeting in January 2008 with the three cardinals.

- Cardinal Re replied to the bishop by letter dated 13 February 2008 and again called on the bishop to resign.

- On 21 February 2008, the Advisory Group was again convened by Bishop Morris. A formal and more developed 'Statement of Position' was prepared in response to the issues raised in the unsigned memorandum of September 2007. These issues had again been emphasised in the January 2008 meeting in Rome with the three cardinals. Once again they requested bishop Morris to resign.

- On 14 March 2008:

  The 'Statement of Position' was sent by Bishop Morris to Cardinals Re (Congregation for Bishops), Levada

(Congregation for the Doctrine of the Faith) and Arinze (Congregation for the Sacraments and Divine Worship). A letter was sent to the Supreme Tribunal of the Apostolic Signatura asking about the right to defence in this instance. (The Apostolic Signatura is the highest court in the Church and the last court of appeal, similar to the High Court of Australia.)

A letter was sent to the Pontifical Council for Legislative Texts, asking for a definition of what constituted 'grave cause' in canon 401 § 2. (This Pontifical Council provides definitive interpretation and definition of legal terminology in all Church law.)

A copy of correspondence sent to each of the Church officials and bodies above was also provided to the other Church officials and bodies.

- On 10 April 2008 the Apostolic Signatura replied saying it was not in their competence as no legal proceedings had taken place.

- In early September 2008, the new Apostolic Nuncio, Archbishop Giuseppe Lazzarotto, informed the bishop that Cardinal Re was still waiting for the bishop's reply. The bishop informed the Nuncio that he had already replied to Cardinal Re on 14 March 2008 when correspondence had been sent to several Roman bodies and officials and only the Apostolic Signatura had replied.

- On 13 September 2008 the Pontifical Council for Legislative Texts replied saying the interpretation of 'grave cause' in canon 401 § 2 was up to the Congregation for Bishops to discern.

- In a letter dated 23 October 2008, Cardinal Re demanded the resignation of the bishop by the end of November 2008 so that an announcement could be made in early January 2009. The letter stated that if the resignation was not forthcoming the bishop would be removed.

- On 19 December 2008 the bishop sent a letter to Cardinal Re, stating that in conscience he could not resign, and outlining his reasons for this position.
- On 24 December 2008 the bishop wrote directly to Pope Benedict XVI.

- In a letter dated 31 January 2009 the Pope wrote to the bishop inviting him to arrange an audience through the Prefect of the Papal Household, Archbishop James M Harvey.

- Archbishop Harvey wrote to the bishop on 10 March 2009 informing him that he and Archbishop Wilson would be received by the pope on 4 June 2009.

- The bishop met with the pope on the 4th of June 2009 with Archbishop Wilson, President of the Australian Catholic Bishops Conference, also in attendance. It was obvious that the pope had been briefed as he reiterated the demands of the three cardinals and indicated that the bishop's talents lay elsewhere than as the bishop of a diocese. The pope urged Archbishop Wilson to work with Bishop Morris to find him a suitable national position in the Australian Church. The bishop left the meeting saying to Archbishop Wilson that he had no intention of resigning as Bishop of Toowoomba.

- On 9 July 2009 Bishop Morris received a letter from Cardinal Re requiring him to submit his resignation as he had promised the pope he would do at their June meeting. The bishop maintained he had not made such a promise.

- On 12 November 2009 Bishop Morris wrote to the pope clarifying his position that in conscience he could not resign from office.

- On 22 December 2009 Pope Benedict replied to Bishop Morris requesting that Bishop Morris resign from office and reminding him that there is no appeal from papal decisions. The pope repeated the serious concerns he had with Bishop Morris's position on the ordination of women and recognition of the orders of Anglicans and other Churches.

- On 25 January 2010 the bishop gathered the College of Consultors with Brian Sparksman and Peter Schultz to update them as to the current situation. The bishop read the pope's December letter. The bishop also informed those present that Archbishop Wilson was currently in Rome and that he had taken with him a proposal that the bishop would retire when he reached the age of seventy (in October 2013). If this offer was not acceptable, the bishop was prepared to retire at an earlier date (in mid-2011) depending on the progress of a recent sexual abuse case in the diocese. [In a later letter to the Holy Father (8 December 2010), Bishop Morris would request more time in office, beyond mid-2011, to attend to the ongoing matters involved in responding to the families and children in the sexual abuse case.]

- On 6 February 2010, Cardinal Re wrote to the bishop, informing him that the pope had decided to accept the bishop's 'proposal', as presented by Archbishop Wilson, to remain in office until mid-2011 (May 2011) but made no reference to the bishop's condition of satisfactorily finalising the current sexual abuse case. While the bishop's offer was to 'retire', the letter used the term 'resign'.

- On 21 July 2010 the bishop wrote to the apostolic nuncio expressing his desire to remain in office beyond May 2011 due to the ongoing pastoral response necessary in the sexual abuse case.

- November 2010: at the Australian Catholic Bishops' Conference (ACBC) the apostolic nuncio informed the bishop his request was declined.

- 8 December 2010: the bishop wrote to the Holy Father informing him of the reasons why he wanted to remain in office beyond May 2011: primarily to deal with the pastoral ramifications of the sexual abuse case involving a former teacher at a parochial school.

- In a letter written on 21 February 2011 (with a typographical error in the dating: it was dated 2010), Archbishop Lazzarotto requested Bishop Morris to tender his resignation which would be effective immediately. The apostolic nuncio informed the bishop that the fact of his resignation would be announced on Monday 2 May 2011. In this same letter, Archbishop Lazzarotto informed the bishop that an 'Apostolic Administrator' would be announced the same day. The Appointment of an Apostolic Administrator removes from the College of Consultors their responsibility to elect a Diocesan Administrator in the event of a vacant See.

- On Friday 11 March 2011 the bishop called the College of Consultors together with Brian Sparksman and Peter Schultz to inform them of these developments.

- The bishop wrote to the Apostolic Nuncio on 15 March 2011 indicating that he had never wavered in his conviction that to resign is a matter of conscience and resignation would mean that he accepted the assessment of himself as breaking *communio*. But he accepts that on 2 May 2011 his proposal presented to the Holy Father and accepted by him for an early *retirement* will be announced.

- On 14 April the bishop met for the last time with the Consultors, Brian Sparksman and Peter Schultz, to tell them of his intention to send a letter to the Priests and Pastoral Leaders and a Pastoral Letter to the people of the diocese. All supported the bishop in this decision. This would mean that the diocese would first hear the news from the bishop and not from the media.

- On Wednesday 27 April 2011, the bishop sent a letter to all priests and pastoral leaders in the Diocese of Toowoomba informing them that he would be accepting early retirement on Monday 2 May 2011. The bishop included a Pastoral Letter to the people of the diocese to be read at all Masses on the weekend of 30 April and 1 May 2011.

- On Friday 29 April 2011, a reflection document on the bishop's early retirement, including this 'Summary History of Events', was sent by the Diocese of Toowoomba College of Consultors, to all priests, pastoral leaders, the Toowoomba Diocesan

Pastoral Council members, Toowoomba Diocesan Pastoral Administration Committee members, Diocesan Finance Board members, directors of diocesan agencies, and heads of churches (Anglican, Lutheran and Uniting) in the Toowoomba region.

1

Learning to Breathe

Brisbane Line: A Personal Story

Deep within you is written your own song. Sing it with all your heart.
William M Morris

Stories are like people, they come in different shapes, colours and sizes. Some are serious, filled with pathos, others are light-hearted, inviting laughter, some tell of relationships past and present, others speak of the past with a smile or a tear, some even try to predict the future. There are legends and fables, sagas and folklore, wives-tales and fairy tales. There is history and fiction, there are myths made up of all kinds of imagery, coloured by widely held but exaggerated beliefs that have become part of the folklore and fabric of life passed on from generation to generation, family to family, under which all of us are born.

I was born in Brisbane, the capital city of the State of Queensland, Australia, in the year 1943, when no building within the city could be higher than the tower of the city hall, and when controversy raged over 'The Brisbane Line'. This was believed to be a plan that, if an invasion of Australia did occur, as General Douglas MacArthur wrote in his memoir, *Reminiscences*, a line of defence following the Darling River from Brisbane to Adelaide would be established. The territory north of the Brisbane Line would be given away while the southern part of Australia would be defended. A Royal Commission was established to determine if such a plan existed. The Commission reported in July 1943 that there was no evidence supporting the existence of an official plan to abandon most of Australia to invading forces, but the myth lives on, or was it indeed a fact?

So my journey commenced in a family of four, surrounded by an extended family of many, with the worry of war but with the hope of

1

victory and peace. A happy childhood filled with love and play prepared me well to be schooled by Sisters of the Franciscan and Mercy kind, in brown and black, to be handed over to the Augustinians and later to the Christian Brothers with whom I completed my schooling. In my final year of schooling I had a strong desire to take up a profession that would be of service to the community. This idea, coupled with the fact that a number in my senior year were interested in following a vocation to the priesthood, was the invitation to ask questions which led eventually to my entering Pius XII Seminary at Banyo, a suburb of Brisbane, to commence my studies for the priesthood in February 1963. A journey that began in a culture and language that had eyes only for the past was to be transformed into a journey in a new culture and language with eyes also for the present as they looked at the Church's rich tradition with vision coloured by the lens of the Second Vatican Council. This was a renewalist, pastoral council seen by Pope John XXIII as a new beginning for the Church, a new Pentecost, where the only culture to be celebrated and the only language to be spoken would be those of love in a spirit of inclusiveness.

It was into this atmosphere of a new Pentecost that I emerged after my ordination in 1969, to be appointed assistant priest to Father Tom Hegerty at Our Lady of Lourdes Parish, Sunnybank, Brisbane. Tom was a larger than life character who had embraced Vatican II with infectious enthusiasm. Cardinal Joseph Cardijn was his hero and the Cardijn pastoral principle of See, Judge and Act became Tom's mantra in his work as Chaplain to the YCW (Young Christian Workers) and in all aspects of his ministry. He had a library that was the envy of many and a parish resource centre of books, tapes, audio visual aids and films unrivalled in the Archdiocese at that time. He was among those chosen to educate the Archdiocese in the documents of Vatican II. It was into this heady atmosphere of the lived teachings of Vatican II that I came in 1970 and for the next three years I was able to live, breathe and put into practice those teachings.

In 1979 my exposure to Vatican II continued. I was appointed Secretary to Archbishop Francis Rush, who was one of the last active bishops in Australia to have attended the Vatican Council. He was strong in his support for the Council of Priests, Parish and Diocesan Pastoral Councils, Liturgical Commissions, Catholic Education, Social Justice, Assemblies for Priests and General Archdiocesan Assemblies and was prepared to implement their findings. He was particularly clear in his understanding of his role as a teacher and he developed pastoral strategies to implement the philosophy and teachings of the Vatican Council. His model of Church was firmly based on the documents of Vatican II, especially its Dogmatic Constitution on the Church, *Lumen Gentium*. Herein, relationships within the Church were seen to be modelled on the mutual relationships of the divine persons within the Trinity; all lay people were called to participate in the mission of the church by virtue of their baptism; a local church was fully the Catholic Church in a particular place; a bishop's participation in the college of bishops came by virtue of his episcopal ordination.

The Archbishop held very strongly to the belief that the Church is the people of God, all having a role to play under the inspiration of the Spirit. On the completion of his theological studies in Rome, he had been ordained to the priesthood just before the election of Pope Pius XII and was present in St Peter's Square with thousands of others for the pope's inaugural address. In many ways, this speech, when Pius XII told the gathered crowd, 'You are the Church', formed the foundational belief of Rush's ecclesiology. As Secretary, I was exposed to Rush's ecclesiology and his strong belief in his role as teacher which became evident in the area of the Communal Rite of Reconciliation with General Absolution. The Second Rite with General Absolution (commonly known as the Third Rite) was widely celebrated in the Archdiocese of Brisbane, mainly during the Christmas and Easter Seasons. It was accepted universally by the people who flocked in their hundreds during the times when the Rite was celebrated. It not only offered them the opportunity to celebrate God's forgiveness as individuals but it developed in the community a sense of social sin and an opportunity to offer each other forgiveness.

To prepare for these celebrations, Rush requested that there be a catechetical preparation in each community before he would give permission for the sacrament to be celebrated. In the early 1980s Rome demanded that he refrain from giving permission. He argued that if Rome took that 'right' from him they would be denying his role as teacher, taking away from him that responsibility and duty. If this happened, the local pastor then had the responsibility under the sacramental and canonical discipline of the Church to make the decision for the pastoral needs of his community. Rush made the point that, if they took this role of teacher from him, abuses would creep in without any oversight. The rest, as they say, is history . . .

At the extraordinary Synod of 1985 called to commemorate twenty years since the closing of Vatican II, Archbishop Rush, as President of the Australian Catholic Bishops' Conference, thanked God for the Second Vatican Council and then identified two major concerns that the bishops of Australia had.

The first had to do with an aspect of *Lumen Gentium*, embracing the questions of collegiality, the relationship of the local Church to the universal Church, and the principle of subsidiarity, which argues that local solutions should be found for local problems, as long as these solutions did not jeopardise the unity of the local Church with and under the Holy Father.[1] The Australian bishops felt that the orthodoxy of bishops and theologians seemed to be lightly questioned without an appreciation of their difficulties and their industry, and that this led to a loss of trust which only damaged the Church. They believed there was need for a more refined theology of, and a more effective use of Episcopal Conferences.

The second concern had to do with *Gaudium et Spes* in that its message had not succeeded in giving men and women a sufficiently clear and inspiring vision of the Church's role in the world of our time. Too many people, even among Catholics, found the Church peripheral to their concerns and more discussion was needed, especially around questions such as what was the mission of the Church for the world today. Rush's final remarks were these: 'The Church needs to search for and shape an answer to the only ultimate question, *who is Christ for the world of today?*'[2]

This question has not changed: it has echoed through the years and has found a response in the call for a New Evangelisation. Pope Benedict XVI took up the beat and called for a Synod in Rome to

---

1. 'A local church that wants to be Catholic without unity with Rome, would thereby lose its very Catholicity because a Catholicity that foregoes Rome is not Catholic anymore. In turn, a local church that wants to be only "Roman" would negate itself and merely turn into a sect, because a church that wants only to be Roman could not be Catholic anymore.' Joseph Ratzinger C/f *Embers in the Ashes: New Life in the Church* by Martin Werlen, OSB (New York: Paulist Press, 2013).

2. C/F Appendix 1. Speech of Archbishop Rush at the 1985 Extraordinary Synod of Bishops.

articulate a vision and a strategy for this to happen. It is the same call that was articulated in the words of Rush: how do you make new the Gospel to individuals and a culture that has largely been shaped by it? In the words of Father Ronald Rolheiser, OMI, how do we do that? How do we make the gospel fresh for those for whom it has become stale? How do we, as GK Chesterton put it, help people to look at the familiar until it looks unfamiliar again? How do we try to Christianise someone who is already a Christian?

Bishop Morris with his father and sister. Photo taken on family holiday in Queensland, 1946.

Bishop Morris as a seminarian at Banyo, Queensland, with his mother. Photo taken in 1963.

Family holiday photo, Queensland, 1946. Bishop Morris with this mother and sister.

2

Pastoral Vision

One of the fundamental challenges for our local Church is to present our leadership as an image of the Kingdom. We can only achieve this if our leadership is relational, radically person-centred, an expression of love. The image of leadership as the washing of dusty feet remains as a powerful reminder of the mind of Jesus for he says to us, 'I have set the example, and you should do for each other exactly what I have done for you' (John 13:15). Jesus is the inspiration for leadership for he came amongst us as one who serves (Luke 22:7). The service of leadership is one of the ministries named by Paul in the first Christian communities (1 Cor 12:28). For Paul, this ministry involves a recognition and utilisation of gifts within the community. It recognises participation and collaboration and is built on being present and sharing wisdom.

William M Morris (Role Statement for Principals)

The year was 1994, my second year as bishop of the local Church (Diocese) of Toowoomba, and words from the opening address of Pope John XXIII began ringing in my ears as I looked at the pastoral needs of the diocese, and heard a mixed chorus of voices looking for direction.

> As I go about my daily work as pope, I sometimes have to listen, with much regret to voices of persons who, though burning with zeal, are not endowed with too much sense of discretion or measure. These people can see nothing but a decline of truth and the ruin of the Church in these modern times. They say that our era, in comparison with past ones, is getting worse, and they behave as though they had learned nothing from history,

7

which is, nonetheless, the teacher of life. They behave as though at the time of former Councils, everything was a full triumph for the Christian idea and religious liberty. I feel I must disagree with these prophets of gloom who are always forecasting disaster as though the end of the world was at hand. In fact, at the present time, Divine Providence is leading us to a new order of human relations which, by the very effort of the people of this time, is directed toward fulfilment of God's great plans for us. Everything, even human indifferences, leads to a greater good for the Church. It's easy to see this if you look casually through history.

(Pope John XXIII - extract from his opening speech, Vatican II)

Also at that time the Church throughout Australia was preparing for the beatification of Mary MacKillop, whom journalist Max Harris described as 'the Wild Colonial Girl and a true Aussie Saint'. Mary was a prophetic voice of her time and she stands as an example and model of one who read the signs of the times, interpreted them in the light of the Gospel and responded courageously without fear. This context gave me the invitation to introduce the concept of pastoral planning to the diocese in an attempt to discern with the priests, religious and laity the signs of the times, to interpret them in the light of the gospel and then, like Mary MacKillop, to respond to the challenge of being agents of change. In this way, the Church could be enabled to respond wisely to the needs of all, both spiritually and pastorally.

It was in November 1996 that I had my first contact with a Roman Dicastery (a department of the Vatican's Curia, which makes up the governing body for the Catholic Church), the Congregation for the Clergy, through a letter from the Apostolic Pro-Nuncio, Archbishop Franco Brambilla, asking for information about lay persons involved in the pastoral leadership of parishes. They wanted to know whether there were any parishes or churches in the diocese entrusted to lay persons, including religious sisters, and if so in what way these lay persons had a share in the exercise of the pastoral care of a parish such as in planning, administration or liturgy. I was able to inform the Congregation that in pastoral planning in the diocese the stress was always that the community of faith was centred on the Eucharist. In those parishes where there was no resident priest, the community, normally through the Parish Pastoral Council or the Finance Committee, undertook the pastoral care of the parish in planning, administration and finance in collaboration with the priest who had been designated as 'moderator' (priest director), according to Canon 517.

To date this role had been undertaken by the priest who was 'Director of Pastoral Planning' in the diocese. It had been our experience that where lay people were entrusted with key roles in their parishes, they carried them out with the utmost diligence. I must also mention that the diocese had been blessed to have the assistance of the Missionaries of the Sacred Heart who maintained a school in the diocese, Downlands College, and who had traditionally been available for pastoral work.

Over the next few years we took up the response to Pope John Paul II's invitation to all local churches to develop a pastoral plan. The plan should involve all the people and all the organisations and movements within the diocese. It called for participation, dialogue and community discernment and should flow from the spirit and spirituality of the Second Vatican Council, which is the spirituality of communion. As the momentum grew, a team was formed under the direction of Sr Monica Cavanagh, RSJ, and engaged in a process of discerning a way forward which involved conducting workshops in each parish called 'Creating Our Future'. This material was then used to plan our first Diocesan Gathering in Roma and Toowoomba, scheduled for 1998.

As anticipation grew and excitement rose, so did the waters in Dogwood Creek outside the township of Miles, two and a half hours west of Toowoomba, making it impossible for those in the East to travel to Roma for the Diocesan Gathering. Those in the West were already gathering in Roma so a decision was made for some of us to fly on the Saturday morning 29 August 1998 and gather with those already assembled, about sixty in number. The rest of the diocese would gather in Toowoomba in a couple of weeks' time. It had been recommended that as many as possible, both priests and laity, take part in the assembly and for the rest of the diocese to gather either for Mass or a Lay Led Liturgy and pray for the success of the Gathering.

Earlier in that year, on 1 June 1998 I had received a letter from the Apostolic Pro-Nuncio, Franco Brambilla, who had received a complaint about an alleged weekend meeting of priests in Roma which would leave the people without Sunday Mass. He drew my attention to the very negative reaction that such an experiment had already provoked some years ago in another diocese and suggested that I reconsider the matter since the administration of the sacraments, especially the Eucharist, takes priority over any kind of meeting. I informed him on 3 June that no such decision had been taken to withhold Sunday Masses. Some communities would be without Mass that weekend but would gather for a liturgy, which happens on a regular basis in some communities because of the distances that have to be travelled between towns.

Some priests in the diocese travel close to 500 kilometres on a Sunday to celebrate Eucharist in the various communities of their parishes. I pointed out to the Nuncio that I thought it would have been wise to check with me first to find out what the true facts were before he wrote his letter and I believed the woman concerned owed an apology to the priests and people of the diocese for not checking her facts before making a rash judgment. Brambilla replied that his letter had been carefully worded referring to an 'alleged' and 'supposed' meeting, and invited me either to write to him again or to write directly to the Congregation for Bishops; alternatively, he could send a copy of my letter to the Congregation regarding the matter as the complainant had also written to the Congregation. As I had no knowledge of the questions the Congregation were asking and what information they required, I was happy for him to send a copy of my letter.

From the two Gatherings, which were a great success, came our Diocesan Pastoral Plan containing the following Vision Statement:

> we are a Pilgrim people living God's dream 'To bring good news to the poor, to proclaim release to captives and recovery of sight to the blind, to let the oppressed go free, to proclaim the year of the Lord's favour' (Luke 4:18–19).

The Mission Statement declared:

> we are Christian faith communities called to work together in a spirit of trust and openness, to bring about hope, love, justice and peace in our world, and the Key Pastoral Directions: through baptism we are called to live out God's dream by embracing action for social justice; evangelising life and culture; respecting and honouring faith traditions; promoting and celebrating life-giving liturgy; developing and updating faith education and spirituality; exploring and implementing various pastoral leadership models.

For the diocese, the Vision Statement was an expression of our basic hopes and dreams, the Mission Statement was the way we saw ourselves as a group of people living out that dream, and the 'Key Pastoral Directions' were the ways that we, as baptised Christians, were called to strive to accomplish our mission. The Pastoral Directions clarified the Vision by giving all in the diocese a sense of direction. It energised those carrying it out by giving a sense of purpose. It did not define the total picture but gave a desired goal towards which to move.

Above: Bishop Morris with Pope John Paul II during Ad Limina visit, 1998

Right: Bishop Morris with Pope Benedict XVI, during Anglaphone Professional Standards meeting, Rome, 2008.

Below: Bishop Morris with Pope John Paul II presenting painting of Our Lady of the Southern Cross, Rome, 2004.

3

Synod of Oceania

We are all seeking the summit of the holy mountain; but shall not our road be shorter if we consider the past a chart and not a guide?

Kahlil Gibran

As the fruits from the Diocesan Gathering were being absorbed, processes were being put into place for the formation of a Diocesan Pastoral Council.[1] Energies were also focussed at that time on preparation for the Synod of Bishops of Oceania which was to be held in Rome, November 22 – 12 December 1998. It was one in a series of continental assemblies called by Pope John Paul II to prepare the Church for the new millennium. Bishops of Oceania were joined by bishops from other continents and heads of Dicasteries of the Roman Curia. Other participants included priests, lay people, and religious as well as fraternal delegates from other churches and ecclesial communities. The assembly was to analyse and discuss the present situation of the church in Oceania in order to plan more effectively for the future. "It also focussed the attention of the universal Church on the hopes and challenges, the needs and opportunities, the sorrows and joys of the vast human tapestry which is Oceania".[2] With the inspiration and excitement of our local assembly fresh in mind, I commenced writing my eight minute intervention for the Synod. 'Collegiality', the word that was echoing for me, and the 'Dialogue of Salvation', which had been a focus of Pope Paul VI's first encyclical,

---

1. The Priests Council and the Diocesan Pastoral Council together would form the body through which Diocesan Policies were formulated and approved.
2. Post-Synodal Apostolic Exhortation Ecclesia in Oceania; Introduction No 2 Page 4.

Ecclesiam Suam (The Church in the Modern World 1964), became the foundations on which I would build. I wrote the following which became my intervention:

> In this encyclical we are called to take part in this unfailing and trustful dialogue, a dialogue initiated and established with us through Christ in the Holy Spirit. Pope Paul VI said that we must examine it closely if we want to understand the relationship which we, the Church, should establish and foster with the human race.
>
> In this dialogue of salvation on which all conversations are based, God takes the initiative and this dialogue springs from the goodness and love of God. The dialogue of salvation does not depend on the merits of those with whom it is initiated nor on the results it would be likely to achieve. No physical pressure is brought on anybody to accept it. All are left free to respond to it or to reject it and this dialogue of salvation must be made accessible to all, applied to everyone without distinction; it is universal, Catholic.
>
> Our dialogue demands that what we say be intelligent, that it is clear, easy to understand, able to be grasped by all in the current idiom. Our dialogue needs to be meek, not arrogant, its authority comes from the truth it affirms, shares with others the gifts of charity, is itself an example of virtue, avoiding peremptory language, making no demands.
>
> Trust is another important aspect of the dialogue of salvation, promoting intimacy and friendship on all sides, uniting in the truth and excluding self-seeking. The dialogue needs to be prudent which enables truth to be wedded to charity, and understanding to love.
>
> This is the dialogue that enables the word of God to come alive and to take root in the hearts of all. It takes into account people's cultures, their backgrounds, their relationships, helping them to recognise their dignity as being created in the image and likeness of God.

When our Holy Father, Pope John Paul II, visited Alice Springs in Central Australia in 1986, he spoke to the Aboriginal people there in these words: '(the) Gospel now invites you to become through and through Aboriginal Christians'. He then went on to say, 'and the Church herself in Australia will not be fully the Church that Jesus wants her to be until you have made your contribution to her life and until that contribution has been joyfully received by others'. That fullness in the Church will not occur in isolation because the growth in faith of Indigenous Australians must walk hand in hand with the growth in faith of all Australians. This will surely result in expressions of faith that are uniquely Australian.

I come from an inland diocese, two times the size of Italy, that stretches from the richly cultivated lands in the east to the red sands of the desert in the west, filled with life and loved by people who are isolated by distance, but not by spirit, faith or hope. There is an evolving culture flowing out of this land which demands forms of faith expression. We have to be conscious of our tradition that has been passed on faithfully. But in the light of our evolving culture, in the dialogue of salvation, we need to look at our tradition with vision so that the God whom Jesus revealed becomes known, and the Body of Christ is set free, experiencing the compassion of a God who loves all creation unconditionally. For this to be achieved, we need to work together, we need to be a Church that listens, learns and grows in trust.

We need to respond to the challenge and invitation of the Holy Father in his 1995 encyclical letter, *Ut Unum Sint,* where he invited patience and fraternal dialogue to help find ways of carrying out the ministry of Peter. He says there must be new ways of doing it as we approach the Third Millennium and that the church does not separate the office of Pope from the mission entrusted to the whole body of bishops who are also 'vicars and ambassadors of Christ'.

He goes on to say that the bishop of Rome is a member of the 'College', and the bishops are his brothers in ministry (*Ut Unum Sint, 95)*. Collegiality does not exist when bishops are passive, but when they take the initiative in bringing forward problems and possibilities, as they share the roles of teaching, sanctifying and governing. If we are to make the faith come alive in our various cultures, if the word is going to be understood in all languages, if evangelisation is to be a reality with truth and vision, and not just a theological principle, then we need to take the Pope's challenge in patience and fraternal dialogue, and work together collegially and in collaboration and with the deepest trust and respect.

Collegiality is not new, for it was known in the early centuries of the Church and simply expresses the apostolic origin of Church, entrusted by Christ to the Apostles and by them to their successors. 'All this points clearly to the collegiate character and structure of the Episcopal order' (*Lumen Gentium 22*).

Cardinal Ratzinger stated during Vatican II that 'conciliarity is something that belongs to the essence of the Church: however it has worked historically, the conciliary principle lies at the heart of the Church and ever presses from within towards realisation'. *J Ratzinger, Das neue Volk Gottes (Dusseldorf 1970)*. As expressed in *Lumen Gentium 22*, this perspective both preserves and enriches the unity of the Church:-

• It preserves it, because each member of the College of the Apostles does not operate as an isolated entity, but 'in communion with one another and with the Roman Pontiff, in a bond of unity, charity and peace'.
• It enriches it, because the Universal Church exists in each diocese, gathered around one of the Apostolic College. With his awareness of the needs of the local flock, he can continue the mission of the Good Shepherd, using all the gifts that God has given him, including the guidance of the Holy Spirit promised

to the Apostles. This is not just a theory, but the theological reality of the Church.

I have become more and more convinced of the principle of collegiality expounded by Vatican II, which I believe guarantees and protects the truth to be taught, lived and celebrated. The dialogue of salvation needs to be kept open; it can never be closed. We need to take the initiative and to participate in the conversation of our brothers and sisters, no matter what the topic may be. We need to be like the College of Apostles who accepted Thomas into their midst, even though he did not believe that the Lord had risen. It was in the continued dialogue that Thomas saw the risen Lord. It is in our continued dialogue as bishops within our local Churches, united with the Holy Father, and in our teaching, sanctifying and governing roles that we enable the faith to be inculturated into the local community (John Huels, *More Disputed Questions in the Liturgy* [Chicago: LTP, 1996]).

We need the trust and freedom to let our brothers and sisters, like Thomas, speak about the divorced, celibacy, married clergy, the unspoken issue of women, appointment of bishops, the adaptation and translation of liturgical texts, the problems surrounding general absolution and Communal Rite of Reconciliation, inculturation of liturgy and many more. We need to be trusted, for we love the Church, and it is in love that these conversations take place. Ears will be closed and hearts will be hardened only when there is a refusal to create a forum in which people can talk of their hopes and dreams, their hurts and failures, their relationships and their life. It is in this dialogue of salvation that we experience the compassion of God, and with Thomas place our fingers where the nails were put, our hands into his side and say, 'My Lord and my God' (*John 20:28*).

This is the ground in which the seed will produce, not tenfold, but a hundredfold. Trust us that in Australia,

we will pass on that same faith, the faith of the Apostles
in ways that also 'show forth all the more resplendently
the Catholicity of the undivided Church' (*Lumen
Gentium 23*).

My speech was one of the last of the day. Present was Pope John Paul
II and a number of the cardinals from the various dicasteries (Roman
'Congregations'). As the assembly arose and the pope made his way
up the ramp leading out of the Synod Hall he looked down at me as
I was waiting to leave and in a strong guttural voice said, 'collegiality'
and kept walking. The next day John Paul II spoke of the importance
of the foundation of truth and our responsibility to both support and
proclaim it.

Coinciding with the Synod was the *ad limina* meeting for the
Australian bishops. At the Australian Bishops Conference that
year (May 1998) we had been told of an inter-dicasterial meeting
(meeting with various ones of the Roman congregations) with a
representation of the Australian bishops to be held in Rome, 17–20
November 1998, in the days leading up to the synod. We were told it
was the wish of the Holy Father that this meeting take place between
the Congregations for the Doctrine of the Faith, Divine Worship
and the Discipline of the Sacraments, Bishops, Clergy, Institutes of
Religious Life and Societies of Apostolic Life and Catholic Education,
together with the Archbishops of the Australian Catholic Bishops
Conference and the chairs and secretaries of the Bishops' Conference
Committees for Clergy and Religious, Doctrine and Morals,
Education, Evangelisation and Missions, and Liturgy. It was said that
this body composed a representative group for the discussions that
were going to take place to better understand the situation of the
Church in Australia. It was an opportunity for a fraternal exchange
of views and proposals. We were told that similar meetings held with
other episcopal conferences had proved to be equally beneficial as
expressions of ecclesial communion.

As history has shown, the Australian bishops were ambushed.
There had been for some time correspondence between a number of
disaffected Catholic bodies who were not happy with the direction the
Church was taking in Australia. It was believed that members from
these conservative bodies had obtained meetings with a number of

Roman Dicasteries expressing their opinions and giving a lopsided view of the Australian Church and misrepresenting the view of the vast majority of the Catholic population in Australia. Unfortunately, they were believed and the so-called fraternal exchange of views and proposals was really a witch-hunt. I was Secretary for the Committee for Evangelisation and Missions and was present at this meeting. It was friendly enough but we were there to be told rather than to have a fraternal dialogue. There was a whisper through the place that Australia was viewed as the Netherlands of the South, and in a way this was affirmed by the response of Cardinal Ratzinger as he drew the conversation on the Communal Rite with General Absolution to a close. I sat there in disbelief after what I thought had been a very pastoral and theological exchange, when Ratzinger said: 'It did not work in the Netherlands, therefore it is not going to work in Australia.' On a number of occasions during the discussions, Ratzinger referred to a 'wrong understanding' of anthropology as the basis of the difficulties the Church was facing in the world today. The 'Statement of Conclusions' mentioned that there was a profound paradigmatic change in anthropology that was opposed to classical anthropology. It was characterised, for example, by an extreme individualism, seen especially in a concept of conscience that elevated the individual conscience to the level of an absolute, thus raising the subjective criterion above all objective factors and having no point of reference beyond itself. Another example was a change in the relations between creation, nature, body and spirit, resulting in certain forms of feminism which expressed an anthropology profoundly different from classical anthropology.

In an article by Francine Cardman in a *Theology and Life Series on Vatican II* entitled '*The Church Would Look Foolish Without Them*' *Women and Laity Since Vatican II*, she writes that:

> *Women and Laity Since Vatican II* not only speaks of a predictable institutional reluctance to share the putative power of the clergy with women and laymen; another force has worked to hold back change in personal and structural relationships between men and women. That force is the theological anthropology implicit in most of the Council's documents and in later Vatican

pronouncements concerning women. The relation of the sexes presumed in this Roman anthropology might be characterised simply as 'complementary but unequal'. In this view, women and men are held to have clearly differentiated and God-given traits and qualities, so that there is not only a physical or biological distinction between them but also an ontological one. As a result, different spheres of influence and activity have been divinely assigned them; 'progress for women, whether in Church or society, is limited to the assumption of 'their full and proper role in accordance with their own nature' (*Gaudium et Spes*, 60).[3]

I have seen nothing in the writings of Joseph Ratzinger or the Church's documents to show that there has been a shift in the understanding of anthropology.

Martin Werlen, OSB, Abbott of the Einsiedeln Monastery and a member of Switzerland's Conference of Bishops, during a celebration commemorating the fiftieth anniversary of the Second Vatican Council, and the opening of the 'Year of Faith', gave a talk in which his small but challenging book, *Embers in the Ashes,* has its origins. In it he comments that if God affirms humans so must the Church strive to join that affirmation all over again with all its heart. Humans are men or women. The Church finds it difficult to say yes to women. He continues in this chapter, referring to the 1994 missive *Ordinatio Sacerdotalis* of Pope John Paul II, where he affirmed that priestly ordination is reserved for men and declared the question beyond discussion. Yet the question remains: is a person's gender a matter of faith? Does it belong to the immutable core of the faith? Werlen goes on to say that after 1994 we can at least still discuss this even more basic question.[4]

As the days of the meeting in Rome went by I started to have a deeper appreciation of the Inquisition during the Middle Ages, with the shadowy secretive presence of Archbishop Bertone and the raised

---

3. Vatican II Theological and Life Series 8, page 123. Francine Cardman (Dublin: Dominican Publications, 1984), 109.

4. Martin Werlen, OSB *Embers in the Ashes: New Life in the Church* (New York: Paulist Press, 2013), 24–25.

voices of various cardinals ringing through the meeting room and telling us to take control of the religious and get them back into habits and convents. The conversation showed no appreciation of the prophetic dimension of religious life, wanting to impose on active apostolic communities a monastic model, and it did not recognise that religious congregations of men and women were initially formed to respond to the needs of the times and that these had changed. As a body, we sat there in disbelief and through silence and word responded that we would not be doing this. Eventually a document was produced called the 'Statement of Conclusions'[5] which, according to the press release, contained proposals and directions for the mission of the Church in Australia, and spoke in general terms to avoid mention of specific persons, groups, institutions or publications that might be considered problematic. It was seen to provide guidance to the local bishop so that he might affirm, admonish and correct, according to what the specific circumstances required. Its focus was in the context of the Church in Australia, the role of Bishop, the role of the clergy, the role of persons in consecrated life, the sacraments, liturgy and Catholic education. The 'Statement of Conclusions' was signed by the Prefects of the Congregations involved, the President of the Australian Catholic Bishops Conference and the Presidents of the Conference Committees present at the meeting. The document was prepared by an editorial committee composed of Cardinal Edward Clancy, an Australian, Archbishop (now Cardinal) Tarcisio Bertone, Archbishop Giuseppe Pittau and Bishop Michael Putney of Townsville. At the press conference Cardinal Joseph Ratzinger said 'the signing of the document signifies that it is a fair representation of the dialogue that took place during the interdicasterial meeting regarding some of the doctrinal and pastoral issues challenging the Church in Australia.'[6]

When the document was released in Australia, its reception was negative and many were distressed by the tone and much of the content of the Statement of Conclusions. These feelings were magnified by the disappointment many felt after their spirits had been uplifted by the speeches at the Synod that had filled them with encouragement and hope. Participants at a National Colloquium on the Statement,

---

5. C/f Appendix 2 Statement of Conclusions.
6. Presentation of the Statement of Conclusions to the Australian Bishops

co-sponsored by the Australian Conference of Leaders of Religious Institutes and the National Council of Priests, felt that underpinning the document's negative evaluation of the Australian Church was a prevailing understanding of Church which seemed to be inconsistent with the liberating ecclesiology of the Second Vatican Council. This was so, particularly in relation to the lay faithful, whose essential role in the mission of the Church was consistently overlooked.[7]

7.   From A National Colloquium, Sydney, 22–24 February 1999.

4

Reconciliation and General Absolution

Forgiveness is the fragrance the violet sheds on the heel that crushed it.
Mark Twain

Our *ad limina* visit was drawn to a conclusion on 14 December 1998 with a meeting with Pope John Paul II who delivered his final remarks to us flowing out of the Statement of Conclusions.[1] This was not a happy ending to our Roman visit. The only thing that uplifted our spirits was that we were heading home for Christmas. The disappointment we were experiencing was in many ways similar to the disappointment our communities were feeling back at home as they wondered what this might imply for them and for the whole of Australia. To them there seemed to be no recognition of Vatican II's emphasis on collegiality and subsidiarity, nor of the emphasis that Vatican II had placed on the Church as the people of God and on appreciation of the faith of the whole people (*sensus fidei*[2]).

The Synod of Oceania became lost in the shadow of the 'Statement of Conclusions' and the conversations that were taking place were focussed on models of Church, liturgy, religious life, ministry, the

---

1. Appendix 3 Pope John Paul II: 'Address to the Australian Bishops', 14 December 1998.
2. *Sensus fidei* (sense of the faith), also called *sensus fidelium* (sense of the faithful) when exercised by the body of the faithful as a whole. Vatican II expressed this in the following way: 'The whole body of the faithful who have an annointing that comes from the holy one (cf 1 John 2:20, 27) cannot err in matters of belief. This characteristic is shown in the supernatural appreciation of the faith (*sensus fidei*) of the whole people, when, 'from the bishops to the last of the faithful' (St Augustine), they manifest a universal consent in matters of faith and morals.' (from Vatican II document 'Lumen Gentium Dogmatic Constitution on the Church', paragraph 12).

lack of reference to Scripture, and especially the Communal Rite of Reconciliation with General Absolution. It was the Communal Rite with General Absolution that was the main concern for the vast majority of priests and people of the local Church of Toowoomba. This Rite had been part of the celebration of their lives for many years. The first point addressed in the 'Statement of Conclusions' concerning the sacrament of penance or Reconciliation focussed on individual confession and absolution which was, and always had been, the ordinary means of reconciliation in the Toowoomba Diocese. The Statement then moved on to speak of the Communal celebration of the sacrament of penance with either individual or general absolution. It encouraged the celebration of the communal rite with individual confession and absolution, especially in the seasons of Advent and Lent, but condemned the use of general absolution if it did not reflect the teaching of the Church in the precise terms required by the 'Code of Canon Law' (c/f especially canons 959–964).[3]

As I read and re-read the pope's message to us and the 'Statement of Conclusions' concerning the Communal Celebration of Reconciliation, I decided to ask our Diocesan Liturgical Commission to look at the needs of our diocese in the light of the liturgical and canon law norms laid down by the Church for the celebration of the Communal Rite with General Absolution. From the conversations that had taken place in Rome and amongst many of the bishops, I believed we had valid reasons for its use.

The Commission was led by Father James Cronin, Chair of the Commission, and Sr Catherine White, mfic, the Executive Officer. Reverend Dr Michael McClure, a moral theologian, was used as a consultant. Through their research they opened to the people of the diocese a greater appreciation of the history and development of the sacrament of reconciliation. As outlined in the following pages, they found that within Catholicism there had always been a number of explicit ways, other than sacramental penance, in which we could open our lives to the healing and reconciling presence of God. It was our responsibility as pastors to help the people of God to discover, understand, and celebrate in a variety of ways the many paths to forgiveness. Only in this way would we nourish a genuine sense of sin and reconciliation as the Holy Father had called us to do.

---

3. C/F Statement of Conclusions Number 45.

The eucharist has always been the primary sacrament of reconciliation within the Catholic Church. Week after week, we celebrate and are drawn into the reconciling life, death and resurrection of Jesus.

In the early Church, public penance was called the 'second plank' for those who had fallen into serious sin after baptism. It afforded an explicit sign of life, and of reconciliation with God and with the Church. A bishop reserved this rigorous, public rite for those with the 'capital sins' of apostasy, adultery and murder. In time, through the influence of the Irish monastic structures, the practice of private confession was gradually introduced. It is of note that this rite itself was at first considered to be an abuse.

Until the Fourth Lateran Council of 1215, when it was stated that the faithful should confess serious sin and receive communion at least once a year at Easter, the Sunday eucharist was the normal way of asking for forgiveness for sin. However, people began to assume incorrectly that confession was necessary prior to the reception of communion. Over the years, the clergy reinforced this misconception, so that the practice of going regularly to confession prior to the reception of communion overshadowed the eucharist as the primary means of forgiving sins. Thus, the Sacrament of Reconciliation came to be understood as the only means of attaining forgiveness for even the most minor sins.

The Council of Trent reiterated the teaching that the Mass 'is truly propitiatory' insofar as the person is contrite and penitent.[4] Furthermore, Trent stated that the Mass 'grants the grace and gift of penitence and pardons *even the gravest sins*'. The revisions of Vatican II have not lessened this understanding. Every Eucharistic Prayer proclaims that we 'do this', in memory of Jesus, 'so that sins may be forgiven' (the recent new translation has it as 'for the forgiveness of sins'!) The Third Eucharistic Prayer prays: 'Look with favour on your Church's offering and see the victim whose death has reconciled us to yourself' (New translation: 'Look, we pray, upon the oblation of your Church and, recognising the sacrificial Victim by whose death you willed to reconcile us to yourself'). It goes on: 'may this sacrifice which has made our peace with you . . .' (New translation: 'may this Sacrifice of our reconciliation, we pray, O Lord, advance the peace

---

4. Trent, *Sess* XXII, 11 September 1582, chapter 2, sections 1393, 1434 and 1520.

and the salvation of all the world'). The fourth Eucharistic Prayer asks God to accept the 'acceptable sacrifice which brings salvation to the world'. (New translation: 'the sacrifice acceptable to you which brings salvation to the whole world').

Within the Mass, the penitential rite, too, allows us to focus on our need for reconciliation and forgiveness before we approach the altar. One option for this part of the rite is the great prayer of contrition: 'I confess to almighty God and to you here present that I have sinned . . .' Other options include the litany of praise, which is punctuated by the proclamation of God's mercy, 'Lord have mercy; Christ have mercy; Lord have mercy'. Every penitential rite contains the words, 'May almighty God have mercy on us, forgive us our sins. . .'

Similarly, *the sign of peace* is a ritual gesture that responds to the command of Jesus: 'When you are offering your gift at the altar, if you remember that your brother or sister has something against you, leave your gift there before the altar and go; first be reconciled to your brother and sister, and then come and offer your gift' (Mt. 5:23-4). By this ritual action, we make clear our intention to be reconciled with every member of the Body of Christ gathered at the altar. We forgive and are forgiven.

Again and again, the prayers of the proper of the Mass express the propitiatory nature of eucharist. The Eucharistic Prayers for reconciliation are recommended for use 'when the mystery of reconciliation is a special theme of the celebration'. These texts are replete with images and texts that help the faithful understand that the eucharist is a 'sacrament of reconciliation'. This is truly an ancient and venerable belief that stands at the heart of our Catholic tradition.

The Church has always taught that an act of perfect contrition forgives serious sin, though sacramental penance is still necessary when it can be obtained. Many people feel that they can never make an act of 'perfect contrition', since the word 'perfect' conjures up the idea of 'without fault', and images such as the saints with their profound and singular sense of sorrow for sin. 'Ordinary' Catholics possess a deep humility that often makes them believe that they can never be perfectly contrite, and that such an act of contrition is therefore beyond their capacity. The language needs to be explained within the context of the theology that gave it birth. 'Perfect contrition' is simply a matter of turning to God and sincerely asking for God's mercy and forgiveness with the resolve not to sin again.

'Imperfect contrition', also known as attrition, is sorrow for sin that comes from a source other than the love of God. A person, for example, may only be sorry because of the punishment that accompanies wrongdoing, and not because of their love for God and their care and love for one another. Church discipline states that an act of contrition is sufficient for the forgiveness of venial sins, and for the forgiveness of mortal sin for the purpose of receiving communion, if the person has the firm resolution to have recourse to sacramental confession as soon as possible *(Catechism 1453)*. The Diocesan Liturgical Commission pointed out that when the act of contrition is explained it would be important to use language that resonates with people. Words such as 'a sincere act of contrition' would perhaps be preferable. Other words might be heartfelt, genuine, or honest. Such contrition would certainly be well within the grasp of all who came to eucharist.

The Diocesan Liturgical Commission went on to speak of 'Penitential Services' as celebrations focussing on the community's need for forgiveness within the context of the merciful love of God. After gathering, listening to, and reflecting on the Word of God, the assembly acknowledges its sinfulness, the broken relationships that are the result, and the need for God's forgiveness. Such celebrations help the community to become more aware of the personal and communal sin that stands in the way of a loving response to God's call. Such sin harms the integrity and holiness of the Body of Christ, tarnishes its ability to be sacrament for the world, and compromises the mission of the people of God.

Penitential services help to bring the community, as a people, to general sorrow for sin, and a resolution to amend their lives. Such services allow for a greater degree of flexibility since they may be led by a lay presider in the absence of an ordained minister. They may also be celebrated by particular groups who wish to ask forgiveness of God and each other for a particular reason.

The Commission further noted that the sacrament of the 'Anointing of the Sick' is available to those people seriously ill, either through sickness or old age, and not only to those persons in imminent danger of death. The rite has its origins in the healing ministry of Jesus, as well as in the practice of the early church as found in the letter of James:

> Are any among you sick? They should call for the elders
> of the church and have them pray over them, anointing
> them with oil in the name of the Lord. The prayer of
> faith will save the sick, and the Lord will raise them up;
> and anyone who has committed sins will be forgiven
> (James 5:14f).

Quite clearly, this sacrament has a twofold purpose: the healing of the
sick and the forgiveness of sins. The Council of Trent described the
sacrament in this way: 'This reality is in fact the grace of the Holy Spirit,
whose anointing takes away sins, and if any remain, the remnants of
sin'. The prayer of anointing indicates that the forgiveness of sin is
central to the sacrament: 'May the Lord who frees you from sin save
you, and raise you up.' Where it is the practice to regularly anoint
those who have become frail due to advancing years or ill health, the
pastor should make clear to those persons that the rite of anointing
has forgiven their sins.

Thus, the Commission's research showed how the tradition of the
Church has always included a variety of ways to receive forgiveness
for sin. The *Catechism of the Catholic Church* (1434ff) lists many
forms of penance in Christian life.

God's grace, the gift of being invited to enter into God's own life,
is a free offer. We choose to accept, reject, or ignore the offer—but the
offer is always there. Similarly, God's offer of forgiveness does not rely
on our request, but is a free gift born of the extraordinary love that
God has for us. A love which is pure gift, not earned, can never be
lost. God cannot help but forgive (Hildegard of Bingen).

The Church must celebrate God's forgiveness in as many ways
as it can. The Church must help people to believe that their sins are
really forgiven in many ways. It would be wrong to let people believe
that God wants us to suffer because of our sins, or that we have to
jump through fifty hoops to find forgiveness. If we believe the Good
News, we know that God asks only that we are sorry and that we
come back. We will always find compassion, mercy and forgiveness
in abundance. Surely, we, the Church can offer no less.

It was in this spirit that I decided to meet with the priests and
pastoral leaders of the parishes, to hear from them the conversations
that were taking place in their communities about the 'Statement of

Conclusions' and what effect it was having. There were two meetings held, one for the Far West in the parish of Mitchell, the other in Toowoomba. Both meetings were lively with the main focus being on what effect the Statement of Conclusions would have on their pastoral ministry, especially in the area of reconciliation. Over the years the diocese, through the wonderful work of its pastors, had developed a deep sense of social justice which they saw as constitutive of the Gospel and the foundation of all relationships. This had developed an understanding of the social aspect of sin, and the communal celebration of reconciliation, with either individual or general absolution, gave them an opportunity to celebrate forgiveness and healing in the presence of their brothers and sisters. The question arose: keeping in mind that general absolution must always be considered an exception, and may only be celebrated within a strict (not restrictive) interpretation of the canonical and liturgical norms of the Church, do the needs of the diocese fit within the guidelines? (Canon 961 Number. 1, 2)

The Diocesan Liturgical Commission came to the conclusion that the Communal Rite with general absolution, as described in the ritual, might be celebrated in parishes where genuine needs existed, in keeping with canonical and liturgical norms. The diocesan bishop should normally be consulted prior to the celebration of this rite, since the law grants him the competence to judge whether the conditions required for general absolution are met. The bishop would remain open to hear of those special cases where moral, pastoral and other reasons would make the celebration of General Absolution a necessary and rightful option. The Commission also concluded that confessors might act in cases of serious necessity without the prior permission of the bishop.

The Diocesan Liturgical Commission also pointed out that the Pontifical Commission which revised the present 'Code of Canon Law' had recognised the need for pastors to discern when to celebrate General Absolution in cases of serious necessity in accord with the principles of moral theology. Within this area of Church discipline some of the more pastorally sensitive issues, which have made the celebration of General Absolution a necessity in some contexts, could be taken into consideration when decisions were made. Such issues could, in many cases, be rightly judged to be causes which would excuse a less than strict adherence to the law because of the situations which presented moral and physical impossibility. The Commission pointed out that in this rural diocese, the difficulty many people experienced in maintaining their anonymity without having to travel excessive distances and the breakdown of relationships that prevented a person from feeling able to approach a particular priest in a one-on-one situation, might be real grounds for claiming moral or physical impossibility. Negative experiences of the confessional, and even the reality of physical and sexual abuse, might also need to be taken into account when decisions about this rite were to be made.

As a local Church we affirmed that the sacrament of penance celebrated according to the First Rite, often called 'Confession', is the normal way by which a person, conscious of grave sin, is forgiven and reconciled to God and to the Church. It was important to note, further, that catechesis for the sacrament of penance, as well as for penitential services, should make it clear that Church teaching has always held that the sacrament of penance is not the only way sin is forgiven. The Catholic Catechism, for example, notes that the forgiveness of sins is also attained in baptism, the eucharist and the anointing of the sick; in martyrdom, efforts at reconciliation with one's neighbour, sincere repentance, concern for the salvation of one's neighbour, the intercession of saints, the practice of charity, or an act of perfect contrition (see, for example, Canons 1393, 1434, 1520). It should also be made clear that after the celebration of such an act, the sin is already forgiven, even in the case of serious sin. The requirement to later confess grave sin in a one-to-one situation allows for a ritual expression of sorrow and of reconciliation with God and with the Church, to take place. The practice of individual confession also allows for guidance and direction to be given in specific and individual cases.

The whole discussion led the diocese to appreciate the three Rites of Reconciliation, each of which must be respected and celebrated according to liturgical and canonical norms. The image placed before the Bishops of Australia by the Holy Father in regard to penance was that of the loving father and the prodigal son. Like the father in that story, and like Jesus in the Gospel stories, we too must run out to search for those who are in need of compassion, mercy, understanding and forgiveness. In this way we, too, would be sacraments of God's forgiveness and mercy for the world to see. If we celebrated the rites well, if we were faithful to the richness of the Church's tradition, and to the Gospel, we would be richly blessed and would truly be faithful ambassadors of the Christ we served.

When the Diocesan Liturgical Commission completed its research, it published 'Guidelines on the Celebration of the Sacrament of Penance' (1999) and two auxiliary papers, one on what constituted serious sin and the other quoted above. I published the conditions which would validate the exceptional pastoral realities on which permission would be granted for general absolution. For the country areas those reasons were:

- There are clearly not sufficient confessors necessary to offer the additional sessions of the First Rite required to meet the spiritual needs of the many penitents who ask for Reconciliation in this privileged season, given that priests currently have pastoral responsibility for a number of Mass centres;
- the isolated position of parishes and the excessive distances which priests and parishioners would need to travel to celebrate the First or Second Rites fittingly;
- the impossibility of rightly hearing all of the confessions of parishioners on a one-to-one basis within a reasonable time;
- the difficulty in maintaining privacy and anonymity in the confessional;
- the earnest desire of the parishioners to make their confession and be reconciled prior to the Solemnity of Easter/Christmas;
- the possibility of real grounds for moral and physical impossibility.[5]

For the city:
- there are clearly not sufficient confessors necessary to offer the additional sessions of the First Rite required to meet the spiritual needs of the penitents who ask for Reconciliation in this privileged season;
- the many hundreds of penitents who gather from Toowoomba and neighbouring areas to celebrate

---

5. C/f Appendix 4 'The Faithful Have Charge of Their Sacramental Needs'.

the Sacrament of Reconciliation make it impossible to celebrate the First or Second Rites fittingly, and within a reasonable time;
- the earnest desire of the parishioners, along with their actual requests, to make their confession and be reconciled prior to the Solemnity of Easter/ Christmas;
- the possibility of real grounds for moral and physical impossibility.

This permission was given only on the understanding that:

a) a well-publicised, regular opportunity is provided for celebration of the First Rite of Reconciliation so that those who wish to avail themselves of that form of the Sacrament can do so without embarrassment or great delay;
b) the celebrant must explain to the faithful the need for those who are aware of *grave sin* in their lives to confess and seek advice from a priest as soon as possible, and prior to another celebration of the communal rite;
c) the celebration of the Communal Rite is arranged according to the Guidelines in the Ritual.

The requests I received for the celebration of the Communal Rite with General Absolution reflected the pastoral reality of the life of the parish communities, and in the majority of cases fulfilled the criteria laid down for a strict interpretation of the canonical and liturgical norms, not a restrictive one. On the moral and physical grounds there were strong personal and private reasons (in particular, as a result of sexual abuse by Church personnel) why people were unable to approach a priest for individual reconciliation. This had been reinforced in the press when it was claimed that a priest's sexual misconduct occurred in the confessional. In the city, but especially in the country, because of the psychology of the small town syndrome, persuading people to avail themselves of the First Rite of Reconciliation was sometimes difficult, because there was a strong fear of a lack of anonymity. Also in country areas, having only one priest available eliminates any choice of confessor unless parishioners are prepared to undertake long inconvenient journeys to other centres to see a priest.

The view often expressed to the priests by their parishioners was that they found the communal rite of reconciliation, with either individual or general absolution, a genuine, prayerful sacramental experience and an important part of their faith life. It heightened their awareness of the communal aspect of sin, and the importance of being reconciled. It helped them in a most prayerful way to be touched by God's mercy and compassion, to deepen their relationship with God, the Church, with members of their family, faith community and with their brothers and sisters.

It is important to note here that the First Rite of Reconciliation was always considered the ordinary and primary rite; communal rites (with individual and general absolution) were always the exception to meet the pastoral needs of the communities and were governed by Canon 961.

On 30 December 1999, I received a letter from the Apostolic Nuncio, Archbishop Francesco Canalini, stating that he had been informed that the sacrament of penance was administered according to the Third Rite[6] in St Patrick's Cathedral on 20 December 1999. His letter recognised that I had issued guidelines for the celebration of the communal rite with general absolution in keeping with canonical and liturgical norms but questioned whether, even in a rural diocese, some of these presented too broad an interpretation of the above mentioned norms. He said that the Toowoomba guidelines should reflect more accurately the response of the Congregation for Divine Worship and the Discipline of the Sacraments given in its letter of 19 March 1999.

I responded to the letter saying that I would re-look at our guidelines with the Diocesan Liturgical Commission to make sure that we had not missed anything. After another look at the documents, canons and sacramental norms we were convinced, especially on moral and physical grounds, that our guidelines fell within the strict (but not restrictive) interpretation of the Church's laws and norms. There was a growing sense of outrage within the

---

6. Note: This is the popular way of speaking of the Communal Rite with general absolution. The Third Rite is a specific rite of its own which was never celebrated in the diocese.

Australian community, reflected within the local church, concerning child sexual abuse by church personnel. Both victims and non-victims were expressing views that they were not going to expose themselves or their children to the First Rite of Reconciliation, and were asking for a safe environment in which to celebrate the sacraments. It was the view of the Liturgical Commission, a moral theologian and the vast majority of priests, pastoral leaders and myself that it was important to create opportunities for the sacrament of reconciliation to be celebrated so that those who felt they could not attend a First Rite had an opportunity to celebrate the sacrament.

On 4 January 2001, I received another letter from the Apostolic Nuncio, Archbishop Canalini, advising me that he had received letters regarding the advertising of the 'Communal Rite of Reconciliation' in several Toowoomba parishes and asked for information. I assured him that all the sacraments to my knowledge were celebrated in accordance with the canonical and liturgical norms of the Church, and the permissions I had granted for the Communal Rite with General Absolution were given according to those norms.

In response to my letter I received a phone call from Archbishop Canalini requesting a meeting to discuss the celebration of the Communal Rite with General Absolution, commonly called the Third Rite. The meeting took place at the Brisbane Airport in the Chairman's Lounge at 10.45 am on Wednesday 27 June 2001. Archbishop John Bathersby, as Metropolitan,[7] was asked to be present. The meeting was cordial and the conversation was focussed on the guidelines I used to give permission. The conversation took place between myself and Archbishop Canalini with Archbishop Bathersby a silent witness. I found Canalini open but quite focussed on a restrictive interpretation of the law, and he believed my interpretation was too broad. It seemed to me that he had no real appreciation of the moral and physical difficulties under which people struggled to receive the sacrament. There was no depth of understanding of the devastating effects that clerical sexual abuse was having on the lives of families and communities throughout Australia, and he did not see it as

---

7. In the Catholic Church, dioceses are grouped into ecclesiatical provinces which as a rule have the same boundaries as states. The province is presided over by the bishop of one of the dioceses, who is known as the metropolitan with the title arcbishop. At that time the Metropolitan of Queensland was Archbishop John Bathersby of Brisbane.

moral grounds for the celebration of the Communal Rite with general absolution.

At the end of the meeting, he requested that I put in writing the guidelines we had been using and give him some background to the intensive education program that we had undergone on the celebration of the sacrament of penance. In my response to him on 5 July 2001, I pointed out how we had explored the richness of the Church's tradition and that the communities not only celebrated the First Rite of reconciliation as the ordinary rite, but availed themselves of the Second Rite where possible, as well as penitential services and Masses of reconciliation. It was because of the exceptional pastoral realities which come under the umbrella of phyical/moral impossibilities that I had given permission for the celebration of the Communal Rite with general absolution. If there is a doubt, interpretation must favour the right of the faithful to receive the sacrament and it must always be kept in mind that the supreme law is the salvation of souls. (Canon 1752)

In January 2002 Archbishop Canalini advised that he had received more letters of complaint concerning the celebration of the Communal Rite. My response referred him to my letter of 5 July 2001.

Another meeting was held between myself and Archbishop Canalini on 8 November 2002 in Sydney at which further discussion took place concerning the guidelines used to grant permission for the Communal Rite with general absolution. Archbishop Canalini believed that they would be unacceptable to the Congregation for Bishops and it was his duty to forward a copy to that Congregation. He then suggested that those who struggled to attend a First Rite of reconciliation, because of moral grounds, be encouraged to make a perfect act of contrition. I challenged this approach on the grounds that everybody has the right to receive the sacraments and it would be treating those who have a difficulty with the First Rite as second class citizens. The Dicastery for Bishops was not happy with the guidelines and requested that I refrain from giving permission. I found it impossible to make a response to this request as the Dicastery had not laid down its reasons for believing that, in light of the exceptional pastoral realities existing in the local church, the guidelines were insufficient and that they did not adequately represent the canonical and liturgical norms under which the sacrament could be celebrated. I wrote to Canalini requesting an explanation as to why the guidelines were inadequate and how they did not follow the canonical and liturgical norms of our tradition, adding that I looked forward to receiving their reasons so that we could dialogue to bring about the best possible practice of celebrating the sacrament of reconciliation in the Church of the Diocese of Toowoomba.

On 3 April I received an unsigned letter from the Congregation for Divine Worship and Discipline of the Sacraments concerning my request for an explanation. The letter ignored completely the moral and pastoral grounds which formed the basis of our reasoning.[8]

With a focus on the pastoral care and the availability of the sacrament of reconciliation for all in the diocese, I appealed (in a letter dated 7 April 2003) the directives contained in the Congregation's letter and informed them that in the most expedient time possible I would prepare a fuller argument based on the faith of the people, on the circumstances of the diocese, the law and in accord with Canon 1734 §1. This petition, in my letter of 7 April 2003, requested the suspension of the directives in the letter from the Congregation. On 24 April, I received a letter from Cardinal Re, Prefect of the Congregation for Bishops, informing me that they had written to the Congregation for Divine Worship and Discipline of the Sacraments requesting its authorised interpretation of the liturgical norms and the law of the Church in regard to the authorised use of general absolution. After receiving a reply from that Congregation (Divine Worship and Discipline of the Sacraments), Cardinal Re responded that the Congregation for Bishops fully supported the instructions issued by the Congregation for Divine Worship and Discipline of the Sacraments regarding the celebration of the sacrament of penance in the Toowoomba diocese, and that he was confident that I would now thoroughly comply with the wishes of the Holy See and the universal law of the Church in this matter.

---

8. C/F Appendix 5 *Congregatio de Cultu Divina et Disciplina Sacramentorum.*

5

First Meeting

The fruit of truth must grow and mature on the tree of the subject before it can be plucked and placed in its absolute realms.

Bernard Lonergan SJ

Under the guiding hands of the two canon lawyers, Diocesan Chancellor, Reverend Dr Brian Sparksman, and Reverend Peter F Schultz, Diocesan Canonical Advisor, a survey was undertaken of those parishes which in the past had requested the use of Communal Rite with General Absolution. Ultimately the results of the survey and a document based on it were handed to me, to which I added my own observations giving an honest appraisal of the conditions that I saw were prevailing in the diocese. The findings of the survey convinced me even more of the need for the Communal Rite with General Absolution, and the extraordinarily rich blessings which flowed from its still limited use. I was equally convinced of the claim that some priests were making, that the celebration did bring some people back to the practice of the First Rite, and did deepen people's appreciation of their communal responsibility. The report contained two parts, one addressing the history of the use of General Absolution in the Toowoomba diocese, based on the survey. The second part contained responses to questionnaires for priests, for lay people, copies of my letters in response to applications from city and country parishes, general handouts regarding communal rites, diocesan guidelines for the celebration of the sacraments of penance and extracts from newspapers.[1]

---

1.   C/f Appendix 6 The Report.

On 23 December 2003, under a covering letter to Most Reverend Francesco Pio Tamburino of the Congregation of Divine Worship and Discipline of the Sacraments, I sent the report with a request for a meeting to discuss the whole issue while in Rome for the *ad limina* visit in March 2004.

As I arrived in Milan for that meeting, my connection to Rome was just pulling out of the station. I approached the information desk and was informed in broken English that I could board a waiting train which would take me express to Rome, but what they forgot to say was that it was an express train only between major stations. It was an interesting trip filled with locals who were travelling home after a Sunday of visiting families, attending football games or just celebrating a sunny Sunday. Having no seat, I sat on my suitcase in the corridor and participated in the life of the travelling community. I passed wine, bread and other edibles of which I was invited to partake, and helped convey babies up and down the corridor as they passed from one family member to another. Upon arriving in Rome on the evening before the beginning of our *ad limina* visit I was greeted excitedly by a number of the Australian bishops who wanted to point out that there was a letter awaiting me at the Casa Santa Marta where we were staying. I was tired after a long train journey from Paris where I had been staying with friends.

Next morning I opened the letter addressed to me from Monsignor Mario Marini, Under Secretary to the Congregation for Divine Worship and Discipline of the Sacraments, inviting me to confirm a meeting with His Eminence Cardinal Francis Arinze. The purpose of the meeting was to discuss matters pertaining to the discipline of the Sacrament of Penance and, in particular, the question of recourse to General Absolution. I was to phone Monsignor Thomas Fucinaro to confirm the time of meeting set for Thursday 18 March 2004 at 11.30 a.m. Because of our *ad limina* commitments, the meeting had to be re-arranged for Saturday March 20, at 11 am.

Present at the meeting were Cardinal Arinze, Archbishop Domenico Sorrentino, Father Anthony Ward SM, Monsignor Thomas Fucinaro and myself. The following is a record of that meeting which I committed to paper as soon as I returned to my room in Casa Santa Marta. I believed from Cardinal Arinze's initial greeting that he had either read my submission or had been briefed, as Father Anthony

Ward and Monsignor Thomas Fucinaro were certainly familiar with it. I sat at a small table facing Cardinal Arinze and to my left and slightly behind me sat the other three on a couch. On the table was a map of Australia and I was invited by Arinze to indicate the area of the Toowoomba diocese. The conversation was cordial. We spoke of the vastness of the diocese, that Italy would fit into it at least one and a half times, the tyranny of distance, the isolation of many communities and the vast distances priests had to travel to minister to their communities.

He then asked me to speak to the report and the reasons for giving permission for the celebration of the Communal Rite with General Absolution. I realised very quickly that they did not have any concept of Australian culture. Nor did they have an understanding of the pastoral intimacy that priests in Australia have with their people, the distances that have to be travelled, the Australian climate, or an appreciation and understanding of the devastating effect sexual abuse has had on our communities, and the lack of trust this has engendered in many concerning the First Rite of Reconciliation. They had no idea how it would be almost impossible for a person who has been sexually abused in the confessional or any other place to go back into a room, no matter how large, to have a one-to-one confession again. Arinze said that a person should recognise the fact that all priests are not like that and should get on with their lives. I tried to explain how abuse damages the psyche of a community, having a debilitating effect on some individuals to the degree that they mistrust the church and its ministers, but Arinze would have nothing of this. He would not accept as valid grounds how pastorally effective the Communal Rite with General Absolution had been, how healing people had found it and for some, how it had become the gateway back into the Church and the celebration of the First Rite.

Arinze did not want to hear that the Diocesan Guidelines kept the celebration of communal rites under the liturgical and canonical norms of the Church and stopped abuses. The conversation also touched on other areas such as para-liturgical celebrations and Masses of Reconciliation. Arinze, in speaking of the Second Rite of Reconciliation with individual absolution and how efficient and fast it could be, down-played the importance of an integral confession by stating that the penitent would only have to indicate some fault in their life, without details, so that the time element would not be extended. I made sure that I understood exactly what he was saying so that we could implement this practice of celebrating the Second Rite. I remember smiling at this point of the meeting as he became quite insistent on how easy it was to celebrate the Second Rite with individual absolution with large crowds. To me this was giving purely lip-service to a restrictive interpretation of the law.

He went on to say he understood that General Absolution was now part of our culture and that it would take a long time to reverse. To address this question he wanted the priests and people of the diocese to be re-educated in their understanding of the sacramental rites of Reconciliation, which would be addressed through our on-going In-Service days held each year. I found his interpretation of the canonical and liturgical norms for the celebration of the sacrament, and the *Motu Proprio Misericordia Dei*,[2] quite restrictive and without any sensitivity to the pastoral needs of communities. It came down to the fact that 'rules are rules' and must be kept and that people just have to understand this. I disagreed with his interpretation that our guidelines did not fit within the liturgical and canonical structures of our Church. But I had nowhere else to go, so I acknowledged that I would accept their interpretation, even though I did not agree with it.

He asked how confessions were heard in some of the isolated communities that did not have a church building. I informed him that as priests, if we were approached for reconciliation we would celebrate it under a tree, walking down the street, on the veranda of the pub, or in any place where a person felt comfortable and where it was private. He responded by saying that if he came into one of his isolated villages the people would have constructed a little confessional, to which I replied that it would not happen in Australia.

Cardinal Arinze then went on to criticise the survey we had presented to the Congregation on the use of the Communal Rite in the diocese. He said we had given the priests and the people a vote and they would certainly vote for something that was not hard, such as General Absolution, which was an easy way to celebrate the sacrament compared to the First Rite. At this point I was drawn back in memory to that famous meeting in 1998 from which came the

---

2. John Paul II, *Motu Proprio, Misericordia Dei*, On Certain Aspects of the Celebration of the Sacrament of Penance, 7 April 2002.

'Statement of Conclusions'. At that meeting the cardinals were saying to us bishops that we needed to tell the priests, the people and the religious what to do, without any suggestion that we should be in dialogue, as called for by Vatican II.

To make his point he said that in his culture, if he gave a person a vote, for example in a situation where a man wanted sons but his wife only produced daughters, then the husband would certainly choose another wife to have sons. Therefore it just stood to reason that our priests and people would choose General Absolution. I took exception to his criticism and told him that I did not understand his culture, in the same way as I believed he did not understand mine, and it would be wrong of me, as it was wrong of him, to be critical of each other's culture. At that point, the three who were sitting to my left and behind rose to their feet in defence of the cardinal, saying that he was not being critical and apologised for any misunderstanding that may have taken place. The bells began to ring in twelve noon so Cardinal Arinze brought the meeting to an end, threatening to hand me over to the CDF (Congregation for the Doctrine of the Faith) if I did not do exactly what he told me to do, adding the comment, 'You wouldn't like that, would you?' We all stood, walked into the corridor, prayed the Angelus[3] and I was shown the door.

As I headed back to my room at Casa Santa Marta to write the minutes of the meeting, it was plain to me that they had already made their decision before I had entered the room and before any discussion had been held. If General Absolution was happening around the world, they really did not want to know about it but would take action if they had to and would quote the law in a restrictive manner. They did leave the door open a little by saying that they understood how culturally ingrained it had become, and realised it would take time to change the practice, but they were closed to any understanding of how pastorally effective the celebration of the Communal Rite with General Absolution was for the people. They were more interested in the mode of the sacrament than in contrition. A few days later the Australian bishops held an afternoon tea inviting the Prefects of the

---

3. Angelus –Latin for 'Angel'. Prayer at 6 am, 12 noon and 6 pm, part of Catholic devotion where a bell is rung and the faithful kneel and remember the Angel Gabriel, Mary, the mother of God and the announcement to Mary of her being the mother of Jesus.

various Dicasteries to gather and meet in an informal fashion. Arinze was present but ignored me as he moved through the room greeting people.

On arriving home from Rome, I informed my brother priests of the decision that the Congregation for Divine Worship and Discipline of the Sacraments had made concerning our application. Unfortunately, as demanded by Cardinal Arinze, I would have to apply a more restrictive interpretation of any application for permission for General Absolution. This was gradually implemented over the next twelve months to two years, with our 'In-Service' education sessions focussing on the sacraments, in particular the eucharist and reconciliation. During this time, use of the Communal Rite with General Absolution gradually ceased and was replaced by the Communal Rite with 'individual absolution'. In accord with the agreement I had reached with Arinze in 2004, I since gave permission only on two occasions for the Communal Rite with General Absolution. On both occasions, the pastors were unwell and unable to spend long hours in the confessional or to travel long distances. By Easter 2007, the Communal Rite with General Absolution had been gradually replaced.

6
Future Planning

There go the people.
I must follow them for I am their leader.
Alexandre Ledru-Rollin

At a Priests Council Meeting held in Taroom in July 2003 the question
of future staffing of the diocese was discussed. On the world scene,
Toowoomba would have overall a better ratio of clergy to people than
many other dioceses, but looking to the future it could be different
due to retirement, death and fewer vocations to the priesthood. To
make sure we were well prepared for the future, a sub-committee was
formed at that meeting to prepare a discussion paper presenting some
important facts about the priests currently serving in the diocese. It was
a paper to stimulate conversation, to help discern pastoral leadership
and planning and it addressed the sixth key pastoral directive of the
Diocesan Pastoral Plan which was to explore and implement various
pastoral leadership models.[1] Consultation was held throughout the
diocese and a working document was produced to plan for the future
pastoral care of the local Church. In November 2003 at a meeting of
the Priests Council, all of the priests of the diocese were invited to
attend and participate in this conversation.

On 5 January 2004 I received a letter from the Congregation for
Clergy seeking my valued input concerning a recent letter received
by the Congregation containing information about our proposed
diocesan initiative regarding the Pastoral Leadership Proposal. The
Congregation's letter went on to say that if this information was
accurate, the Dicastery would have certain concerns regarding this

---

1. Appendix 13 – Diocesan Pastoral Plan

supposed initiative in the light of the Instruction from Rome, *Ecclesiae de mysterio.* The Congregation asked for a detailed description of this proposed policy together with all associated documentation and my own *votum.*[2]

I responded to Archbishop Csaba Ternyak on the presumption that the document he had received was the discussion paper presenting some important facts about the priests currently serving in the diocese. If this presumption was correct, I pointed out to Ternyák that the paper was prepared to stimulate conversation, and to help discern pastoral leadership and planning. It was for priests and pastoral leaders to work on and to come up with a paper that could be used in discussions throughout the Local Church. I invited the Congregation to comment on the document or they could wait until we had gone through the various levels of consultation and had come up with a working document that would be used as a foundation for further discussion and pastoral planning. I asked Ternyák for the name or names of those who sent the document so that I could speak with them personally, pastorally care for them and clarify any misunderstanding they may have with the discussion paper.

On 22 April 2004 I received the Congregation's response, clarifying its policy about divulging information that had been sent to the Holy See. Communication with the Holy See, it went on to say, is the right of every member of the faithful, along with its associated confidentiality. Except for those cases which are involved in formal administration or judicial processes, which was not the case in this instance, the identity of those in correspondence with the Holy See remains confidential. Concerning the proposed Pastoral Leadership Proposal, the Congregation thought a careful study of this proposal would be useful to me and was therefore prepared to offer its help. To aid such a study, they asked for a detailed description of the proposed policy together with all associated documentation and my *votum.*

In the meantime, I had received a letter from the Apostolic Nuncio, Archbishop Francesco Canalini, informing me that it had been reported to him that Toowoomba was experiencing a shortage of priests. Because of this, he had been told, the Council of Priests had proposed some alternatives to help alleviate this pastoral situation. Canalini offered the Apostolic Nunciature's help if needed. In reply,

---

2. Votum- my preferred option with an explanation.

I thanked him and informed him that if he would like to look at the numbers, Toowoomba would have a better ratio of clergy to people than many other dioceses around the world, and I told him what we were doing to plan for the future pastoral care of the local Church.

Further meetings of the priests were held in May and June 2004 to clarify aspects of the Pastoral Leadership Plan, culminating in November 2004 when, following a Priests Council Meeting at St Monica's Parish, Oakey, all the priests of the diocese, and pastoral leaders, gathered to discuss and vote on the final draft of the proposed Leadership Plan. It was accepted through consensus and would commence from Easter 2005, with increments of three years, for a period of nine years. Only three priests opposed the Pastoral Leadership Plan. This meeting was the fruit of consultation that had been held with Parish Pastoral Councils (or local equivalent bodies) across the diocese on the topic of Pastoral Leadership over the next nine years. Thirty-two of the thirty-five Parish Councils (or local equivalent bodies) supported it, two were opposed and one remained uncertain. There had been a strong endorsement by people, parishes, pastoral councils and priests to pursue and explore the six key statements. These were that leadership in every Catholic faith community was to be a collaborative role involving lay people and priests; that a well-defined and commissioned leadership structure (for example, a Pastoral Council) was to be in place in every faith community; and that a designated Pastoral Leadership Team was to be in place in every faith community where there was no resident full-time active priest appointed.

A change was later made to the above statement which now reads as follows: An approved and commissioned lay leadership structure be established in every parish in the diocese of Toowoomba whether there is a resident priest or not. This lay leadership structure— appropriate to each parish community situation—would be expected to work collaboratively with the Priest appointed to that community; that the principle of cooperation and sharing resources, both personnel and material, be practised across 'Regions' or 'Deaneries'; that appropriate training be offered to people in each faith community so that ministries can be provided confidently, effectively and in a pastorally sensitive way; and finally that the basic minimum allocation of priests available for full-time pastoral ministry be according to the number of priests to work in each region, based on the accepted tables for 2005–2007; 2008–2010; 2011–2013. Over the following two years, the Pastoral Leadership Plan was implemented, varying in degrees of success. As local Pastoral Councils took up the challenge, local pastoral leaders were appointed, appropriate training was implemented and the sharing of resources started to bear fruit.

This helped the Diocesan Pastoral Council and the Council of Priests to focus on a new policy and related procedures for the appointment of priests and pastoral leaders in the diocese. To support this I used my Advent Pastoral Letter of 2006 to re-focus the local Church on our new Diocesan Pastoral Leadership Plan with its associated staffing plan and appointments policy for priests and pastoral leaders.[3] Its focus was to encourage the communities to re-read the policies covering 'Ministry Appointments Policy and Procedures', the time-line this would cover, and the history of making appointments in the diocese with a focus on the key elements in the new appointments policy. The Letter encouraged all to look to the future with hope. I pointed out that we were not alone in searching for a response to the number of priests available to minister and serve the diocese, for many communities were discussing various options to address this question. So, as a pilgrim people who journey in hope, we needed to remain open to the Spirit so that we could be agents of change and respond wisely to the needs of all members of the local Church of Toowoomba.

Little did I know at the time what a controversial Advent Pastoral Letter it would become.

---

3. Appendix 7 Advent Pastoral Letter 2006

7

The 2006 Advent Pastoral Letter

Pastoral Planning has imagining the future at its heart. It is aspiration carried by imagination. Pastoral Planning aims to create a better Church, and through it a better World, as a direct outcome of its imagining. So it takes a critical look at where the Church is now, imagines a better future, then pictures in a practical way the steps to achieve that future.

B Cussen

To put the 2006 Advent Pastoral Letter into context we need to go back to the year 1994, my second year in the diocese. In an attempt to discern the signs of the times and interpret them in the light of the Gospel and then respond both spiritually and pastorally to the needs of all members of the diocese, a diocese covering 487,000 sq. kms, I decided to introduce the concept of Pastoral Planning. My motto, 'Christ is My Hope', spelt out my vision for the diocese for it was my hope that we would all work together to bring about the Kingdom of God through encouraging and enabling all to use their gifts. In this way the local Church would become more missionary and visionary and fulfil its role as servant through listening and then responding to the needs of all.

I based this on the Vatican II document, the Pastoral Constitution on the Church in the Modern World, (*Gaudium et Spes*, paragraph 4, from the documents of the Second Vatican Council). 'At all times the church carries the responsibility of reading the signs of the time and interpreting them in the light of the Gospel if it is to carry out its task. In language intelligible to every generation, she should be able to answer the ever recurring questions which the human person asks about the meaning of this present life and of the life to come, and how one is related to the other'. Other Second Vatican Council documents that encouraged me were *Lumen Gentium* (Dogmatic Constitution on the Church), and *Apostolicam Actuositatem* (Decree on the Apostolate of the Laity). All these documents gave encouragement to work cooperatively with our baptised sisters and brothers to bring about the Kingdom of God of which the church is servant.

In my Advent Pastoral Letter of that year, 1994, I invited the diocese to be open to the process of Pastoral Planning and to respond to the challenge of being agents of change so that we could respond wisely and serve the needs of all the local communities. As this work began I appointed Father Peter Doohan as Director for the Office of Pastoral Planning and I encouraged the diocese to recognise that we were living in exciting times and were experiencing the springtime[1] of new life rather than a time of death and decay. Some of our old structures and customs were falling away so that the great tree that is the Church could grow new shoots and blossom again. Some of the signs that began to emerge showed that it was not possible for the Eucharist to be celebrated in some parishes every Sunday. At first there was great sadness and a feeling that the Church was slipping into oblivion. But later, dedicated men and women stepped forward to lead Celebrations of the Word as well as Celebration of the Word with Communion. Parish Communities recognised that they were the Church, that they were able to gather and pray even when Eucharist was not possible. These parishes came to recognise that when they were able to celebrate Eucharist again they would have grown considerably. Through pain and loss and grief, the love of God had shown them their own dignity as a holy and priestly people. From decay and brokenness, new life began to spring.

In 1997 the Office of the Diocesan Pastoral Planning Ministry was changed to the Diocesan Ministry for Pastoral Vision (DMPV), and Sister Monica Cavanagh, rsj, was appointed Executive Officer. With this change the focus now became one of vision rather than planning and over the next two years every parish community in the diocese was visited by members of the Office for Pastoral Vision who helped

---

1. Pope John Paul II in *Redemptoris Missio* 'As the third millennium approaches God is preparing a great springtime for Christianity' (No 86). Thomas Merton reflects 'we are living in the greatest revolution in history, a huge spontaneous upheaval of the entire human race'.

them create the story of their parish entitled 'Creating Our Future'. With the support of a small committee, Sister Cavanagh collated this information in preparation for the first Diocesan Gathering[2] in 1998 out of which the Diocesan Pastoral Plan was created and the Diocesan Pastoral Council[3] was formed.

As I moved about the diocese, I could see signs of hope growing for the Diocesan Gathering. This hope was fed by the preparation that was taking place involving parish communities and diocesan organisations whose members were showing a willingness to take up roles in ministry and to search for an understanding of how to be church today. I had a strong sense that seeds were taking root and a new way of church was emerging. This church was being built on the memory of the past, a memory that had the ability to empower people to bring the past into the present so as to influence it and to provide hope for the future. We experienced this new growth brought about by the Spirit as signs of hope: more collaborative church structures, evangelisation, ecumenism, social justice, and a new understanding of the mission and shape of the church in the modern world. This indeed heralded a new springtime for the church.

Each year since the Diocesan Gathering in 1998 we had made advances in many of the areas of our Key Pastoral Directions, in some more than in others. An area of concern for me was the sixth item of our Key Pastoral Directives which was to explore and implement various pastoral leadership models. For some time I had been concerned for the welfare of the priests of the diocese as they took on more pastoral responsibilities as their numbers decreased. As a diocese, we had a better ratio of priests to people compared to many other dioceses both in Australia and around the World. But our numbers were decreasing through age and death so we needed to look at the best possible way to support the available priests and to make sure the parish communities and the various pastoral ministries in the diocese could be supported.

As outlined in Chapter Six, the Council of Priests Meeting held in Taroom, July 2003, authorised, with my approval, four priests to meet and develop a proposal for the future allocation of priests in the diocese. This was the catalyst that began the conversation to explore

---

2. C/f Page 15 of the Diocesan Pastoral Statement, text is in Appendix 13.
3. C/f Page 16 of the Diocesan Pastoral Statement, text is in Appendix 13.

and implement various pastoral leadership models.[4] By September the priests had developed, for prayerful consideration and discussion, a proposal addressing future pastoral leadership needs of the diocese. They were conscious that they themselves were participants in the process and challenged by it as much as everybody else. They were aware, too, of the fact that to do nothing other than continue in the 'old' way was hardly an option to keep the Local Church alive and true to the Gospel. The Pastoral Leadership Proposal had the full support of the Diocesan Pastoral Council.

The Pastoral Leadership Proposal contained several elements. The first of these elements was to recognise that there were thirty-five parish communities across the diocese which currently had a parish priest or had a recent history of having a parish priest. These thirty-five communities were grouped into six regions; four of these were the same as existing deaneries; two new regions were proposed for the Toowoomba area. Each of the thirty-five parish communities was to have an effective Parish Pastoral Council (or equivalent local body) and a designated pastoral leader, whether Priest or Pastoral Coordinator. Other faith communities within or beyond parish boundaries might well consider similar leadership structures. Teams of priests were to be formed in each region, for three-year periods (covering the next nine years) and the teams of priests in each region were to work with the Parish Pastoral Councils to determine where Pastoral Coordinators would be best located. Priests and Pastoral Coordinators together were to work as a Pastoral Team for the region as well as for each parish community. As the number of priests in a region decreased, the number of Pastoral Coordinators increased and the existing Pastoral Team was to work with the Parish Pastoral Councils to determine where new Pastoral Coordinators would be best located. Priests, Pastoral Coordinators and Parish Pastoral Councils were the primary partners in pastoral leadership in each community in each region, and Pastoral Associates, Parish Workers, Retired Priests in Residence, Religious Presence in a community, and Parish School personnel provided support to those in pastoral leadership.

---

4. See Appendix 13.

In presenting this proposal for discussion, the following foundational principles were offered:

a) *The Church is a pilgrim people living God's dream.* We are Christian faith communities called to work together in a spirit of trust and openness to bring about hope, love, justice and peace in our world. Through baptism we are called to live out God's dream by embracing action for social justice, developing and updating faith education and spirituality, respecting and honouring faith traditions, promoting and celebrating life-giving liturgy, evangelising life and culture and exploring various pastoral leadership models (Diocesan Pastoral Statement 1999).

b) *Every faith community is gifted with the ministry gifts of the Spirit.* The community exercises ministry through the particular gifts of those within its fold. In a profound sense, derived from baptism, the community itself is priestly and eucharistic. It is called to worship God, called to respond compassionately to human need both within and beyond the faith community, called to build communion in which all are welcomed and valued.

c) Where the faith community includes (or shares) an ordained Priest, the community and its life is profoundly enriched through the regular celebration of eucharist. Here the community finds its ultimate meaning, life and encouragement, and gives worship to God.

d) The ordained ministry is a particular call to leadership and service within the local Church.

e) Each parish community needs to have an effective Parish Pastoral Council or in smaller communities, a leadership group based on the leadership style of the Parish Pastoral Council. The Parish Pastoral Council works in partnership with the Priest or Pastoral Coordinator in providing leadership and planning in the community.

f) A Pastoral Coordinator is a person (other than a priest) who is entrusted with a share in the pastoral care of a parish community by the Bishop, on advice from the Parish Pastoral Council. This person exercises a leadership role of responsibility for the day to day functioning of a parish community in partnership with the Pastoral Council and the priests in the regional team.

g) Pastoral leadership is a particular ministry gift: a gift of service to the faith community. In their ministry of pastoral leadership, Priests, Pastoral Coordinators and Parish Pastoral Councils embody, in a profound sense, the deeper leadership responsibility that resides in the whole faith community to be a source of life to the world. All the baptised share responsibility for the life and mission of the Church. Designated leaders, in and through their ministry of pastoral leadership, are immersed in their communities, sharing faith and life, wisdom and responsibility.

h) Each faith community in the diocese (whether within or beyond parishes) is to have reasonable access to the sacraments and the ministries only a Priest can provide. When faith communities are unable to celebrate Sunday eucharist they are encouraged to maintain their sense of identity and belonging by coming together each Sunday as a worshipping community for a Liturgy of the Word and by finding alternative ways to celebrate the life experiences of the community.

i) The diocese is to provide support and training, formation and education to those involved in pastoral leadership.

j) While renewing existing communities, we need to affirm the primacy of the family and to support and encourage all families in their effort to form their children in the faith. Parish communities need to pray and call forth leadership at family and community level and to encourage vocations to ordained leadership and to the witness of religious life.

k) *Parish communities have the right and the responsibility to retain their identity and existence.* Through baptism, they are called to be the servant of the reign of God within that part of the world in which they live and work. Each community is called to recognise and affirm the ministry gifts of those within its fold. It is only by building and maintaining strong, vibrant, gospel-centred communities with a missionary outlook that the continued existence of faith communities may be ensured.

l) *Every Priest needs a support community* and a place to call 'home'. Where a priest works across a region and is involved in one or more communities, his residency and 'home' in one place does not mean favouritism for that particular community but is for his benefit as a person.

The next Council of Priests meeting was held in Warwick on 11 and 12 November 2003. All Priests of the diocese were invited to participate in an open forum on the second day of the meeting to discuss the Pastoral Leadership Proposal. In the meantime, communities were invited to discuss the proposal and the committee of four were available to participate in these discussions. They requested responses before the November Council meeting. Those present at the November meeting agreed that the discussion of the proposal be widened to include all Parish Pastoral Councils (or equivalent local bodies) as the next stage, and extensive conversations within all the faith communities were promoted.

New material was sent out for discussion focussing on two basic questions which were of deep concern to all and to which there was, hopefully, the possibility of finding a practical solution: How could we as Diocesan Priests best serve the Toowoomba Diocese over the next nine years and how could we ensure that effective pastoral leadership would be provided within every faith community? There were also a number of related important issues which needed to be addressed. These included attracting, preparing and ordaining from within our Diocese significant numbers of new Priests; training and formation for lay people in pastoral leadership positions; recruiting, preparing, supporting and sensitively placing priests from outside the Diocese; finding funds, from both local and diocesan sources, for wages and training of personnel. None of these were simple issues but they deserved detailed and thorough discussion.

Born out of these conversations, and as previously mentioned, accepted through consensus, the final draft of the Proposed Leadership Plan would commence from Easter 2005 with increments of three years for a period of nine years.[5] This had the support of the Priests' Council as well as the Diocesan Pastoral Council.

To drive this proposal through ongoing education, and to monitor its implementation, a combined committee of representatives from the Priests Council and the Diocesan Pastoral Council was formed. This group became conscious that there were gaps in people's knowledge throughout the diocese which affected the implementation of some aspects of the proposed plan. To help alleviate this, communities were invited to take up the offer of the Director of the Office of Pastoral Formation and/or members of the combined committee to help in the ongoing education process and to discern the strengths and the weaknesses of the proposed plan. During 2006 I became aware that there were still gaps in people's knowledge and further clarification was necessary. To respond to this need, and to stimulate discussion, I decided to use my Advent Pastoral Letter of 2006 as a way to refocus all communities of the diocese on the key elements of the Diocesan Pastoral Leadership Plan,[6] with a special focus on the new Policy and related Procedures for the Appointment of Priests and Pastoral Leaders in the diocese. It was my hope that the letter would help communities appreciate their call to contribute and participate in whatever way they could, so that the diocese would become more missionary and visionary, and they would fulfil their baptismal calling through listening and then responding to the needs of their brothers and sisters. To show them that they were not alone, that other communities around the world were struggling to find solutions to similar pastoral problems, I used examples of discussions that were taking place around the world, not as proposals for them to adopt, but to help them look for options that would ensure that Eucharist might be celebrated. The reference in the Advent Letter: 'While we continue to reflect carefully on these options . . .' did not refer to the

---

5. See chapter 6.
6. See Chapter 6.

several responses that were being discussed *internationally, nationally and locally* but to the invitation to the local communities to offer suggestions of how best to implement the Proposed Leadership Plan for ensuring that Eucharist might be celebrated.

I did not have to worry about the letter not stimulating discussion for it became the centrepiece of conversations far beyond the Toowoomba Diocese.[7]

I began the letter by saying that:

At the start of this year [23 January 2006] on the recommendation of the Diocesan Pastoral Council and the Council of Priests, I wrote to you about the new Policy and related Procedures for the appointment of Priests and Pastoral Leaders in our diocese.

With that letter I included a copy of the:
a) Ministry Appointments Policy and Procedures document;
b) Timeline covering the years 2005 to 2013 and
c) Background Comments on the history of making appointments in our diocese and on the key elements in the new Appointments Policy.

I would encourage you to read this material again. It remains the basis for implementing our Diocesan Pastoral Leadership Plan over the nine year period that will draw to a close in Easter 2014.

This letter invites you to look to the future with hope.

Our new Diocesan Pastoral Leadership Plan with its associated Staffing Plan and Appointment Policy for Priests and Pastoral Leaders is a transitional measure covering nine years, beginning Easter 2005. As with any interim measure, it calls into play uncertainties and worries. We do face an uncertain future with regard to the number of active priests in our diocese and we have yet to design what shape priest staffing may take at Easter 2014 when this transitional period draws to a close.

But this in-between time is not all doom and gloom! Already we have witnessed a flowering in lay-led ministry at a local level: Pastoral Councils are being established or consolidated, Finance Councils are being resourced and inserviced, Liturgy Committees and Baptism, Marriage, Funeral, Confirmation and Eucharist, Social Justice and

---

7. See Appendix 7 for the full text.

Ecumenism ministry groups are being developed, St Vincent de Paul Conferences and Care and Concern Groups continue their works of compassion, School Boards are in place in many schools. In several Parish communities Priests already work side by side with Pastoral Leaders, Pastoral Associates, Co-Workers and coordinators.

This interim period invites us into deeper faith in God's Spirit at work in our own time, trust in one another and hope for the future. We undertake this task together as best we can with the human and material resources we have to hand. We know this transitional time is neither ideal nor preferable but necessary: we accept the pastoral situation of our own day and work within it as people of faith and hope.

The **immediate task** before us is to develop the procedure for making appointments of priests in the diocese in the light of the discussion, discernment and appointment decisions made in these last twelve months. The new Ministry Appointment Policy and Procedures for Priests and Pastoral Leaders addresses this task.

The **long-term task** that remains as yet unaddressed is the development of a priest Staffing Plan for **Easter 2014**, once again within the wider context of a vision for Diocesan Pastoral Leadership. Current information on ages and numbers of priests currently working in the diocese presents a challenge.

In parish-based ministry in 2014, there will be:
- 65 years and younger: 6 priests with 3 in the 61-65 year group
- 66-70 years: 8 priests (with the option to retire)

In diocesan ministry in 2014, there will be:
- 65 years and younger: 2 priests
- 66-70 years: 2 priests (with the option to retire)
- 71-75 years: 1 Bishop

We may well be moving towards a Staffing Plan that places two Priests in the larger towns or communities in each of the six regions, one priest 65 years or younger and the second priest from the older group (66–70), with the surrounding faith communities served by an increased number of Pastoral Leaders.

Given our deeply held belief in the primacy of Eucharist for the identity, continuity and life of each parish community, we may well need to be much more open towards other options for ensuring that

Eucharist may be celebrated; as has been discussed internationally, nationally and locally, the ideas of:

- ordaining married, single or widowed men who are chosen and endorsed by their local parish community;
- welcoming former priests, married or single, back to active ministry;
- ordaining women, married or single;
- recognising Anglican, Lutheran and Uniting Church Orders.

While we continue to reflect carefully on these options, we remain committed to actively promoting vocations to the current celibate male priesthood and open to inviting priests from overseas.

What is certain is that Easter 2014 is irrevocably approaching!

Please take some time to give these matters serious thought and reflection. In Advent this year, we begin preparing for the second three-year period of our Pastoral Leadership Plan by asking the priests two questions:

a) where are you willing and able to work for the next three years?
b) where would you prefer to work for the next three years?

Responses will be collated and used as the basis for discussion and discernment at our next Presbyteral Forum, to be held during Lent 2007. From the Presbyteral Forum will come advice on Priest Staffing for the period 2008 to 2010. As a pilgrim people who journey in hope we need to remain open to the Spirit so that we can be agents of change and respond wisely to the needs of all members of the local Church of Toowoomba.

I ended the letter by acknowledging an acute awareness of the pain many of our brothers and sisters in the diocese affected by drought and inviting all to hold each other in prayer knowing our God is with us and wishing all the joy and peace of Christmas and every blessing for 2007.

Birdsville, Queensland, in the dry season.

Birdsville, Queensland, in wet season.

8

Continuing Correspondence From Rome

Critical intelligence is the gift God gave humanity.
To use it in the cause of human dignity and insight
is one of the great ways of serving God. When
faith suppresses questions, it dies, when it accepts
superficial answers, it withers. Faith is not opposed to
doubt. What it is opposed to is the shallow certainty
that what we understand is all there is.

Rabbi Jonathon Sacks

As the Catholic 'world' was focussing on World Youth Day in August 2005 in Cologne, Germany, and I was preparing with other Queensland bishops to accompany the Queensland contingent, a letter arrived from Cardinal Arinze. This letter was also copied to the Apostolic Nuncio, Archbishop Ambrose de Paoli, Archbishop Carroll, the President of the Australian Bishop's Conference and Archbishop John Bathersby, Archbishop of Brisbane. The letter focussed on my visit to the Dicastery (Congregation) during the *ad limina* visit in 2004, mentioning how I had put forward many reasons for collective absolution in the diocese. Arinze pointed out how he had explained that both the Code of Canon Law and the Apostolic Letter *Misericordia Dei* laid down stringent conditions which make General Absolution altogether exceptional and individual confession with individual absolution the ordinary form of the sacrament. It was now more than a year since my visit and the Congregation of Divine Worship and Discipline of the Sacraments would be interested to hear if individual confession with absolution had now replaced collective absolution in the diocese. Before I left for World Youth Day, I penned a letter to Arinze pointing out that individual confessions with individual absolution had always been the ordinary form of the sacrament in the diocese of Toowoomba. I pointed out that General Absolution had been the exception. I also noted that in the discussion at the meeting in Rome in the previous year, it was my understanding that we had differed on the reasons that would fulfil both the Code of Canon Law and the Apostolic Letter *Misericordia Dei*. However, I had agreed to put into place a process that would, over time, replace the Communal Rite with General Absolution with the Communal Rite with 'individual' Absolution. Further, I had undertaken that I would give permission for the celebration of the Communal Rite with General Absolution only in exceptional circumstances which did fulfil the requirements according to the Code of Canon Law and *Misericordia Dei*. I added in the letter that I still believed that our diocesan reasons—to meet a moral and physical need in the life of the diocese—did fulfil the stringent conditions laid down for the administration of the sacrament of penance. I assured him that we had an ongoing programme of education with a particular focus in 2005 on the eucharist and that the sacraments were being celebrated according to the Church's highest law, namely, the salvation of souls, further noting that any law that did not put one in touch with a compassionate and loving God would not be a good law.

At this time I also received a letter from Cardinal Re, Prefect of the Congregation for Bishops, commenting on the Quinquennial Report for the Diocese of Toowoomba 1998 – 2003. He made comments about the diocese being in the Southern Region of the State of Queensland with the western parts of the diocese considered more 'remote', and that, as a local Church, we should strongly uphold the authority of the Magisterium of the Church[1] as it had been expressed in the teaching of the Second Vatican Council and in papal documents since then. He then went on to say that we (the Diocese of Toowoomba) had

1. The Magisterium in Catholic teaching refers to the authority that lays down what is the authentic teaching of the Church. For the Catholic Church, that authority is vested uniquely in the pope and the bishops who are in communion (*communio*) with the pope. Scripture and tradition in Catholicism 'make up a single sacred deposit of the Word of God, which is entrusted to the Church' (Vatican II Dogmatic Constitution on Divine Revelation, *Dei Verbum*, No 10), and the magisterium is not independent of this, since 'all that it proposes for belief as being divinely revealed is derived from this single deposit of faith'. *Catechism of the Catholic Church*, No 86.

inherited a situation where the so-called Third Rite of Reconciliation had been practised as an acceptable form of receiving the sacrament of penance. He was confident that, in solidarity with my brother bishops throughout Australia who had also dealt with similar challenges, we would continue to find ways to catechise the faithful and to promote the true and authentic discipline of the sacrament of penance.

In October 2005, I received further correspondence from Cardinal Arinze claiming that my characterisation of the outcome of the meeting held on 20 March, 2004 was not exact. He went on to say that, after a review of the minutes of the aforementioned meeting, the Congregation of Divine Worship and Discipline of the Sacraments had not found anything outside of its presentation of the requisites which would allow for 'general absolution' to be licitly administered. The question, he said, was not a case of my opinion versus your opinion but the requirement of the Code of Canon Law, canon 961, which alone gave the conditions for the granting of General Absolution. These conditions, he noted, had been made even more precise by Pope John Paul II's *Motu Proprio, Misericordia Dei,* Number 4. This was followed by a question as to whether or not, as a diocesan bishop, I accepted these directives and they awaited my response.

The question, in my view, had never been whether or not I accepted the directives of the Code of Canon Law, or those of the *Motu Proprio, Misericordia Dei.* I did. The question was, rather, whether or not the material that I presented to the Congregation (Congregation of Divine Worship and Discipline of the Sacraments) could be fairly interpreted as adequately complying with the canonical and liturgical norms under which the sacrament could be celebrated to meet the exceptional pastoral realities existing in the local Church of Toowoomba. My minutes of the March 2004 meeting reflect this so in my reply to Arinze in November 2005 I asked for a copy of their minutes, so that I too could review them, before I responded any further to their communication.

It was early December 2005 when a reply came from Cardinal Arinze informing me that their minutes were internal notes of the Congregation of Divine Worship and Discipline of the Sacraments and were not for publication. He went on and quoted extracts from his letter of October 2005, asking me the same question so that the Dicastery (Congregation of Divine Worship and Discipline of the Sacraments) would know how it must proceed in this matter. In early

July 2006, I received a phone call and a letter from the Apostolic Nuncio, Archbishop Ambrose de Paoli. In his letter he referred to some correspondence he had received from a few people in the diocese complaining about the Communal Rite of Reconciliation. I was able to advise him that General Absolution was gradually being replaced by individual absolution in the Communal Rites as directed by the Congregation for Divine Worship and the Discipline of the Sacraments and as accepted by me at the meeting held in March 2004. He asked me if I would respond to Cardinal Arinze, saying, 'Don't try to discuss anything with him, just give him what he wants and get him out of your hair'.

On 12 July 2006 I took Archbishop Ambrose's advice and wrote to Cardinal Arinze, apologising for not having answered his letter earlier and assuring him that I had never not accepted the directives, and that individual confessions with individual absolution had always been the ordinary form of the sacrament in the Diocese of Toowoomba. All other forms were an exception. I said that I would have been happy to continue the dialogue as I believed the Communal Rite of Reconciliation in both its forms had great pastoral benefits, not only for the general community at large, but especially in the exceptional moral circumstances in which many members of our rural communities found themselves. This was not to be.

9

Lead Up to the Apostolic Visitation

*In the torment of the insufficiency of everything attainable we finally
learn that here in this life all symphonies remain unfinished.*
Karl Rahner SJ

It was 21 December 2006 when final preparations were being put into
place for the celebration of Christmas, offices were preparing to close
and families were busy preparing to celebrate this great feast when I
received a fax from Cardinal Arinze. He informed me that the Holy
Father had instructed the three Cardinal Prefects of the Congregations
for the Doctrine of the Faith, for Bishops and for Divine Worship and
the Discipline of the Sacraments to hold a discussion with me on the
practice of General Absolution in the Diocese of Toowoomba. Two
dates were suggested: Tuesday 13 February or Friday 23 February
2007 at 10 a.m in the offices of the Congregation for Bishops. He
requested my reply as soon as possible so he could communicate the
dates to the other two cardinals, and extended to me best wishes for
Christmas, expressing his religious esteem.

The next day, 22 December 2006, I replied that I would be in Rome
in May 2007 for the Anglophone Meeting on Professional Standards,
and asked would it be possible to change the meeting date to May. I also
pointed out that I would be heavily committed in the next few months
because of my responsibilities in the area of Professional Standards
in which I represented the Australian Episcopal Conference. There
were also the immediate pastoral responsibilities in the Province of
Queensland and the Diocese of Toowoomba, which included being
present with one of my priests who was dying, as well as giving
support for a dying family friend.

After seeking advice, I informed them that it would be my intention to be accompanied by at least one canon lawyer, possibly two. I pointed out that I was surprised by the letter for, since my meeting with Cardinal Arinze in March 2004, I had not given permission for the celebration of the Communal Rite with General Absolution apart from two exceptional circumstances. I added that I had encouraged the priests of the diocese to make sure they always celebrated the Rites of Reconciliation according to the canonical and liturgical norms of the Church's tradition. I explained that we also had an ongoing education programme concerning the sacraments and that I had employed a religious priest to travel around the diocese to spend time in all the communities, especially in some of the most isolated ones, giving people the chance of a visiting confessor. I went on to say that the Australian Bishops' Conference was in the process of drawing up guidelines for the practice of the Communal Rite, with General Absolution, for Australian conditions, and after the Australian Catholic Bishops Conference meeting in May we should have a clearer guide as to what these conditions would be. I finished off the letter by informing them that our fax machine was not secure and I would appreciate any further correspondence to be sent by confidential mail.

In the first week of January 2007, while I was on retreat, a fax arrived at my office from Cardinal Arinze informing me that, after due consideration of my letter, the three cardinals wished to say that the proposed meeting with them was important enough to take precedence over the possible schedules that I had mentioned. I was requested to choose one of the two dates in February 2007. Cardinal Arinze went on to say that the meeting, of its nature, should be between myself and the three cardinals without the necessity to bring a canon lawyer into it, and that if I wished to bring a brother bishop, that would be all right. If I insisted on bringing a canon lawyer, they would accept this.

In response, I took the opportunity to explain to the three cardinals that, as I was sure they would understand, my prime responsibility was to my diocese and therefore my pastoral responsibilities to the local Church would not allow me to be in Rome on 13 or 23 February 2007. But I went on to say that I would be happy to meet with them while I was in Rome for the Anglophone Meeting on Professional

Standards which would be during the week of 21–28 May 2007. It was only at that time that I could have the support of another brother bishop to accompany me to the meeting. Concerning a canon lawyer being present, I said I would keep my options open. The next three sentences in my response to Arinze were, I believe, the beginning of the grounds upon which the decision was made for my dismissal:

> In 2004 when I had a meeting with yourself, Cardinal Arinze, I was foolish enough to think that the meeting was between brothers searching for the truth and reflecting together on the pastoral needs of the people of God. I will never place myself in that situation again and it is only in the company of a brother bishop and possibly a canon lawyer would I attend another meeting. So that I can prepare myself, I would like to receive an agenda for the meeting with the questions that are going to be addressed.

Based on information arising from my initial meeting with Archbishop Charles Chaput, Archbishop of Denver, USA, the Apostolic Visitator to the Diocese of Toowoomba in 2007, I believe the above statement was the cause of much upheaval in Rome. Chaput's comments to me, as well as his statements to the chancellor, Father Brian Sparksman, led me to the view that he believed that this was the crux of the problem between me and Rome. He said that, in comparison to the reaction to my letter, we should disregard all the other letters of complaint sent to Rome about my leadership of the diocese.

The Queensland bishops gathered for their Provincial meeting at Wynberg, New Farm (the Brisbane residence of Archbishop Bathersby), in early March 2007. Present at the meeting was the Apostolic Nuncio, Archbishop Ambrose de Paoli, who was to bless and lay the foundation stone for the new Holy Spirit Seminary at Banyo. He knew I was going to Rome in May and asked why. I explained to him about the Anglophone Meeting on Professional Standards, dealing with sexual abuse within the Church, and how important it was for the English speaking world. We had been given permission to meet inside the Vatican at the Casa Santa Marta, which was an important witness to the world that at last the Vatican acknowledged, not only that the meeting was taking place, but that it was taking place within the Vatican itself. Two days later I received a phone call at Wynberg from Ambrose de Paoli, informing me that Pope Benedict, after consulting with the three cardinals of the Congregations for the Doctrine of the Faith, the Bishops and Divine Worship, had decided to send an Apostolic Visitator to the Toowoomba Diocese. This was to be Archbishop Charles Chaput OFM Cap, the Archbishop of Denver, Colorado, USA.

Archbishop Ambrose was very sympathetic about the concerns raised by such a visit. However, he thought it could be a good thing to have as he believed Archbishop Chaput came from a pastoral background and would therefore be able to understand the importance of the implications concerning the pastoral effectiveness that I had placed on the celebration of the Communal Rite with General Absolution. In experiencing the diocese at first hand, he might become an advocate and help develop a better understanding of the pastoral effectiveness of collective absolution.

A few days later I received a letter from Cardinal Re informing me of the Visitation and the reasons behind it. The reason for the visit was that the doctrinal and disciplinary line that I was following seemed not to be in accord with the Magisterium of the Church, and an expression of this was to be found in some phrases of my Advent Pastoral Letter of 2006. This was the first time that the Advent Letter was referred to and eventually it became the grounds on which I was dismissed.[1] I was informed that Archbishop Chaput would be arriving in Australia on 23 April 2007, that the Apostolic Nuncio would provide me with further details and that I would offer full collaboration and hospitality to Chaput, enabling him to fulfil the specific mission entrusted to him by Pope Benedict XVI. Thus, planning for the visitation began.

---

1. Appendix 7, Advent Pastoral Letter 2006.

10

The Announcement of The Visitation

One ailment that antibiotics will never stamp out is premature formation of opinion.

Anon

The letter from the Congregation for Bishops appointing Archbishop Charles Chaput, OFM Cap, as Apostolic Visitator to the diocese of Toowoomba read:

> His Holiness Pope Benedict XVI does, through this letter of appointment by the Congregation for Bishops, commit His Excellency, Charles J Chaput to the office of Visitator to the Diocese of Toowoomba to diligently discover and review the state of Catholic Doctrine and governance there, and to report on it accordingly.
>
> The Sacred Congregation has confidence that the same Most Reverend Archbishop of Denver will carry out this assigned task zealously and in comformity with the Apostolic mandate, as he is so authorized to do by this document.
>
> Given in Rome, from the offices of the Sacred Congregation for Bishops, on the 12th day of March, in the year 2007.
>
> Giovanni B Cardinal Re, Prefect Bishop; Franciso Monterisi, Secretary

On 23 March, 2007, I received my first fax from Archbishop Charles Chaput informing me that, after a conversation with the Nuncio, Archbishop de Paoli, he would be arriving in Brisbane on April 23 and departing for Denver on April 29, that he was looking forward to meeting me and seeing the diocese first hand, that he was grateful for my willingness to receive him and while the matter at hand was serious, he was arriving with no pre-determined outcome. He also mentioned that his elderly mother was quite ill and he would be spending some time with her and he looked forward to speaking with me by phone. I responded by email assuring him of a remembrance in our prayers and masses for his mother and, as I had received no correspondence from Rome at this time, I would appreciate any information he could give me concerning the visit and what he had been asked to investigate.

He faxed an immediate reply saying that he had not yet completed reading the latest Quinquennial Report and other materials provided to him by Cardinal Re. He wrote that the Vatican was seriously concerned by the continuing widespread use of General Absolution, and that my Advent Pastoral Letter of 2006 had increased that apprehension by resurfacing the issues of married clergy, women priests and the possibility of recognising Protestant orders. Rome was also concerned by the vocation situation in the diocese and the general theological climate, and he suspected that the Holy See viewed some of my responses as inadequate and unhelpful. All of this, he said, had raised the level of uneasiness about the viability of my pastoral leadership in the diocese. He went on to say that he regretted the need to be so direct and he had no desire to diminish my service to the Church and the people of the diocese. He would need to speak privately with each of my senior advisors and assistants and see some of the life of the diocese first hand; he would need to talk personally with a selection of key people, both supportive and critical of my leadership; and he would probably have other questions to pursue once he familiarised himself with Toowoomba circumstances. His focus then would be the Communal Rite, the Advent Letter, my pastoral style and the lack of vocations. There was no mention of the four ordinations we had celebrated in the last few years.

On Thursday morning 29 March 2007, at a meeting of the Priests and Pastoral Leaders to discuss future staffing of parishes in line with our Diocesan Pastoral Leadership Policy, I informed those gathered of the imminent Apostolic visitation and stated the reasons for the formal visit. There was shock, anger and tears but a commitment to participate fully in the process, and to make sure that the Apostolic Visitor would gain insight into the life of our rural diocese and that they would have an opportunity to meet with the Visitor.

At the same time, Father Brian Noonan, Chair of the Toowoomba Diocesan Council of Priests, emailed Archbishop Chaput on behalf of the priests of the diocese extending a warm welcome in anticipation of his arrival, and stated that the priests would welcome the opportunity to meet with him as a body during his time in the diocese. Archbishop Chaput's reply to me and to Father Noonan focused on the fact that he believed his visit was intended by the Holy See to be as discreet as possible and not a matter of public disclosure, and that he would be happy to meet confidentially with the Council of Priests but did not think a general discussion with the priests would be a useful way of approaching this task. He did not want a public meeting with the priests of the diocese because he said his time in Toowoomba was not a matter for public discussion or general disclosure, but it would be useful if he had a list of the priests whom he could visit individually. He went on to say that he would like to meet with five of the most recently ordained, three priests from the middle age group of the diocese and three from the senior group, as well as the Vicar General, the Vicar for Clergy and the Judicial Vicar.

On arriving back from Cunnamulla, one of the towns I was hoping he would visit, I spoke to Father Sparksman and it was agreed that a meeting with the Council of Priests would be arranged and further meetings organised with those he would like to see. I informed Archbishop Chaput of this and suggested that on the Wednesday we would take a trip around the diocese which would enable him to see first-hand the country as well as a number of towns and communities where he could meet some of the priests, people and religious, and a cross-section of people from various communities. I assured him that the trip and the meetings would be as discreet as possible.

The Vicar General of the Toowoomba Diocese, Father Peter Dorfield, wrote to the bishops of the Province of Queensland on 3 April 2007 seeking their support. He pinpointed for them the issues that Chaput was to enquire into, such as, the doctrinal and disciplinary line that I follow in my pastoral leadership. He went on to identify for the bishops the five areas of concern that Chaput had identified: the use of General Absolution; the mentioning of issues such as married and women priests; the possibility of recognising Protestant Orders; the vocations situation; and the general theological climate in the diocese. Father Dorfield asked them for their support in upholding the record of my doctrinal and disciplinary orthodoxy and the quality of my pastoral leadership. He put this request in the context of the fact that, as brother bishops working closely in addressing the pastoral needs of the Province of Queensland, they as a body would have special insight into the lives and convictions of one another; he was asking that some of that wisdom about myself not be left unsaid.

On, or about the same date, Fr Peter Dorfield received a communication from Archbishop John Bathersby which was also forwarded to me. Bathersby suggested that he should meet with Archbishop Chaput on the morning of Tuesday the 24th of April 2007, which was eventually changed to the afternoon of the 23rd of April so that Chaput could travel to the diocese on the Tuesday. Bathersby went on to suggest that, because it would be difficult to travel in the diocese, he recommended restricting his interviews to the larger cities of Toowoomba, Warwick and Dalby since they were reasonably close together. He also suggested that he stay at the Cathedral presbytery which would give us both appropriate independence and he could use the Cathedral presbytery interview rooms. He also called Chaput's attention to the fact that April 25, Anzac Day, was a major remembrance day in Australia, and that bishops and most priests are involved in public ceremonies. Chaput, in recognising this fact, asked if it was possible to work on the 25th April even though it would have some difficulties.

I contacted Archbishop Bathersby about his suggested itinerary. As Bathersby had not contacted me, he was unaware that I had been in communication with Chaput but was happy to change the Tuesday meeting to either the afternoon or the evening of the 23rd April which allowed Chaput to travel to Toowoomba on Tuesday morning the 24th of April. I went on to suggest that he be picked up at 8.30 a.m. from the Archbishop's House in Brisbane to arrive in Toowoomba around 10 a.m. for morning tea and a meeting with the Council of Priests, with other interviews arranged for the afternoon.

On Wednesday, Anzac Day, a public holiday in Australia, I suggested that we begin our diocesan tour so that he could visit some of our smaller communities and speak with as many people, priests, and pastoral leaders as possible. We would then spend the night in Charleville and I would bring him back the next day to do the same thing. We would then arrange more interviews again in Toowoomba on Friday and, if he so desired, also on the Saturday. He could then depart for Brisbane on Saturday or Sunday depending on his plans. In looking at a map, Chaput thought the offer of Charleville was generous but too far as it would mean a lot of time in the car. He would rather stay closer to Toowoomba to meet more people more easily and to avoid caving into jet-lag. He thought one day and evening travelling locally around the Toowoomba area might be a better use of his time and, if we were going to be away overnight, he would like to be back next day to rest and perhaps do some afternoon interviews.

In a meeting with Father Peter Dorfield, Vicar General, and Father Brian Sparksman, Chancellor, I shared Archbishop Chaput's concern about travelling to Charleville as we looked at a possible itinerary for his visit. I informed Chaput that both my vicar general and chancellor agreed that it would be important for him to travel for the two days visiting various communities so that he would gain an appreciation of the geographic spread of the diocese. While conscious of jet-lag and the need to rest, I informed him that if we did not travel then it would be impossible for him to be able to fully appreciate the life of the local Church, and that he would be able to rest in the car while I drove. I asked him how many priests and people he would like to interview and how long he would like to spend with each person so that we could make the best use of time.

I suggested that it would be important for him to meet the Diocesan Pastoral Council, which I believed would help him gain a picture of the great work that was happening in the diocese and, if he agreed, this could happen on Saturday morning. For his privacy and comfort I offered my residence here in Toowoomba where he would be able to conduct his interviews in private. On Saturday 14 April 2007, I received an email from Chaput informing me that the Holy See had approved of one of his permanent deacons, Deacon John Neal, husband, father and former business executive, who served as the chief operating officer of the theological seminary in Denver (reporting to the Rector), to accompany him. Chaput said he would need personal access to a private phone for diocesan calls, internet access and a residency away from my home for both Deacon Neal and himself, as well as the need for a driver if necessary. He went on to say that he regretted burdening me with these things but, given the Holy See's mandate for his visit, he must insist. He thought travelling over one night could be useful if I thought so but he would need to be back in Toowoomba the next afternoon for interviews. He explained that he understood the challenges of a vast diocese because he had served as the Bishop of Rapid City, South Dakota, before going to Denver, Colorado. He pointed out that both these US dioceses were geographically quite large and diverse, and he could not spend two days on the road because there simply was not time.

Taking into account all the requests that Archbishop Chaput had made, Fathers' Sparksman and Dorfield at last put together a proposed itinerary and emailed the information to the Visitator in the USA.

Early on Sunday morning the 15th of April 2007, one of our youngest priests, Father Tony O'Keefe, lost his battle with a brain tumour. This brought to an end a journey of over two years filled with much suffering.

11

The Visitation

Loyalty to a petrified opinion never broke a chain or freed a human soul
Mark Twain

On Tuesday morning, 24 April 2007, Fathers Dorfield, and Sparksman arrived at Archbishop Bathersby's residence, Wynberg, Brisbane to collect Archbishop Chaput and Deacon Neal. They arrived in Toowoomba at Bishop's House around 10 a.m. While I met with Chaput, Dorfield took Deacon Neal to their arranged accommodation at Grammar View Motel, within five minutes walking distance from my residence. After a short initial meeting, Chaput was taken to the Cathedral Centre for a meeting with the Council of Priests.

The meeting with the Council of Priests was chaired by Father Brian Noonan, who was the official Chair at the time. Archbishop Chaput introduced himself and announced his task: at the direction of the Holy See, he was to investigate my pastoral leadership in a number of specific areas and the pastoral life of the diocese. He handed Father Peter Dorfield a photocopy of the letter (in Latin) authorising this mission which stated that he was 'to diligently discover and review the state of Catholic doctrine and governance there, and to report on it accordingly'. This letter was from the Congregation of Bishops, signed by Cardinal Re and dated 12 March 2007.

As I understand it, what followed was a somewhat one-sided discussion. As matters were tabled by Archbishop Chaput, responses flowed from the priests of the diocese, who indicated that he needed to understand both the pastoral context in which these matters occurred and the broader and distinctive setting of the Church across the Toowoomba Diocese.

Efforts were made by the priests to describe the use of General Absolution as being appropriate, given the nature of our diocese and the liturgical and canonical boundaries that had been provided by me. The Advent Pastoral Letter of 2006 that had caused so much angst in Vatican minds was set in context. No women had been ordained. No plans were in place for the ordination of women. Church communities all over the world were discussing the ordination of women, in spite of the Vatican decree that no such discussion should take place. Were these dioceses also subject to Apostolic Visitations and investigation?

Ecumenical relationships in our diocese between Anglican, Uniting and Lutheran Churches were well-established, with clear lines of respect for the particular and distinctive teachings of each Church body. In practice, everyone knew how this worked in local rural communities, often separated from each other by considerable distances. The allegations of formal recognition of Anglican orders, or of recognition of the pastoral roles of Uniting and Lutheran pastors, simply missed the point and rendered effective ecumenical collaboration within agreed limits questionable, or even worse, of no account.

It was reported to me following the meeting that the priests' responses were met with Archbishop Chaput's inflexible demand for adherence to the Magisterium as outlined in the Catechism and in the teachings of the Holy Father.

A whole range of curious other matters then began to emerge: priests wearing ties; words in eucharistic prayers being changed; having my face painted and wearing a colourful stole at a diocesan youth gathering; quality and extent of prayer in the life of the diocese; liturgical abuses that confused the laity on the distinction of role of priest and people; inaccurate information on vocations and ordinations; support of lay leadership to the detriment of priests; insufficient energy and involvement in the diocese on pro-life issues.

In this early meeting with the Council of Priests, in spite of inadequate discussion of issues, Archbishop Chaput gave the impression that he was willing to listen. One priest would later say to me that he thought the Archbishop was a smooth and professional operator, deliberately giving the impression of labouring under an unwelcome task, almost seeking our sympathy or at least our understanding. As the days progressed and individual interviews with priests and lay people took place, he seemed to come across in a different light. Many have said to me that Archbishop Chaput was direct, blunt, accusatory and in some instances, offensive. Some believed that his approach to his visit was becoming inquisitorial and confrontational.

After lunch at Bishop's House I met privately with Chaput without Deacon Neal. The meeting was cordial, respectful and focussed on the topics of my letter to Cardinal Arinze: General Absolution, abuses in liturgy, forum of conscience, the Catechism of the Catholic Church, vocations to the priesthood and my Advent Pastoral Letter of 2006. Chaput was armed with files that he had been given from Rome which contained not only my correspondence, but letters of complaint written over the years I had been in Toowoomba.

One of the first comments that Archbishop Chaput made to me directly was to say that in his view I was brave to write the letter I did to Cardinal Arinze, that he would never have had the courage to write such a letter, and if they had asked him to be in Rome, he would have been there yesterday.[1]

From his comments and general tone, and from the way future conversations and meetings with the three Cardinals, Levada, Arinze and Re, developed, I would say that this letter was the tipping point on which the decision was made for my dismissal.[2] He then asked me a curious question: 'Why am I here?' He went on to say that he had not read anything in the material handed to him that he had not read about or heard happening in other places, and being said by other bishops around the world. So he asked me the question again: Why did I think he was asked to do the Visitation, as he had never done one before? He said he had asked Archbishop John Bathersby the same question and Bathersby did not know. At this stage I was a little guarded in my response as I was uncertain what Chaput's motives were, and I presumed he would have been well briefed by Cardinal Re and possibly others. However, I then spoke of my letters to the three cardinals in trying to rearrange the original meeting date, which I believed did not go down well, and perhaps they had decided to put me in my place, for they did not like being treated as equals. This, I believed, was basic to my problems. In recent times it

---

1. C/f Appendix 9 Letters A B C & D.
2. C/f Appendix 9 Letter D.

has been heartening to hear Pope Francis say that Roman officials do not outrank diocesan bishops, but must serve as aids to the bishops' ministry.[3]

Out of the file he produced a photo of me with my face painted, celebrating a liturgy titled, 'Leap into Life', with students from state schools and nine Catholic diocesan high schools. The liturgy had been focussed on the gifts of youthfulness, community, justice and service, and was held in 'The Founders Pavilion', Toowoomba Showgrounds in 1996. It was a wonderful celebration filled with many symbols and images, respecting our rich tradition and speaking to the youth of the day. It appeared that someone had sent a photograph to Rome complaining that I allowed the youth to paint my face as part of the celebration. Out of this large file filled with many letters, he focussed on liturgies that had been held in some of our secondary schools.

Apparently Rome had received letters of complaint that the schools had not followed the liturgical laws of the Church. Some of the letters I was already familiar with and I could inform him that when such complaints were brought to my notice, I dealt with them appropriately, with the assistance of the Diocesan Liturgy Office. There were others that he mentioned which had never been brought to my notice but which had been sent directly to Rome without any reference to me or the Diocesan Liturgy Office. It seemed clear that a climate of writing directly to Rome had developed among a small group of people in the diocese. If some people were not happy with the way things were done, whether they were appropriate or inappropriate, they would complain directly to Rome without the courtesy of any reference to the priest, the school, the liturgy office or to myself as bishop. A number of them would move from parish to parish, from school to school, with note-pad in hand, and would take down every variation of rubrics that they believed was not authorised by the Magisterium. They would also do this on in-service days, and often became quite rude to guest speakers with whom they disagreed.[4]

The Communal Rite with General Absolution formed a major part of our conversation that afternoon. I took the earlier advice of the Nuncio, Archbishop Ambrose de Paoli, and reflected on the pastoral effectiveness of this celebration, how it opened the door for

---

3. Quoted by Fr William Grimm, MM, Tokyo December 2, 2013.
4. These people have often been called the 'Temple Police'.

those who could not approach the First Rite of Reconciliation on moral grounds and how spiritually formative it was in helping people come to a deeper appreciation of communal sin and the celebration of forgiveness in their lives.

Unfortunately, Chaput was interested only in whether or not I was obeying the canonical and liturgical norms of the Church, and not in how effective the rite was pastorally. I could and did assure him that, since my meeting with Cardinal Arinze in March 2004, now over three years ago, I had given permission for the Communal Rite with General Absolution only in two exceptional circumstances of which I had spoken.

Referring to his large file again, Chaput said that there had been complaints that the diocese had ignored the Catechism of the Catholic Church. He referred to an occasion when it was reported that I had said the role of the Catechism was not to hit people over the head with, but that it was to be used as a reference text and a source of Church teaching. I referred him to the catechetical programme used in our schools which was clearly based on the Catechism of the Catholic Church.

In this, my first meeting with Archbishop Chaput, we then moved on to my Advent Pastoral Letter of 2006. He stated that he thought I had been unwise to write such a letter, referring to teachings that the Holy Father and Councils had affirmed were not possible. Realising that he, like others, had misread and misinterpreted the Pastoral Letter, I pointed out to him that the items he was referring to such as: ordaining married, single or widowed men, chosen and endorsed by their local parish community; welcoming back to active ministry former priests, married or single; ordaining women, married or single; and recognising Anglican, Lutheran and Uniting Church Orders, were all topics being discussed internationally, nationally and locally. I was referring to them, I pointed out, as examples of discussions that were taking place. I also referred him to a number of articles in various newspapers where I had said that I would not ordain married men or women against the teachings of the Church and that it was important to keep dialoguing so that our understanding would grow. If the Church's teaching did change then I, like many other bishops around the world, would welcome such a change. Our conversation continued for some time on my Advent Letter.

I discussed with Chaput that Rome and others seemed to have forgotten the point of the Advent Letter, which was to invite the diocese to look to the future with hope and not with a mood of despair. It had been intended as an invitation to look with excitement at the emergence and flowering of lay-led ministries at a local level: for example, the establishment and consolidation of pastoral councils, the resourcing and in-servicing of finance councils, the development of liturgy committees and ministry groups in catechetics, baptism, marriage, funerals, ecumenical hospital pastoral care, confirmation and eucharist, social justice, ecumenism, and many other pastoral initiatives. The Pastoral Letter also described how, in several parish communities, priests worked side-by-side with pastoral leaders, pastoral associates, pastoral co-workers and ministry coordinators in pastorally effective partnerships. It had invited communities to be open towards other options for ensuring that the eucharist might be celebrated and, while continuing to reflect carefully on these options, to actively promote vocations to the current celibate male priesthood, and to be open to inviting priests from overseas.

It was almost time for Chaput's meeting with the Diocesan College of Consultors and he spent the last part of our initial meeting speaking about the importance of promoting vocations to the priesthood, what he did in his Archdiocese of Denver, the number of students who were entering his seminary and what he was doing to support this work. The procedure we followed for this in the diocese was to ask the pastoral councils as a body to appoint a representative to support the work of the two vocation directors, who worked in their own way, in their own time, over and above their pastoral duties to do whatever they could in this promotional work. They were available to interview and support any prospective candidate for priesthood. From the time of my arrival in the diocese we had seven prospective candidates for the priesthood who spent some time in formation, a number who made serious enquiries, and four ordinations.

The College of Consultors gathered in the boardroom of Bishop's House to meet Archbishop Chaput, where once again he repeated his self-introduction and explanation of his mission as given at the morning meeting with the Council of Priests.

In his opening comments, Chaput identified as concerns the continuing use of General Absolution, support for the ordination of women, recognition of Anglican and other Church orders (both drawn from the Advent Letter, 2006), lack of vocations to the priesthood, and reported liturgical abuses over which no disciplinary action had been taken. None of these matters came as a surprise to the College of Consultors as I had briefed them on the correspondence which had taken place over the last five years between myself and the Vatican.

I was told later that when pressed on various matters related to these issues, his attitude suggested that the Vatican had not listened to the replies and explanations provided earlier by me, and that when further matters came up in segue (for example, the non-reception of the teaching of *Humanae Vitae* on artificial birth control, the inappropriate words of the Holy Father on violence in Islam), Archbishop Chaput became testy and defensive. I was told that he repeatedly insisted that the role of a bishop was to teach in faithful obedience to Rome.

It was becoming obvious to some of the priests that Archbishop Chaput had every intention of straying beyond what he had declared was his limited brief and considered that he could investigate any dimension of the life of the diocese and the liturgical and leadership practice of the bishop in any area of his pastoral activity.

One of the priests reflecting on the Gospel reading of the day spoke simply and directly to Chaput of the need for respect for truth and for appreciation of the valued pastoral leadership of myself as bishop. Another priest, when responding to a question from Archbishop Chaput about the wearing of diocesan ties rather than clerical collars, expressed the opinion that he thought it extraordinary that an archbishop would be sent from the other side of the world to deal with such a weighty matter. Chaput, no doubt fuelled by letters of complaint, seemed to have in mind that I was in some way diminishing the ministerial priesthood.

The College of Consultors developed a view that Archbishop Chaput thought he already understood the pastoral reality of the rural Toowoomba Diocese, on the declared basis that he had worked in rural dioceses in the United States. Even in this meeting with priests who were well informed about the deteriorating relationship between myself and the Vatican authorities, it was becoming apparent that Chaput came with a closed mind and a set agenda, defined by the substantial folders of complaint material which he had brought with him (later visually sighted during interviews). It seemed that he intended primarily to substantiate these criticisms with local comment from detractors and critics.

To those involved in these meetings, the Archbishop gave no impression at all of understanding that he might need to listen to local wisdom and pastoral experience about the diocese. In his view, the touchstone of a bishop's authenticity was complete and unquestioning obedience to the Magisterium of the universal Church, as outlined in the Catechism and the teachings of the Holy Father (the pope).

Several members of the College of Consultors spoke strongly and firmly to Archbishop Chaput about the apparent lack of understanding by some Vatican authorities regarding the pastoral and theological life of the diocese. They also conveyed to Chaput their great disappointment that Rome, while seeming unable or unwilling to take into account the actual pastoral needs of the diocese, was yet willing to give an uncritical and ready hearing to those who wrote letters of complaint. At one point Chaput did concede that he would not be influenced by the unfair and unreasonable critics of my leadership because, after all, every bishop, including himself, had to deal with people of this bent. But as time went on, he too seemed to be quite ready to give such people undue weight in his assessment of the life of the diocese and of my pastoral leadership.

Following the Consultors meeting, Chaput met with Father Peter Schultz, Diocesan Canonical Advisor, who mentioned to me that the meeting had been cordial and brief. Chaput, he said, first commented on how impressed he was by the meeting of the Council of Priests and how articulate he found the group. Father Schultz noted that Chaput seemed somewhat surprised by this. The interview had then focussed on my Advent Pastoral Letter of 2006 and Chaput showed surprise to learn that I had not shown the Letter to Schultz prior to it being published. Schultz sensed that Chaput was somewhat shocked and had said that nothing of such significance would leave his office that had not been read at least by his chancellor, a canonist and his vicar general. Father Schultz said that was not my practice and that he had drafted one pastoral letter and had input into one or two others, as they were in areas that touched on his expertise and interest. He went on to say that he himself might have nuanced some of the statements a little more, but that essentially it was a factual statement, and despite

Roman comments to the contrary, no such discussions were actually going on, but that they were indeed topics of conversation both inside and outside of the Church. Schultz responded to Archbishop Chaput's enquiries that I did consult with him and said he did provide both oral and written responses to me, depending on what was required.

The conversation then focussed on my orthodoxy which had been brought into question from letters received by Roman Congregations concerning some aspects of my leadership. Father Schultz affirmed, as he had done at the Council of Priests meeting, that I was indeed orthodox and outlined for Chaput a brief history of the diocese and the fact that there were conservative people who from the start had opposed my leadership as a bishop. Some were clergy, but mainly laity, who would tolerate no deviation from what they believed was the authentic articulation of the faith. Schultz commented that he had also been accused by some of the same people of liturgical abuses and unorthodox teaching and that he would be prepared to defend both of us before any tribunal. Schultz commented that the most notable aspect of the interview at the level of process was that in most other instances the Apostolic Visitor interviewed people and groups in the presence of his notary, Deacon Neal, and with a file at easy access. Schultz was interviewed alone in his office and there were no files at the meeting.

The Chancellor, Father Brian Sparksman, was then interviewed. Sparksman told me later that this first interview was casual and non-threatening. The Deacon was not present and Archbishop Chaput asked Sparksman for his personal history, and queried him about his relationship with myself as bishop. Sparksman walked him through some of the history of the diocese and credited me for my ministry, in the diocese, to the priests, and for bringing about an atmosphere of unity. The question of ecumenism arose and Sparksman who, as Diocesan Ecumenical Officer, had been a leader in this area for many years in the diocese, and throughout Queensland and Australia, could assure him that all our dealings with other churches were in accord with the 1993 *Directory for the Application of the Principles and Norms of Ecumenism*. Chaput, being tired, cancelled his scheduled interview with the Vicar General, Father Peter Dorfield. So began the Visitation of the Diocese of Toowoomba.

Left:
Bishop Morris blessing of the Covenant between the Anglican Archdiocese of Brisbane, the Catholic Archdioces of Brisbane and the Catholic Diocese of Toowoomba, 2009

Right: Bishop Morris on visitation of the far western district of the diocese in the 1990's.

Left:
Bishop Morris with a group of Josephite Sisters in the 1990's.

12

On The Road and Back Again

It is the journey that is important not the destination.
William M Morris

Wednesday 25 April, Anzac Day 2007, dawned as a perfect autumn day and commenced with the celebration of Mass in my chapel at Bishop's House at 6.30 a.m. Following breakfast, our journey to the western part of the diocese began. Archbishop Chaput was in the front passenger seat and Deacon John Neal in the back seat while I drove. Our first stop was at the town of Miles where Father Brian Noonan, the parish priest of Chinchilla and priest director of Miles, had arranged a meeting over morning tea with the local pastoral team. Driving out of Miles, Chaput's conversation was filled with praise for the pastoral leadership team and how impressed he was with them. As we headed for Roma, it was all eyes on the look-out to see if we could spot a kangaroo, emu or both which they desperately wanted to see, Deacon Neal, so he could tell his grandchildren, and Archbishop Chaput as he had never seen either of these animals in the wild.

The town of Roma was waiting for us. Present was a parishioner, together with Father Peter Doohan, parish priest of Charleville and Dean of the Far West deanery, who had travelled for three hours to be present, and Father Mervyn Ziesing, a retired priest in residence of Wallumbilla/Surat, whose travel time had been just over half an hour from Wallumbilla.

All three were interviewed. The most interesting comments afterwards came from Mervyn Ziesing who later shared with me his reflections of the day. Ziesing began:

> Charles and John were dressed in black, crosses on chains around their necks, white collars, black shoes and socks.

At the beginning Charles said that the use of the Third
Rite, and the resurfacing of questions of married clergy,
ordination of women and recognition of Protestant
Orders (mentioned in Bill's pastoral letter) needed to be
investigated. He had been selected as an outside person
to carry out the visitation and to report on it in writing.
I blew it badly! I gave my views on the above, views that
raised questions I considered reasonable. Charles was
not happy. After about ten minutes of my monologue,
Charles gave me an academic and personality
assessment: academically shallow and personality-
wise arrogant, adding that it was no use continuing the
interview. He could be correct of course; I just wish that
he had taken a little more than ten minutes to find out.
He wanted my comments relative to the diocese, not my
personal views on the topics.

Our journey out west continued to the town of St George. About an
hour into the trip we spotted our first kangaroo, followed closely by
a few emus. The two visitors were delighted and extremely excited to
be able to go home and describe what they had seen.

On arriving at St George, Archbishop Chaput and Deacon Neal
set themselves up in a motel where the following interviews occurred:
Father Jamie Collins, parish priest of St George, the joint vocation
director, Father Michael O'Brien, parish priest of Goondiwindi, and
a parishioner who was the chair of the parish pastoral council in St
George. All three later told me that they thought that Archbishop
Chaput was more interested in being a teacher and disciplinarian than
in listening, and did not really want to hear about the local Church
in that area. At a meal that evening at the presbytery, I remember
the chair of the pastoral council being upset as she reflected on her
interview; she was astounded at the way he spoke down to her, at
Archbishop Chaput's refusal to listen and at his arrogance.

Next morning, Thursday 26 April, we began our journey back to
Toowoomba along the Moonie Highway. The conversation for a good
part of the journey centred around the difficulty Archbishop Chaput
was facing concerning the sexual abuse cases in his archdiocese, and
how important it was to protect the archdiocese from being sued by
having it incorporated, which had been a directive from Rome to the

Church in the United States. After three hours we arrived in Dalby where he interviewed Father Michael Cooney, parish priest, head of the local deanery and joint vocation director. While the interview was taking place, I phoned the Chancellor, Father Brian Sparksman, inviting him to join us for lunch as there were items that Archbishop Chaput wished to discuss.

At the lunch in Toowoomba the archbishop asked Father Sparksman why no religious sisters were included in the list of interviews. Sparksman replied that if he had gone to Mitchell, which had originally been intended, he would have met Sr Amy Caldwell, an Ursuline Sister, who was the parish pastoral leader. He added that if the archbishop had followed our original advice, and travelled to Charleville and Cunnamulla, he would have met religious sisters from the Josephite and Mercy Orders.

As we sat at the dining room table, the archbishop asked for fewer interviews and that the list should start with the most senior positions, including the youth officer. Archbishop Chaput was becoming more assertive and much more business-like than before. The softly, softly approach that he seemed to be taking when he first arrived was gradually disappearing. Chaput and the Deacon retired to their motel and began interviewing various people. Some of these people we knew because we had arranged their interviews, but there were others whom he had arranged personally and so we did not know who they were. We also knew of one woman who followed him up the street asking for an interview. We had arranged a balance of those who were in many ways opposed to my leadership, those who were supportive and others who were prepared to be part of the dialogue for building a more pastoral, collaborative, participative and ecumenical Church, where justice and charity would be the foundation stones of all relationships.

The pattern of interviews on Friday 27 included breaks of fifteen and thirty minutes. During these intervals Father Sparksman received further questions and observations from Archbishop Chaput. There were some questions that centred on education, and Sparksman, after checking with the appropriate bodies, assured him that the cases he was raising were historical and had been dealt with appropriately. Archbishop Chaput suggested to Father Sparksman that some witnesses had been primed, that the priests all said the same thing and that it was like pressing a button because the same message kept on coming out. Sparksman responded that if there were such similarities, would not that be an indicator of the unity of the priests of the diocese that had been brought about by the bishop's ministry.

Chaput continued to bring up issues such as whether there had ever been teaching on the Catechism of the Catholic Church. He was shown a list where there was reference to the Catechism in 'In-Services' and catechetical programmes. The questions continued. One was that the bishop (that is, me) did not wear a chasuble while celebrating Mass. Sparksman expressed surprise, and that he had never seen this. Chaput explained that he meant for morning Mass in my own chapel. Another question was to do with something he had been told about priests wearing T-shirts during the annual retreat when Mass was being celebrated. He wanted to know if this was true. Sparksman replied that it is often very hot in January and the principal celebrant always wore vestments and led his brothers in the eucharist.

At one point on Friday I happened to be in Sparksman's office when Chaput, during one of the breaks, came in to ask for further clarification. During this conversation he spoke about the inappropriateness of my letter to Cardinal Arinze[1] and said that he thought this was the crux of the problem and that we should disregard all the complaint letters in comparison to this. I then took the opportunity to describe to Chaput the meeting I had had with Arinze, what had happened, and that I believed it was because of that meeting, and my letter, that he, Arinze, had orchestrated the Apostolic Visitation. Chaput's reply was, 'Now I understand', and referred to Arinze as 'a big boss'.

On Friday afternoon I had my final meeting with Archbishop Chaput. As always, he was friendly and respectful and, without referring to any names, he asked for clarification on a number of questions. He asked why I had been giving the anointing of the sick (a sacrament in the Catholic tradition and therefore for baptised Catholics) to a person who was not a Catholic and had given them communion. I explained to him that my actions were based on the 'Directory for the Application of the Principles and Norms of Ecumenism', issued by the Pontifical Council for Promoting Christian Unity. He became a little defensive and in the course of our

---

1. C/f Appendix 9 Letter D.

discussion, I tried to unwrap for him how effective our ecumenical ministry was in the diocese.

The agreement between ourselves and the Anglican Church in ministering to each other's communities had been approved by the competent Roman Congregations who had examined the diocesan document.[2] The conversation concerning the question of this anointing of the sick went on and on, and he said enough for me to realise that it had been a complaint from one of the 'temple police' concerning a relative, and for whatever reason, he was unable to move on for some time. It was almost like an obsession.

Earlier in the day he had asked Sparksman about an Internal Forum (forum of conscience) matter and because of Sparksman's involvement in the particular case, Sparksman advised him that it would be better to speak directly to me about it and to leave him out of the discussion. Before he left for Australia, Chaput had asked Rome for clarification concerning the question of Internal Forum, for he believed my interpretation was not accurate. I asked him what his interpretation was and he responded that the couple had to live as brother and sister if they wished to participate fully in the life of the Church and receive the sacraments. My reply was, 'Sorry, that just won't happen!' After a couple have exhausted all available avenues open to them, and through the process have developed an informed conscience, and if they believe there is no sacramental covenant remaining in a previous marriage, then in their informed conscience they can apply the principle of Internal Forum. It is in the Internal Forum that they make the decision that their marriage is sacramental, and God is their judge, not us. He did not agree with me, told me my understanding of Internal Forum was wrong and not in line with the advice he had been given by Rome.

Focus then moved to liturgies that had been celebrated within some of our schools, and about which Rome had received various direct complaints. Of some of the liturgies he referred to, I had no knowledge, while there were others which had been brought to my attention. These had been dealt with appropriately with the support of both the education and the liturgical offices in the diocese. Some of the situations were over ten years old but were given a life as though

---

2. C/f Appendix 8 Statement of Agreement with the Anglican Church.

they were still happening, without any appreciation of the work that the diocese, through its various educational arms, had been doing over the intervening time. The liturgical errors that had been made, and were referred to, were historical and no longer an issue.

Another subject of concern to which he referred was sex education in schools. That had been a burning topic in the 1990s and, except for a few people who still carried the issue with them, was no longer a problem. Such education had become an accepted part of the holistic approach to education in schools in the diocese.

We then moved on to the topic of clerical dress and collars. Archbishop Chaput said that he had been told that priests who wanted to wear Roman collars were subject to ridicule. I understood that he had already been told by the Council of Priests that I had not forced anyone to wear ties and so I believed it was no longer an issue to be discussed. Thus I reaffirmed what the Priests Council had said and assured him that no priest, no matter what their dress, had ever been ridiculed, that all priests in the diocese were treated with the utmost respect and dignity, not only by myself but by their fellow priests in the diocese. Over the years I had noticed that this acceptance and respect had grown, and I told him that I did not accept the observation he was making as I believed it was untrue. On Saturday morning Father Sparksman was asked the same question and he assured Archbishop Chaput that it was not so.

Archbishop Chaput then commented that some of the priests were retiring early. I referred him to our diocesan 'Policy on Retirement' that had been a practice in the diocese before I arrived and which I fully supported. No priest was forced to retire and those who did take the opportunity became very active pastorally.

My Advent Pastoral Letter of 2006, General Absolution and Vocations to the priesthood then formed part of the general conversation.

At no point on that Friday afternoon did Chaput mention what he was going to put in the report, except that he would be busy over the next few days in writing it, as he had to have it in Rome as early as possible in May. I believed the urgency was because of my visit to Rome for the Anglophone Conference due to be held later in May, at which time I understood that I would be meeting with the three Cardinals, Arinze, Re and Levada.

After he concluded his interview with me, I had no knowledge of whether he had further interviews at his motel with other people.

On Saturday morning he met with the Toowoomba Diocesan Pastoral Council, followed by a formal interview with the Chancellor, Father Brian Sparksman and the Vicar General, Father Peter Dorfield. As he left the meeting with the Pastoral Council he commented to me, 'they certainly love you and I am sure they would like to see you'. As I entered the room there was a quiet stillness and it was only after Chaput and his Deacon had left the building that members of the Council began to express their anger and disbelief at what had just taken place. Instead of being the listener, Chaput had become the teacher and disciplinarian. His aggressiveness was met with aggression; they challenged and he responded.

As he sat down for his interview with Father Sparksman, the Diocesan Chancellor, I am told that Chaput commented that the meeting with the Diocesan Pastoral Council was the hardest meeting that he had ever attended. With the Deacon nodding furiously in agreement, Chaput commented that they were aggressive and moved from the point at issue, namely, the bishop, to attack Church teaching. Sparksman commented that he was shocked at the amount of material that Chaput was carrying from Rome. He became aware of this when the Deacon was asked to check a particular name from that material. Two large folders were produced out of what seemed a mountain of material, one folder contained the Quinquennial report which in itself was substantial and to which Chaput had referred.

He then enquired of Sparksman about the fact that some people addressed the bishop as Bill or Billy, and did this come from the casual Australian lifestyle.[3] When Sparksman answered in the affirmative he replied, 'I thought so'. He also enquired of Sparksman how influential were the priests over the bishop in running the diocese, because it had been suggested to him that the bishop was too influenced by the priests. Sparksman responded that the bishop worked through the

3. 'Believe me brothers and sisters, if what I am for you frightens me, what I am with you reassures me. For you, I am the bishop; with you I am a Christian. "Bishop" this is the title of an office one has accepted to discharge; "Christian" that is the name of a grace one receives. Dangerous title! Salutary name!' (Augustine Sermon 340.1).

clergy of the diocese in a collaborative way.[4] Sparksman told me that Archbishop Chaput commented that 'there are those who would say that the bishop is a lightweight intellectually, that he hasn't any brains'. Sparksman's response was that the bishop can be 'incisive' which to him meant that he was no lightweight.

Chaput then interviewed Father Dorfield whom he had intended to interview earlier in the week. But he had decided that he was too exhausted with his ongoing task and this interview could wait until the end. Dorfield commented to me later that after almost curt preliminaries, and with the customary seating of the deacon behind the person being interviewed, it began with a short and blunt lecture on the responsibilities of a competent Vicar General. The archbishop said that the role was to 'look after' his bishop and, when necessary, to 'pull him into line' and, as it were, to protect him from himself. Dorfield reported to me that he was stumped by this line of approach and was getting the sense that he was being personally blamed for what was happening to me, and generally for the state of the diocese under his (the bishop's) uncorrected leadership. Chaput then made this quite explicit by saying to him, 'You helped him into this trouble with Rome, now you help him out of it.'

Chaput then instructed Dorfield to influence me to be concessional, submissive and apologetic when I went to Rome in about four weeks, in May 2007. I was not to be confrontational or conflictual. I was to openly accept the judgment of Rome on General Absolution. I was to affirm the ordination of single males and to apologise for imprudent comments on the ordination of women and the recognition of other church orders, and to admit that I had allowed contemporary discussion on these issues in the wider community to intrude into a Church teaching document, the 2006 Advent Letter. I was to reassure Roman officials of the practice and belief in the centrality of the eucharist in the diocese and the necessity of the ordained priesthood. I was to reassure the cardinals that I was currently dealing with any specific liturgical issues brought to my attention. I was to state that I was willing to work cooperatively[5] with Rome in these pastoral,

---

4. It is true that I am a strong believer in a collaborative and participative ministry and the principle of collegiality and subsidiarity which I believe flowed out of the teachings of Vatican II.
5. In my experience to work 'cooperatively' with the Roman Curia was to be treated as a branch manager, to do what you are told without any respect for the local

liturgical and sacramental areas, and was being faithful and obedient to the Magisterium as well as in my teaching. Finally, I was to apologise for personal conflict with or offence to Cardinal Arinze.

Father Dorfield encapsulated Archbishop Chaput's reflections about me and the diocese in these words: I was a good, humane and prayerful bishop but innocent and naïve and open to manipulation because of my great desire to see good in everyone, and that people had taken advantage of my goodness and trust. I had been captured, manipulated and misled by a so-called progressive group of priests in the diocese who were in fact 'running the diocese'; as a result of the actions of these priests, I had been led astray and now needed to recant, and in effect throw myself on the mercy of the Vatican authorities, promising a more orthodox and obedient future.

Father Dorfield told me that his response was to suggest that in Archbishop Chaput's short time here he had learnt very little about the personality and character of myself as the leader of the diocese and that his comments were in fact quite offensive and insulting to me; they were a back-handed way of saying that I was weak and accommodating, and unable to assert my own leadership and authority, that I was not my own person.

Dorfield then tried to show that the Advent Pastoral Letter 2006 needed to be seen in the context of the process of pastoral planning in the diocese. This involved the placement of priests (and their participation in decisions affecting their appointment), the development of lay leadership in partnership with priests in communities across the diocese, and the significant role of parish pastoral councils or similar bodies in each community. The few comments at the end of the Advent Pastoral Letter were an attempt to help people understand that we were not the only diocese struggling with these important matters around pastoral leadership. Dorfield's attempt to defend my practice of writing Advent Letters as pastoral documents in collaboration with diocesan people with particular competence and expertise fell on deaf ears.[6]

Church and the principles of subsidiarity and collegiality, endorsed by Vatican II.

6. I believe some of this agenda would have come from a discussion document on pastoral planning that was sent to Rome and signed by the Council of Priests Committee responsible for the Discussion document. C/f Chapter Six—Future Planning 'Discussion Paper on Pastoral Planning'.

In the interview, Chaput then used the focus of what he described to Dorfield as 'outrageous liturgies' that had been celebrated in the diocese to accuse Dorfield. He flourished a piece of paper in his face saying that he, Dorfield, had also been guilty of liturgical abuses in the diocese. He did not allow Dorfield to see the complaint but just made general accusations. Dorfield was caught off guard and found himself defending the accusations. Chaput then moved swiftly to make a series of denigrating comments about different priests whom he had interviewed or met during his short time in the diocese. Some of this negative commentary, Dorfield sensed, came from or was consolidated by Chaput's interviews with individual priests and lay people, from what others had to say in the absence of the person about whom they were speaking. He then took several priests to task. At this stage, Dorfield found himself becoming quite angry and, on reflection, thought that this was probably the purpose of Archbishop Chaput's comments to him.

Dorfield was restrained in his response but gave Chaput a short blast on the many years of committed pastoral and priestly service which these priests had given to the diocese, many in the far-west, a most difficult and remote part of the diocese and of Australia. He defended their personal integrity and suitability for pastoral office, which Chaput had questioned, and the extent and quality of on-going formation in theology which was common among them. At times they had all lived and worked with bishops of questionable ability and competence, only now to be found severely wanting by a visiting bishop who had been with the priests for four days and who knew next to nothing of the history, culture and life of the diocese. Dorfield commented that, at this moment in the interview, Chaput suggested it might be time for a new Vicar General because of his perceived undue influence over me as bishop and my personal inadequacies in theological practice.

Chaput continued the interview by naming several of the matters he intended to cover in his final report to the Vatican. He said that he would acknowledge my positive qualities: prayerful, empowering, respectful and seeing the good in others, although of limited theological ability; willing, however, to seek the support of others, genuine care of the priests, compassionate, active in social justice matters, locally and nationally (child protection, industrial relations, Australian Catholic Social Justice Council). Then came the negatives: untenable position on the use of general absolution, imprudent comments in the 2006 Advent Letter on settled matters of Church teaching, insufficient action on promoting vocations to the priesthood, lack of vigilance on liturgical abuses, disrespectful of Vatican authorities, unduly influenced by a group of senior priests who needed to be displaced from advisory positions.

Dorfield's understanding was that Chaput would raise these matters with me prior to his departure. As indicated, in the days leading up to his departure, the Archbishop had discussed a number of issues with me similar to some of those mentioned above, but he never advised me of what he was going to put in his report.

At the end of the interview, Dorfield noted that he had lost hope, for not only was the report going to be negative, but he realised it was clear that Chaput had learnt nothing of the distinctive life of the diocese in so many areas: pastoral, liturgical, ecumenical, social justice, spirituality, faith formation, confidence in lay leadership in partnership with priests, mature planning for the future. This was confirmed by a number of priests who expressed to me their strong dissatisfaction with the process of the visit. Archbishop Chaput arrived with a softly, softly approach which turned slowly and progressively into what appeared to be aggression and that he was a man on a mission, becoming a teacher and a disciplinarian and he seemed unable to listen. Some saw him as dishonest for he would make a statement like, 'I don't know what I am here to do', then would bring up issues which would be refuted, to which he seemed to then turn a deaf ear.

On reading Dorfield's notes of the meeting, I was saddened by the way he was treated and the unjust attack and judgment on priests and people of the diocese by one who had spent just four days in a diocese larger than Germany. He had arrived around 10 a.m. on Tuesday 24 April 2007, and departed around 1 p.m. on Saturday 28 April 2007.

The local Church of Toowoomba is made up of hundreds of communities, rich in life and diversity, displaying hospitality to friend and stranger, and my brother priests who breathe this same air and celebrate this life are gifted and generous pastors embraced by their communities. I have been privileged to have been loved and supported by my brother priests and my diocesan family, and I would defend their integrity, prayerfulness, sense of social justice, theological ability, their openness to keep learning and growing and being surprised each day by the love of God, whom they serve and who calls them by name.

Chaput and Deacon Neal were driven to Brisbane by Sparksman and Dorfield. The following is Sparksman's record of the conversation that took place in the car. Chaput commented that the bishop did not understand Internal Forum (forum of conscience) and neither did some of the priests. Sparksman brought up the fact that he had it on good authority that in the Vatican, Australia was referred to as the Netherlands of the south. That is, that we were revolutionary and untrustworthy in matters of the Catholic faith. Sparksman suggested that he believed this was a harsh judgment and that the visitation by Archbishop Chaput was in part due to that attitude. Then out of the blue, Chaput said to Sparksman: 'I would be astonished if you were to lose your bishop.'

Chaput and Deacon Neal stayed in Brisbane with Archbishop John Bathersby on Saturday night, 28 April 2007 and flew to Sydney on Sunday morning 29 April and on to Denver later in the day. Of the exact location where he stayed during that day, or with whom he spoke while in Sydney, before flying out of the country I am unaware. But from somewhere in Sydney, Chaput sent an email to Sparksman looking for additional information which had come to his attention since leaving Toowoomba. Where this matter came up, and from whom, neither Sparksman or myself are clear. Nor have we been able to find out.

Archbishop Chaput wrote in the correspondence that he understood that two formerly active priests were now working in the diocese, one in charge of religious education, and one the 'Director of Pastoral Vision and Planning'. A concern had been expressed to him, Chaput, that they might not share the real vision of the Church but might have their 'own' agendas. He asked for their names, their positions and whether or not they had been dispensed from the obligations of the Catholic priesthood and celibacy, and what was their general theological orientation. He then went on to say that he would let Sparksman know when his task was finished and the report was sent to Rome.

A copy of the email was also sent to me. In it, Chaput thanked me for my kindness and openness during the time of the Apostolic

Visitation, and said that my fraternal kindness was extraordinary, and hospitality impeccable. In the same email he also mentioned that he was at that time in a hotel in Sydney, waiting for the plane to Denver and was working on the report along the way.

Sparksman later replied to the email from Sydney and gave Chaput the information he requested, emphasising the fact that he had never heard any question concerning the orthodoxy of either man and that both had been quietly helpful in their ecumenical role in the diocese.

On 4 May 2007 I received an email from Chaput informing me that he had mailed the report of his visitation to Cardinal Re at the Congregation for Bishops and that he had also faxed him a copy. He thanked me once again for making him welcome under such difficult circumstances, and that I was a brother to him at every moment (I wish he had displayed the same sensitivity to others in the diocese as he displayed to me). He ended the email by saying that he would hold myself, the clergy, the religious and the people of the Diocese of Toowoomba in his prayers. He also informed Sparksman that he had sent the report and that he had been requested to destroy his copies and all documentation he had.

In the intervening weeks before my trip to Rome to attend the Anglophone Conference on Professional Standards, to be held in the Vatican at the Casa Santa Marta towards the end of May, I attended the Australian Catholic Bishops Conference in Sydney where I shared my experience of the visitation with some of my brother bishops and spoke of it at some length at the Queensland Bishops Meeting. Archbishop Wilson, who was President of the Bishops' Conference at that time, offered his support and encouragement to me. He, with Bishop Brian Finnigan, Auxiliary Bishop in the Archdiocese of Brisbane, were also attending the Anglophone Conference and Finnigan would be accompanying me to my meeting with the three Cardinals, Arinze, Re and Levada.

Many of the bishops commented that they thought it was an insult to the Australian Episcopate (the Australian bishops) that an Australian was not chosen for the Apostolic Visitation, as it would not be possible for a thoroughly American bishop, in four days, to appreciate the Australian culture, let alone a diocese almost twice the size of Italy. However, that was the way it played out.

Bishop Morris at the Queensland–South Australian Border in the 1990's
with the local priest.

Bishop Morris with group of people on 'Big Red', a sand hill between
Birdsville and the Northern Territory.

13

The Days That Followed

<hr />

I am not made or unmade by the things that happen to me but by my reaction to them.

William M Morris

There was a numbness in the life of the diocese. For many of those with whom I spoke who had participated in the process of the Apostolic Visitation, and whose experience has been referred to in the previous chapter, Archbishop Chaput had left behind him an unease that ate into the heart of hope. This hope had been injected with some life by Chaput's parting words to Sparksman: 'I would be astonished if you were to lose your Bishop.' We had been respectful of the wishes of the Vatican by keeping the whole matter confidential, except for those directly involved: the priests, pastoral leaders, members of the diocesan pastoral council and those invited to meet with Chaput and those whom he invited, of whom we have no knowledge. The vast majority of the diocese were completely unaware of the Apostolic Visitation and only gradually, as time went by, did knowledge of the visitation begin to seep out.

Rumours started to grow and journalists' curiosity led them to ask questions. These found no answers because of the fidelity of those involved in the confidentiality of the process. Questions were asked of the Australian Catholic Bishops' Conference Secretariat as well as of the Apostolic Nuncio, Archbishop Ambrose de Paoli, but very little information was forthcoming. Eventually an article was published from an extremely right wing source which posts on the CathNews discussion board, that Archbishop Chaput, the extremist and fundamentalist Capuchin Archbishop from Denver USA, had been the one delegated by the Vatican to undertake the investigation of myself as the Bishop of the Diocese of Toowoomba. Commenting in a letter to the Apostolic Nuncio, Brian Coyne, the editor and publisher of *Catholica Australia,* said that if there was any substance to this then it certainly should be viewed with enormous alarm. This alarm was shared by some of my brother bishops whom I had taken into my confidence at the time.

While I was at the Australian Catholic Bishops Conference, the Chair of the Council of Priests in the diocese invited the priests and pastoral leaders of the diocese to meet and reflect on the Apostolic Visitation. Twenty-eight priests attended, three apologies were received. Four pastoral leaders were present and the open meeting resulted in a clear expression of solidarity with and for me. It was decided at the meeting that letters from the priests of the diocese expressing support for me be written to Cardinal Re, Prefect of the Congregation for Bishops. At the time of the meeting, there were forty-four priests incardinated (assigned) in the diocese. Three of these priests work in other dioceses and one was on leave. Of the forty priests living and working in the diocese, thirteen were retired. Three of these priests work as retired priests in residence and the remaining ten were available for supply and support work. Twenty-seven diocesan priests were involved in active full-time ministry with one religious priest at that time working in the diocese. The package sent to Cardinal Re contained thirty-six letters of support for me from the priests of the diocese. Two priests were physically unavailable, one in India and the other in far-western Queensland. Three priests chose not to sign the letter. Also enclosed were letters written privately by the four pastoral leaders. The letter read:

> We, the priests of the diocese of Toowoomba, are aware that our Bishop, Bishop William Morris, is to meet with you during his time in Rome in late May 2007. From the 24th to the 28th April 2007, an Apostolic Visitation was conducted in our diocese by an Apostolic Visitor bearing a mandate from the Holy Father. Most of the priests and a number of lay people were interviewed either individually or as part of meetings between the Visitor and diocesan bodies.
>
> Bishop Morris has been the leader of the local Church of Toowoomba for the past fourteen years and in that

time had led with compassion and gentleness in the example of the Good Shepherd. As bishop he is admired and appreciated by the vast majority of clergy and people of this diocese. It is our firm belief that Bishop Morris is a loyal bishop of the Church and a conscientious member of the College of Bishops.

We wish to express our personal and presbyteral support for Bishop Morris and his pastoral leadership in our diocese. We commit ourselves to working with Bishop Morris to address matters that may be brought to his attention as the Chief Pastor of our diocese.

Sincerely yours in Christ.

The priests and pastoral leaders of the diocese are still to this day waiting for a response to their letters.

On arriving home from the Australian Catholic Bishops Conference and before leaving for Rome, a number of people spoke to me about their experience (reflected in the previous chapter) of being interviewed by Chaput. To many he was quite respectful but to others he was aggressive, becoming the disciplinarian and teacher; he did not listen, treating the interview as a teaching session. An example of this was the interview he held with Father Ray Crowley.

Crowley told me that the room was set up in such a way that Deacon Neal, who was present at the meeting to take notes, sat behind Crowley with Archbishop Chaput in front of Crowley. At the appropriate time in the discussion, which centred not only on myself, but in a particular way on Crowley's pastoral practice—especially in the area of liturgy— Deacon Neal would, when prompted, in Crowley's words, 'throw things over my shoulder' to Chaput. It was material that had been sent to Rome complaining about certain liturgies at which Crowley had presided. These letters were sent directly to Rome without any reference to myself as the Bishop of Toowoomba, or to those concerned most intimately with the celebrations. Archbishop Chaput intimated that someone had said to him that I was influenced by my friendship with Crowley and therefore did not challenge his behaviour, especially in the area of liturgy, and that this had led to some of the controversy around me as a bishop.

After the meeting, Crowley responded to all of this in a letter to Chaput dated 27 July 2007 which he later shared with me: 'I am sure your visit would have confirmed the fact that Bishop Morris is very much his own person. In fact, his courage, compassion and ability to challenge, without shaming his priests and *people,* are some of the reasons I freely renew my allegiance to my bishop each year.' Crowley went on to say that if he had known that Deacon Neal was not there just to take notes, but to be actively involved in the interview, then he would have invited him to sit next to Chaput. This still would have been an imbalance of power but would have given Crowley a little more dignity than the way it was done. Crowley remarked that his perceptions might be off the mark but he would be open to Chaput explaining to him the gospel value or the gospel lesson he needed to learn from the way things were done. His concern, he said, was not so much around the content Chaput had shared with him, and the discussion on those issues, but the process that was used.

Chaput responded to Crowley's letter by stating his great respect and affection for me and that he was simply sharing with Crowley what several people whom he had interviewed had suggested: that is, that Crowley did have an influence on me. He refuted Crowley's interpretation of Deacon Neal throwing things over his shoulder and that he was simply responding to his request to share material that had been received from others. Chaput finished off his letter to Crowley by stating that the Church was not about balancing power but about each person fulfilling the responsibilities and duties that God gives each through baptism, ordination or through the mission entrusted by the Church.

14

What Meeting?

The tendency to turn human judgments into divine commands makes religion one of the most dangerous forces in the world.

Georgia Harkness

The flight to Rome was uneventful and gave me a chance to do some reading in preparation for our Diocesan Gathering in June 2007. I always find airports fascinating and Rome is no exception. The first impression is that the place is deserted but eventually you see people in uniform looking very serious and official, but with a few looks up and down to make sure you match the photo on your passport and some impressive stamp action, you are set free to retrieve your luggage. I love Roman taxis and have had some wonderful journeys, feeling as if I were in a James Bond movie, being chased and needing to get to my destination safely and as quickly as possible. This ride was no exception, arriving at the Casa Santa Marta in impressive time. After finding my room, I checked to see if there were any messages for me, but there were none. The last time in Rome when I was expecting a meeting with Cardinal Arinze, a message had been left for me with phone numbers and the contact person to arrange the time, place and day for the meeting.

It was Wednesday and I still had not heard from anyone concerning time and place for my expected meeting. It could not be that they did not know I was in Rome because the urgency and pressure under which Chaput was put to do the visitation and have his report in as early as possible in May was, I believe, so that a meeting could be arranged. In my earlier correspondence I had told Arinze that I would be in Rome in May and would be happy to meet with himself, Re and Levada. The Apostolic Nuncio, Ambrose de Paoli, had asked me as early as March about the Anglophone Meeting I was attending in Rome in May. I had spoken to Bishop Brian Finnigan before leaving Australia, asking if he would accompany me to the meeting as he would also be in Rome at that time, being a member of the National Committee for Professional Standards.

As the day and our meeting drew to an end on that Wednesday, Archbishop Philip Wilson (who was also attending the Anglophone meeting), Bishop Finnigan and myself were stepping out for dinner. Walking across St Peter's Square, I spoke of my unease at not having heard anything about the possibility of a meeting and whether or not I should be making contact with Arinze who had been the instigator of the whole process, having threatened me with the CDF (Congregation for the Doctrine of the Faith) if I did not do exactly what he directed. Archbishop Wilson was adamant that I should make no approach to Cardinals Arinze, Re or anybody else, for if they wanted to see me, they would be the ones to make contact. In Wilson's words, 'Bill, don't rock the boat'. The Anglophone meeting finished on Friday and that evening I found out that Cardinal Arinze was out of the country.

On arriving home I had a gathering with the priests and pastoral leaders of the diocese to inform them of the outcome of the meeting that never happened. I walked them through the history of my dealings and relationship with the Roman Curia and the various Congregations and we left the meeting with the hope that the worst was over. We would just have to wait for the next chapter. There was even a feeling among some that we might not hear anything.

One afternoon in early September 2007, I received a phone call from Archbishop Ambrose de Paoli, the Apostolic Nuncio in Australia, requesting that I come to Canberra for a meeting. He had received a communication from Rome which he had to hand to me personally. I asked whether it was concerning the Visitation and whether he could tell me what was in it. He said it was but he had to hand it to me personally. I was going to Sydney in the next few days for a meeting with the Australian Bishops Conference Commission for Church Ministry so I arranged to go to Canberra in the morning to see the Nuncio and then fly back to Sydney for the Commission meeting.

I was met at the Canberra airport by Monsignor Jude Okolo, Charge d'Affaires a.i. and taken to the Nunciature. Archbishop Ambrose was there to greet me and with an arm around my shoulders led me into a room where he invited me to sit on a couch and he sat beside me. Still holding my hand, he handed me an envelope. I looked into his face and saw tears in his eyes and asked, 'They want to get rid of me don't they'? He replied, 'Yes, I can honestly say this is the worst day of my life. Read the letter.' He let go of my hand to give me the freedom to open the envelope while he continued to hold my arm.

It was quite a bleak day in Canberra and as I opened the envelope that bleakness seemed to creep into the room and there was a coldness gripping my heart. The Memorandum consisted of four pages on the letterhead of the Congregatio Pro Episcopis, Congregation for Bishops, unsigned but dated Vatican City, 28 June 2007 and stamped with the Congregations stamp. It read as follows:

Bishop William M Morris and the Diocese of Toowoomba

1. Bishop Morris is generally well liked by the priests and the faithful of his diocese. He is generous, sensitive to people's needs and works hard, especially in the area of social justice. There are no questions regarding his personal moral integrity.

   However, the local Church in Toowoomba is moving in a different direction than that of the Catholic Church. One expression of this is seen in Bishop Morris's 2006 Advent Pastoral Letter, in which he claims one may continue to be 'open to other options' while 'discussing' issues already decided by the Magisterium such as the ordination of 'married, single or widowed men who are chosen and endorsed by their local parish community' and the reintegration of married ex-priests. Even more serious is his declaration that we must be open to the ordination of women, married or single (while the very opposite is held by the Catholic Church, 'definitive *tenenda*'), and to 'the recognition of Anglican, Lutheran, and Uniting Church Orders' (contrary to Catholic teaching and practice). An attentive reading of this pastoral letter reveals a flawed ecclesiology resembling that of a Protestant church.

2. The Diocese of Toowoomba is going through a severe crisis that spreads its roots back over the last ten years. The way out of such a crisis is by strengthening a solid faith and an authentic and committed Christian life of the faithful. It is not found by inviting discussion about issues such as the ordination of married men or women.

It is the duty of every bishop to guide the faithful in fidelity to the doctrine and discipline of the Church, working hard to promote new priestly vocations and to offer solid theological, spiritual and human formation to his priests. It is counterproductive for the formation of clergy and faithful to suggest discussion about topics already decided upon by the Church and which no Bishop can change.

3. In the Diocese of Toowoomba, there are liturgical abuses, such as unapproved modifications in the language of the Mass and the Rites of the Sacraments, including Marriage and Baptism, and Bishop Morris does not generally intervene to correct them.

4. On the basis of an unacceptable extension of the conditions required for grave necessity, 'General Absolution' is still common. Moreover, there is a tendency to abandon or to reduce individual confession, with consequent serious harm to the spiritual life of the faithful and to the holiness of the Church. This continues even after the promulgation by Pope John Paul II on April 7, 2002, of the Apostolic Letter, *Misericordia Dei*. Despite a history of admonitions from the Holy See to change course, Bishop Morris adamantly resists fulfilling his responsibility to apply Church norms properly.

5. The general theological climate of the diocese, and especially of its priests, needs to move toward a more authentic Catholic identity, as found in the 'Catechism of the Catholic Church'.

6. In the past seven years there has been no priestly ordination. The Diocese does not seem to have an effective and sufficiently dynamic pastoral programme for promoting vocations or finding priests from elsewhere and the bishop does not offer the leadership necessary to reverse the situation. For example, the marginalization of priests (e.g. through early retirement) and their substitution by deacons or laity in providing alternative Sunday worship can have a negative impact on vocations.

CONCLUSION:
The good of the diocese requires a bishop who will approach in a different way the challenges facing the Church today. Toowoomba needs a Bishop who, with determination and courage, will tackle the problems and rectify what is not in conformity with the doctrine and the discipline of the Catholic Church. Bishop Morris's theological preparation and type of leadership are inadequate to confront the crisis of the Church of Toowoomba, despite his good intentions.

I took my time reading the unsigned memorandum and kept getting surprised by inaccuracies contained in it. I mentioned these to Ambrose and asked him how could they get it so wrong and did I have a right of appeal to correct the errors. He said I could respond and point out the errors contained in the unsigned memorandum, that it was my right, but it would make no difference as they had already made up their minds and wanted my resignation as soon as possible. I then asked what if I did not resign, what would happen then! He said that popes no longer depose bishops, they no longer bring in their armies to overthrow them, and that there would have to be a meeting with the Queensland Bishops, and then some form of process would be put into place to discuss the whole question. As I got ready to leave, he said he would like to know my answer within a couple of weeks as his health was failing quickly and he would be heading home to America very soon. That was the last time I saw and spoke to Ambrose. He died on 10 October 2007 in Miami, Florida, USA, after a long battle with leukemia.

The trip back to Sydney was pensive and it was a little difficult to focus that afternoon for the remainder of the meeting for the Bishops Commission for Ministry. In the days that followed, I tried to get canonical advice as to my position. I was counselled to take my time and remain true to myself. Archbishop Philip Wilson, at the time the President of the Australian Catholic Bishops Conference, had been made aware of my position and together it was decided that I would write to Cardinal Re, Prefect for the Congregation of Bishops, which I did on 17 September 2007. In that letter I acknowledged having received his unsigned document from the hands of the Nuncio and in discussion with the Nuncio it was accepted that I had the right to respond. I acknowledged the seriousness of the situation and said I would like to take the opportunity to respond to the document and to dialogue with various aspects of it. As I was about to go on annual leave in October, I would take the opportunity to pray and think about my response so that my letter could form a basis for future dialogue. I shared my thoughts with Monsignor Jude Okolo. He acknowledged that it was the way to proceed and that he would send the letter to Rome via the Diplomatic Bag. On Friday night 28 September 2007 I was at Tugun on the Gold Coast, Queensland, preparing for a wedding on the Saturday and met up with Archbishop Wilson, as he was visiting the area. Our conversation centred around the preparation that would be required to get ready for a meeting with Cardinals Re, Arinze and Levada to discuss the erroneous unsigned memorandum. He was concerned that various forces were at work.

15

The Next Chapter

There is nothing so powerful as truth—and often nothing so strange.
Daniel Webster (1782–1852) Orator, Lawyer and Statesman

In mid-October 2007 a letter arrived from Cardinal Re in which he ignored the contents of my letter of 17 September 2007. I had suggested that while on annual leave I would reflect on my response to the unsigned memorandum so that it could form a basis for future dialogue. Cardinal Re turned my letter around and said that I had informed him that I would be going on annual leave, during which time I would reflect on the request for my resignation as Bishop of Toowoomba and would pray about the resolution. I had said no such thing. He also went on to say that during these days he hoped that the Lord would enlighten me and give me the courage to take this step which would be painful but also essential.

He asked that I consider this for the good of the Diocese of Toowoomba, which should have a solid bishop who was in accord with the pope and the universal Catholic Church; he was saying that I was out of communion with the Church and Rome.[1] Finally, he said, 'in the name of the Holy Father, I ask you to submit your resignation' because, as stated in the memorandum, my 'theological preparation and type of leadership are inadequate to confront the crisis of the Church in Toowoomba', despite my good intentions. He said that he

---

1. Communion or *communio,* is a theological term referring to the unity of the Church wherein each member of the College of the Apostles, that is bishops in the Catholic tradition, does not operate as an isolated entity, but in communion with one another and with the Roman Pontiff, in a bond of unity, charity and peace. I was accused of breaking *communio* in the contents of my Advent Pastoral Letter of 2006.

expected to receive my letter of resignation by the end of October. This, he suggested, was for the good of the Church of Toowoomba.

To this day, no one I know can identify the crisis of the Church of Toowoomba, except maybe a group referred to as the 'temple police' who have their own agenda which is subjective and judgmental and certainly not gospel based.

The last week of my holidays was not relaxed as I was trying to put together a response to Cardinal Re's letter, with Archbishop Ambrose's words in the back ground as a mantra: 'Popes don't depose bishops anymore; they have made up their mind Bill, they want to get rid of you.' On 6 November 2007 I replied to Cardinal Re's letter, sharing with him also my concern for the good of all the Catholic faithful in the Diocese of Toowoomba and the wider Australian Church, and pointed out that it was for that reason we needed to approach these issues in a collaborative spirit, ensuring that all the ramifications of the request being made of me were fully considered. With this in mind, I wrote that I would like to present a detailed reply to the comments in the memorandum, which on reflection I knew I would find difficult in some areas, in view of the general nature of some of these comments. One example I gave was that I was not sure how one would assess 'the general theological climate of the diocese', or what would be a 'sufficiently dynamic pastoral programme for promoting vocations'. Another example was that, having followed the earlier directions of Cardinal Arinze, I did not believe that General Absolution was still common.

I acknowledged the important responsibilities of the Congregation of Bishops but had no intention of entering into any controversy that did not move all people forward to a better understanding of the issues and how to resolve them. I wrote that I had to assume that the unsigned memorandum had been drafted in the light of information which the Congregation had to hand. As I was not aware of that information, nor had I had any opportunity to respond to it, I said I would welcome receiving more specific details of the material that had formed the basis for the conclusions which had been set out in the unsigned memorandum. I advised him that, on receipt of the material, I would undertake to deliver my response within fourteen days which would then form a basis for a face-to-face discussion. Because the then-President of the Australian Catholic Bishops

Conference, Archbishop Philip Wilson, would be in Rome in the last two weeks of January 2008, and was willing to accompany me, I asked would it be possible to have our face-to-face meeting during that time, and as appropriate with the Holy Father. The Metropolitan, Archbishop John Bathersby, would also be available to come to Rome.

November is always a busy month with many diocesan pastoral responsibilities, school break-ups, the winding down of diocesan meetings, the Australian Catholic Bishops Conference final meeting for the year and preparations for Christmas. As we moved into December, another strictly confidential, for my eyes only, letter arrived. Cardinal Re responded that after prayerful reflection he wanted to communicate to me that he accepted my request to meet with him in Rome the following January and that Cardinals Arinze and Levada would be with him. However, the Holy Father would only receive me after my resignation. However, as was clear later from comments by Pope Benedict XVI to me, any bishop may request to have a meeting with the Holy Father as a brother bishop.

Cardinal Re said that he saw no reason why Archbishop Bathersby should make such a long journey to accompany me to the meeting as he believed it was sufficient that Archbishop Philip Wilson be with me. He suggested that the meeting take place on Saturday 19 January at 9 a.m. at the office of the Congregation for Bishops. My request for more detailed information was dismissed and I was referred to re-read my 2006 Advent Pastoral Letter written by me as Bishop of Toowoomba, which he, Cardinal Re, went on to say presented a vision and a pastoral approach which did not conform with the doctrine and discipline of the Catholic Church. He stated that he was grateful to learn that General Absolution was no longer a common practice and that I had followed the directions of Cardinal Arinze to intervene and limit such a practice only to the exceptional circumstances proposed in the *Motu Proprio* of the Holy Father entitled *Misericordia Dei*. He also welcomed my collaboration and general desire to move towards a decision for the good of the Diocese of Toowoomba and the wider Australian Church, and that he would pray for me over Christmas to find the courage and the humility to take the step that the Holy Father wished for the good of the Diocese of Toowoomba.

I love Christmas. I was not going to let the meeting with the three Prefects of Congregations of the Roman Curia cloud the wonderful diocesan family Christmas celebration we always had in St Patrick's Cathedral, and I did not let this happen. At this time I had kept my counsel close to my heart and shared it only with a few people, hoping that I would be able to resolve the matter without worrying my diocesan family. With the encouragement of those who knew, I gathered together a small group to respond to the unsigned memorandum, especially identifying those areas that were incorrect and in error. This small group came together between Christmas and New Year, and collaboratively, with fingers reaching overseas to both canonists and theologians, put together a response for the meeting with Cardinals Re, Arinze and Levada.

On Tuesday evening, 15 January 2008, after celebrating a diamond wedding anniversary, I boarded the plane for Rome. I always find it difficult to sleep on planes so it gives me a wonderful opportunity for reading and reflection. During the hours of flight, I was able to consume two books. I arrived in Rome on a day that was cold and wet, to be told that my luggage was still in Dubai with the promise that it would be delivered next day. After arriving at my accommodation, I purchased an umbrella and went walking for the next few hours through the cobble-stone streets of Rome that glistened in the rain and invited me to keep walking in the mysterious beauty of the old city. Archbishop Philip Wilson and Father Brian Lucas, Secretary to the Australian Bishops Conference, were staying at the same venue and we met that evening over a meal. The next day, true to their word, my luggage arrived and I spent the day walking, reading, resting and thinking about the forthcoming meeting. Wilson and Lucas were in Rome for meetings with the Prefects of the various Dicasteries and on Friday they met with Cardinal Re, Prefect for the Congregation for Bishops. Earlier that day we had arranged to gather late in the afternoon to prepare for the meeting the next day. When we gathered, Wilson and Lucas looked worried and suggested that we find a place where we could sit and talk over coffee. We walked for some time and at one stage passed close to Campo de Fiori, the Field of Flowers, where in the centre is a sculpture of a dark hooded figure on a pedestal whose name is Giordano Bruno, burned on this spot in the 1600s after being accused of heresy. He was the last to be consumed by flames in Rome, but not the last to be burnt. And I wondered if this was an ominous sign!

We found a place to sit and talk. Wilson and Lucas then started to give an account of the meeting they had had with Cardinal Re who, they said, seemed to be totally fixated on my situation and that this had taken up most of the meeting time. They had been surprised to see among the papers on the desk in front of Re a copy of *Lepanto*, a small conservative fundamentalist bulletin which is published by Lepanto League Australia Incorporated and which can be quite scurrilous, judgmental and self-righteous in a very un-Christian way. The gospel values of mercy, love and justice are hard to find in its contents. Wilson and Lucas were worried about how the meeting would go the next day as Re seemed to be focussed on nothing else except my resignation. They were convinced that the only thing they had was my 2006 Advent Pastoral Letter and that they would use this against me. Once more the voice of the Nuncio, Archbishop Ambrose de Paoli, came echoing back to me: 'Bill, they want to get rid of you.'

Saturday morning arrived ringing in a fine cold day. Earlier we had celebrated Mass in one of the small chapels beneath the Basilica of St Peter's and after breakfast we made our way to the building that housed the office of the Congregation for Bishops. Wilson and I were greeted in a most friendly manner and invited to take our positions opposite the three Cardinals Re, Arinze and Levada, with the Archbishop Secretary to the Congregation also present to take a record of the meeting. After the initial greeting, Cardinal Re thanked Archbishop Wilson, as President of the Australian Catholic Bishops Conference, for accompanying me. He went on to say that he, and Cardinals Arinze and Levada, would be happy to listen to me but first he thought it would be useful to explain the mind of the Holy See before discussing the matter together.[2] He identified that secularisation and other such problems existed in all dioceses throughout the world but the reasons for worrying about the ecclesial situation in the Diocese of Toowoomba, he believed, had gone beyond acceptable limits. He then focussed on the fact that, even though I was well motivated by good will and generosity and was close to my priests and people, my leadership did not correct nor rectify what was incompatible with the doctrine and discipline of the Catholic Church. Consequently, because of this the local Church in Toowoomba was moving in a

---

2.   C/f Appendix 11 Cardinals Re, Arinze, Levada's statement at meeting 19 January 2008 Rome.

direction different from that of the Catholic Church. He then went on to offer some concrete examples.

He first mentioned my Advent Pastoral Letter of 2006 which he said focussed on a serious and important problem, namely, the ever-diminishing number of priests for the celebration of the Eucharist and pastoral work. However, in the Advent Pastoral Letter there was no reference to that liturgical season or to the coming of Christ, not even a minimum of theological content, but only pragmatic considerations. These included an invitation to be 'more open towards options for ensuring that the Eucharist might be celebrated' by inviting discussion on the recognition of Anglican orders which had been declared invalid by Pope Leo XIII, a decision which was '*definitive tenenda*'. So what was the point in discussing something that was in fact impossible? In the same way Lutheran ordinations were not sacraments, they were not valid ordinations because they were not ordinations at all. With emphasis in voice and gesture, Cardinal Re continued to read that I had invited discussion even about the ordination of women. Was I not aware of a document called *Ordinatio Sacerdotalis* written by Pope John Paul II in 1994, which stated that 'the Church has no authority whatsoever to confer priestly ordination on women (N4)', and this was a decision in the category of 'definitive *tenenda*'. To invite discussion on this topic meant that I did not accept the pope's decision and a bishop cannot go against a decision of the Holy Father.

As he was reading from his typed notes, I could see what Wilson and Lucas meant: the three cardinals were going to use the 2006 Advent Letter against me by misquoting it and making it read as something other than what was actually written. I remember at the time thinking, why not be honest, why not give the true reasons, that they saw me as recalcitrant in my continual efforts to give a voice to the people and that they saw their authority being challenged. I had not refused to meet with them but I had put my pastoral responsibilities to my diocesan family first, before their chosen time of meeting and that was anathema. This was the real reason confirmed by Chaput when he spoke to me about my letter to Arinze. He had commented that he would have been there yesterday, no matter what. Then Cardinal Re summed up this first part by saying that to present these questions as topics for public discussion was to separate myself from the teachings of the Catholic Church, that the letter revealed a very poor theology and ecclesiology that was not Catholic and that the bishop must be the 'Teacher of the Faith'. There was a pause, and I remember noting later as I reflected on the meeting that they want to control what people think and talk about and that is not going to happen in today's world. The world is evolving and maturing and, as part of that process, so are human beings and as mature adults they do not need permission to imagine options and choose from among them. It is a human being's freedom to do so, it is the passport to understanding mystery which encapsulates the truth. By being involved in dialogue, each response leads to another question in the search for truth and understanding.[3]

Cardinal Re continued, pointing out that in the past eight years there had been no priestly ordinations in Toowoomba and the diocese did not seem to have an effective and sufficiently dynamic pastoral programme for promoting vocations or finding priests from elsewhere, and that I, as bishop, was not offering the necessary leadership to reverse the situation. Furthermore, the early retirement of priests still in good health and their substitution by deacons or laity in providing alternative Sunday worship was not a valid solution in a situation where there was a shortage of priests (c/f chapter 16, 'My Response').

Cardinal Re then moved on to General Absolution, saying that they were glad to hear that it was no longer common and that, for the last two years, they had been trying to get a clear indication that the diocese was in fact adhering to the regulations as stipulated in the 2002 *Motu Proprio, Misericordia Dei* of Pope John Paul II. It was to discuss this, and then he added, other problems which were not mentioned in the original letter, that I had been given two possible dates to come to Rome. He looked at me, and then read on, that my reply, in not accepting either date and wanting to postpone the encounter for a later time, indicated that I was treating the whole thing as unimportant.

I looked at Cardinal Arinze. He was watching me. I was wishing that I had a copy of the letters I had written to him over the last two years in which I had stated that the diocese was adhering to Church teaching on the sacraments. In those letters I had stated

---

3. Judy Cannato, *Field of Compassion: How the New Cosmology is Transforming Spiritual Life* (Green Press, 2010).

that the sacrament of reconciliation was being celebrated according to the canonical and liturgical norms of the Church, and that the Communal Rite with General Absolution was never the ordinary form of reconciliation as Arinze continually suggested. I had adhered to his order by not giving permission on the pastoral, moral, liturgical and canonical grounds that we had developed as a diocese.

Cardinal Re's voice broke into my thoughts, speaking of liturgical abuses which in general, he said, I had not intervened to correct as if I considered them of little importance, and did I not know that the proper administration of the sacraments was at the heart of the pastoral responsibility of a diocesan bishop? He also said that the general theological climate of the diocese, especially of its priests, needed to move towards a more authentic, Catholic identity as found in the 'Catechism of the Catholic Church'.

I was tempted to break into Re's presentation, critique and misrepresentation of the priests of the diocese by quoting how impressed the Apostolic Visitor, Archbishop Chaput, had been in his meeting with the Council of Priests, and how articulate he had found them. Cardinal Re concluded his statement by commenting that the Holy Father was deeply concerned about the conditions in the diocese of Toowoomba and that the good of the diocese required a bishop who would approach, in a different way, the challenges facing the Church today. Toowoomba needed a bishop who, with determination and courage, would tackle the problems and rectify what was not in conformity with the doctrine and discipline of the Catholic Church. He said that my theological preparation and type of leadership were inadequate to confront the crisis of the Church of Toowoomba, despite what may have been my good intentions.

He went on to say that I was a person of integrity and morals, a man of goodwill and other gifts, and that I could continue to do much good, but the right role for me was not that of Diocesan Bishop of Toowoomba. I should be given another assignment with special duties. With this in mind, the Holy Father was asking the Metropolitan Archbishop of Brisbane and the President of the Australian Catholic Bishops Conference to help find the most appropriate responsibility in which I could continue to effectively serve the Church elsewhere in Australia, while obviously being assured of financial security for a suitable living. Cardinal Re looked up and with a contented, you could almost say, satisfied smile on this face, sat back and invited me to respond.

16

My Response

---

*When faith suppresses questions, it dies. When it accepts superficial
answers it withers. Faith is not opposed to doubt. What it is opposed to
is shallow certainty that what we understand is all there is.*

Rabbi Jonathan Sacks

The only noise in the room was the scratch of the pen of the Archbishop
Secretary to the Congregation for Bishops who was crouched over
his papers as though to protect from invisible eyes. The group who
had helped me put together my response thought that my directness
may have offended Cardinal Arinze, so with that in mind I began
by simply saying that if I had unintentionally offended any of them,
in particular Cardinal Arinze, in past contact and correspondence, I
apologised for any hurt caused.

I then presented my response as follows.

> A diocesan Bishop is required to offer his resignation
> from Office for one of two reasons: reaching seventy-
> five years or ill-health [Canon 401; *Christus Dominus*
> Para 21]. Neither of which applies to me.
>
> It appears that your Eminences are suggesting that the
> real causes for suggested resignation are contained in
> the unsigned Memorandum of 28 June 2007. The lack
> of truth in the unsigned memorandum leads to a lack of
> justice in the request for resignation.
>
> I am unable to respond fully to issues raised against
> me because I have not been provided with a copy of the
> material carried by the Apostolic Visitor when he came

to our diocese in April 2007, nor have I seen the final Report.

Canon 220 guarantees my right to a good name and Canon 221 a right to defence.

I am exercising my right to defence as far as possible by responding to matters raised in the unsigned memorandum. I wish to respond to these six points, paragraph by paragraph.

1) A different direction . . .
Never once as a bishop have I taught anything contrary to Catholic faith and morals. I wish to propose that the local Church of Toowoomba is quite in harmony with the Universal Church in spite of the comments in the unsigned Memorandum about the Advent 2006 Pastoral Letter. In my letter I referred to well-known discussions throughout the world. However my letter stated, 'we remain committed to actively promoting vocations to the current celibate male priesthood and open to inviting priests from overseas'.[1]

2) A severe crisis . . .
Never once during my episcopate has there been official or sponsored discussion within the Diocese of Toowoomba of the ordination of married men. It is well known that such discussions occur throughout the world [for example, Synod of Oceania 1998; Synod of Bishops on the Eucharist 2006]. The Diocese of Toowoomba is as normal and steady as anywhere else in spite of a small number of disaffected members. The diocese is loyal to the Catholic Church and the Holy See. I as a bishop have always professed fidelity to the Holy See. The challenges that we face in Toowoomba do not differ from other dioceses in Australia and overseas.

3) Liturgical abuses . . .
It is my well-publicised view that the authorised

---

1. C/f Appendix 12 Correction on Website

liturgical books must be used throughout the diocese. Liturgical abuses are in fact comparatively rare. Reports of aberration have been addressed immediately, when referred to me.

4) General absolution . . .
I guarantee that every parish in this diocese has individual confession frequently and it is the ordinary form of celebration of the sacrament. In the past three years I have given permission only twice for general absolution by virtue of the provisions of Canon 961. Each of these permissions involved a situation in which the priest was seriously ill. It has been my constant concern to maintain a keen appreciation of the value and importance of sacramental absolution.

5) Theological Climate . . .
The Catechism of the Catholic Church is used as the basis for all catechesis in the Catholic schools of the Diocese. The Catechism has always provided and continues to provide the basis for in-service and formation of priests and pastoral leaders. The Catechism is at the centre of adult faith education in parishes.

6) Ordinations - Vocations - Marginalisation of Priests -Alternative Sunday worship . . .
This is an unfortunate and inaccurate presentation of the facts. In fact, there have been four priests ordained in the last eight years with the last ordained four years ago. Two priests are engaged in promoting vocations to the priesthood; they have been in this ministry for seven years. Five priests are on loan to us from outside the diocese. As we have no deacons, I wonder if you are confusing us with another place.
No priest under the age of seventy-five is retired except for serious health issues or at the priest's own request.

At this point in my presentation Cardinal Re interrupted and asked the archbishop secretary to take note of the fact of the inaccuracies.

He asked him to amend the following: that there had been four ordinations and that the diocese does not have any deacons, and that no priest is asked to retire unless it is at their own request, except when they reach the age of seventy-five.

> Sunday Celebration of the Word in the absence of a priest is provided only as an alternative in situations of necessity where a priest is not available and is celebrated in accordance with Vatican guidelines.
> Programmes used . . .
> Parish Vocations Awareness Committee Guidelines – Fostering a 'Vocations Culture' across Australia. A Pastoral Letter of the Bishops of Queensland on Vocations to the Priesthood.
>
> When Archbishop Chaput made his Apostolic Visitation to the Diocese in April 2007, he was in possession of documentation of complaint of which I was not aware. I have always responded immediately to matters not in conformity with the doctrine and the discipline of the Catholic Church that have been brought to my attention.
>
> As a priest and bishop, I have always encouraged people to be faithful to their vocation. This has been my practice with married people, Religious, Deacons and Priests. In times of difficulty, I have encouraged people to stay committed to their particular vocation. It is now the same for me. The call to be a bishop is a vocation. I cannot in conscience before God, resign.
>
> After long and prayerful consideration and after taking counsel discreetly from trusted advisors, I do not intend to offer my resignation from the Office of Bishop of Toowoomba as suggested in the letters of 3 October 2007 and 30 November 2007.

I had not given a copy of my response to the three cardinals, so when I had finished there was surprise written on their faces, and the sound of the scratchy pen of the archbishop secretary filled the silence that followed. Cardinal Re broke the silence by saying that he was disappointed with my closing remarks as it was the Holy Father who was asking me to resign. When I said I would be willing to speak to the Holy Father to explain my position to him, Cardinal Re responded that I could only see the Holy Father after I had resigned, to which I reaffirmed my intention that I would not be resigning.

Cardinal Arinze then entered the conversation, supporting Cardinal Re by saying that a bishop has to support Church teaching and must not downplay Instructions given by Rome. He then referred to the Instruction, 'On Certain Questions Regarding the Collaboration of the Non-Ordained Faithful in the Sacred Ministry of the Priest', and how I had dismissed it as if it were of no importance. I explained to him that at a meeting of the Australian Catholic Bishops Conference we were advised that this 'Instruction' was not intended primarily for the Australian Church because the particular abuses identified were not considered prevalent in Australia. But he insisted that it was an 'Instruction' from Rome and must be obeyed and taken seriously. I assured him that we did take things seriously, even if they had no practical application to our situation. He then spoke of inter-communion and how holy communion, the eucharist, was given too freely to those who were not of the Catholic faith. I was able to refer him to the diocesan document, 'May All Be One' (produced by our Diocesan Ecumenical Commission, and based on the 'Directory for the Application of the Principles and Norms of Ecumenism', 1993), which provided pastoral guidelines for eucharistic hospitality and was followed throughout the diocese. Seemingly ignoring my response, he focussed on the permission I had given to an Anglican hospital chaplain to place his 'Pyx'[2] in a tabernacle in a Catholic hospital chapel. I tried to explain the process I had gone through in making this pastoral judgment to offer hospitality but his focus was purely on showing how pastorally inadequate my ministry was as a bishop.

Up to this point there had been no reference in the conversation to General Absolution, for by now, I believed, they realised that as a diocese we had put into practice what Cardinal Arinze had asked and, in trying to make a case for my dismissal, they were struggling to find serious grounds to fulfil the requirements of canon law. It was at this point that Cardinal Levada, who up until now had sat silently, took over the proceedings by stating that I was teaching things that

---

2. A small container which holds the host from a eucharistic celebration.

the Holy Father had said could not be taught or spoken of. He then referred to the four dot points in the 2006 Advent Pastoral Letter. He said the Holy Father did not want any conversation concerning the ordination of married men or welcoming former priests back to active ministry. As for discussing the recognition of Anglican, Lutheran and Uniting Church orders, that was impossible, as was discussing the ordination of women. However, in their view, I had gone ahead and given people in the diocese permission to discuss these issues, issues which it was impossible to discuss.

From the time Arinze had threatened to hand me over to the Congregation for the Doctrine of the Faith (if I did not do exactly what he demanded), I knew Cardinal Levada was there to use his power and authority to pressure me either to resign or be dismissed. Since the Nuncio, Archbishop Ambrose de Paoli, had told me that 'they' wanted to remove me, I knew that Cardinal Levada was there to work on me to resign, under the threat of dismissal if I did not do so. I also knew from what had been said that they were struggling to find grounds and were going to use what I had written to accuse me of being disloyal to the Holy Father and not in communion with him.

I responded to Cardinal Levada by pointing out that with my 'Letter' I had not given permission to anyone in the diocese to discuss any particular option, but rather I had noted what was being discussed internationally, nationally and locally. I said that he was misrepresenting the text of my letter by giving it an interpretation that was not valid. He denied any misinterpretation of the text and continued to say that I was teaching and giving permission for things to be discussed against the 'wishes' of the Holy Father. I realised at that moment that Levada had recognised they had a problem and needed something to show that I had broken communion with the teaching authority of the Church, by accusing me of not teaching what the Church teaches. The discussion was not moving beyond the stance being taken by Levada. On the one side, there was his insistence on his interpretation of what I had meant, and from my side, a denial of his interpretation.

Cardinal Re interrupted and redirected the proceedings, inquiring of me my itinerary. He was saying that they would like my letter of resignation before I left Rome to return to Australia. I reaffirmed that in conscience I could not resign. He asked that I reconsider my position and said they would wait for my letter before I left for Australia. Archbishop Wilson, who had sat silently through the proceedings as all the questions had been directed to me, asked Cardinal Re why they had a copy of the *Lepanto* journal on the table among the files. He pointed out that this journal reflected a particular view of the Church that had little credibility in the eyes of most Australians. Its promoters, he said, were obsessed with finding instances of a lack of orthodoxy and their articles were exaggerated and lacked context. In many instances, because of their exaggeration and obsessiveness, there was a lack of truth in it. Cardinal Re responded by saying that they took no notice of journals such as this, and that they received such publications from all over the world. I was thinking that, if these journals meant nothing to them, why would they have one such as this among their files. Cardinal Re drew the meeting to a close and said they would look forward to receiving my response. As Wilson and I left the room after saying goodbye to Levada and Re, I was surprised to see Arinze already outside, seemingly anxious to engage me in conversation. As we shook hands he said: 'It is not personal, I am only doing my job, just like you'. We said our goodbyes and left. I wondered later why Arinze would rush out of the room and make such a statement if it was not indeed a personal matter.

As Archbishop Wilson and I walked back to our accommodation, we decided to gather later in the day with Fathers Brian Lucas and Ian Waters (a canon lawyer who happened to be in Rome at that time for a meeting) to discuss my options and the mornings proceedings. After we reflected on what had taken place that morning in the offices of the Congregation for Bishops, I decided I would write to Cardinal Re when I arrived home.[3] I would thank him for the meeting and inform him that, at this initial stage, I reaffirmed the position I had made clear at the meeting, that is, that in conscience I was unable to resign. However, I would also say that I would be giving careful consideration in prayer to all the reasons surrounding his request for my resignation. I decided I would point out that I had many issues to reflect upon about my future and the future of the priests and people of the Diocese of Toowoomba, and my intention would be to reply more fully before Easter.

---

3. C/f Appendix 10, Letter of 24 January 2008.

In February 2008, I received a response from Cardinal Re saying that, after the meeting together with Cardinals Levada and Arinze a few weeks before on 19 January 2008, he was deeply surprised at my determination. He said that he would attentively read my detailed reply which I had promised to send. He went on to say that, for the good of the Diocese of Toowoomba, he hoped that I would accept the invitation to find the courage to take the necessary steps and submit my resignation as bishop of the diocese. He continued by saying that the reason for such an invitation was that my type of leadership of the diocese was seriously defective, and it would be very sad for me if the Holy Father had to proceed towards my removal when confronted with my refusal.[4]

---

4. A full copy of the letter from Cardinal Re is to be found in Appendix 10, Letter of 13 February 2008.

17

Statement of Position

To be persuasive, we must be believable.
To be believable, we must be credible,
To be credible, we must be truthful

Edward R Murrow (1908–1965) Broadcast Journalist

On 14 March 2008 I wrote to Cardinals Re, Arinze and Levada enclosing a more detailed response covering the matters that had been raised in the January 2008 meeting. I also pointed out the claim that my 'type of leadership of the diocese [was] seriously defective' was not substantiated in the material that was presented to me. Furthermore, the conclusion appeared to be based on the report of the Apostolic Visitation, which I had not seen and which I had not been given any opportunity to address. I then asked Re, Arinze and Levada for the 'grave cause' (Canon 401§2)[1] for which my resignation was being sought, and the arguments, accompanied by the concrete documents and proofs, that they had used in coming to the opinion that such a 'grave cause' existed. I informed them that I would be writing to the Pontifical Council for the Interpretation of Legislative Texts to ascertain the true interpretation of 'grave cause' in Canon 401§2 and to the Supreme Tribunal of the Apostolic Signatura for advice as to my entitlement to 'defence' in accordance with Canon 221 and Canon 1620, 7°.[2]

---

1. Canon 401§2: 'A diocesan bishop who, because of illness or some other grave reason, has become unsuited for the fulfilment of this office, is earnestly requested to offer his resignation from office.'
2. Canon 221§1: 'Christ's faithful may lawfully vindicate and defend the rights they enjoy in the Church, before the competent ecclesiastical forum in accordance with the law. Canon 1620 'A judgement is null with a nullity which cannot be

In the more detailed response, which I had promised, I started with their critique of the pragmatic nature of my 2006 Advent Letter. The document that was read and handed to me at the meeting with Cardinals Re, Arinze and Levada in Rome on Saturday 19 January 2008 stated that my Advent Letter lacked theological content, made no reference to the liturgical season of Advent, and was substantially a 'pragmatic' document. In one sense, that assessment was accurate. However, I believed that my letter had been taken out of context and, because of that, its practical character had been given an undue and misconstrued emphasis. I never intended it to be a theological teaching letter, and certainly in no sense was it an exercise of the episcopal Magisterium.

I deliberately wrote a practical letter. I knew this letter would be read in every parish community. I wrote because I had been concerned for several years about the need to prepare our local Church for a time when there would be a shortage of priests. I wanted to alert them to the need for greater participation of laity and religious in general non-sacramental areas of pastoral leadership.

The priests were generous, prayerful and committed, but they were also very human and none of us were comfortable with the decreasing number of priests and the increased workload placed on them. In light of this reality, there was the need to develop adequately formed, educated and resourced lay leaders who might take up a larger role in pastoral ministry in collaboration with the priests.

The diocese was 487,000 sq km. This was 130,000 sq km larger than Germany which consisted of 27 dioceses and 24,000,000 Catholics. The diocese of Toowoomba had a Catholic population of 66,000, approximately thirty per cent of the total population. The knowledge that my Advent Letter would at least be read out and published in every parish community during November 2006, and subsequently discussed, offered me the opportunity to ensure that this pressing pastoral issue associated with the decreasing numbers of priests in our diocese would simultaneously be brought directly to people's attention right across the diocese. This would assist in overcoming some of the inertia in a few places where people hoped the problem would just go away.[3]

---

remedied, if: 7° the right of defence was denied to one or other party.'
3. C/f Appendix 7, Advent Pastoral Letter.

Most of my earlier Advent Letters could be produced to indicate that usually I had dwelt on the liturgical and theological significance of Advent and Christmas. On this occasion, I had made a discretionary judgment that the pastoral life of the diocese would be better served by a direct and practical letter on these matters.

It is common practice for Australian bishops to write a pastoral letter in Advent or Lent, or at another time, that might deal with subjects other than these liturgical or seasonal themes.

In the time since the 2006 Advent Letter, many people in many parishes had spoken positively in response to this Letter and the basic pastoral leadership issues it addressed. A much smaller number in only a couple of parishes complained. My sense was that the greater majority of the faithful of the diocese appreciated my frankness and the willingness as a diocese simultaneously to promote vocations to the priesthood and to adequately form and resource lay leaders within their areas of appropriate pastoral competence.

In my response, I then addressed the 'permissive' impression on matters of settled teaching. The primary focus of the Advent Letter fell on encouraging those who were already seriously addressing pastoral leadership needs in the light of the decreasing numbers of available priests. It was also an urgent reminder to those who had yet to address these issues.

The Advent Letter was explicit in its emphasis on the centrality and primacy of Eucharist for all our parish communities. It reminded the people of the diocese of our commitment to promoting vocations to the priesthood. It reinforced our efforts in recent years in the important and urgent task of pastoral planning across the diocese.

In the latter part of the Letter, I made reference to a range of efforts that other communities and forums, both international and national, had been considering in the overall task of addressing pastoral leadership in the absence of priests.

At the time of the Apostolic Visitation, in his meeting with the College of Consultors, Archbishop Chaput conceded that I was not the only church leader to seem to have made an unwise imprudent public statement. He then made reference to the comments by Pope Benedict XVI in his Regensberg address on Islamic faith that, when taken out of the wider context, were considered offensive by some Islamic leaders. The same could be said of the Advent Letter, and in my response I acknowledged that my wording, too, could be considered clumsy, and maybe even misleading and imprudent, if the wider context of the particular pastoral reality of the diocese was not familiar to the reader.

Any sense that my Letter gave 'permission' to the reader to take up a position in opposition to the definitive teaching of the Church was not intended, nor do I believe that a fair reading would reach this conclusion. For those seeking to find fault, of course, this was their interpretation. In my mind, I was acknowledging that discussions around these issues were actively taking place in a range of other forums, indicative of the extensive nature of these issues and the widespread concern of many people of faith beyond our diocese. By referring to these 'matters in discussion', I was trying to reassure the diocese that we were not alone in facing the issue of priest shortage and its pastoral consequences for pastoral leadership in our local parish communities. I was showing that the problem was such that very radical, and from a Catholic perspective, doctrinally unacceptable solutions, were being canvassed.

My intention was to encourage the diocese to think and prayerfully reflect on our pastoral situation, so that we could work towards the solutions that would best apply to the particular circumstances of this sparsely populated diocese, but always in conformity with the mind of the Church.

At no point did I assert that these options might be implemented in the diocese. At no time in my service to this diocese as bishop had I ever acted to implement any of these options under discussion in various parts of the world. Nor had I taught them, as had been suggested and used against me to show that my teaching was unorthodox.

In meeting with people across the diocese since the 2006 Advent Letter, it had been clear to me that the vast majority had not taken my Letter as giving them permission to call Church teaching into question. Like all searchers for truth, discussions are held on all aspects of Church teaching, questions are asked, answers are sought, all to help develop a greater understanding. Pope Paul VI, speaking of the hunger for truth in everyone, gave advice worth taking on board which I paraphrase here:

> So the search continues and, as you know, in an ocean
> of truths and mysteries, in a drama in which each one

of us has his/her own part to play. This is life. Can it be exhausted in this temporal existence of ours? No. In spite of the immense light of our Catholic religion, the search and expectation of future revelation are not complete; on the contrary, they are still at the beginning. Faith is not complete knowledge; it is the source of hope. [Heb 11:1] Now we see religious realities even in their incontrovertible reality, in mystery, in their impossibility of being reduced to the purely rational yardstick; we know these realities 'in a mirror dimly'. Study, research and—let us say the word that comprises the whole human—religious process—love, remain active and dynamic.

The Jesuit Karl Rahner, too, has written pertinently in this regard:

> . . . . it is the bitter grief of theology and its blessed task, too, always to have to seek (because it does not clearly have present to it at the time) what in a true sense—in its historical memory—it has always known . . . always providing that one has the courage to ask questions, to be dissatisfied, to think with the mind and the heart one actually has, and not with the mind and the heart one is supposed to have.[4]

On the other hand, a small number of continuously critical people were only too happy to seize on my wording, taken in a contextual-excluding sense, to reinforce their personal dissatisfaction with me as their bishop. Their search for truth is very narrow, based on a child-like absolute acceptance of following significant others in an uncritical way, locking them into what Fowler would call Stage 3:

> Synthetic-Conventional faith development. It is a 'conformist' stage in the sense that it is acutely tuned to the expectations and judgments of significant others and as yet does not have a sure enough grasp on its own

---

4. Quote in the preliminary pages of James Carroll, *Constantine's Sword* (Mariner book, 2001).

identity and autonomous judgment to construct and
maintain an independent perspective.[5]

In my letter I then responded to the statement of Cardinal Re at
the January 2008 meeting, and related comments from Cardinals
Arinze and Levada, that my Advent Letter amounted to a rejection
of the teaching of the Catholic Church on the ordination of women
and Anglican Orders. Levada also made much of the fact that I had
had the audacity to allow conversation on the possible ordination of
married men and welcoming back to active ministry priests, either
married or single, who had left, when the Holy Father had said 'No' to
this. This was dropped in further conversations as these subjects had
been and were continuing to be discussed in Synods and other official
forums. I pointed out once again, as I did on the day, that I had never
rejected the teaching of the Church.

Even in that part of the 2006 Advent Pastoral Letter where I had
suggested that 'we may well need to be much more open towards
other options for ensuring that eucharist may be celebrated', I was
trying to place increased emphasis on the prior need for us to cherish
'our deeply held belief in the primacy of the eucharist for the identity,
continuity and life of each parish community'.

My invitation to the diocese that we needed to reflect on all these
matters did not mean that we, or I, rejected the current teaching of
the Church. On the contrary, once I became aware of some level
of misconstrued reading of my 2006 Advent Letter, I responded
through the local, state and national media immediately, and later
through our diocesan website to correct this misunderstanding and
misrepresentation of my words by writing:

> In my Advent Pastoral Letter of 2006, I outlined some
> of the challenges facing the diocese into the future. In
> that letter I made reference to various options about
> ordination that were and are being talked about in
> various places, as part of an exercise in the further
> investigation of truth in these matters. Unfortunately,

---

5. Fowler's theory of Growth and Development. Taken from *Women's Spirituality:
Resources for Christian Development,* edited by Joann Wolski Conn (New York:
Paulist Press, 1986), 226–232.

some people seem to have interpreted that reference as suggesting that I was personally initiating options that are contrary to the doctrine and discipline of the Church. As a bishop I cannot and would not do that and I indicated this in the local media at the time. I and all the bishops of the Catholic Church form a college with the Holy Father and cannot act contrary to the teaching and practice of the Universal Church. Encouraging vocations to the priesthood must remain a priority for our local Church and we pray this Christmas and as we begin the New Year that more young men will consider deeply their response to God's call.[6]

With hindsight, the Advent Letter could have been better worded to prevent even the slightest possibility of such misunderstanding. But the Letter itself, even as it stands, does not call for a rejection of current Church teaching or point to any official teaching on these matters by me.

In my response, I took the time to show that my Advent Letters over the years since 1994 provided independent and historical evidence of my faithfulness to the official teaching of the Church. The Pastoral Directions developed through our Diocesan Gathering in 1998 and reviewed and endorsed in subsequent Diocesan Gatherings in 2001, 2004 and 2007 expressed the willingness of the diocesan Church and myself to be in line with official teaching. These Diocesan Gatherings had brought together people of active faith from every parish community and diocesan agency. And they had always provided space for those critical of the life, practice and leadership of the diocese to be given a hearing.[7]

My response continued by addressing the question of the 'general theological climate' of the diocese. This had been mentioned in both the unsigned Memorandum and the statement from the January 2008 meeting, where particular reference had been made to priests of the diocese being at variance with authentic Catholic identity as portrayed in the Catechism of the Catholic Church. As the Cardinals did not know the Toowoomba diocese or its priests, this reference

---

6. Appendix 12, Correction on Website.
7. Appendix 13, Diocesan Pastoral Statement.

could only have come from the Apostolic Visitor, Chaput. This concerned me for, after Chaput's meeting with the Council of Priests, he had commented to Father Peter Schultz, the Canonical Advisor of the diocese, that he was surprised at how articulate the clergy were. This seemed to challenge the mindset that he had brought with him and seemed to indicate a recognition of the theological and pastoral competence of the priests, who, I believed, would be the equals in theology, spirituality and pastoral practice of priests of any diocese, anywhere.

I pointed out to the cardinals that our normal practice each year was to have two diocesan 'In-Services' for priests, usually in March and September, and that there had always been a priest who, in addition to his normal pastoral responsibilities, was formally appointed to the ministry of 'Director of Continuing Education of Clergy'.

Diocesan In-services, usually of two or three days duration, had focused on key pastoral areas in the life of the diocese. These In-services had drawn on the expertise of a range of priests, bishops and lay people, all theologically, academically and pastorally competent in their respective fields and acknowledged as such in the Australian Church.[8]

All of those who led these 'In-Services' had ensured that the official teaching of the Church was given due weight in their presentations. Priests, as part of their continuing education in ministry and theology, had been encouraged to think and reflect on these matters, but they had never been led to reject official teaching in any matter.

Priests of the diocese had been encouraged to undertake sabbatical study when time and diocesan resources allowed. Approximately one third of the currently serving priests had attended sabbatical programs offered in Catholic institutions in Europe and North America. When St Peter's Centre for the Continuing Education of Clergy was operating in Canberra, over a third of the priests of the diocese attended. Over the last few years, the diocese had sponsored

---

8. Diocesan In-Services covered areas such as: Ecclesiology, Eucharist, Marriage (theology and law), Family Perspectives in Ministry, Sacrament of Penance, Rites of Reconciliation, Ecumenism and Inter-Faith Relations, Mariology, Catholic Social Teaching, Media, Psychosexual Development, Order of Christian Funerals, Canon Law, Indigenous Issues, Pastoral Planning, Evangelisation and Culture, Youth Ministry, Priestly Well-Being, Evangelisation, Liturgy, Catechesis (Catechism of the Catholic Church)

and organised a sabbatical program for the priests of Australia at the James Byrne Diocesan Conference Centre in Toowoomba.

Priests were encouraged to keep up their private reading whenever the daily pressures and responsibilities of pastoral life permitted. The diocese had a well-established 'Resource Centre', available to all members of the diocese. For many years, we had had our own diocesan Family Bookshop operating as a ministry in adult faith education. In recent years, this diocesan initiative had been taken over by The Society of St Paul. This ensured that access to reading and study material in a range of pastoral, spiritual and theological areas remained available. Priests and people made good use of this facility to keep themselves in touch with the 'mind of the Church'.

At the beginning of each year we had a 'Diocesan Retreat' for the priests which had always been a valued part of their lives and an important aspect of the life of the diocese. Over the years the retreat directors had provided direction and spiritual input. Priests were also encouraged to take advantage of other retreat opportunities offered elsewhere in Australia. I had always attended this retreat.

I must say that I found the allegation that the general theological climate of the diocese was at variance with the authentic identity of the Church to be an unfair and unsubstantiated assertion. If this matter had been one of the issues raised by the Apostolic Visitor, then I found it difficult to understand how, in the space of a few days, such a widespread assessment could possibly have been made. I knew some of the people whom the Visitor had interviewed. Several of these people had been discontented from the beginning of my time as bishop and had been persistent in their complaints to the Holy See. They held particular theological positions. They were hardly an accurate indicator of the general theological climate of the diocese. Similarly, within the body of priests, there were a few who had been disgruntled with my leadership since I had arrived in the diocese. However, the overwhelming majority had indicated to me their consistent support and their appreciation of the encouragement and growth that my leadership had provided for them.

After the Apostolic Visitation, all but three of the priests signed letters of support and sent these to the Congregation of Bishops, unbeknown to me at the time. None of them have ever received a reply.

In my Statement of Position I addressed specific issues raised by Cardinal Arinze. The first was the placement of an Anglican Pyx in the Tabernacle of St Vincent's Hospital chapel, Toowoomba. When the Anglican chaplain asked if he could place his Pyx in the tabernacle in the hospital chapel in cases of emergency, I took appropriate counsel and found from my investigations that the practice of offering this ecumenical hospitality within hospitals and other chapels happens in various places throughout the world. Out of a sense of respect and appreciation for the Anglican 'Hospital Ministry', and on the condition that the Anglican Pyx would be clearly identifiable and not confused with any other sacred vessels and, given that this was a private chapel not a public Church, I gave permission for this to take place. However, it never actually eventuated. It was unlikely that any scandal or *admiratio* would have been caused. I should add that in this part of Australia, Anglican faith in the real presence is similar to Catholic faith.

Once I was notified that the Congregation for Divine Worship and Discipline of the Sacraments disagreed with this pastoral judgment, I notified the local Anglican bishop who accepted the decision and expressed gratitude for our pastoral concern and sensitivity.

Cardinal Arinze had also asserted that intercommunion was too widely allowed. The diocese followed the practice whereby no open or unqualified invitations were extended. In 1996, the diocese, through the 'Diocesan Ecumenical Commission', developed a policy document on intercommunion, based on the *Directory for the Application of the Principles and Norms of Ecumenism* (1993). This diocesan document, *May All Be One*, provided pastoral guidelines for Eucharistic Hospitality and was followed throughout the diocese.[9]

Cardinal Arinze was concerned that I had downplayed the 1997 Instruction 'On Certain Questions Regarding the Collaboration of the Non-Ordained Faithful in the Sacred Ministry of the Priest'. At a meeting of the Australian Catholic Bishops Conference, not long after the publication of this 'Instruction', we were advised that this 'Instruction' was not intended primarily for the Australian Church because the particular abuses identified were not considered prevalent within Australia.

---

9.   Appendix 14, May All Be One: PastoralGuidlines for Eucharistic Hospitality.

Acting on the advice presented to the Australian Catholic Bishops Conference, I responded to a complaint from a person in Toowoomba, mentioning this general advice we had received. This personal letter was then sent to the Congregation for Divine Worship and Discipline of the Sacraments and was the basis of this complaint. An enquiry to the Australian Catholic Bishops Conference National Director of Liturgy confirmed that the abuses referred to in the document were not then, and are not now, widespread in Australia. As for the reference to the supposed 'well-noted liturgical abuses' in the document handed to me at the January 2008 meeting, I could assure them that whenever liturgical abuses of any kind had been referred to me, I would direct the person to speak with the priest concerned. If they were not satisfied with his response, I indicated to them that the next step in the process would be to contact the Diocesan Liturgical Commission. If they were still not satisfied, and came to me, I would address the situation in collaboration with the priest and the Diocesan Liturgical Commission in a pastorally sensitive way.

Some of the 'liturgical abuses' referred to never came as a complaint to the priest, to the Diocesan Liturgical Commission or to myself, but were referred directly to the Apostolic Nuncio or to Rome. In reality, what were sometimes referred to as 'abuses' were in fact minor rubrical irregularities, such as this: I once received a complaint that a priest did not wear the chasuble on a Sunday in a remote place where the temperature had passed 42° Celsius.

I also responded to Cardinal Arinze's suggestion of what he called my dismissive attitude towards attending a meeting in Rome, which he said indicated that I thought the proposed meeting was not important. This was not the case. I had indicated a willingness to meet in Rome but asked that the meeting be deferred to a later date to coincide with my presence in Rome representing the Australian Catholic Bishops at the Anglophone Meeting on Professional Standards. I had asked for this deferral on the grounds of pastoral considerations of the diocese, as well as on account of provincial and national responsibilities in which I was involved at that time. In particular, one of the younger priests in the diocese had been in the final stages of dying from an aggressive cancer, and I wanted to be with him and the diocesan family. At no time did I consider the need to meet in Rome as a matter of no importance.

Finally, to complete the picture, I added some comments concerning General Absolution which had been the reason for being called to Rome at the beginning of this story. It was not discussed in the January 2008 meeting, for by then it had been realised there was no case to answer as I had followed Cardinal Arinze's demands. I pointed out that in all my lengthy correspondence with the Holy See over the pastoral use of General Absolution, I had never considered it to be the Ordinary Form of the Sacrament of Reconciliation.

The First Rite of Individual Reconciliation had always been the stated Ordinary Form of the Sacrament in the diocese. General Absolution had always been understood as an Extraordinary Form of the Sacrament and, where used in the past, in response to pressing pastoral needs, had been celebrated in accord with diocesan guidelines based on the liturgical and canonical norms laid down by the Church. In more recent times, and as agreed in a discussion with Cardinal Arinze in 2004, priests had been directed to seek my permission on each occasion to judge whether there was a 'grave necessity' as outlined in Canon 961 and the *Motu Proprio, Misericordia Dei,* for the use of general absolution. Only two occasions had occurred since 2004, conforming precisely to the canonical and liturgical norms. As mentioned before, when it was realised that there was no case to answer in this area the Advent Letter was seized upon.

My response also addressed what had been alleged in the unsigned memorandum, namely, that there had not been any ordinations in the diocese in the previous seven years. This was incorrect. There had been four ordinations in the past eight years. Two priests were engaged in promoting vocations. It had been claimed that I had handed parish leadership to permanent deacons. There were no permanent deacons in the diocese. It had been alleged that I encouraged priests to retire before the age of seventy-five. No priest had retired prior to that age unless for serious health reasons or at his own request, and even then within the diocesan guidelines and without any encouragement from me.

Sunday celebration of the eucharist without a priest occurred only in cases of necessity when a priest was not available and in accordance with the law. It should be understood that there were parishes in excess of a five hour round trip from their neighbour. It should not be overlooked, either, that there had been some candidates for priesthood who, for reasons of health, scholastic ability or other personal reasons, had not proceeded to ordination. In comparison, considering our Catholic population of only 66,000, there had been a better response with young men offering themselves for ordination than in places with larger populations.

In the document from the January 2008 meeting with the cardinals, reference had been made to the Apostolic Visitation that took place in April 2007. In my 'Statement of Position', my final remarks concerned this Apostolic Visitation, referred to in this January document, but not discussed at the meeting. This left me with the question of just how important *was* this Apostolic Report. There had been a number of comments concerning this Apostolic Report which, as far as I knew, no one other than Chaput, the three Cardinals and maybe members of their Congregations had seen. These comments indicated that the Report had been favourable to me, and not what Cardinals Re, Arinze and Levada had been looking for. This was the reason Levada eventually used, and misused, the Advent Letter to build a case against me.

When Chaput arrived in Toowoomba, in his initial meeting with me, he expressed a measure of surprise that he was being asked to investigate me because, as far as he could see from the material provided to him, things that I had reportedly said and done were happening in other places as well. I have mentioned before that I discovered in conversation with the Metropolitan, Archbishop John Bathersby, that Chaput had asked Bathersby the same question. I believe that this would suggest that in the mind of Chaput there was uncertainty and doubt as to the necessity and purpose of his task.

At the end of the Apostolic Visitation, when Chaput was being driven back to Brisbane, he remarked to the Diocesan Chancellor, 'I would be astonished if you were to lose your bishop'.

A final impression I had was that Chaput did not observe an appropriate process in making the Visitation. Several of those interviewed had complained to me about the manner of the interview. Many of the priests felt that he came with a preconceived agenda and made little substantial effort to understand the prayer and pastoral life of the diocese. In my view, he was unduly swayed by prior critical comment.

Some of the laity to whom Chaput had spoken were known to me. They reflected a particular view of Church life. They saw me as exemplifying all that they thought was wrong with the 'post Vatican II Church'. On the table in front of Cardinal Re there had been the *Lepanto Journal*, which has little credibility amongst the bishops, priests and the vast majority of people in Australia. The journal's promoters seemed obsessed with finding instances of lack of orthodoxy. Their reports were exaggerated and lacked context. I had not had any opportunity to deal with any specific complaints they had made, nor had they been referred to me by the Congregation. As mentioned before, Cardinal Re had assured Archbishop Philip Wilson and myself that they received hundreds of such journals of which they took no notice. The question then remains, why was this particular issue on the table at this meeting if it held no reference to me?

In my Statement I took the opportunity to offer these few personal reflections that had been shared with me by several priests and people to indicate a measure of unease with both the process and content of the Apostolic Visitation, as well as its subsequent Report. None of us had ever seen this Report, nor had we had any opportunity to respond to it. I was afforded only a limited opportunity in conversation with the Visitor to answer some questions arising from material he had brought with him, and from some interviewees.

I made these observations, I said, by way of response to matters raised in the unsigned Memorandum (September 2007), the document from the January 2008 meeting, and matters raised in discussion with Cardinals Re, Arinze, and Levada at that meeting.

I pointed out to Cardinals Re, Arinze and Levada that this had been a painful, draining and difficult time for me. However, after considerable prayer and reflection, and after seeking appropriate counsel, I remained firm in my position in conscience not to resign as requested. As stated before, the lack of truth and the inaccurate presentation of facts in the unsigned Memorandum led to the lack of justice in the request for resignation. The claim had been that my 'style of leadership of the diocese is seriously defective'. I responded to all matters that had been raised that might suggest this. I did not and still do not believe that there were grounds on which the request for my resignation was lawfully and justly based, and certainly not 'grave cause' as required by Canon 401 §2. Hence, I asked how in conscience before God, could I resign.

I finished my Statement by saying that I would welcome any response to it and that I was willing to deal in more detail with any of these issues.

In concluding my reply to Cardinals Re, Arinze and Levada, I said, it had became clear to me that I needed some clarification of the proper meaning of 'grave cause'. As I had not reached the completion of my seventy-fifth year, as mentioned in Canon 401§1, and was not suffering from ill-health, the only criteria on which the request for my resignation could be made was that of 'grave cause'.

The second part of Canon 401§2 states that, ' . . . or some other grave reason, has become unsuited for the fulfilment of his office, is earnestly requested to offer his resignation from office'. I wrote to Archbishop Francesco Coccopalmerio, President of the Pontifical Council for Legislative Texts, enclosing copies of letters sent to Cardinals Re, Arinze and Levada with all the materials provided to them, asking Coccopalmerio, given the circumstances, to confirm the interpretation of Canon 401§2. I also requested his advice as to the proper meaning of 'grave cause' in the circumstance of the request put to me.

I followed this up with a letter to Cardinal Agostini Vallini, Prefect of the Supreme Tribunal of the Apostolic Signatura, seeking information as to how the right to defence enunciated in Canons 221 and 1620, 7° could and should be applied when the notion of 'grave cause' under Canon 401§2 was being relied upon by the Prefect of the Congregation for Bishops to invite a diocesan Bishop to resign. With this request, I enclosed the same materials as provided to Coccopalmerio. As I posted all this correspondence, I felt that, at last, I might be getting somewhere. Then I remembered the words of Archbishop Ambrose de Paoli: 'You can respond, correct the errors and show where they have got things wrong, but it won't make any difference because they want to get rid of you'.

After all of this going on in my head and all the material I had sent off, the celebration of Easter that year, 2008, was very meaningful and powerful for me.

Diocesan Quilt.

18

Waiting for a Response

All men dream: but not equally. Those who dream by night in the dusty recesses of their minds wake in the day to find that it was vanity: but the dreamers of the day are dangerous men, for they may act their dream with open eyes, to make it possible.

TE Lawrence, *Seven Pillars of Wisdom*, Chapter 1

In the weeks that followed Easter 2008, I was diagnosed with a melanoma. It was situated behind my right ear and from April to November I had a series of six operations. These operations have been successful and after six years I am still clear of melanoma. I will be forever grateful to my doctors, nurses and surgical staff who took such great care of me, as well as my family, friends and all who supported me during that time. An amusing side to my ordeal was that I was able to be admitted to the local Catholic Hospital, be operated on, be admitted to a four bed surgical ward where I enjoyed the company of three other surgical patients, and it was only as I was walking out the front door to leave the hospital that I was recognised.

Cardinal Levada was in Brisbane in early May for the blessing and opening of The Holy Spirit Seminary, Banyo, and because of my situation I was unable to attend. I missed the Australian Catholic Bishops Conference Meeting in May 2008, much of its focus being on the preparation for World Youth Day to be held in Sydney during August which I was able to attend between operations. In May 2008 I received a reply from the Supreme Tribunal of the Apostolic Signatura. The letter was signed by Archbishop Velasio de Paolis, CS, Secretary, and informed me that the 'right to defence' cited in Canons 221 and 1620,7° concerned exclusively a judicial context, that is, within the proceedings of a judicial process in an ecclesiastical tribunal. It was only later I realised that my 'right to defence' had been swept aside, under the guise that this was a pastoral process, being carefully managed so it would not become a judicial process which would have given me the 'right to defence' under canon law.

Father Peter Schultz was my advocate and submitted the following to the Apostolic Signatura based on the facts that are outlined in this book and the Canons in Appendix 15.[1] The advocate's letter of 10 March 2008 was the law applied to the facts:

> While there can be no appeal against a judgment of the Supreme Pontiff or the Apostolic Signatura, no such judgement has been communicated as of this date, therefore, I submit that Bishop Morris has the right to appeal to the Apostolic Signatura. In accord with canon 1445 § 3, 1º and article 124, 1 of the Apostolic Constitution Pastor Bonus, it is the responsibility of the Apostolic Signatura to exercise vigilance over the correct administration of justice. It is the position of Bishop Morris that he has been denied justice by the way matters have been handled by the Congregation for Bishops and others.
>
> Canon 220 guarantees the right of all the faithful to a good name. I submit that there can be no greater attack on the good name of a bishop than to call into question his exercise of the *tria munera*: to sanctify, to teach and to govern, in hierarchical communion with the head of the college and its members. I submit that it is the very exercise of his episcopal ministry that is being called into question and therefore it is his good name that is under threat from the proceedings of the Congregation for Bishops.
>
> With the right to a good name comes the right of all Christ's Faithful to vindicate this, canon 221. For Bishop Morris to effectively vindicate this right all allegations against him need to be detailed. But as he has never been given a copy of all the material that the Apostolic Visitor brought with him, nor has he been given a copy

---

1. Appendix 15, The Law.

of the report that the Apostolic Visitor made, his ability to vindicate his right to a good name has, I submit, been denied him.

Further Bishop Morris has never been formally summoned to trial before a competent tribunal, which would be in his case the Holy Roman Rota. I submit that a proper judicial review of the case with full disclosure of all allegations and evidence in accord with law as required might reach a very different conclusion.

It is without doubt that, under Article 79 of 'Pastor Bonus', the Congregation for Bishops has the right and obligation when it is deemed necessary to initiate Apostolic Visitations and to make recommendations to the Holy Father as to what action, if any, is to be taken as a result of such an Apostolic Visitation. However, when such a recommendation amounts to an effective sanction then, I submit, the due processes of the law need to be followed.

I submit that the efforts of the Apostolic Visitor are equivalent to the preliminary investigation as it is defined in Canons 1717–1719. If the results of the Apostolic Visitation are such as to support a prima facie case requiring action, then in the case of Bishop Morris the result should be a trial unless the Holy Father chooses to act *motu proprio* as is always his right.

By asking Bishop Morris to submit his resignation the Congregation is asking him to act against the law that identifies only two criteria for a diocesan bishop to resign, the completion of his seventy-fifth year or ill health. Neither of these criteria apply to Bishop Morris. In suggesting that the Bishop might find another role in leadership in the Church in Australia, I submit that the Congregation for Bishops is suggesting an effective sanction because as a diocesan bishop it is Bishop Morris's right to exercise a deliberative vote in the Australian Conference of Bishops but if he is no longer a diocesan bishop he has only a consultative vote, an effective demotion.

I submit that if Bishop Morris were to submit his resignation at this time it would be, in this case, invalid. The Bishop has made it plain that he has no intention of resigning because he does not accept the conclusions of the Congregation of Bishops. If he were to resign it would be as a result of pressure placed on him and he would lack the necessary freedom to place a valid judicial act. I submit that this would amount to an act under grave fear.

Much of the material used by the Apostolic Visitor appeared to be letters of complaint sent by people dissatisfied with the leadership and decisions of Bishop Morris. Because Bishop Morris was not privy to these documents there is no certainty as to what exactly they were. In his comments to the Cardinal Prefects, Bishop Morris indicated that he had always responded when complaints were made to him. The fact that fourteen years of letters had been collated and used as the basis for the Apostolic Visitor's investigation is one thing, but I submit that the fact that these letters had not been returned to Bishop Morris for action, or to the people responsible for them, requiring that they approach the Bishop for recourse before approaching a higher authority, is to ignore the requirements of Canon 1734 and the other canons on recourse. I submit that no one can respond effectively to complaints when he does not even know that the complaint exists.

In summary I submit that the actions of the Congregation for Bishops have lacked proper process. The Congregation may be acting on its own particular law but if this is the case it has not been revealed to Bishop Morris so he can understand it and respond accordingly. I submit that fundamental rights belonging to all Christ's Faithful have been denied Bishop Morris and some, especially his right to a good name, have been attacked without the right to proper defence.

With respect I request that the Supreme Tribunal of the Apostolic Signatura investigate these matters in the interest of justice. Dated at Toowoomba the 10th day of March 2008.

I shared this response with a few of the bishops who knew my situation and whose wisdom and counsel I respected. They were convinced that I would hear no more until after World Youth Day, for the last thing Rome would want at this stage was any distraction or controversy, and they were right. The new Nuncio for Australia was Archbishop Giuseppe Lazzarotto. It was at the dinner for Pope Benedict hosted by the Australian Bishops during World Youth Day that I met Lazzarotto for the first time. At the end of the meal as I was about to leave he sought me out, introducing himself, enquiring of my health and with the hope that all would be well for me into the future. World Youth Day came to an end and it was not long after this that Lazzarotto enquired of me when was I going to respond to Cardinal Re as he was waiting for my reply. Mystified at this request, I informed Lazzarotto that I had written to Cardinals Re, Arinze and Levada in March. I had also written to the Supreme Tribunal of the Apostolic Signatura and the President of the Pontifical Council for Legislative Texts at the same time, and the only reply I had received was from the Apostolic Signatura. I found his response curious as he then asked would I like a reply.

Within a few weeks I received a letter from Archbishop Juan Ignacio Arrieta, Secretary of the Pontifical Council for Legislative Texts, apologising for not responding sooner, remarking that it was only received just after Easter . . . It was now the end of September. My letter to this Pontifical Council had stated that 'as I have not reached the completion of my seventy-fifth year, as mentioned in Canon 401§1 and I am not suffering from ill-health, the only criterion on which such a request for resignation could be made would be that of *grave cause*'. I proceeded to ask the Dicastery to confirm that this interpretation of Canon 401§2 was correct and to provide 'advice as to the proper meaning of "grave cause" in the circumstances of the request' that had been put to me by Cardinal Re, Prefect of the Congregation for Bishops.

The letter had gone on to say that 'after carefully examining my correspondence, it seems to this Pontifical Council that the question is actually not one of interpretation (the phrase "grave cause" is unambiguous and well-established in canonical tradition) but rather of evaluating whether the law is being correctly applied in a concrete case, a judgment that ordinarily falls outside the institutional competence of this Dicastery'. The letter finished by stating that 'with respect to the Latin Rite Church in Australia, questions concerning the proper application of the Canon 401 CIC would need to be addressed to the Congregation for Bishops'.

It was November 2008 when I received a reply from Cardinal Re who remarked that he had waited until now to reply after learning of my health problems, as he did not want to disturb me until after I had finished the prescribed treatment and hoped that I would continue to improve and would be feeling better after my time of rest. Then came his critique of my 'Statement of Position' which he encapsulated in the misreading and wrong interpretation of the 2006 Advent Letter which had been the focus of Cardinal Levada during the meeting of January 2008. Cardinal Re was dismissive of the practical reasons and the particular pastoral focus for writing such a letter, stating that the letter led in a direction that opposed the teaching of the Church and a bishop should teach in accordance with the truths of the faith, not in contrast with its doctrine and discipline even in 'pragmatic' matters.

Trying to make his argument stronger, he mixed the contents of the Advent Letter with statements from the unsigned Memorandum that Archbishop Ambrose de Paoli had handed to me in September 2007. It had stated that we had no ordinations—we had four—which was just one of the errors I had pointed out in that particular document. Cardinal Re was disparaging of this, saying that it was a positive fact, but so small a number, and the Advent Letter speaking of the scarcity of priests presented no programme for promoting vocations or even a recommendation to pray for priestly vocations. At the same time he ignored completely the strategies I had outlined in my response, as well as the material that had been given to Chaput, the Apostolic Visitor. He went on to say that instead of promoting vocations to the ministerial priesthood, hope had been placed on 'a flowering in lay-led ministry at a local level' and the discussion of 'other options'. Then again, taking words out of context to prove a point, he wrote, 'almost as an afterthought' had I said in the Advent Letter 'we remain committed to actively promoting vocations to the current celibate male priesthood', but failing to include the quote, 'and open to inviting priests from overseas'.

Cardinal Re's criticism then moved into areas that the Advent Letter did not enter. That is that the Letter was permissive and undermined Church teaching and discipline by saying that 'we may well need to be much more open towards other options' when faced with the scarcity of priests. Then he quoted the examples from the Letter of what was being discussed in various parts of the world and accused me of inviting the clergy and faithful of Toowoomba to discuss matters that were to be 'definitively held', and of being 'only open to a reflection that wants to put them into practice and not one that proceeds in the opposite direction, putting them in doubt'. I had acknowledged in my 'Statement of Position' that, if taken out of context, my words could be misleading and in this light you could call them clumsy. Cardinal Re used this acknowledgment against me by saying that 'this clumsy wording which places before the public matters which are not open to discussion is another indication of your inability to teach clearly what the Church teaches'. The letter had not called for rejection of current Church teaching, nor had that been my official teaching on these 'definitively held' matters as indicated by Cardinal Re and supported by Cardinals Arinze and Levada. Cardinal Re finished this part of his critique of the Advent Letter by focussing on the invitation he said the letter had given the diocese to reflect on those issues which were 'definitively held' matters and by quoting the line that 'this does not mean that we or I reject the current teaching of the Church'. This line had not been in the Advent Letter, but he used it to give validity to his incorrect accusation.

It is worth noting that in the life of the Church there are examples of traditions and seemingly 'irreformable doctrines' that have changed over the years, changes in many cases that had already taken root in the Catholic community. Some examples are the dispute over usury, where eventually concerned laity, the Jesuits and other theologians brought the Church doctrine into conformity with changes in the European economic system, already widely accepted but condemned by the hierarchy; Galileo's attempts to reconcile the new science with the old faith; John Courtney Murray's long crusade against the traditional Church state doctrine which had been in practice for 200 years in America but contradicted centuries of European practice.

In these three examples, the struggle for change was difficult because the doctrines in dispute had been presented by the Church for many years as definitive, fixed and 'irreformable'. The Magisterium did not believe that it was authorised to alter them. Only in retrospect, after the change occurred, did the whole Church, from bottom to top, see that these doctrines had been in development and subject to change because of new information or insight.[2]

Yves Congar, a French Dominican Priest, who was one of the pioneers in the Church's theology of ecumenism, as well as the place of laity in the Church and one of the most influential theologians of the Second Vatican Council, believed that a knowledge of history was the best way to ensure confidence in the Church. He wrote that 'acquiring knowledge of history is the surest way of acquiring confidence in the Church. History teaches that nothing is new and that the Church has survived sadder and more difficult situations. History is a school of wisdom and of limitless patience.'[3]

Cardinal Re continued by quoting the specific issues raised by Cardinal Arinze, saying that I had 'failed to promote the discipline of the universal Church, as seen in the convergence of liturgical abuses that had been brought to my attention', without any reference to the way these matters had been addressed when brought to my attention or that of the Diocesan Liturgical Commission. He then wrote of the general theological climate of the diocese by referring to the report of the Apostolic Visitor, which he said confirmed the general theological and disciplinary decline of the diocese. That these had existed through the years, he said, was another sign of inadequate and defective leadership.

I am of course unable to comment on the Report of the Apostolic Visitation as I am unaware of its contents, but I found this accusation surprising after some of the statements made by Chaput, who had praised the priests of the diocese for their 'eloquence' and mentioned this to me. He was critical of some of the priests, quite unfairly I believe, as he did not know them, spent so little time with them and his interview manner at times was, I was told, quite judgmental and affronting. He was adversarial on many occasions, not looking for information but playing the devil's advocate, with his Deacon Neal

---

2. Robert McClory, *Faithful Dissenters: Stories of Men and Women Who Loved and Changed the Church* (Mayknoll, New York: Orbis, 2000), 161–162

3. Quoted by Thomas O'Meara OP, 'Raid on the Dominicans: The Repression of 1954', *America*, Volume 170/4 (2/5/1994): 16.

sitting behind the person being interviewed and passing documents over the shoulders of the interviewees.

Cardinal Re had started his letter by stating that my leadership had not been in accord with the doctrine and discipline of the Church and therefore I had not fulfilled the essential role of a bishop as the bond of communion between the universal Church and the local Church, of which the Bishop was the 'visible principle and foundation of unity', (*Lumen Gentium,* No 23; cf Canon 392*)*. He continued by saying that these fundamental defects, evident over many years, constituted the 'grave cause' which made necessary my resignation as the Bishop of Toowoomba.

He concluded his response by stating that he believed he had now addressed all the essential elements of my 'Statement of Position':

> In conclusion, as was stated to you in the 19 January, 2008 meeting here in Rome, despite good intentions, your pastoral governance has been judged as seriously and substantially flawed, and the ecclesial condition of the diocese of Toowoomba is a cause of deep concern to the Holy Father. In fact, it was he who specifically authorised this Congregation to ask for your resignation.
>
> Your resignation according to Canon 401§2 of the Code of Canon Law does not suggest that Your Excellency is lacking in personal, intellectual or moral character. In fact, you have demonstrated that you are a prayerful, forthright and personable man who embodies Christian and human virtues. You are generally well-liked by the priests and faithful of the diocese of Toowoomba and you are both generous and sensitive to the needs of others. The problem is your flawed pastoral leadership.
>
> Unfortunately, at this stage there is no other option but to ask Your Excellency to tender your resignation before the end of November 2008, so that it can be published at the beginning of January next year. As an act of filial obedience to the Holy Father, your resignation will avoid embarrassment for yourself and will potentially avoid misunderstanding and division among the priests, religious and faithful of the diocese of Toowoomba.

> The Apostolic Nuncio will be in contact with Your Excellency concerning some options for your future ministry.
>
> If Your Excellency should sadly refuse to comply with this invitation, the Holy See will be obliged to announce that you have been relieved of your office as the Bishop of Toowoomba and have been assigned a Titular See.
>
> I fraternally implore you to accept this decision with solicitude for the good of the diocese of Toowoomba and also for the Universal Church.

My offer to deal with, to clarify, and participate in a dialogue concerning any of the issues that had been raised was once again ignored.

As the Australian Bishops gathered in Conference in Sydney in late November that year, I was approached by the Apostolic Nuncio, Archbishop Giuseppe Lazzarotto. He was present at the Conference on the first morning of our meeting to address us and then stayed for a short time to be available. He approached me the night before the meeting started and said he needed to see me to discuss options for my future ministry and we made a time directly after he had addressed the conference. He began our meeting by informing me that earlier in the year when he was in Rome preparing for his appointment in Australia he had tried to solve the problem that had arisen between myself and some of the Dicasteries in the Vatican. He said he was told that the decision was already made and there would be no turning back, so he was here now to talk about my future. As he was speaking, I realised that he would have been in Rome when I was having my meeting with the three Cardinals, Re, Arinze and Levada in January of 2008.

He spoke about possibilities of what might be future roles for me within the Australian Church. I could have a national role or one of the bishops might have a position for me in their archdiocese or diocese, but before any of this could happen I needed to resign as requested by Cardinal Re. Lazzarotto was friendly but insistent that I send my letter of resignation as soon as I arrived home from the conference, and finished with the words, that 'he had tried his best but they have made up their minds'.

Our meeting over, I went back to the conference, a little distracted with what was happening and relieved that I did not have to make my reports until the following days. That evening I shared this next chapter of my story with one of the bishops who had been supporting me. We shared a meal, saw a film and I came back to the conference much refreshed.

On arriving home, I called a meeting of the Diocesan Consultors on 18 December 2008 to keep them up-to-date with the recent proceedings. I wanted to make sure that there was a group in the diocese who knew what was happening, and to prepare them for the possibility that Rome could go ahead and publish in January 2009 that I had been relieved of my office as Bishop of Toowoomba and assigned a Titular See somewhere. I also needed their prayerful wisdom to guide me in the decision I had to make.

Bishop Morris after confirmation and first communion , Windorah,
Queensland, in the 1990's.

Bishop Morris with his predecessor, Bishop Kelly, in Toowoomba during
the 1990's.

19

My Reply

One can accumulate facts, but one does not always achieve Knowledge. To know, one must be "awake" to the Living. Khaled Bentounes The law is not the truth! Not the only truth! The truth is plural because society is also plural.

Marc-Alain Ouaknin

Should you sit upon a cloud you would not see the boundary lines between one country and another, nor the boundary stone between a farm and a farm. It is a pity you cannot sit upon a cloud.

Kahlil Gibran

On 19 December 2008 I finally wrote to Cardinal Re. In preparing my reply I had prayed, reflected and taken discreet advice on all the events, meetings and letters that had transpired over the last few years. I had always hoped I would be able to address the difficulties that had arisen through a creative dialogue with the three cardinals of the Roman Congregations but unfortunately it had always been a monologue. It was at last clear that they were accusing me of breaking *communio*[1], so I informed Cardinal Re that I believed before God that I could and should not resign because in conscience I believed I had not broken *communion*, and had always been loyal to the teachings of the Church and the Holy Father. I went on to say that throughout this sad matter I believed I had been denied natural justice.

I also pointed out that when the meeting with the Congregations was being negotiated I had indicated that I would bring a canon lawyer with me. I was told this was not desirable. I was permitted to

---

1. *Communio* in the Church is described in chapter 15.

bring a brother bishop, a canon lawyer would be tolerated if I insisted, but that I was in essence alone. I stated that when the meetings took place, I felt bullied and intimidated as I sat opposite three Cardinals without any trusted advisors to support me. Archbishop Wilson, then President of the Australian Catholic Bishops' Conference, was present primarily as a solace.

As a brother bishop in the college of bishops, I believed that I had a right to speak with and explain myself to my immediate superior. When I made the request to have an audience with the Holy Father, I was told this was not an option available to me until I had resigned. At no time had I been shown a 'Papal Mandate' authorising the Prefect of the Congregation of Bishops to ask for my resignation. There had been no canonical process to establish a 'grave cause' for removal, such as a trial. I concluded my reply to Cardinal Re by assuring him that I was in good health. I had recently undergone some surgical procedures that were necessary, but these were not life-threatening or indeed anything abnormal for a man of my age, or for anyone who had grown up under the harshness of Australian climatic conditions. The surgery was successful, so it would be quite dishonest to suggest to the public that I was ill or in poor health.

I stated that the whole process had relied on the presumption that I would be compliant and resign. However, as I said, I could not do so in all conscience because my resignation would be based on my acceptance of a lie. My resignation would mean that I would accept the assessment of my having broken *communion*. I absolutely refuted and rejected this assessment and finished by saying that I was available for open, respectful, and discreet dialogue.

Some of those who were supporting me, especially some bishops and canonists both in Australia and overseas, were fairly certain that Pope Benedict probably knew very little of the whole affair, if anything. This was supported by the statement of the cardinals, that an audience with the Holy Father was not an option available to me until after I had resigned. So when I suggested that I write to the Holy Father informing him of my situation, those who had been offering support were a little hesitant, thinking that I might be opening a door that had been closed or maybe just a little ajar. On Christmas Eve 2008 I finally decided to write to Benedict. I faxed the letter to Archbishop Fernando Filoni in the Secretariat of State, and sent a hard copy to the Apostolic Nunciature to be placed in the Diplomatic Pouch for Rome.

I began the letter by indicating that I was writing to him in extraordinary circumstances essentially concerning his exercise of the Petrine ministry and my own position, before God, as a bishop of a particular local Church. I then went on to explain that there had been serious, protracted and disputed dealings between myself, as Bishop of Toowoomba, and the Cardinal Prefects of the Congregations for Bishops, Divine Worship and Discipline of the Sacraments, and Doctrine of the Faith. I stated that I was now being required by them to resign as Bishop of the Diocese of Toowoomba. Given that our differences had now reached such a polarised and inevitably personalised state, I was unable, in deepest conscience, to accede to their request, as I believed, and knew to be true, that the processes leading to this situation had serious shortcomings and were based on actual errors of fact and misinformation. Such demonstrable defects in process and distortions of facts cannot and could not form a legitimate basis for a move of such gravity in the life of the Church.

I wrote that if I knew that Pope Benedict XVI had received a comprehensive account either personally, or through some forum such as members of the Signatura which stands some steps removed from the Cardinal Prefects who had, up to date, been so closely involved in the matter, then I would be able to submit, with a clear conscience, to whatever the pope might decide and direct. The key issues originally in contention had been resolved and any further remedial measures in this regard I was willing to initiate and see through to an appropriate pastoral conclusion in the local Church. However, it had now been asserted that despite these undertakings, I was not suitable to be the ordinary (bishop) of the diocese and that I had broken *communio* which I absolutely refuted and rejected and still do.

Such a broad judgment surely needed to be objectively tested and further evidence was needed to substantiate this claim. I then pointed out to the Holy Father that, throughout this sad matter, I believed I had been denied natural justice and when I had made the request to have an audience with him, I was told this was not an option available to me until I had resigned. There had been no canonical process to establish a 'grave cause' for removal, such as a trial. I then requested that if possible he review the report of the Apostolic Visitation undertaken by Archbishop Charles Chaput in 2007, my response to the unsigned Memorandum handed to me in September 2006, my meeting with the cardinals (the prefects—heads—of the congregations), and my response, 'Statement of Position', provided in March 2008.

I went on to say that I believed the views of the bishops of the province of Queensland and a select group of Australian bishops needed to be canvassed as well. The assessment of my pastoral effectiveness or otherwise surely needed to be informed by the opinions of other bishops facing similar local issues. I concluded the letter with a request of what I needed in conscience before God, namely, the knowledge that my case had been fairly reviewed and, whatever the pope's ultimate decision might be, that it had been truthfully and adequately informed by the actual facts substantiated from all the evidence and from my personal and respectful dialogue with him. After assuring Pope Benedict of my prayerful support and that of the local Church and wishing him the peace and joy of the birth of Jesus, I walked out of the office to celebrate the Mass of Christmas Eve with a full Cathedral of joy-filled families, happy children alive with expectation and the joyful sound of Christmas carols. As I looked upon the gathered community, I remember thinking that this could be the last Christmas I celebrated with my diocesan family, and with that I immersed myself in their love and happiness.

January 2009 came and there was no announcement that I had been relieved of my office. In mid-January of that year I received a phone call from Father Brian Lucas who was in Rome with Archbishop Philip Wilson, who, as President of the Australian Catholic Bishops Conference, was visiting the Roman Dicasteries. That day they had visited Cardinal Re, Prefect of the Congregation for Bishops. Much of the meeting had been taken up with a discussion about my situation and Cardinal Re had asked questions about my health. Archbishop Wilson defended and was protective of me in the meeting. After the meeting Wilson asked Lucas if he would contact me and obtain a copy of the letter I had sent to Cardinal Re in December 2008. I sent a copy the next day and a few days later I received another phone call, this time from Archbishop Wilson. He had just come out of a meeting with Pope Benedict, a meeting he had requested on previous visits but had been unsuccessful in attaining. This time, however, his request had been granted and a substantial part of this meeting was a discussion concerning myself and my situation.

Archbishop Wilson was upbeat about the meeting and said the Holy Father was critical of the position the cardinals had taken in not allowing me to have an audience with him until after I had resigned. His response to Wilson was that every bishop in the world was free to ask for an audience with him. Wilson assured him that what the cardinals had said was accurately reported because he was present and he told me, with some excitement, that the Holy Father was willing to meet with me and that I would receive a letter. Wilson went on to say that the pope had requested that he accompany me to the meeting, but also said to me that I should not get my hopes up too high but that it did look promising. I was enlivened about the prospect that, at last, I was getting the opportunity to discuss these extraordinary circumstances in which I had found myself with Pope Benedict in whose hands all authority and power rests (Canon 333§1).[2]

In February 2009 I received an animated phone call from the Apostolic Nuncio, Lazzarotto, informing me that I had a letter from the Holy Father and how was I going to collect it. Post it, was my response. This was received in silence, which I broke by suggesting that he could read it to me. The letter was posted and it read:

> To the Venerable Brother William Morris, Bishop of Toowoomba. I wish to acknowledge your letter of 24 December 2008 in which you informed me of your difficulties in presenting your resignation as Bishop of Toowoomba. I have read your letter attentively and I have noted your openness with which you wrote to me. With equal clarity and fraternal love, I would like to tell you that your guidance of the diocese seems to be weak and insufficient for the challenges and the circumstances of Toowoomba. The pastoral demands of the good of the diocese require a bishop who will be able to rectify the course and give fresh vitality to the diocese in steadfast fidelity to the Magisterium of the Church. I read in your letter the expressions of respect which you have towards me and I know that I can fully rely on your obedience

---

2. Canon 333 § 1. 'By virtue of his office, the Roman Pontiff not only has power over the universal Church, but also has pre-eminent ordinary power over all particular Churches and their groupings. This reinforces and defends the proper, ordinary and immediate power which the bishops have in the particular Churches entrusted to their care.'

to the Successor of Peter. Soon after this coming Easter, I would be willing to receive you in Audience and talk with you. Please contact Archbishop James M Harvey, Prefect of the Pontifical Household, to arrange a suitable date. With deep affection I assure you of my prayers and I invoke God's blessing on you and the diocese of Toowoomba. Vatican City, 31 January, 2009. Benedictus XVI.[3]

The tone of the letter confirmed the advice of Archbishop Wilson to me that I should not get my hopes up too high.

I wrote to Archbishop James Harvey informing him of the Holy Father's message and his desire to receive me in audience sometime after Easter. In my letter, I suggested early June 2009, anytime from the 1 to the 5th of the month as both I and Archbishop Wilson (whom the Holy Father had invited to accompany me and be present for the meeting), would be in Rome during those days for the Anglophone Meeting for Professional Standards. I went on to say that if this time was not convenient Archbishop Wilson and I would be available to attend a meeting at a date that was most suitable to the Holy Father. On the 18th of March 2009 I received Harvey's reply that Pope Benedict would be pleased to receive us on Thursday the 4th of June and upon my arrival in Rome I was to contact his office so that the details about time and place could be communicated.

In preparation, I informed the Queensland bishops and asked them for letters of support which I would hand to the Holy Father. I received these letters before my departure for Rome in May of 2009. I had a meeting with the Diocesan Consultors to keep them informed. At the meeting Father Peter Schultz shared the results of his discussion with a number of internationally renowned canonists. These canonists had been aware of my situation and, after reviewing the file, believed the letter from Pope Benedict XVI spelt the end and that my resignation would be demanded at the audience.

Father Ian Waters, then President of the Canon Law Society of Australia and New Zealand, with other canon lawyers from overseas, advised me to stand my ground, indicating that strong pressure would be placed on me to resign. They believed that cardinals from

---

3. Appendix 16, Correspondence from Benedict XVI, dated 31 January 2009.

the Dicasteries would be saying things like the following: 'the pope is very concerned and would be losing sleep over my situation; it is making him sick with worry and I wouldn't want to put the Pope under that pressure, would I?'

I had no intention of resigning but, to make sure my judgment was based on fact and not emotion, I asked the Diocesan Consultors, whom I had kept up-to-date with the information about my relationship with the various Dicasteries, 'was I', and I used the phrase 'out of step', with Rome? If it was genuinely believed that I was 'out of step', and did not have the support of my brother priests in the diocese and the vast majority of the diocesan family, and if they did not approve of my leadership, then I would resign immediately.

General discussion followed, all supporting my ministry and leadership. They affirmed the stance I was taking in not resigning and suggested that copies of the letters of support, signed by the clergy and pastoral leaders[4] after the Apostolic Visitation, be taken with those of the Queensland bishops and presented to the Holy Father. I felt affirmed in the position I had taken.

---

4. C/f Chapter 12.

Bishop Morris with Queensland Premier, Mr Peter Beatie, at the blessing and openng of Mary MacKillop Primary School, Highfield, Queensland.

20

The Audience

It's a mistake to think we listen only with our ears. It's much more important to listen with the mind, the eyes, the body and the heart. Unless you truly want to understand the other person, you will never be able to listen.

Mark Herndon

Arriving in Rome at midday on the 31st of May 2009, I once again enjoyed a frenetic drive from the airport to Vatican City where the Anglophone Meeting on Professional Standards was to take place. The meeting was taking place in the Casa Santa Marta where we were staying. The Casa is situated inside Vatican City, and is now the chosen place of residence of Pope Francis. After finding my room it was time for a walk. To walk and get lost in the narrow cobblestone streets of the Old City can give you the feeling that time has stopped and that you are walking back in history. As I stopped under the arches in the shadow of St Peter's Basilica, I was reminded of a story told by Father Richard Rohr on a visit to the eternal city. He was being shown around by a friend who lived in Rome. On arriving at St Peter's, they were standing just inside the front doors. Rohr's companion asked him had he heard what an elderly Italian gentleman, who was standing near them, had just said. Rohr replied that he had heard him mutter something but did not understand the exact nature of the comments. Rohr's companion translated what the little Italian had murmured with a sigh: 'Some tomb for a fisherman'. As I looked past the Basilica to the Apostolic Palace, I had a feeling of sadness for the successor of 'Peter' . . . living in a museum behind walls of security, both ancient and living, protected from the heartbeat of creation, not being able to get his feet soiled in the messiness of life.

The next morning I made contact with Archbishop James Harvey and the following day received notification that Archbishop Wilson and I would be received in audience on Thursday 4th of June 2009 at 11.15 am in the Appartamento Pontificio. On Wednesday morning the participants at the Anglophone meeting attended the general audience with Pope Benedict XVI in St Peter's Square, which is held every Wednesday depending on the pope's availability. It was there that I met and spoke to Harvey, and was presented with a number of other bishops to Pope Benedict, who made no response to my comment that I was looking forward to our meeting the next day, except to repeat 'Toowoomba' after me when I told him where I was from. I greeted him with the prayerful best wishes from the local Church of the Toowoomba diocese and told him I was a member of the Anglophone Conference on Professional Standards, to which he nodded and smiled. As I walked away, I was hoping for a friendlier meeting the next day.

That evening the Australian contingent at the Anglophone Conference met at one of the restaurants off the Borgo Pio, a street opposite the Santa Anna Gate, a popular eating area with both locals and tourists. We were dining alfresco and enjoying the twilight in the coolness of the evening, as were the passing crowds of tourists and local families with their children playing games. Out of this wonderful mix came a face I recognised. He was a priest whom I had come to know over the years from my visits to Rome and with whom I had contact in his role in the Secretariat of State. In the course of our meeting he mentioned how pleased he was that he had the opportunity to speak with me before my meeting with the Holy Father the next day. He told me not to worry about the meeting and that everything would be all right. He said that the Holy Father would speak of the difficulties that had arisen, ask for my faithfulness to him and the Church's teachings, give me his blessing and that would be the end of the matter. As he went on his way I resumed my place at the table with a lighter heart and enjoyed the evening.

The next day Archbishop Wilson and I arrived at the Appartamento Pontificio around 11am, and were ushered into a large waiting room. Not long after 11.15 am we were led into an even larger room with Pope Benedict seated behind a desk immediately on the right as you entered the room, with his back to the wall, and except for the two chairs in front of the desk the rest of the room was bare, softened only by paintings. Greetings over, we occupied the seats in front of the desk and with a few opening remarks the Holy Father asked me what I wanted to say. Archbishop Wilson and I thanked him for seeing us and I replied that I would like to listen to him, remembering what I had been told the previous evening.

As he began to speak I remember thinking, am I really hearing what Benedict is saying, for I felt as if I was being transported back in time to my meeting with Cardinals Re, Arinze and Levada, that I was listening once again to Levada, stating that I was teaching things that the Holy Father had said could not be taught or spoken of. That is, that I was doing this by raising such matters as discussing the recognition of Anglican, Lutheran and Uniting Church orders as well as discussing the ordination of women, matters which had been spoken of definitively by the pope and the Church. Pope Benedict was using exactly the same language as Levada had used, focussing on the misreading and misinterpretation of matters raised in my Advent Pastoral Letter of 2006 which had addressed local pastoral questions and matters which were and are still in ferment generally across the whole Church. He said my doctrinal teaching around these matters contained errors and, because of this, my pastoral leadership was flawed by teaching on these matters and allowing them to be discussed. At that point I said to the Holy Father that I had not taught these matters and to say so was a misreading and a misinterpretation of the 2006 Advent Letter.

It was like pushing a button on a tape recorder for Benedict repeated the exact statement he had just made, but finishing this time with the words that 'it was God's will that I should resign.' I responded by saying that I did not believe it was God's will that I should resign as I had never broken *communio* or taught against Church teaching. He then went on to say that I was a very gifted and charismatic person but too practical in nature and that I lacked the appropriate charism to be a diocesan bishop, as I was not in step with the theology of the Magisterium of the Church and that my gifts could be used by the Church in other areas but not as a diocesan bishop. I responded once again by saying that I thought that he and the three cardinals were wrong in their reading and interpretation of what I had said in the Advent Letter, and that I had not taught against the Magisterium and had not broken *communio*.

There was no dialogue. It was purely a monologue. The Holy Father was repeating what he had been told by others, making me doubt whether or not he had ever seen or read the 2006 Advent Letter or any of the documentation around my case. Before I could respond again to the inaccurate judgment that was continuously being made by those in Rome and presumably elsewhere, he spoke to Archbishop Wilson. He directed him to find me another position in the Australian Church. At that point he drew the conversation to a conclusion by saying that he knew how painful it must be for me, but for the good of the Church I must resign from my present position as Bishop of Toowoomba. The door opened, the Monsignor who had ushered us in to the meeting was waiting to usher us out. As we departed, I said to the Holy Father that the last thing I wanted would be to cause him any more worry than he already had, thanked him for seeing us, that I would think prayerfully of what he had said and we both assured him of our prayerful support. I handed the letters of support that I had brought with me to the attendant with the request that he would pass them on to Pope Benedict. Then we left. The audience with the pope had lasted about fifteen minutes in total.

As Archbishop Wilson and I left the Apostolic Palace and walked slowly back to the Casa Santa Marta, the route taking us behind the Basilica of St Peter's, I remarked to him that what we heard from the pope was almost identical to what Cardinal Levada had said in our meeting with him twelve months previously. Wilson agreed, thought it was almost word-perfect, and we both wondered whether or not Pope Benedict had ever seen any of the material or whether he had just been briefed by Cardinal Levada and possibly Cardinals Re and Arinze, had taken their advice, and without any conversation with me, had already made his decision, one which he made without ever giving me a chance to discuss the matters with him at length. I said to Archbishop Wilson, as we continued our walk back to the Casa, 'You know in conscience and in justice I can't resign, don't you?' He responded, 'Yes'. We continued in silence, arriving back at the Casa, taking our place at the Anglophone Meeting and looking forward to the lunch break.

In the afternoon before the Anglophone meeting started, I lost myself once again in the old city of Rome and by the time I arrived back at the Casa my spirit had been rejuvenated. That night the Australian contingent once again found a pleasant restaurant and enjoyed each other's company in the Roman twilight. The meeting came to an end on the Friday and that evening the whole group walked to Trastevere, enjoying the atmosphere of the Roman evening and surroundings, grateful for the support and friendship that had developed through our meetings over the last few years.

Before heading off to Trastevere, my contact in the Secretariat of State came looking for me. He wanted to express his utter surprise and shock at what had happened in the morning at the meeting with the pope. He said that in the Secretariat they had not seen this coming at all, had totally misread what was going to happen and were in a state of shock. He then asked me what I was going to do. Would I resign, and if not, what did I think would happen? I was a little guarded in my reply, expressing how I was feeling rather than what I was going to do. In the course of our conversation he warned me that there was strong support for the extreme right of the Church among those who worked in the various congregations, and not to be surprised if word of my meeting with the Holy Father reached Australia before I did. He then asked me, if I did not resign, what did I think the pope would do. I replied, 'Sack me!' With the promise of prayerful support and whatever he could do for me, we went our separate ways.

On Saturday I immersed myself in the sights and smells of Rome and allowed the atmosphere of the ancient city to wash away the disappointment of the last few days. Sunday morning came and, after celebrating the eucharist, Bishop Brian Finnigan and I found an Irish pub where we enjoyed a hearty Irish breakfast with all the trimmings. Finnigan was saddened by what had happened, hoping too, that there might even be, at this late hour, a solution and reversal of the pope's decision.

Bishop Morris at Coopers Creek Queensland.

21

The Next Step

A person must break with the illusion that his life has already been written and his path already determined.

Marc-Alain Ouaknin (20th – 21st century)

A few days after arriving home, I called the Diocesan Consultors together on the 12th of June 2009 to report on the meeting with Pope Benedict in Rome. After briefing them as to what had happened and how surprised I had been that the meeting had taken the turn it did after the advice I had received, I indicated to them that I was becoming a little tired of the fight and was seeking their advice. I had already received advice from canon lawyers to hold firm, based on two grounds. First, that in the end, after much pressure the Holy See would not act. Second, any resignation would be seen as a victory by the extreme right wing of the Church. It had already been spoken of that I was to be the sacrifice for the extreme right and this victory would keep them quiet. I was concerned, not so much for myself, but for the consequences for the diocese. I asked the Consultors whether I should acquiesce, tender my resignation and accept one of the national positions within the Australian Church or the Australian Catholic Bishops Conference which the Holy Father had asked Archbishop Wilson to work on with the Apostolic Nuncio to secure.

The consensus of the Consultors was that I should do whatever I considered best for myself and my integrity. I spoke with the Consultors about 'retirement'. Father Peter Schultz pointed out there was no such thing as retirement for a bishop and that I would have to resign. I repeated what I had said elsewhere, that for me in all good conscience, resigning was impossible. Schultz then offered the possibility of a letter that used the term, 'retirement'. The letter would be extra-canonical, that is, it would have no real standing but would enable me to depart on my own terms and not accept the fundamental untruth of the Holy See's position. There was a long discussion of what the future might hold and a decision was made by the group that, without myself present, they would meet to discuss the situation further in a few days.

The meeting with the Consultors had been on the 12th of June 2009. By the 19th of June I had my reply ready for the Holy Father, thanking him on behalf of Archbishop Wilson and myself for meeting with us in Rome on Thursday 4th June 2009. I informed him that I appreciated that he must have found it a difficult meeting, having to inform me of his decision made on the advice of the three cardinals, the heads of the three congregations. I continued, saying that I was writing to him as a brother bishop asking for his help, and referred to my letter of the 24th December 2008, in which I had assured him that I would undertake to conform to, and abide by, whatever determination in the Petrine ministry he held. I had also requested that what I really needed in conscience before God, was the knowledge that my case had been fairly reviewed. I had asked for this because the process leading to his request for my resignation had very serious shortcomings and was based on errors of fact, misinformation and misrepresentation.

So I indicated that it was in his discernment with the cardinals, the heads of the three congregations, that I needed his help. I informed him that I was supported in asking this of him by a number of my brother bishops in Queensland, from others in Australia, by trusted advisors and by canon lawyers, who had all seen at first hand my ministry and were aware of my faithfulness to the Magisterium. I wrote that none of these people could see how such defects in process and distortions of facts could form a legitimate basis for a move of such gravity in the life of the Church as my being forced to resign as the Bishop of Toowoomba.

I finished my letter by pointing out that Archbishop Charles Chaput, who conducted the Apostolic Visitation, had expressed a measure of surprise that he was being asked to investigate me because, as far as he could see from the material provided to him, things that I had reportedly said and done were happening in other places around the world as well. At the end of the visitation he had also remarked to the Diocesan Chancellor, Father Brian Sparksman, that he would be astounded if our diocese were to lose its bishop.

I then pointed out that it was in the context of this background that I was asking him, as my brother bishop, to help me form my conscience as I had not been shown anything that would establish a 'grave cause' for my removal. I informed him that Archbishop Wilson was away until mid-July 2009 and he had asked me to wait until he returned from overseas before any decision was made.

On the 9th of July 2009 I received two letters. One was a copy of correspondence from Cardinal Re. The second was a covering letter from the Apostolic Nuncio, Archbishop Lazzarotto. Pope Benedict had asked Cardinal Re to write in reply to my letter. Cardinal Re said that first of all the Holy Father wanted to assure me that he had read my letter attentively, as he had the letters of support from some of the bishops in Queensland that I had handed to him on the occasion of my recent visit to Rome. There was no mention of the other letters of support from the priests and people of the diocese. Second, he wrote that the Holy Father continued to hold the same view of the decision he had expressed to me in Rome, namely, that the for good of the diocese of Toowoomba he required that I tender my resignation as Bishop of the Diocese of Toowoomba. His Holiness trusted that I would be faithful to the promise I had made to do so, one that I had made during my visit there. The letter said that Pope Benedict was aware of the sacrifice involved in such a step, but he asked me to resign from my present office out of my love for the Church.

Very interestingly, since that time the 'Vatileaks' fiasco showed how wrongly those in Rome, including the pope, had perceived the whole situation. The Italian journalist, Gianluigi Nuzzi, wrote a book in 2012 with the Italian title translated into English as *His Holiness: The Secret Papers of Benedict XVI*. The book is based on leaked Vatican documents. In the book the journalist had copied a letter I had written to Pope Benedict and a set of notes written by Benedict himself and addressed to Cardinal Re about my 'case'.

The notes were written after my meeting with Pope Benedict in June 2009 and after the letter I had written following the meeting in which I questioned the way my case had been handled, and their continual misreading of the 2006 Advent Letter. The journalist had sent me a translation of what Pope Benedict had written in a note that my 'theological formation . . . is not adequate for his office', citing my views on women's ordination and the possibility of Anglican ministers leading Catholic liturgies. In response to my statement, Benedict wrote of 'lack of care for the truth', blaming it all on a problem of language. 'Obviously there was a misunderstanding, created, it seems to me, by my insufficient knowledge of the English language. In our meeting, I tried to convince him that his resignation was desirable and I thought he expressed his willingness to renounce his functions as Bishop of Toowoomba. From his letter I see this was a misunderstanding. I acknowledge that, but I must say decisively that this isn't a case of "a lack of care for the truth" '. Benedict finished his note to Cardinal Re, writing, 'There's no doubt of his very good pastoral intentions', but 'the Diocesan Bishop must be, above all, a teacher of the faith, since the faith is the foundation of pastoral activity'. Benedict XVI told Re to recommend that Morris accept 'free renunciation of his actual ministry, in favour of a ministry more consistent with his gifts', and asked Re to 'assure him of my prayers'.[1]

On Sunday 3 June 2012, I received an email from the Italian journalist, Gianluigi Nuzzi, in response to my inquiry as to where I could purchase a copy of his book. He thanked me for my request and advised me that it had not yet been translated into English but that I could purchase it in Italian. He then went on to say that my story was incredible and he was sorry for the suffering I had endured, and to let him know if there was anything he could do. On 9 June 2012, Robert Mickens, in *The Tablet*, published an English translation of Pope Benedict's note of 11 December 2009 to Cardinal Re concerning myself, which reads:

> Thank you for drafting the letter. I would further insert the following points: The bishop continuously talks about a 'process', of 'defects in process'. He says: 'I have been denied natural justice and due process', 'there has not been a canonical process', etc. It must be said that in fact there was no process, but a fraternal dialogue and an appeal to his conscience to freely renounce his office as diocesan bishop. We are convinced that his doctrinal formation is not adequate for this office and it was our intention to explain to him the reasons for our conviction.

1. Personal correspondence of Gianlugi Nuzzi to the author.

The bishop speaks of 'a lack of care for the truth' on our part. This statement is unacceptable. But obviously there was a misunderstanding, created—I think—by my insufficient knowledge of English. At our meeting I tried to convince him that his resignation was desirable, and I understood him to have expressed his willingness to renounce his duties as Bishop of Toowoomba. From his letter I can see that this was a misunderstanding. I acknowledge that, but I must state firmly state there was not a 'lack of care for the truth'.

The bishop states that this concerns only cultural differences that do not regard communion. In fact, in his pastoral letter—in addition to pastoral choices that are highly questionable—there are at least two proposals that are incompatible with the doctrine of the Catholic faith: The letter says one could even start ordaining women to overcome the priest shortage. But the Holy Father John Paul II decided in an infallible and irrevocable way that the Church does not have the right to ordain women to the priesthood.

He says furthermore that even ministers of other communities (Anglicans, etc) could help out in the Catholic Church. But according to the doctrine of Catholic faith, the ministries of these communities are not valid, are not 'sacrament' and therefore do not permit them any actions linked to the sacrament of priesthood. There is no doubt about his excellent pastoral intentions, but it is clear that his doctrinal formation is insufficient. A diocesan bishop must also and above all be a teacher of the faith, seeing that faith is the foundation of pastoral work. This is the reason for the invitation to reflect in conscience before God about the free renunciation of his current ministry in favour of a ministry more suited to his gifts. Assure him of my prayers.[2]

Later, the Australian Jesuit, Father Frank Brennan, made this observation about Pope Benedict's comment:

---

2. *The Tablet*, 9 June 2012, 6–7.

In his note of 11 December 2009 following upon his meeting with Bishop Morris on 4 June 2009, Pope Benedict wrote 'that in fact there was no process, but a fraternal dialogue and an appeal to his conscience to freely renounce his office as diocesan bishop'.

Prior to the fraternal dialogue, there was a process of sorts. In April 2007, the Holy See sent Archbishop Chaput to conduct a visitation of Bishop Morris's diocese. Morris never saw the report, and claims never to have been appraised of its contents. In September 2007 an unsigned memorandum dated 28 June 2007 from the Congregation for Bishops was received by Bishop Morris requesting that he resign. On 3 October 2007, the Congregation for Bishops requested his resignation, in the name of the Holy Father. At a meeting on 19 January 2008 attended by three Curial Cardinals, Bishop Morris and Archbishop Wilson, President of the Australian Catholic Bishops Conference, Cardinal Re stated: 'Bishop Morris is a person of integrity in morals, a man of good will and other gifts. He can continue to do much good, but the right role for him is not that of Diocesan Bishop of Toowoomba.' On 23 October 2008, Cardinal Re demanded Morris's resignation by the end of November 2008 so that an announcement could be made in early January 2009. He wrote that if the resignation were not forthcoming the bishop would be removed. The process preceding the Holy Father's 'fraternal dialogue' was neither fair, transparent nor consistent. The process had been premised on Morris's resignation for at least one year and nine months before the Pope met for the fraternal dialogue.

On or after 4 June 2009, the pope decided that the 2006 Advent Pastoral letter was the hanging offence. Benedict identified two theological errors: 'The letter says one could even start ordaining women to overcome the priest shortage.' 'He says furthermore that even ministers of other communities (Anglicans, etc) could help out in the Catholic Church.'

With all respect, Benedict's summary of Morris's position is far too simplistic. This is what Morris wrote: 'Given our deeply held belief in the primacy of Eucharist for the identity, continuity and life of each parish community, we may well need to be much more open towards other options of ensuring that Eucharist may be celebrated. Several responses have been discussed internationally, nationally and locally:

• ordaining married, single or widowed men who are chosen and endorsed by their local parish community
•welcoming former priests, married or single back to active ministry
• ordaining women, married or single
•recognising Anglican, Lutheran and Uniting Church Orders. While we continue to reflect carefully on these options we remain committed to actively promoting vocations to the current celibate male priesthood and open to inviting priests from overseas.'

As soon as the local media started asking Morris if he would take these courses of action, he consistently replied that he would only do what Rome approved. Ultimately, he published a clarification of his pastoral letter on the diocesan website saying:
'In my Advent Pastoral Letter of 2006 I outlined some of the challenges facing the diocese into the future. In that letter I made reference to various options about ordination that were and are being talked about in various places, as part of an exercise in the further investigation of truth in these matters. Unfortunately some people seem to have interpreted that reference as suggesting that I was personally initiating options that are contrary to the doctrine and discipline of the Church. As a bishop I cannot and would not do that and I indicated this in the local media at the time. I and all the bishops of the Catholic Church form a college with the Holy Father and cannot act contrary to the teaching and practice of the Universal Church. Encouraging

vocations to the priesthood must remain a priority for
our local Church and we pray this Christmas and as we
begin the New Year that more young men will consider
deeply their response to God's call.'

In his own minutes from the meeting on 19 January
2008, Cardinal Re wrote: 'To sum it up briefly: to
present these questions as topics for public discussion
is to separate yourself from the teaching of the Catholic
Church.' It seems the Pope agrees.[3]

In Archbishop Lazzarotto's covering letter to me of July 2009, with the
letter of Cardinal Re on behalf of the pope, he requested that, without
further delay, I write to the Holy Father my letter of resignation in
compliance with the promise I made during my last meeting with
him in Rome. However, my resignation would be made public at a
later stage once—with the help of Archbishop Wilson and others of
my brother bishops—I was able to find and assume a suitable and
dignified ministry.

Well, so much for my asking for help and, in the process,
discovering how the Holy Father came to his decision on reading the
Advent Letter and other documentation. Was the pope's view based
purely on the advice of the three cardinals, the prefects of the three
congregations, who had shown at our initial meeting that they had
misconstrued and misinterpreted the Advent Letter? What was clear
was that the pope had not listened to me in our meeting in Rome in
June 2009. As I read the nuncio's letter, and the other letter, the words
of Blessed Cardinal John Henry Newman's toast were ringing in my
ears: 'I shall drink to the pope, if you please, still, to conscience first,
and to the pope afterwards.'[4]

While the Church is not, nor ever will be, a full democracy there
are canon lawyers who argue that it would be possible to establish
a system of law that recognised the separation of powers and that

3. Letter to the Editor *The Tablet*, 9 June 2012, published on the web site of *The
    Tablet* in the letters-extra section.
4. Quoted in *The Tablet*, 16 July 2011. JH Newman, *A Letter Addressed to His Grace
    the Duke of Norfolk on the Occasion of Mr Gladstone's Recent Expostulation* (New
    York: Catholic Publications Society, 1875), 86.

therefore would protect the ideals of justice more fully. The doctrine (separation of powers) would ensure that no one person or group of people could have absolute power and control.

All authority and power rests in the hands of one man, the bishop of Rome, the pope. Because the pope makes the law, he can, if he wishes, change it, *motu proprio*. Likewise, the pope can act without due process. For example, if a bishop wanted to remove a priest from the clerical state or a parish priest from his parish, there are processes he must follow and the priest may appeal this to the Congregation for Clergy against his bishop. However, if the pope wanted to remove a priest from the clerical state or a bishop from office, he can do so simply by signing a decree. There is no competent forum to bring an action against anything done by the Supreme Pontiff; he is chief judge and therefore cannot be judged. (Canon 1404: The First See is judged by no one.) It is my belief that, until there is a separation of powers, there never will be due process or true justice.

On the 18th of September 2009, I received another letter from the Nuncio, Archbishop Lazzarotto, reminding me that I had not replied to the correspondence from Cardinal Re. In reply I informed him that I had been in conversation with Archbishop Wilson and was in the process of drafting a reply to Re, who had written on behalf of the Holy Father, and that I would be forwarding my reply to the Holy Father at the end of October. I pointed out to Lazzarotto that it had been a difficult few years and showed no signs of getting any easier. I had not had a break for twelve months, carrying the normal load of pastoral responsibilities of the diocese, as well as my commitment to the provincial and national Church committees, with the added pressure of having to respond to an unjust process. I asked for his support, which would enable me to have some time and space before responding to the Holy Father.

Refreshed from my month away, in November 2009, I launched into my response to Pope Benedict XVI with renewed vigour, based on the letter I had received from Cardinal Re on the 9th of July 2009 asking for my resignation that the Holy Father said I had promised him at our meeting in June 2009. I commenced by reflecting on my conversation with Archbishop Wilson when he returned from overseas, on his recollection of the meeting with the Holy Father and the conversation that took place. Archbishop Wilson concurred with me that nothing I said could be taken or construed as a promise to resign. In fact, he reminded me that I had said to him as we left the meeting that 'I would not be resigning'. This also accords with my letters to Pope Benedict XVI on the 24th of December 2008 and the 19th of June 2009 in which I stated, that for me, this was a deeply held matter of conscience.

I pointed out in the letter that Cardinal Re's claim that 'I promised my resignation' was but further troubling evidence of a 'lack of care for the truth' which had characterised the whole process or lack thereof, to which I had been subjected. Therefore, it cannot be 'of God' when the truth is not respected and exactness is not preserved. I went on to say to the Holy Father that my dilemma remained intense, for I could not see how such evident defects in process and distortions of facts could form a legitimate basis for a move of such gravity in the life of the diocese for which I was ordained as bishop, and to which I had been committed for the past sixteen and a half years. I stated that I feared for the consequences for the people of the local Church of Toowoomba and indeed the damage and scandal this would cause to the whole Church's authority generally. I then reflected on my own motivation, for in searching this, I had discerned no personal preferences, practical convenience or ambition. It was quite the contrary! This detachment and my reluctance 'to play politics' may have caused or contributed to the situation in which I now found myself. I did not want—let alone seek—any notoriety which would only damage the Church, locally and generally, as I had already stated.[5]

I then went on to explain why in conscience I was unable to offer my resignation, for that would imply an acceptance or at least a compliance with the procedures and processes which had been lacking in natural justice, transparency and truthfulness. My 'unsuitability to be a diocesan bishop' was a most broad, general assertion which had not been adequately substantiated or demonstrated to me. If I was such a danger to the faith of my diocesan family because of my 'insufficient theological formation', to quote Pope Benedict, would I not be the same danger in another ministry, as Benedict put it, more suited to my 'gifts', for the only function that Pope Benedict

---

5. I had come to realise over a period of time through prayerful reflection that 'one's life situation is not one's life'.

wanted to remove from me was that of governance, not the functions of teaching and sanctifying. The areas in which I had been at fault I had corrected, and the matters raised in my Advent Letter, which I acknowledged could have been worded better, were those which are in ferment generally across the Church.[6]

Continuing in my letter to the Holy Father, I reflected that maybe our respective cultural and linguistic backgrounds could have influenced the manner and the words chosen in which we try either to conceal or to confront the problems facing the Church. I admitted that the tone of some of my correspondence may have seemed too direct or too blunt for curial diplomacy, but surely this was more a matter of style rather than of substance—a case of cultural difference rather than broken *communio*. I then mentioned that I did regret the fact that my situation had added to the weight of the Holy Father's concern for all the churches, yet my best efforts at restorative justice and a genuine reconciliation had been severely hampered as the allegations remained unspecific, *vague, undefined, based on a lack of care for the truth*. My words, actions and intentions had always been to preserve rather than pervert *ecclesial communion*. This was supported by my brother bishops in Queensland and other parts of Australia who, if asked, would testify to the worth of my ministry, and who were aware of my fidelity to the Magisterium.

Reading the Advent Letter in its correct context and without distorting its meaning, what I then asked the Holy Father was precisely where, when and exactly how I had failed? I pointed out that I had been denied natural justice and due process; that I had never seen the report prepared by the Apostolic Visitor. The Apostolic Visitor had indicated to me and to others that the conditions in the Toowoomba Diocese were not so very different from those across the English speaking Church. I had not been shown any of the 'evidence' that was gathered, or even the names of my 'accusers'. This to me seemed *contra Scriptura* (Matt 5:23–26, 10:26–27, 18:15–18 etc). There had not been a canonical process to establish a 'grave cause' for removal and the conditions of Canon 401§1§2 had not been met. And the so called

---

6. 'The answer is always contained in the mystery of the question. The mystery will only reveal itself in reflection leading to dialogue. By stating that these questions cannot be spoken of is treating the people of God as children, gagging the Spirit, thereby not allowing the Church to breathe freely or together.' WM Morris.

'fraternal dialogue' had been a monologue based on a misreading and misinterpretation of the Advent Letter, as seen in Pope Benedict's notes to Cardinal Re revealed through the eyes of Vatileaks.

I proceeded, saying, that as I had been denied natural justice and due process, I could not in conscience accept some artificially created, extra-diocesan position, for in Australian culture this would be seen and ridiculed for what it was—a sinecure—and would further damage the Church's standing in this country. I made reference to the marked differences between the adversarial and inquisitorial legal traditions from which we respectively came but it was the vague generality and the evident factual inaccuracies in the very limited information of which I had been made aware that left me unconvinced and unconvicted in my own conscience.

I finished off by saying to the Holy Father that I believed that I had to express myself as forthrightly as possible to capture the moral dilemma in which I found myself embroiled. It was for me a matter of conscience. My resignation would mean that I accepted the assessment of myself as breaking *communio* which I absolutely refuted and rejected, and so it was out of love for the Church that I could not do so. I then pointed out that I was sure both of us would be aware that any discernment based on false premises could not lead to truth.[7]

---

7. Appendix 16, Correspondence to Pope Benedict XVI 0f 12 November 2009.

22

What Next?

When his life's work was threatened, Saint Ignatius Loyola was asked what he would do if Pope Paul IV dissolved or otherwise acted against the Society of Jesus, to which he had devoted his energy and gifts, and he replied: 'I would pray for fifteen minutes, then I would not think of it again'.

Alan Paton

In the first week of each year we priests of the diocese gathered for our annual retreat. It was during this time, in January 2010, that I received a phone call informing me that a letter had arrived from Pope Benedict, dated 22 December 2009.[1] Like St Ignatius, founder of the Jesuits, quoted above, I prayed about this situation and wondered about obtaining the letter or leaving it till the end of the retreat. In the end I decided that if I was going to have any peace for the remaining days of the retreat, I needed to read the letter.

The letter began by acknowledging receipt of my letter of 12 November 2009 in which I had explained why I could not resign. In referring to this, the pope used the word *reluctance* to describe my stance towards offering my resignation as Bishop of the Diocese of Toowoomba, without making any reference to conscience. He then focussed on the closing paragraph of my letter in which I had said that 'I respectfully remain in need of your guidance and wisdom', saying that this inspired him to write to me frankly and fraternally.

He focussed on my claim that there had been 'defects in process'

---

1. .Appendix 16, Correspondence from Pope Benedict XVI dated 22 December 2009.

saying that, rather than any due process and a denial of natural justice, we had been engaged in a fraternal dialogue in which appeals had been made to my conscience to renounce freely the office of diocesan bishop. He said that some of my doctrinal utterances had caused grave concern in view of the responsibility of the bishop to teach the entirety of the doctrine of the faith authentically, and that it had been his intention to explain to me his firm conviction in this matter. He went on to say that canon law did not make provision for a process regarding bishops, 'whom the Successor of Peter nominates and may remove from office'. History shows that this was not always the case.

His letter then shifted to the statement in my letter that there had been a 'lack of care for the truth' on the part of the Holy See. This he swept aside by saying that, clearly, there had been a misunderstanding. This reminded me of the apology Pope John Paul II gave in 1992 for the condemnation of Galileo—that the earth does indeed revolve around the sun—saying that it was 'a tragic mutual incomprehension' between the inquisition and the scientist.[2]

Pope Benedict continued in his letter of December 2009, saying that he had tried to show me why my resignation was necessary and that it was his understanding that I had expressed my openness to comply and resign as Bishop of Toowoomba, but from my letter he realised now that I had no such intention. He then reemphasised that there had not been 'a lack of care for the truth'. Later, VatiLeaks would show that this - that is, his claim that it was because of his lack of ability in English he may have misunderstood what I said - was wrong.[3]

He then alluded to my reference to 'cultural difference' that does not affect ecclesial communion. In fact what I had said was that 'our respective cultural and linguistic backgrounds may influence the manner and the words chosen in which we try either to conceal or to confront the problems facing the Church'. He stated that my Advent Pastoral letter of 2006—besides containing some very questionable pastoral choices—presented at least two options that were incompatible with Catholic faith: a) ordaining women in order

2. James Carroll, *Constantine's Sword* (Boston, Mariner Books Houghton Mifflin, 2002), 384. (When Carroll was interviewing Hans Kung in 1996 his response was 'Galileo was right. The others were wrong.'

3. C/f Journalist Gianluigi Nuzzi in his new book *His Holiness: The Secret Papers of Benedict XVI* (Italian: *Sua Santità. Le carte segrete di Benedetto XVI*, Chiarelettere).

to overcome the priest shortage. 'Yet, the late Pope John Paul II has decided infallibly and irrevocably that the Church has not the right to ordain women to the priesthood'; b) with reference to my 'recognising Anglican, Lutheran and Uniting Church Orders', he replied that 'according to the doctrine of the Catholic faith, ministers from these communities are not validly ordained and therefore do not share in the Sacrament of Holy Orders; and as such their actions are not joined to the ministerial priesthood.'[4]

Once again, while reading this I did not believe that this could be seen in any way other than a deliberate misinterpretation of what I had written. As Father Frank Brennan SJ has written, 'for people all over the world who love the Church and care passionately for its future' are 'also talking and writing about this sort of thing'.[5] I was reminded again of the words of the Apostolic Nuncio, the late Archbishop Ambrose de Paoli, which came flowing back to me when he said to me in Canberra, 'Bill, they want to get rid of you'.

Pope Benedict then went on to say that there was no doubt that my pastoral intentions were good but clearly my doctrinal teaching contained errors. When I read this I was quite certain that the Holy Father had not seen or read the Advent Letter but had depended totally on the advice of the prefects of the three Roman congregations. They, for their part, after finding they had nothing with which to charge me, then accused me, on the basis of the 2006 Advent Letter, of teaching what was incompatible with the Catholic faith and of giving the people the right to discuss questions that had been decided infallibly and irrevocably by the Church. In 1998 Pope John Paul II, in an Apostolic Letter titled *Ad Tuendam Fidem* ('To Defend the Faith'),[6] added Canons stating that one who denies a truth which must be believed with divine and Catholic faith, or who calls it into doubt, or who totally repudiates the Catholic faith, and who does not retract it after having been warned, is to be punished with a just penalty.

---

4. Appendix 16, Correspondence from Pope Benedict XVI of 22 December 2009.
5. Father Frank Brennan, SJ in a note on the *Eureka Street* Site: 'All Bishop Morris said in his pastoral letter of 2006 was that people overseas were talking about this sort of thing. They were, they are, and they will be. So why the need to sack not the theological agitators but the occasional pastoral bishop who merely points out that these things are being discussed? Having been travelling overseas for a couple of weeks, I can assure you they are being discussed by people who love the Church and care passionately for its future.'
6. 'Ad Tuendam Fidem', in *National Catholic Reporter*, July 17, 1998.

I believe this amendment to the Code of Canon Law by Pope John Paul II, and the commentary on this amendment by the then Cardinal Ratzinger, Prefect for the Congregation for the Doctrine of the Faith, was used against me. For Ratzinger had used the example that affirming the right of women to be ordained would place one in contradiction to the Catholic faith by repudiating a teaching that was both infallible and irrevocable. At that time, *The Tablet* in its editorial had commented:

> the recent *moto proprio, Ad Tuendam Fidem,* and above all the commentary on it from Cardinal Ratzinger, are clearly designed to shut down debate on matters about which there was much more to be said . . . Rome's desire to silence theological dissent contradicts the deeply felt commitment to the importance of freedom of speech and intellectual integrity that is characteristic of modern democracies. In the secular world, only dictators silence their opponents and demand unquestioning obedience.[7]

Professor Nicholas Lash from Cambridge, writing in *The Tablet* in April 2012 commented:

> When, for example, Pope John Paul II announced that the Church has no authority to ordain women to the presbyterate, and that the matter was not to be further discussed, two questions immediately came to mind: first, how does he know? (that is to say: what were the warrants, historical and doctrinal, for his assertion?); secondly, what theological note should be attached to his assertion? In view of the fact that, so far as I know, the question has never, in the Church's history, come up for serious and close consideration, that note cannot be very high up the scale. From which it follows that his further instruction that we must not discuss it lacks good grounds.[8]

---

7. *The Tablet*, 19 September 1998.
8. *The Tablet*, Letters 28 April 2012, 217.

As soon as I realised that the local media and others were asking questions about whether I would ordain women, married or single, and recognise Anglican, Lutheran and Uniting Church orders, I published clarification which was reported in the local and national media and on the diocesan website.[9] It would seem that members of the Roman Vatican Curia, and others here in Australia, had not seen what I had written, nor been made aware of it, or, if they had, they had failed to note that this was an important clarification that I had made. Thereby these officials declined to afford me the rights guaranteed under the new canons added by Pope John Paul II in 1998.

Confirming Archbishop de Paoli's words to me, as well as illustrating how deliberately my words in the 2006 Advent Letter had been misconstrued, was Cardinal Re's note in his minutes of the meeting of 19 January 2008: 'To sum it up briefly: to present these questions as topics for public discussion is to separate yourself from the teaching of the Catholic church.' What the pope said in his letter showed that he agreed with the cardinal prefects, for he went on to say that it had been

> made clear to me during the meeting on 19 January 2008 with the Prefects of the three Roman Dicasteries that [my] leadership of the priests and the faithful of the diocese raises serious questions, for the diocesan bishop must above all be an authentic teacher of the faith, which is the foundation of all pastoral ministry.

---

9. 'In my Advent Pastoral Letter of 2006 I outlined some of the challenges facing the diocese into the future. In that letter I made reference to various options about ordination that were and are being talked about in various places, as part of an exercise in the further investigation of truth in these matters. Unfortunately some people seem to have interpreted that reference as suggesting that I was personally initiating options that are contrary to the doctrine and discipline of the Church. As a bishop I cannot and would not do that and I indicated this in the local media at the time. I and all the bishops of the Catholic Church form a college with the Holy Father and cannot act contrary to the teaching and practice of the Universal Church. Encouraging vocations to the priesthood must remain a priority for our local Church and we pray this Christmas and as we begin the New Year that more young men will consider deeply their response to God's call.' See also Appendix 12, Correction on Diocesan Website.

Pope Benedict finished his letter to me by saying that 'before Christ who will one day judge me and himself', he renewed his request to me to tender my resignation as Bishop of Toowoomba and to accept another responsibility, in which I could continue to serve the Church in Australia in another ministry more in keeping with my gifts and talents. He then assured me and the Diocese of Toowoomba of his prayers and that he would invoke God's blessings on us.

Being on retreat gave me the chance to sit prayerfully in my room and reflect on what I had just read. I picked up a pen and started to write. I allowed myself to be open to the Spirit, as the stream of consciousness flowed, and words became visible as my pen moved across the pages.

> Thank you for your letter. At our meeting I did not experience a fraternal dialogue but rather one of having been judged, and any clarification I might offer, rejected. I have some understanding of your suffering when you were misunderstood by our Muslim brothers and sisters and then by your brother bishops because of the way I, too, have been misunderstood. Because of the great respect I have for you, I thought I must be wrong and by what I had written in my Pastoral Letter, had broken communion with you. To make sure, I tested it with a number of my brother bishops, theologians and canon lawyers and they confirmed that my words had not broken communion and that the Cardinal Prefects were misinterpreting what I had written and had given you the wrong advice. A careful reading of my Advent Pastoral Letter of 2006 says this—'Given our deeply held belief in the primacy of Eucharist for the identity, continuity and life of each parish community, we may well need to be much more open towards other options for ensuring that Eucharist may be celebrated. Several responses have been discussed internationally, nationally and locally':
>
> • ordaining married, single or widowed men who are chosen and endorsed by their local parish community;

- welcoming former priests, married or single, back to active ministry;
- ordaining women, married or single;
- recognising Anglican, Lutheran and Uniting Church Orders.

While we continue to reflect carefully on these options, we remain committed to actively promoting vocations to the current celibate male priesthood and open to inviting priests from overseas.'

Very few misunderstood it and when it became clear to me that a small number were reading it the wrong way, I immediately corrected their misunderstanding publicly. You mention that I am not supportive of the priests of the diocese. With all respect I totally reject that judgment, for without any prompting from me and while I was at the Anglophone Meeting of Professional Standards in Rome in 2007, the priests of the diocese had a meeting at which they wrote a letter supportive of my leadership and all signed it except for three. One of those priests has since approached me and confirmed his support for me and my leadership. The letters were sent to Cardinal Re who has never acknowledged them.

You also mentioned that my leadership of the people leaves much to be desired. Once again without my invitation, the Diocesan Pastoral Council wrote letters of support for my leadership. These people are in touch with the Parish Pastoral Councils around the diocese and have a sound understanding and knowledge of what people are thinking. From their reporting 90+% of all the communities are supportive of my pastoral leadership. Their letters were also sent to Cardinal Re and they too have never received any acknowledgment. I would also like to mention here that a letter of support sent by the Metropolitan on behalf of the Bishops of Queensland has never been acknowledged, nor have letters written individually. If I thought that I did not have the support of my brother priests and the vast majority of the people of the diocese and if they did not approve of my leadership I would resign immediately.

So you see, Holy Father, I do need your counsel for if you know more than what I have been told, then please tell me, for on what I have been given, there are no grounds for my resignation and I cannot in conscience resign. The bishops in whom I have confided and who know me, support me in my decision, for they too cannot see any reason for you asking me for my resignation. Holy Father, may I offer a suggestion to this impasse. In three and a half years I turn seventy which maybe an appropriate time for me to apply for early retirement. I am suggesting this as a way around the difficult situation in which we both find ourselves. I would then be free to do whatever work the National Church would ask of me. By resigning now and taking on a National role, I would be confirming that the accusations made of me were correct which I, in conscience, before God refute.

I finished off my prayerful reflection by writing that it was not that I did not trust the Holy Father but in these matters, without further explanation and knowledge, I trusted the judgement of some of my brother bishops, priests and people who knew me, who had read the 2006 Pastoral Letter, and who could affirm that I had not broken *communio* (communion) and that my interpretation of these matters was correct.

Taking the advice of St Ignatius Loyola, I prayed for fifteen minutes, put the reflection away and participated fully in the remaining days of the retreat. This prayerful 'letter' that I wrote while on retreat and which I have quoted above, never became an actual letter that I sent to the pope, or others, but remained in my own personal files.

23

The Decision

They took away what should have been my eyes,
(But I remembered Milton's Paradise)
They took away what should have been my ears,
(Beethoven came and wiped away my tears)
They took away what should have been my tongue,
(But I had talked with God when I was young)
He would not let them take away my soul –
Possessing that, I still possess the whole.

Helen Keller

In the weeks that followed the retreat I had the opportunity to share the letter of 22 December 2009 from Pope Benedict with two of my brother bishops whom I trusted. They were upset with its contents and without any prompting from me, said they believed it was based on a false set of premises. With Benedict's words ringing in our ears, 'Canon Law does not make provision for a process regarding bishops, whom the Successor of Peter nominates and may remove from office',[1] that is, 'I hire and I fire', I shared with them my idea to break the impasse by offering to retire on turning seventy in three and a half years' time, as resigning, in my view, was out of the question. They supported my thinking as possibly the only avenue left open to me.

Archbishop Philip Wilson, still President of the Australian Catholic Bishops' Conference, was heading to Rome at the end of January 2010 for his annual meeting as President of the Conference with the Prefects of the Roman Dicasteries. I discussed with him

---

1. Appendix 16, Correspondence from Pope Benedict XVI, dated 22 December 2009.

the contents of the pope's letter, put forward my proposal to retire on turning seventy as a way forward, and asked him to take my response to the Holy Father. If my offer to retire at age seventy was not acceptable, then at least when a sexual abuse case concerning a school in the diocese was concluded, a case which would take possibly about eighteen months to two years. On 21 February 2010, I received a letter from the Apostolic Nuncio, Archbishop Giuseppe Lazzarotto, enclosing a letter from Cardinal Re of the Congregation for Bishops, informing me of the Holy Father's response to my proposal submitted on my behalf by Archbishop Philip Wilson, and assuring me that the Nunciature would remain at my disposal for any assistance I might need in this matter.

The letter from Re read as follows:

> at a recent Audience with the Holy Father, His Excellency Most Rev Philip Wilson, Archbishop of Adelaide and President of the Australian Conference of Catholic Bishops, presented 'my' proposal of resigning as Bishop of Toowoomba in May 2011.[2]

That had not been my proposal and in conversation with Wilson, I learnt that it was not acceptable to the Holy Father, who made the decision that it would be May 2011. Cardinal Re's letter went on to say that 'the Holy Father had instructed him to tell me that he had decided to meet my desire which I had forcefully expressed, and thus he accepts that the notice of my retirement as Bishop of Toowoomba will be published in May 2011'.

I smiled at the use of the two words, 'resignation' and 'retirement' as I had never wavered in my conviction that in conscience I could not resign.

In July 2010, I wrote to Archbishop Lazzarotto asking for his assistance concerning my retirement, that it might need to be delayed to deal with the child sexual abuse cases. I pointed out that I was sure he would appreciate that my first and highest priority was to look after the children and their families affected by a former teacher's actions. The process to settle the claims made by the families can be

---

2. Appendix 17, Correspondence with Cardinal Re of 2010, letter of 6 February 2010.

both stressful and worrying for them and it would be my hope that these matters could be resolved as considerately and expeditiously as soon as possible. To do this I had acquired the services of a former Justice of the High Court of Australia to mediate the civil claims made by the victims. I went on to say that the most important people here were the victims and their families and that I was doing everything in my power to respect their dignity and needs by putting in place the process I had described. But I had no control over the length of time these negotiations would take; it would be my hope that they would be completed before May 2011 but if not, within a short time afterwards.

I informed Archbishop Lazzarotto that I had spoken with Archbishop Wilson who agreed with me that it would be distressing for the victims and their families if I retired while they were still dealing with this very tragic event in the lives of their children. It would be my proposal to keep him informed of these negotiations so that together we could choose the most appropriate time for the announcement of my retirement. It was not until the November Australian Catholic Bishops Conference in 2010 that I was informed by Lazzarotto that the Congregation for Bishops had decided not to extend my retirement date until later in the year so that I could pastorally care for the victims and their families while mediation was carried out. On hearing, this I decided to write again to Pope Benedict XVI.

On 8 December 2010, I put pen to paper informing the Holy Father of the tragic event that had taken place in one of our schools and how I was sure he could appreciate how devastated the victims and their families were, suffering from stress and anxiety, and looking for support and healing so that they could get on with their lives. It was our hope that the mediation could be finalised as early as possible in the new year of 2011. Unfortunately, these things could not be rushed and I had been advised that the proceedings might not be settled until later in that year. I continued by saying that I realised that I was not the only one who could mediate and help bring about healing for the victims and their families, but that I was the constant Church authority for them at this moment in time, and I believed it would be another abuse of their growing trust in the Church if I retired in May before the mediation was completed.

I was not asking for myself but for the children and their families, that I might be able to walk with them during the final stages of mediation. I added that it was important for the Church to care for the victims, to take the necessary steps to help them, and to make sure they were looked after appropriately. I had spoken to the President of the Australian Catholic Bishops Conference, Archbishop Wilson, and he supported me in my request for an extension of a few months so that the victims and their families could be looked after, and that this sad episode in the life of the Toowoomba Church could be handled with dignity and respect. I concluded my letter by saying that 'you, Holy Father', would have empathy with all victims of sexual abuse, and how 'you would wish to do all in your power to bring about healing in their lives', and would want the Church to do the right thing in looking after the victims. 'Like you, I have the local Church and especially the victims and their families at heart when I ask you for an extension of time to allow me to represent them in the mediation proceedings'. I said I would keep the Apostolic Nuncio, Archbishop Lazzarotto, informed and when the process was completed would write to him (the Holy Father) according to Canon 401§1, requesting retirement.

On the 10th of January 2011 Toowoomba experienced an inland tsunami causing loss of life and devastation to many properties, not only in the city but throughout the Lockyer Valley and environs. Members of the local communities, supported by the Army, Police, Ambulance, Fire Brigade, State Emergency Services, Helicopter Rescue Teams, Church, and other voluntary organisations and many volunteers came together in an extraordinary way to help their brothers and sisters. A few days later Brisbane was flooded. Support flowed in from all over Australia and even as I recall these events today, I am humbled by the financial support given to the Diocesan Relief Fund to help those in greatest need. In a conversation with Archbishop Wilson, who had phoned to give his support, I commented that it would be the wrong time to announce my retirement as it was important for me, not only to continue my support of the families devastated by the sexual abuse case, but also those now affected by the flood waters that flowed through Toowoomba and the Lockyer Valley. He said he would be writing to the Holy Father informing him of the events unfolding in the local Church of Toowoomba and recommending that my retirement date be delayed on pastoral grounds. He was eventually notified, after a lengthy period of time, that his letter had been received.

In February 2011, I was attending a meeting of the Commission for Church Ministry in Sydney when I received a phone call from the Nuncio, Archbishop Lazzarotto, informing me that he had been instructed to convey to me the reply to the letter that I had recently addressed to the Holy Father, through the Secretariat of State. He said that Pope Benedict, after attentively considering what I had outlined in my correspondence, had confirmed his previous decision and asked me to submit, as from now, my resignation as Bishop of Toowoomba. He said my request for an extension of time to minister to the pressing pastoral needs of the local Church was denied, and that my *resignation* would be made public on 2 May 2011.

Towards the end of February I received a letter from Archbishop Lazzarotto confirming his telephone conversation. He went on to say that he understood this to be a painful step for me to take, particularly in the present circumstances of the diocese. However, he was sure that I would accept this definitive decision of the Holy Father in a spirit of ecclesial communion with the Supreme Pastor of the Universal Church.

For the governance of the diocese, and until a new bishop was named, an Apostolic Administrator would be appointed. Lazzarotto said that he had no doubt I would do my best to facilitate, in any way possible, the transition of duties and responsibilities and that in due time I would be informed of what would be decided in this regard. He had also been asked to inform me that my resignation did not affect my present position as Co-Chair of the National Committee for Professional Standards and that even after relinquishing the governance of the Diocese I might retain my responsibilities in the said office.

The end was nigh! There was to be no pastoral consideration given to the extraordinary circumstances in the diocese. So, on 11 March 2011, I gathered with the Consultors for the last time. I took them through the various steps I had taken over the last twelve months, beginning with the letter I had received from the Holy Father back in January 2010, asking me to renounce the Office of Diocesan Bishop through resignation, on the grounds of failure to teach the entirety of the doctrine of faith authentically. I informed the Diocesan

Consultors that I could not do this, that for me not to resign was a matter of conscience, for my resignation would mean that I accepted the assessment of myself as breaking *communio*, and on the advice of canon lawyers none of the conditions of Canon 401 were applicable. So with this in mind I had spoken with Archbishop Wilson who was going to Rome in January 2010 about the possibility of my retiring at the age of seventy as a way around the conundrum, for the Pope had made it clear that there was no canonical process regarding bishops, whom he nominates and may remove. If this time was not acceptable, then at least when the sexual abuse case was concluded, which I had been informed would take at least eighteen months to two years. I told them that I had received a phone call from Archbishop Wilson within hours of his audience with the Holy Father, informing me that my request to retire at seventy had been rejected and that the pope would be announcing my retirement in fifteen months, which would be early May 2011.

I advised the Diocesan Consultors that I was conscious I would need more time to minister to the victims and their families and by July I was convinced this would be so. I had then written to the Apostolic Nuncio, Lazzarotto, requesting his assistance that, if it was possible, the proposed date of my retirement be delayed. I had to wait until November at the Australian Catholic Bishops Conference in Sydney to be informed by him that my request was denied. Refusing to give up, I had written to the Holy Father on 8 December 2010 regarding the above request. This had been denied by a phone call from Lazzarotto, followed by a letter which arrived in February 2011.

The College of Consultors expressed their personal appreciation of my pastoral leadership and the patience, endurance and charity I had displayed in my struggle with Rome. They expressed their awareness of the personal cost to me and of the constant stress involved over such a long period of time. All present expressed gratitude for my presence in our diocese for the last eighteen years. I informed the Diocesan Consultors that I would be preparing a letter to the diocese informing the priests, pastoral leaders and people of the decision of the Holy Father and the Prefects of the three Dicasteries of the Holy See.

On 15 March 2011 I once again wrote to Archbishop Lazzarotto in response to his letter in which he stated that Pope Benedict, in confirming his decision, asked me to submit my resignation, as from now, as Bishop of Toowoomba. I pointed out that as my request to postpone my early retirement for the pastoral reasons mentioned had been denied, I would not be resigning but accepted that on 2 May 2011, my proposal presented to the Holy Father and accepted by him for retirement would be announced.

On 18 April 2011, the Nuncio, Archbishop Lazzarotto, wrote confirming the 2 May 2011 announcement, that my resignation as Bishop of Toowoomba would be made public at 8 pm, and at the same time it would be announced that the Most Rev Brian Finnigan, Auxiliary Bishop of Brisbane, would be Apostolic Administrator *ad nutum Sanctae Sedis* of the Diocese of Toowoomba.

On 21 April 2011, I wrote to Lazzarotto to clarify the wording in his letter, that the Holy Father had accepted my offer of early retirement, not resignation. I said that his letter stating my 'resignation' would be announced was but further troubling evidence of a lack of care for the truth which had characterised this whole process to which I had been subjected. I also pointed out that I had mentioned this to the Holy Father, that this cannot be 'of God' when the truth is not respected and exactness is not preserved. I also informed him that I would be notifying the priests and people of the diocese and the bishops of Australia that I had not resigned, that I had never written a letter of resignation, but had negotiated early retirement.

Archbishop Lazzarotto responded on 27 April 2011, assuring me that he had attentively read what I shared with him concerning my early retirement and that he understood perfectly that the step I was taking was not an easy one, neither for myself nor for the diocese that I had served for many years. The press release on Monday 2 May 2011 at 8 pm would have no reference to a 'resignation' on my behalf but would read 'His Holiness Pope Benedict XVI has accepted the retirement of Most Rev William M Morris and has released him from the governance of the diocese of Toowoomba' and that Bishop Brian Finnigan has been appointed Apostolic Administrator of the same diocese.[3] He finished off his letter by saying that he would appreciate it if no public announcement would be made prior to the date and time indicated.

---

3. Appendix 18, Correspondence with Papal Nuncio 2010 – 2011, letter of the Nuncio dated 27 April 2011.

BIshop Morris at St Finbarr's Primary School, Quilpie, Queensland.

24

The Day

It is just as well that justice is blind; she might not like some of the things done in her name if she could see them.

Anon

It had always been my hope that a solution would be found. Pope Benedict, in his letter, said that we had been involved in a 'fraternal dialogue'. We had never been involved in a dialogue and my mistake from the outset was that I treated my brother bishops in Rome as equals. I had thought that I would be able to work with them to bring about pastoral solutions to pastoral problems, whereas really, as expressed in the words of the French Dominican theologian and ecumenist, Yves Congar, 'What put me wrong (in their eyes) is not having said false things, but having said things they do not like to have said.'[1]

With the imminent announcement of my retirement, and out of love and respect for my diocesan family, I believed that it was important to inform my brother priests of the decision that had been made and to make sure the communities for which they were responsible received the information over the weekend or before the announcement at 8 pm on Monday 2 May 2011. I asked that the information be embargoed until 12 noon on Saturday 30 April 2011.

This was my letter to the Priests and Pastoral Leaders of the Diocese:

> I had been hoping that I would never have to write
> this letter to you as it had always been my desire that

---

1. Quoting Yves Congar, in 'Silenced for Saying Things Rome Didn't Like to Have Said', *National Catholic Reporter*, 2 June 2000.

the difficulties experienced between myself and the Congregations for Bishops, Divine Worship and Doctrine of the Faith would be able to be resolved. Unfortunately without due process it has been impossible to resolve these matters, denying me natural justice without any possibility of appropriate defence and advocacy on my behalf. This has been confirmed in a letter from Pope Benedict stating: 'Canon Law does not make provision for a process regarding bishops, whom the Successor of Peter nominates and may remove from office.'

It has been my experience and the experience of others that Rome controls Bishops by fear and if you ask questions or speak openly on subjects that Rome declares closed or does not wish to be discussed, you are censored very quickly, told your leadership is defective, that you are being unfaithful to the Magisterium, that you have broken *communio* and are threatened with dismissal.[2]

I have never seen the Report prepared by the Apostolic Visitor, Archbishop Charles Chaput; I have never been shown any of the 'evidence' that was gathered except for an unsigned memorandum handed to me by the Apostolic Nuncio, Archbishop Ambrose de Paoli, which was filled with errors. There has been no canonical process to establish a 'grave cause' for removal; the accusations that my doctrinal teaching contains errors and that I have a flawed pastoral leadership has never

---

2. Congar writes in his journal of 9 February 1954: 'The bishops have bent over backwards in passiveness and servility: they have an honest, childlike reverence for Rome, even a childish and infantile reverence. For them, this is "the church" . . . In concrete Rome is the pope, the whole system of congregations which appear as if they are this church which Jesus has built on the rock. And it is the "Holy Office". The "Holy Office" in practice rules the church and makes everyone bow down to it through fear or through interventions. It is the supreme Gestapo, unyielding, whose decisions cannot be discussed . . . So the foundation of the debate is a new conception of the church which they want to impose on us, the basis of which is first a reduction of everything to obedience and a relationship between authority and subjects; and secondly a new conception of obedience, of a *"style super jésuitique"*.' Quoted in *My Struggle for Freedom: Memoirs by Hans Kung*, Hans Kung (Novalis: 2002), 104.

been backed by facts except by some broad statements based on my Advent Pastoral Letter of 2006 which has been read inaccurately and interpreted incorrectly and used against me.

In a letter of 12 November 2009, I pointed out to Pope Benedict that such evident defects in the process, distortion of facts and a lack of care for the truth, which has characterised this whole process, cannot be 'of God' when the truth is not respected and exactness is not preserved. Pope Benedict responded by focusing on the matters raised in my Advent Pastoral Letter of 2006 which addressed local pastoral questions and matters which are in ferment generally across the Church. I quote from his letter:

> In your Advent Pastoral Letter 2006—besides containing some very questionable pastoral choices—there are at least two options presented that are incompatible with the Catholic faith:
> a) Ordaining women in order to overcome the priest shortage. Yet, the late Pope John Paul II has decided infallibly and irrevocably that the Church has not the right to ordain women to the priesthood:
> 'b) recognizing Anglican, Lutheran and Uniting Church Orders'. But according to the doctrine of the Catholic faith, ministers from these communities are not validly ordained and therefore do not share in the Sacrament of Holy Orders; and as such their actions are not joined to the ministerial priesthood.

How it can be said that my Pastoral Letter teaches these things is beyond me when it purely refers to the fact that these are among many questions being discussed internationally, nationally and locally. To me this shows a total misreading and misinterpretation of what my Pastoral Letter is saying. Pope Benedict further states that my leadership of the priests and faithful of the diocese raises serious questions and that the diocesan bishop must above all be an authentic teacher of the faith, which is the foundation of all pastoral ministry. This is said without any foundation or proof. I was also told by Pope Benedict that I am too practical and it is the will of God that I resign.

The whole process has relied on the presumption that I would be compliant and resign. However, I cannot do so in conscience because my resignation would be based on my acceptance of a lie. My resignation would mean that I accept the assessment of myself as being unfaithful to the Magisterium and breaking *communio*. I absolutely refute and reject this assessment. I do not accept that there is any grave reason for me to resign and the conditions of Canon 401 §§ 1,2 not being met, it would be dishonest of me to suggest that they had.

To negotiate a way through this stalemate I was offered an extra-diocesan position, to be artificially created, in which I was told I could continue to serve the Church in Australia in another ministry more in keeping with my gifts and talents; that I was too practical and it was the will of God that I should accept this decision. As I have been denied natural justice and due process, in conscience I could not accept such an artificially created position for in Australian culture it would be seen and ridiculed for what it is—a sinecure.

Given the circumstances that there is no canonical process regarding bishops, that there is no separation of powers, meaning the Successor of Peter is Legislator, Judge and Jury [See Canon 333 § 1,2,3 'There is neither appeal nor recourse against a judgment or a decree of the Roman Pontiff'. Also Canon 1404, 'The First See is judged by no one'], my position as Bishop of Toowoomba is untenable. I have never wavered in my conviction that for me to resign is a matter of conscience and my resignation would mean that I accept the assessment of myself as breaking *communio* which I absolutely refute and reject, so it is out of my love for the Church that I cannot do so. I have never written a letter of resignation.

To find a way through this moral dilemma I asked Archbishop Philip Wilson, President of the Australian

Catholic Bishops Conference, when he met with the Holy Father in January 2010, to affirm my position that I would not resign, but instead to put forward a proposal that I was prepared to negotiate an early retirement. My proposal was that I would retire at seventy but this was found to be unacceptable. The other possibility was to retire in eighteen months depending on whether or not the sexual abuse cases I was dealing with here in the diocese were finalised. It became evident that more time would be needed to finalise these cases and to pastorally care for the victims and their families. Unfortunately, this extension of time was denied, the eighteen months was reduced to fifteen by Pope Benedict and my retirement will be announced on Monday 2 May 2011.

The Consultors are aware of all the facts as I have met with them on a regular basis to keep them up to date with what was happening. They will meet with you to give you the full story.

I wish to thank you for your friendship and prayerful support over the eighteen years of my ministry here in the diocese. It has been a gift and a privilege to serve you and I have deeply appreciated your care for me and your unselfish ministry to your brothers and sisters in the Local Church. It has been my experience through the giftedness of your ministry that the people who are the Church, the Body of Christ, have come to appreciate their baptismal calling more and more and are living it out in their service of one another. This has led to a strong sense of shared responsibility which empowers the lives of the members of each community, giving them a willingness to participate.

I am one with the diocese as I am one with you and in my retirement you will continue to have a remembrance in my prayers and Masses. You will always have my love and friendship and if there is anything I can ever do for you it would be my privilege.

I have enclosed a good-bye letter to the people of the diocese. I would ask that you read it to them at all

Masses this weekend, Saturday 30 April and Sunday 1 May, thanking them for all they have been to me and given to me over the past eighteen years, and assuring them that they will always have my love and friendship and be remembered in my prayers and Masses. As the quote below (from *A Man for All Seasons,* an alternative ending) says in the last line, *'If we should bump into one another, recognise me'.* In the London production of this play at the Globe Theatre the play ended as follows:

Instead of the CROMWELL and CHAPUYS entrance after the HEADSMAN'S line 'Behold—the head—of a traitor!, the COMMON MAN came to the centre stage, having taken off his mask as the executioner, and said:

I'm breathing . . . Are you breathing too? . . . It's nice isn't it? It isn't difficult to keep alive friends . . . just don't make trouble – or if you must make trouble, make the sort of trouble that's expected. Well, I don't need to tell you that. Good night. If we should bump into one another, recognise me.'

Below is my letter to my diocesan family:

Just over eighteen years ago on 10 February 1993 I was ordained as your Bishop, responding to an invitation from Pope John Paul II. On that day I told you a story about an old priest who was invited by a couple whom he had married twenty-five years previously. Also invited to the celebration was a friend of theirs who was a Shakespearian actor and quite famous around the theatres of London. As often happens at such celebrations those who have certain gifts are asked to entertain the group and so our Shakespearian actor was asked to do just that.

A conversation occurred between himself and the guests as to what they would like to hear him recite, and finally the elderly priest suggested that he might like to recite the 23rd Psalm . . . The Lord is my Shepherd. He responded by saying that he would do so if the priest would recite it after him, which he willingly agreed to.

The actor began his recitation and as he finished reciting the words of the Psalm the voice of the little old Padre could be heard. A deep silence spread throughout the room as the priest recited the Psalm . . . and when he had finished there was a hush that enfolded the room and a number of guests had tears in their eyes.

The Shakespearian actor, seeing this, turned to the priest and said: 'I am an actor, a very good one and I know I have the skills to hold people's attention and to capture their imagination, but the difference between you and I in reciting this Psalm is that I know the words but you know the Shepherd.'

It would be my hope that as I say good-bye to you as your Pastor, that we can both say, because of our relationship over the last eighteen years we all know the Shepherd a little better.

I came to the diocese from the Gold Coast with little knowledge of this wonderful local Church, or you the people who are the local Church. I found welcome, friendship, encouragement, challenge, prayerful support, a home among you and a real sense of belonging. It is with true sadness therefore that I write this letter to you.

While the overwhelming majority of you have been supportive of me and have worked collaboratively with me to ensure the ongoing life of the diocese, and its mission to be a bearer of the Gospel to the wider world, a small group have found my leadership and the direction of the diocese not to their liking.

While I have tried to deal with all people fairly and to involve all in the ministry and mission of the diocese I have not always been able to succeed. Some of those who have been disaffected by my leadership have exercised the option of making complaints about me, some of these complaints being based on my Advent Pastoral Letter of 2006 which has been misread and I believe deliberately misinterpreted. This led to an Apostolic Visitation and an ongoing dialogue between myself and the Congregations for Bishops, Divine Worship and

Doctrine of the Faith and eventually Pope Benedict. The substance of these complaints is of no real import now but the consequences are that is has been determined by Pope Benedict that the diocese would be better served by the leadership of a new bishop.

I have never seen the Report prepared by the Apostolic Visitor, Archbishop Charles Chaput, and without due process it has been impossible to resolve these matters, denying me natural justice without any possibility of appropriate defence and advocacy on my behalf. Pope Benedict confirmed this to me by stating 'Canon Law does not make provision for a process regarding bishops, whom the Successor of Peter nominates and may remove from Office'. This makes my position as Bishop of Toowoomba untenable. I have never wavered in my conviction that for me to resign is a matter of conscience and my resignation would mean that I accept the assessment of myself as breaking *communio* which I absolutely refute and reject and it is out of my love for the Church that I cannot do so. I have never written a letter of resignation.

To find a way through this moral dilemma I put forward the proposal that I was prepared to negotiate early retirement. As Canon Law does not make provision for a process regarding bishops this seemed the only course open to me. I do so with profound sadness, knowing that I still enjoy the support of the vast majority of the people and priests of the diocese. The Consultors are aware of all the facts as I have met with them on a regular basis to keep them up-to-date with what was happening. Through them, the priests and the pastoral leaders, you will be given the full story.

To the entire Diocese I say a heartfelt thanks for your support, friendship, love and prayers over the last eighteen years. You have been a great gift to me and it has been a privilege to serve you.

I make my own the words of St Paul to the Philippians:

I thank my God every time I remember you, constantly praying with joy in every one of my prayers for all of you, because of your sharing in the gospel from the first day until now. I am confident of this, that the one who began a good work among you will bring it to completion by the day of Jesus Christ. It is right for me to think this way about all of you, because you hold me in your heart, for all of you share in God's grace with me, in the defence and confirmation of the gospel. For God is my witness, how I long for all of you with the compassion of Christ Jesus. And this is my prayer, that your love may overflow more and more with knowledge and full insight to help you to determine what is best, so that in the day of Christ you may be pure and blameless, having produced the harvest of righteousness that comes through Jesus Christ for the glory and praise of God (Phil 1:3–7a, 7c–11).

Whatever the future holds for me you will always have a place in my heart and prayers. I thank you once again for your love, friendship and support, you will always have mine, and until we meet again may God bless you with every good gift.

I wrote a letter to the Australian Bishops in the same vein as I did to the priests of the diocese with only a small variation: 'I had been told that it is the Bishop's role to support the Pope in whatever he says without question, to teach from the Catechism and the documents of the Church and not to ask questions about topics that had been declared definitive or closed. I ask you, where is the Spirit in this?'

The letter to the diocese brought an immediate reaction from the priests and the people of the diocese who were in total shock. I had kept the Consultors, the Chancellor and the Judicial Vicar informed of the ongoing struggle with Rome, while the rest of the diocese had hoped that they had seen the end of the investigation after the

Apostolic Visitation had been completed. There was consternation throughout the diocese as the news broke, showing an extraordinary support of love and friendship that was quite overwhelming. As the news broke the telephone rang constantly and emails, faxes, letters and cards arrived in their thousands from around Australia and overseas.

From the moment the announcement became public the media wore a path to my office seeking interviews over the next few days. A candlelight vigil procession was organised by the people of the diocese on Tuesday evening to show solidarity with me by the whole community. It assembled opposite Bishop's House in prayer and reflection and proceeded in silence in a candlelight procession to St Patrick's Cathedral. Those unable to join the walk were invited to wait in prayer and reflection for the arrival of the procession. The feeling of grief and support was palpable. I could never have envisaged the positive emails, cards, letters and phone calls received in my office in the weeks following my retirement which came to a climax in a Thanksgiving Mass celebrated at St Patrick's Cathedral on Sunday 28 August 2011, amongst fifteen hundred people, priests and bishops, in an extraordinary outpouring of love, appreciation and many tears quietly shed.

In the days that followed, local, provincial and national media carried the story of my retirement with headlines that encapsulated the feelings and frustrations of the local community in colourful headlines such as:

> *Diocese in shock as Bishop Bill calls it quits . . .Bishop's treatment unpalatable . . .Faithful express anger at Bishop's dismissal . . . Bishop quits in row with Vatican . . . Outrage over Bishop's fate . . . Bishop falls to Zealots . . . 'Whistle-blower' raised concerns with Vatican . . . Parishioners rally behind Bishop . . . Bishop's removal 'heavy-handed', Vatican punishing a crusader against school sexual abuse . . . 'Temple Police' blamed for Bishop's downfall . . . Bishop Bill not deserving of outrageous treatment . . . Bishop remains faithful to the Church . . . And Only God knows why . . .*

Conversations, printed and unprinted, asked questions concerning the lack of due process, denial of natural justice and procedural fairness.

> Isn't the Church supposed to be a source of justice, fairness, compassion and have a deep respect for the dignity of each person? One would think ordinary Christian values would allow for a fairer process. We hope that his experience will precipitate Roman authorities to consider better processes, which are demanded by at least our Western society in this 21st Century world . . . When the Vatican effectively sacked an admired bishop in the bush, it raised questions about justice, and about how Roman discipline will shape the future of the Catholic Church in Australia.[3]

Questions kept appearing about the Apostolic Report and if the 2006 Advent Letter were the grounds on which the Vatican made its decision to dismiss me, how could it make such a judgment that there was a departure from Church doctrine and dogma.

Articles in a number of different magazines and some local publications supported stories that were unfactual and gave a disfigured picture of the local Church of Toowoomba. Statements appeared such as—in some Catholic School classes the Church's teaching was now allowing abortion. To the credit of members of the diocese, this was refuted in many letters to the local media. A letter on a website titled, 'Catholics in Toowoomba see prayers answered through adoration', credited my ouster to the power of prayer and eucharistic adoration. They noted that they were praying for my conversion for 'at the end of the day he is a soul and nobody wants to see him lost'.

The suggestion that 'This Diocese was divided quite badly' and regarding the critics of the pope's decision that 'there's a predictable chorus from a minority', was rebuffed by many letters to the *Toowoomba Chronicle,* showing how out of touch those who made the comments were about the life of the diocese. Also there was a

---

3. Stephen Crittenden 'The Inside Story Of How Rome Ousted A Bold Bush Bishop', in *The Global Mail,* 14 February 2012.

full page article taken out in the *Toowoomba Chronicle* by a group of clergy and laity under the title of the 'Toowoomba Diocesan Leadership Group' representing the Diocesan Consultors, priests, heads of diocesan agencies and members of the Diocesan Finance Board and Diocesan Pastoral Council. The article under the heading, 'We call for Natural Justice in the Catholic Church' and sub-titled 'The Bishop Bill Morris Story', refuted the suggestion that the diocese was divided quite badly:

> We would like to inform the readers of this newspaper that in our experience, this is not the case. The majority of Catholics in the Toowoomba Diocese do support Bishop Morris and are concerned with the circumstances surrounding his forced retirement.
>
> There have been thousands of messages of support worldwide for Bishop Morris and at a local level we are angry, sad and disappointed that Bishop Morris—a selfless, caring, just and compassionate human being has been treated in this way.
>
> Over 18 years he has provided us with strong effective leadership as Bishop of the Diocese.
>
> A website—www.bishopbillstory.com.au—sets out the facts and some correspondence and may be useful for those wanting to understand more fully the worrying nature of this troubling issue.
>
> A copy of the Investigation into our Diocese, prepared and sent to Rome by Archbishop Charles Chaput, has never been sighted by Bishop Morris. This is a denial of natural justice no matter what legal system is involved.
>
> We ask those concerned to join with us in communicating with the Australian Bishops to express the need to have an enquiry into this matter . . .

Another article suggested nailing protests to St Pat's door. The media including programmes on television, radio, local, national and overseas continued for months. Articles appeared in overseas journals, the product of many hours of phone interviews.

There were other articles that appeared on web, blog sites and in journals that just plainly got the whole story wrong. There was always an element of truth, but without context, rendered factually inaccurate. That is why it has been important that I write this book.

Milton Erickson once said, 'Each person's map of the world is as unique as their thumb print. There are no two people alike. No two people who understand the same sentence the same way. Try not to fit them into your concept of what they should be.'

Bishop Morris with his mother and sister at his ordination as a bishop,
Toowoomba, 1993.

25

Reflections

The pendulum of the mind oscillates between sense and nonsense, not between right and wrong.

CG Jung

Justice and power must be brought together, so whatever is just may be powerful, and whatever is powerful may be just.

Blaise Pascal

The Toowoomba Diocesan Leadership Group (TDLG), after receiving an unsatisfactory response from the Australian Catholic Bishops Conference concerning their motion[1] for an independent enquiry into my removal, resolved to appoint the Honourable WJ Carter, QC, a retired Queensland Supreme Court Judge,[2] to conduct

---

1. The Motion sent to the Bishops Conference on Thursday night 5 May 2011 through Fr Brian Lucas, to be tabled on Friday 6 May 2011 at the Conference read:

   'This gathering of Priests, Pastoral Leaders and Responsible Leaders in Diocesan Councils and Agencies requests the Australian Catholic Bishops Conference to initiate an open, honest, professionally conducted study of the forced retirement of Bishop Bill Morris: this study to examine the process and the conclusions from canonical, pastoral, theological and natural justice perspectives.'

2. Judge Carter is a well-known and highly respected Queensland Jurist.
   - Barrister in private practice at the Queensland Bar between 1960 and 1980. Took silk in 1978
   - Appointed a Judge of the Queensland District Court in 1980
   - Appointed a Judge of the Queensland Supreme Court in 1983
   - Retired from the Supreme Court in 1990 and since that time has been appointed to a number of public enquires and a Royal Commission.

an independent review of the process which forced me out of office. Their decision was based on the fact that the Australian Catholic Bishops Conference made no acknowledgement that my retirement was a forced one, and in particular their concern was the denial of natural justice.[3]

Carter, after reviewing the correspondence between myself, Pope Benedict XVI, and Cardinals Re, Arinze and Levada who were involved in the process, and after meeting with me, presented the Toowoomba Diocesan Leadership Group with a lengthy Memorandum which can be found in Appendix 19. I will quote here its final section:

The serious deficits in that process can be readily summarised:

1. In advising Bishop Morris by letter dated 16th March 2007 of the Apostolic Visit to the Diocese in April 2007, Cardinal Re stated that 'the reason for the visit is that the doctrinal and disciplinary line you are following seems not to accord with the Magisterium of the Church'.

2. Cardinal Re failed to identify or particularise for Bishop Morris the facts or matters relied on to support the Bishop's alleged departure in matters of doctrine and of discipline which were not in accord with the Magisterium.

3. The Apostolic Visitor did not at any time during his visit to Toowoomba inform the Bishop of any of the matters alleged against him as being the reasons for the visit, nor did he do so after the visit, nor did he give Bishop Morris the opportunity to respond to any such allegations nor did he identify to Bishop Morris the evidence relied upon to support the various allegations nor the identity of the accusers.

4. The unsigned document of 28th June 2007, which made

---

3. Letter received by the Diocesan Leadership Group from the Australian Catholic Bishops Conference through Bishop Brian Finnigan dated 12 May 2011. Letter to Australian Bishops Conference from the Diocesan Leadership Group. Appendix 20.

serious and damaging accusations against him, failed to provide any evidentiary material relied upon by the author or its compiler to support such allegations.

5. Those responsible for the compilation of such documented allegations failed to identify the person who wrote the document nor any person or source who could support the allegations with the evidence relied on.

6. Bishop Morris therefore was denied knowledge of the allegations and access to them and to the evidence relied upon by the author of the document to support them at any material time before or after the compilation of the unsigned document.

7. Having on or about 17th September 2007 received and read the unsigned document, Bishop Morris advised Cardinal Re by letter dated 17th September that he wished to respond to it and that he would respond upon his return from annual leave (due in October 2007).

8. Cardinal Re, on 3rd October 2007, before Bishop Morris had the opportunity to respond, wrote to the Bishop and asked him in the name of the Holy Father 'to submit your resignation', because—'as stated in the memorandum which the Apostolic Nuncio delivered to you" (that is the unsigned document) 'your theological preparation and type of leadership are inadequate to confront the crisis of the Church of Toowoomba'.

9. Bishop Morris intended to fully and comprehensively respond to the allegations, all of which he firmly refutes and denies, but before being able to do so, Cardinal Re concluded his 3rd October letter saying 'I expect to receive your letter of resignation by the end of this October'.

10. Cardinal Re and his Cardinal colleagues had decided by 3rd October 2007 to require the Bishop's resignation before he had had the opportunity to respond and when the Bishop, in his response on 6th November 2007, requested detailed information upon which

the allegations were made so that he 'could present a detailed reply', these were denied and again Cardinal Re persisted in requiring the Bishop's resignation before hearing any response from Bishop Morris.

11. The Vatican document which purports to be minutes of the meeting between the three Cardinals and Bishop Morris on 19th January 2008 in Rome records Cardinal Re as follows:

12. 'I think it would be useful to explain the mind of the Holy See and then we will listen to what Bishop Morris . . . wants to say.'

The Cardinal then repeated the contents of the unsigned document with emphasis only on that part of the Advent Letter referred to in the document. He concluded this presentation by again requesting Bishop Morris' resignation before he had had a chance to respond. The Cardinal's conclusion simply repeated what Cardinal Re had determined and had already expressed in his letters of 3rd and 30th November 2007 before providing to Bishop Morris the details of the allegations and before hearing Bishop Morris' response.

Accordingly Bishop Morris' response delivered later in the meeting fell on deaf ears but he maintained his refusal to resign. He had not then or later received the detailed evidence relied on to support the allegations.

13. The biased and preconceived conclusions of the Cardinals at the 19th January meeting is well evidenced by Cardinal Re's reference to Bishop Morris' response to the original Cardinal Arinze request for a meeting in February 2007 in relation to the general absolution issue when the Bishop requested a later date because of pressing pastoral responsibilities.

The minutes of the meeting record Cardinal Re saying:-

'He (Bishop Morris) replied (to the original Arinze letter dated 21st December 2006) by not accepting either date and postponing the encounter (sic) for a later time as if it were something that was not important.'

At no time before his ultimate retirement did Bishop Morris ever receive the factual or evidentiary material relied upon to support the allegations before the decision was made to require his resignation, at the latest by 3rd October 2007.

All that emerged with any semblance of particularity were two matters—the communal rite issue and the 'phrases' in the 2006 Advent Pastoral Letter—both of which the Bishop had effectively dealt with. In his final appeal to Pope Benedict, Bishop Morris insisted that the communal rite issue had been resolved. (Even Cardinal Re had conceded that). And he confirmed that he had publically corrected and clarified 'any ambiguity in my Advent 2006 Pastoral Letter'. He therefore sought the Pope's intervention.

In his letter of refusal dated 22nd December 2009, when responding to the Bishop's concern about the process to which he had been subjected since December 2006, the Pope wrote:

'Canon Law does not make provision or a process regarding Bishops whom the Successor of Peter nominates and may remove from office.'

That statement is perhaps the most compelling confirmation that Bishop Morris was denied procedural fairness and natural justice.

Canon Law does expressly empower the request for a Bishop's resignation for 'grave cause'. That is an administrative decision which has the capacity to seriously damage the reputation of a Bishop, if resorted to without a sound and valid basis. The notion that that can be done unfairly and without resort to principles of natural justice offends basis principles of morality and justice.

The proposition that, because 'I appointed you to a particular office, so I can remove you' by an unfair process and in breach of the principles of natural justice, is offensive not only to the requirements of the Civil Law but also to those of the Canon Law.

Hon W J Carter QC.

Bishop Putney and Bishop Morris, Geneva, Switzerland, 1998.

26
Canonical Reflection and Theological Overview

Loyalty to a petrified opinion never broke a chain or freed a human soul.

Mark Twain

The Toowoomba Diocesan Leadership Group (TDLG), after receiving the Carter Report, noted that Judge Carter, having regard for the principles of both civil law and canon law, requested that the Memorandum be given to a canon lawyer for his opinion, as some may have considered that Carter had stepped outside his area of expertise. With this in mind, the TDLG asked Father Ian Waters,[1] a canon lawyer, to appraise the Carter Report. Here is what he wrote:

> I have been invited to provide a brief canonical reflection on the Carter Report. I have read the report. My reflection is solely in response to the report, as I have not read the documentation examined by Hon. W.J. Carter, QC.
>
> I presume that I have been invited because I am not a Queenslander. I have never met Mr Carter, although I know that he is an eminent and highly respected jurist.
>
> **1. Grants and Termination of Ecclesiastical Office**
> In the Catholic Church at present, an ecclesiastical office is defined as any post which by divine or ecclesiastical disposition is established in a stable manner to further

---

1. Very Reverend Professor Ian B Waters, MChA, JCL, MCL, JCD, Phd, is Professor of Canon Law at Catholic Theological College, Melbourne, within the University of Divinity.

a spiritual purpose (canon 145). Furthermore, an ecclesiastical office cannot be validly obtained without canonical provision. The provision of every ecclesiastical office is effected in one of five ways, namely: 1) by it being freely conferred by a competent ecclesiastical authority; 2) by appointment after presentation; 3) by confirmation or admission after an election; 4) by confirmation or admission after postulation; 5) by acceptance of an election which does not require confirmation. In this brief reflection, it is sufficient to note here that at present in the Catholic Church the Pope freely appoints most bishops; and he confirms the election of the diocesan bishops of about 130 dioceses which have the right to have their bishops elected. In other words, the Pope confers office on every bishop, either by freely appointing them (as in the Diocese of Toowoomba) or by confirming their election.

An ecclesiastical office is lost naturally by the death of the incumbent. Besides death, there are six other ways in which an ecclesiastical office can be lost, namely 1) expiry of a predetermined time; 2) on reaching the age limit defined by law; 3) by resignation; 4) by transfer to another office; 5) by removal; 6) by deprivation.

Many offices in the Church are conferred for a predetermined time. Examples include parish priests in Australia being appointed for terms of six years. However, the vast majority of bishops (including the Bishop of Toowoomba) are appointed without any limitation of time, which means they have permanent tenure of their see.

At present, some office bearers (including diocesan bishops, auxiliary bishops and parish priests) are requested to submit their resignation from office on the completion of the seventy-fifth year of age, or if they become unsuited for the fulfilment of their office because of illness or some other grave reason. All the circumstances surrounding the offered resignation will then be examined, and the resignation will be either accepted or deferred. The Carter Report reveals that Bishop Morris was repeatedly urged to submit his resignation to the Pope. If he had done so, presumably the Pope would have accepted it.

A resignation can be made by anyone capable of personal responsibility for a just reason. A resignation made as a result of grave fear unjustly inflicted, or of deceit, or of substantial error is invalid; and the authority accepting the resignation is forbidden to accept it if it is not based on a just and proportionate reason. The Carter Report noted that Bishop Morris felt compromised by the exceedingly robust tone of the 2004 meeting (p. 3); it details the subsequent correspondence and meetings between Bishop Morris and three Roman Curial cardinals which the Bishop perceived to be accusations founded on errors of fact and generalised assertions, culminating with a meeting on 19 January 2008 at which his resignation was insisted upon. If a resignation had been offered then, many canonists would certainly have questioned whether a bishop in such a situation would be capable of the personal freedom necessary to make an informed decision.

The possibility of the transfer of Bishop Morris to another office does not appear to have been considered. Not infrequently a bishop is transferred from one office to another, although normally in the context of a perceived 'promotion'. Canon law provides a specific process for the transfer of parish priests. If a bishop is transferred, the principles of consultation with him, hearing some of his peers, weighing the reasons to favour or oppose the transfer, and consideration of the general good of the bishop and the Church would no doubt be employed. The fact that a transfer was not considered in this case is probably consistent with Cardinal Re's written opinion that Bishop Morris was not 'a solid bishop who is in accord with the Pope and the universal Church'.

The next possibility was removal. No one may be removed from an office which is conferred on a person for an indeterminate period of time, except for grave reasons and in accordance with the procedure defined by law. While there are canonical processes for removal in general (Canon 1732–1739), and specifically for parish priests (canon 1740–1747), there is no specified process for the removal of a bishop. If the process for removing a parish priest were adapted for the case of Bishop Morris, it would involve: identifying the reasons for his removal; discussion about the reasons for removal by the Pope with two Australian bishops elected by the bishops conference; an invitation to Bishop Morris to reply in writing to the specified accusations; an inspection by Bishop Morris of all the evidence gathered and an invitation to him to respond or produce contrary evidence; a weighing up of the evidence by the two elected bishops and their recommendation to the Pope; and a decision by the Pope. Such a process would ensure procedural fairness and natural justice which the Carter Report found were denied to Bishop Morris.

The final possibility was deprivation of office, which is being deprived of office as a punishment for an offence. Deprivation may be effected only in accordance with the provisions of the canons concerning penal law. The penal process may be either judicial (a hearing by a Church tribunal) or extra-judicial (an administrative process). However, both the judicial and extra-judicial processes require that the accused be assisted by an advocate; that his good name not be called into question; and that procedural fairness and the right of defence be respected. Moreover, a perpetual penalty may be imposed only after a judicial process, not after an extra-judicial process.

The Code of Canon Law lists many offences for which a member of the Church—if found guilty—can be punished. Most of these offences are to be punished with 'a just penalty' which is to be determined by the judge or the presiding ordinary. The only offences for which deprivation of office is specified as a penalty are the offences of apostasy from the faith, heresy or schism committed by a cleric; the abuse of ecclesiastical power or an office; and grave violation of the obligation of residence to which he is bound because of an ecclesiastical office.

While the unsigned document dated 17 September 2007 on letterhead from the Congregation of Bishops (of which Cardinal Re was the Prefect) made serious allegations about Bishop Morris and the Diocese of Toowoomba, such as the Diocese was moving in a different direction to that of the Catholic Church, and that the Bishop had failed to guide the faithful in fidelity to the doctrine and discipline of the Church, it fell short of the specific accusation of heresy or schism. Consequently, it is most unlikely that a penal process would have been able to find the Bishop guilty, and therefore able to deprived of office as a punishment.

In summary, as Bishop Morris had permanent tenure of his See, there was no possibility of his tenure terminating because it was limited by a predetermined term or an age limit. While there was the possibility of Bishop Morris freely offering his resignation if he became convinced he was unsuited for the fulfilment of his office, the Carter Report indicates that he was unable to offer his resignation. Transfer to another episcopal office was not suggested by the Holy See, which left only two possibilities, namely removal or deprivation. Although the Holy See identified what it believed to be a canonical reason for removal or deprivation ('leadership of the diocese is seriously defective'), it consistently refused to permit a canonical process for either to commence. Instead, the Pope himself wrote, 'Canon law does not make provision for a process regarding bishops whom the Successor of Peter nominates and may remove from office.'

In fact, canon 19 of the current Code of Canon Law states,

> If on a particular matter there is not an express provision of either universal or particular law, nor a

custom, then, provided it is not a penal matter, the question is to be decided by taking into account laws enacted in similar matters, the general principles of law observed with canonical equity, the jurisprudence and practice of the Roman Curia, and the common and constant opinion of learned authors.

2. Historical Precedents

Bishop Morris is not the first Australian Bishop to have his resignation requested by the Holy See. At present, the archives at the Holy See are open to researchers officially until 1938, although in practice it is very difficult to access records later than 1930. There were four episcopal casualties until then, and a resignation was demanded from each. When Bishop John Brady of Perth refused to resign in 1850, he was forbidden to live in his diocese; he returned to Ireland and acted as an auxiliary to the Bishop of Kilmore; an apostolic administrator was appointed to govern the Diocese of Perth; but Brady remained Bishop of Perth until his death in 1871. In 1867, Auxiliary Bishop-elect Austin Sheehy of Sydney humbly submitted his resignation and worked as a parish priest until his death in 1910. In 1877, Bishop Timothy O'Mahony of Armidale most unwillingly resigned under pressure, and then was appointed Auxiliary Bishop of Toronto (Canada). In 1910, Bishop Matthew Gibney of Perth resigned most unwillingly, and then lived as a recluse until his death in 1925.

Of these cases, only Bishop-Elect Sheehy acted willingly. He immediately declined the episcopate, returned the apostolic brief of appointment, and asked the identity of the accusers. The Cardinal Prefect declined to reveal the accusers, praised Sheehy's humble renunciation, and told him to trust the Pope's judgement. On 14 June 1868, Pope Pius IX, after being advised that the charge could not be sustained, judged "in the Lord" that this resignation of 'a virtuous man' from episcopal promotion be accepted.

Bishops O'Mahony and Gibney tried to negotiate; but each eventually resigned under pressure. In contrast Bishop Brady was not forced to resign, although he was ordered to leave Australia. In 2011, Brady's body was exhumed, and was solemnly re-interred with his successors in the Perth cathedral, as he is now being rehabilitated as the zealous and selfless pioneer of the Church in Western Australia who ensured that it be established against impossible odds. In contrast, in 1850 the Holy See saw him as defying instructions; possibly mentally unstable; and the product of a Parisian seminary with Gallican traits that expressed themselves in his referring to his rights under canon law, the Council of Trent and natural justice! These three bishops were denied any process.

The Vatican archives have not been accessed for the resignation of Coadjutor Archbishop Michael Sheehan of Sydney in 1937. However, Sheehan's own account includes, 'On 25 May (a black day for me), the Delegate sent for me; he said he had *triste notizia* for me; he read me a letter from Cardinal Fumasoni saying at an audience with His Holiness, the Pope had decided that I was at once to retire from Sydney, occupy myself with literary work, and receive any yearly allowance the Delegate thought reasonable.' On 29 May, Sheehan cabled Pope Pius XI to reconsider. The cable was not answered, and news of the resignation was published in Sydney on 3 June. Sheehan acquiesced, returned to Ireland in retirement, and mused that the charge seems to have been that 'I have been an absolute cipher'.

3. The Removal of Bishop Morris

Since the removal of Bishop Morris, there has been much comment. Father Jesus Miñanbres Fernandez, of the canon law faculty at the prestigious Pontifical University of the Holy Cross, Rome, is reported as saying:

> In cases involving the conduct of bishops, the visitator would make a report to the Vatican. The report

would be secret, to be read only by the Pope and the Vatican congregation that ordered the investigation. It could be harmful to release all the information. The investigation probably includes the names of other bishops in Australia. It is probably not convenient that he knows all the details. There have been different conversations with people that are protected.

Father Fernandez was of the opinion that this was an administrative act. He continued:

If this act is signed by the Pope, it cannot be overturned. If it's just from a congregation, it can be. If it's that grave that it was signed by the Pope, no. The actions of the Pope are definitive.

I have no reason to doubt that Father Fernandez knows how the Roman Curia really functions, and that the process he has described—a secret administrative inquiry with no right of defence by the accused—is what does happen, and has happened since the nineteenth century.

Consequently, on 11 May 2011, the weekly edition in English of *L'Osservatore Romano* carried the following advice under Changes in Episcopate:

The Holy Father relieved Bishop William Martin Morris of his office as Bishop of Toowoomba, Australia (2 May).

This is in marked contrast to the usual announcement of The Holy Father accepted the resignation of Bishop Xxxxxxx of Yyyyyyyy. It was presented in accord with canon 401 §2 of the Code of Canon Law.

In accordance with Canon 19, the Holy See, departing from the earlier precedents for the removal of Australian bishops, could have designed a process similar to the process for removal of a parish priest, thereby according procedural fairness and natural justice consistent with the Code of Canon Law. This was not done. I respectfully concur with Mr Carter's conclusion that "Bishop Morris was denied procedural fairness and natural justice."

Father Michael Kelly, an Australian Jesuit living in Bangkok, where he is Executive Director of UCAN NEWS, was requested to write an article for *The Tablet* and other media outlets. His article, *Bishop's Sacking and the Vatican,* in many ways summed up the conversation that was taking place around the world and is as follows:

> Independent and expert Civil and Canon law reviews of the removal of Bishop William Morris of Toowoomba in May 2011 on grounds of 'defective pastoral leadership' have concluded there was a denial of 'procedural fairness and natural justice' in the process of his sacking.
>
> A retired judge of the Supreme Court of the Australian State of Queensland, the Hon William Carter QC, found it 'an unfair process and in breach of the principles of natural justice', 'offensive not only to the requirements of Civil Law but also to those of Canon Law'. Carter found the breaches were regularly exercised by three Roman Dicasteries and reached as far as Pope Benedict between 2006 and 2011.
>
> The eminent Canonist and head of the Matrimonial Tribunal in the Archdiocese of Melbourne, Fr Ian Waters, concurred, saying that 'the Holy See' departing from the earlier precedents for the removal of Australian bishops, 'could have designed a process similar to the process for removal of a parish priest, thereby according procedural fairness and natural justice consistent with the Code of Canon Law. This was not done.'
>
> The first step in what ended with Morris's involuntary removal from office was taken in 2004 when he was invited to meet Cardinal Arinze, then the Prefect of the Congregation for Worship and Sacraments. He was surprised when he arrived alone for the meeting with the Cardinal flanked by an archbishop and two monsignors, apparently Canon lawyers. What he found to be an ambush hinged on the claims of unnamed accusers about the bishop permitting the Third Rite of Reconciliation in his diocese.
>
> That diocese, Toowoomba, is one covering approximately 500,000 square kilometers where priests

are few, and ageing. With 66,000 Catholics, and 36 parishes served by 28 active priests, pastoral visitation and celebration of the sacraments is rare in many places.

The bishop explained that in these conditions, some flexibility was needed if the sacraments were to be available. The cardinal and his companions said the practice was forbidden and should cease. Morris complied and from that date Third Rite celebrations gradually ceased in Toowoomba over the next two years as agreed upon.

Two years later, in December 2006, Cardinal Arinze did not so much as invite but demand that Morris be in Rome on either of two dates in the following February to discuss matters which the cardinal did not specify. Morris explained that for pastoral and administrative reasons, the dates did not work for him but that he would be in Rome in May. Morris sought an agenda for the meeting so that he might prepare.

No agenda but rather an order that he be in Rome in February was the response and that Arinze would also have the Prefects of the Congregation for Bishops and the Doctrine of the Faith attending.

Morris replied that he was unavailable and would be in Rome in May. Without delay, Cardinal Re announced the appointment of an Apostolic Visitor to the diocese— Archbishop Charles Chaput then of Denver and recently translated to the more significant See of Philadelphia. He was booked to be in Toowoomba in April 2007. Cardinal Re made no reference to the Third Rite and the now settled controversy. Rather he alleged to Morris: 'The doctrinal and disciplinary line you are following seems not in accordance with the Magisterium of the Church.'

Such a serious claim was based on documents, letters and representations to Rome from parties hostile to Morris which he has not seen to this day and was never asked to respond to. They came from a small and unrepresentative group according to Morris and the lay and clerical leadership of the diocese.

The Apostolic Visitation—of four days to such an immense area—followed a now well established pattern. Morris was never really told (the) nature of, reason for or the terms of reference guiding the Visit. He never saw any documents in the possession of the Visitor. He never learnt who had accused him of what.

Even now, he has never seen the Visitor's report. Father Jesus Minanbres Fernandez, a Canon Lawyer from the Roman University of Opus Dei, says non-disclosure is 'for the good of the Church': whose interest would not be served by the revelation of who supplied information to the Vatican and what that information was.

The Visit was followed in mid 2007 by an unsigned document on the letterhead of the Congregation for Bishops detailing why it believed Morris was a 'defective' leader in Toowoomba and had to go.

Carter found that this pivotal document, which came to Morris from the Nuncio, displays 'an appalling lack of evidence and particularity', containing 'demonstrable errors of fact' and reflecting a 'process of decision making by high ranking Church officials more likely based on gossip and hearsay' than on factual evidence.

Carter nominates fourteen points at which Morris was denied natural justice and due process over a period from mid 2006 to late 2009. He finds that Cardinal Re had made up his mind that Morris had to go as early as June 2007 (when the unsigned document from the Congregation for Bishops materialised and following the Visitation in April 2007) and no later than October 2007 when he demanded Morris's resignation.

Morris has never seen the evidence or testimony on which that demand was made and told Cardinal Re that in conscience he could not comply. Ian Waters, the Canonist who reviewed the case, has said that a forced resignation of a bishop in the absence of grave cause or illness, is an invalid exercise of authority in the Church.

Carter and Waters are at one in their conclusion that 'Bishop Morris was denied procedural fairness and natural justice' by all key Vatican officials including

Pope Benedict who wrote, 'Canon Law does not make provision for a process regarding Bishops whom the Successor of Peter names and may remove from office'.

At their recent *ad limina* visit to Rome [October 2011], the Australian bishops had up to five meetings with the Prefects of the Congregations for Bishops and the Doctrine of the Faith. According to one of the bishops present, Morris 'says one thing and the Prefects say another'. However, Morris is the only party to surrender his documentation to independent scrutiny.

Responses in Australia to Morris's forced resignation have been varied. Leadership—clerical and lay— in the Church in Toowoomba wrote to the Vatican both following the Apostolic Visitor and following Morris's removal. The correspondence has not been acknowledged.

Fallout in the diocese and across the country has been considerable. In response, the Australian bishops published a joint letter over its President's signature that recognized the dismay of many, promised that the matters would be addressed at their forthcoming *ad limina* and, significantly, endorsed the effective and sustained pastoral leadership Morris has shown, in contrast to the Vatican's judgment of 'defective leadership' as the reason for his removal.

The endorsement notwithstanding, the letter was from the President, Archbishop Philip Wilson of Adelaide who had accompanied Morris on some of his visits to Vatican officials. The letter gave as the reason Morris was removed what amounted to that used in divorce proceedings: irreconcilable differences.

The bishops promised in the letter that they would take their own and many others' concerns up with Roman authorities. What resulted was a subsequent statement that one member of the Conference described as 'a lowest common denominator outcome'—a statement that pledged loyalty to the Pope and fraternal affection for Morris. It reported no progress on the outstanding issues addressed by Carter and Waters: due process and respect for Morris's natural rights.

As Carter observed in his report, 'The principles of natural justice and fairness lie at the heart of the maxim "Not only must justice be done, it must manifestly be seen to be done"'.

If the Morris affair is anything to go by, the light of natural justice and due process is yet to penetrate the dark corridors of the Vatican.[2]

Copies of the Memorandum (Carter Report) and the Canonical Reflection were sent to the cardinals of the relevant Congregations involved in the process as well as to the Supreme Court of the Church, The Signatura.

---

2.   'Rites and Wrongs', in *The Tablet*, 21 January 2012: 4–5.

Bishop Morris sailing in the Whitsundays, Queensland.

27

Ad Limina Visit 2011

Facts do not cease to exist because they are ignored.
Aldous Huxley, Complete Essays 2, 1926-29

Men occasionally stumble over the truth, but most of them pick themselves up and hurry off as if nothing ever happened.
Winston Churchill

Statement from the Australian Catholic Bishops in Rome
Our letter to Bishop Brian Finnigan in May said that, during the *Ad Limina* visit in October [2011], we would have discussions concerning the events which led to the departure of Bishop William Morris from the pastoral care of the Diocese of Toowoomba. That has been done.

We had individual meetings with Cardinal Marc Ouellet, Prefect of the Congregation for Bishops, and Cardinal William Levada, Prefect of the Congregation for the Doctrine of the Faith. Subsequently we had a joint meeting with Cardinal Ouellet and Cardinal Levada. As well, we ourselves met several times.

We were very appreciative of the time given to us by the Cardinals and the personal and pastoral concern which they expressed. Our discussions with them were substantial, serious and candid.

These meetings have given us a more adequate understanding of what was done by the Holy See in an attempt to resolve the difficulties with Bishop Morris, which concerned not only matters of Church discipline but also of Church doctrine definitively taught, such as on the ministerial priesthood. What the Holy See did was fraternal and pastoral rather than juridical in character. Although efforts continued over many years, a critical point came when Bishop Morris failed to clarify his position to the satisfaction of the Holy See and then found himself unable to resign as Bishop of the Diocese when the Holy Father made the request.

What was at stake was the Church's unity in faith and the ecclesial communion between the Pope and the other Bishops in the College of Bishops. Eventually Bishop Morris was unable to agree to what this communion requires and at that point the Pope acted as the Successor of Peter, who has the task of deciding what constitutes unity and communion in the Church.

We express our acceptance of the Holy Father's exercise of his Petrine ministry, and we reaffirm our communion with and under Peter. We return to Australia determined to do whatever we can to heal any wounds of division, to extend our fraternal care to Bishop Morris, and to strengthen the bonds of charity in the Church in Australia.

From the time the bishops arrived back in Australia there had been a number of reports of the conversations they had amongst themselves, with Cardinals Marc Ouellet, Prefect of the Congregation for Bishops, and William Levada, Prefect for the Congregation for the Doctrine of the Faith. These reports vary in their support of the contents of the statement made by the Australian Catholic Bishops in Rome. From the beginnings of my communication with Pope Benedict, there has never been a question of my loyalty and acceptance of his role as the Successor of Peter and my acceptance of the exercise of his petrine ministry. It was because of this that I approached him for his guidance and wisdom to help me clarify and understand, how, on the evidence provided, it could be said that I had broken communion, when there was evidence and processes that were lacking in natural justice, transparency and truthfulness.

None of the reports that I have received since the *ad limina* visit of 2011 have been critical of the Holy Father but some have asked questions about the lack of process, the truthfulness of the accusations, and the so called pastoral and fraternal dialogue. Some thought that I should have immediately resigned, others respected my right to defend myself against false accusations. Others at the *ad limina* had the feeling that what happened to me was a 'done deal', as mentioned to me by Archbishop Lazzarotto in a meeting with him, and they were just there to be told rather than to have a fraternal dialogue. Others reflected on the fact that when Rome is dealing with Australia, the 1998 Statement of Conclusions still colours Rome's judgement and my Advent Letter was proof of this thinking.

It was mentioned that if I had written another letter clarifying my position this would have resolved the matter . . . As I have stated in my story, I clarified my position immediately in the national, provincial and local media as well as on the diocesan website. It was also mentioned at the *ad limina* visit that the four page unsigned memorandum handed to me by Archbishop Ambrose de Paoli was a four page summary of the Visitor's Report, which had never been referred to in any conversation I had with any of the Vatican Officials.

It was said that Cardinals Ouellet and Levada made the observation that the Holy See had been very patient, and there was a careful process but I had refused to resolve the matter. I find this perplexing as I had tried to dialogue with Cardinals Arinze, Re and Levada but found they were not interested as they had already made their decision and the process was a monologue. As for the accusation that I came to Rome and made no contact, I have already shown that this was inaccurate, since I had received the advice—'if the Cardinals want to see you they make the contact, don't rock the boat'.

There is also an interesting section in the statement made by the Australian Catholic Bishops in Rome that

> these meetings have given us a more adequate understanding of what was done by the Holy See in an attempt to resolve the difficulties with Bishop Morris, which concerned not only matters of church discipline but also of church doctrine definitively taught, such as on the ministerial priesthood

I find this section interesting. Interesting, because I was never part of this conversation. It would be my understanding that if parties were genuine in their desire to arrive at the truth then the main players involved need to be present and part of the dialogue. Otherwise it is like looking into a mirror where one party sees its own reflection while blocking the reflection of the other.

After the publication of the statement from the Catholic Bishops in Rome following their *ad limina* visit, the Toowoomba Diocesan Leadership Group, Co-chaired by Father Ray Crowley and Mr John Elich, wrote to the President of the Australian Catholic Bishops Conference, Archbishop Philip Wilson. In the letter they thanked him for publishing the 'Statement' and asked when it would be possible for him to share with the Leadership Group his understanding of the reasons the cardinals gave for making the strong recommendations they did to the pope for my resignation. They went on to say that 'we understand fully that the Pope has the right to make the decision he did . . .however we remain concerned about the accuracy of the information provided to Pope Benedict by the Cardinals'.

The Leadership Group continued by referring to a letter dated 11 August 2011 from Archbishop Wilson in which he said that, to assist with the questions raised by the Leadership Group, 'the Permanent Committee [of the Australian Catholic Bishops Conference] has resolved to refer the issues of process and the doctrinal matter of infallibility of the teaching on women's ordination respectively to the Congregation for Bishops and the Congregation for the Doctrine of the Faith'. The Group said that they would appreciate further comments and discussion about these matters. They went on to say that if healing was to take place then 'truth telling' was important and the release of Archbishop Chaput's Report, following his visit to the diocese, was a vital part of the 'truth telling'. The Group believed this was important if the diocese was to move on and to move forward, but even so at this point they were positive and confident about the future of the Catholic community in the diocese, and rejected references to the diocese being divided as untrue and without basis.

The Australian Catholic Bishops' 'Statement' had concluded by saying 'we return to Australia determined to do whatever we can to heal any wounds of division, to extend our fraternal care to Bishop Morris, and to strengthen the bond of charity in the Church in Australia'. The Leadership Group finished its letter, adding that it appreciated the offer of healing so with this in mind they asked

Wilson or his representative to visit Toowoomba and engage with them in information sharing, truth telling and mediation, for they were concerned about the faith of the diocese being their spiritual home and they wanted to leave no stone unturned in continuing to be the People of God in this Place.

The bishops' reply came in the form of a motion which was passed at the Australian Catholic Bishops Conference in late November 2011. The motion read:

> That the President of the Conference reply to the recent correspondence from Toowoomba indicating that the Apostolic Administrator and, as he wishes, accompanied by some bishops from the Province, will meet with them to discuss the present situation and the process for healing.

Bishop Finnigan, the Apostolic Administrator, in consultation with the Queensland Bishops and representatives of the Toowoomba Leadership Group, was finally able to arrange a meeting on Thursday 12 April 2012 in Brisbane at the residence of the Archbishop.

The Toowoomba Leadership Group, at a meeting on 17 January 2012, finalised the issues that they wished to discuss. They covered four areas in their letter forwarded to Bishop Finnigan by Mr John Elich and Father Ray Crowley, Co-Chairs of the Group:

> 1. The factual circumstances surrounding Bishop Morris's retirement are quite clear but the reasoning behind the action taken is still not clear (as seen in the Report of Carter who had access to the correspondence between Bishop Morris and the Vatican). The Australian Bishops stated that they left their *ad limina* visit with a better understanding of the situation. If that be the case, we would be very grateful to receive any additional information that was provided to the Australian bishops during the *ad limina* visit.
>
> If there is something more to the story, we would be grateful to know what that additional information is.

Further, to ensure that we all have a complete understanding of the situation, we believe that it is essential that Bishop Morris attend the meeting so that any factual misunderstandings or uncertainties can be clarified.

2. As you would appreciate from our correspondence to the Australian Catholic Bishops Conference and perhaps also from our media releases, we are obviously concerned that Bishop Morris has been treated unjustly.

As you are also aware, we have called upon the Australian Bishops to provide a meaningful response to what we perceive to be a significant issue. In short, we would like the opportunity to discuss with you what can or is to be done about the grave injustice that has occurred.

3. You might also recall that in our correspondence to the Australian Catholic Bishops Conference we sought the opportunity for further comment and discussion in relation to the doctrinal matter of infallibility of the teaching on women's ordination. This issue remains important to us.

5. Finally, we have been concerned to read/see/hear in the media statements by senior Australian churchmen that the people of our diocese are deeply divided on the issue of Bishop Morris's treatment and that this deep division requires some kind of healing or repair.

6. We wish to make it plain to you that this is simply not the case and that whilst there are a small number of individuals who have been critical of Bishop Morris, the greater majority of our diocese share the concerns expressed by this group from the outset.

These are the issues that we seek to discuss with you.

Present at the meeting on 12 April 2012 in Brisbane were ten representatives of the Toowoomba Diocesan Leadership Group, the bishops of Queensland, (except for the Archdiocese of Brisbane which was awaiting a new appointment) and myself. The meeting was chaired by Bishop Brian Heenan of Rockhampton, Senior Suffragan (the senior bishop in the group).

At the beginning of the meeting the bishops' clarified their status saying they carried no official authority from the Australian Catholic Bishops Conference or from Rome. As Queensland Bishops they expressed their hope that the meeting might affirm the priests and people of the Diocese of Toowoomba and address in some way the deep hurt experienced over my retirement. The representatives of the Toowoomba Leadership Group then reiterated their belief that natural justice and due process had been denied and that this was supported by the findings of Judge Carter and Canon Lawyer, Father Ian Waters, and that there must be truth telling before the diocese could heal and move on. During the discussion the following points were covered.

The Australian Bishops had not received any new information during their *ad limina* visit. All the bishops present stated unequivocally that there was no 'hidden' information: there were no grave matters concerning myself that had not already been aired. The implication that there was 'new' information rose from the fact that many Australian bishops were unaware of the ongoing conflict between myself and Rome. It was important for the Toowoomba Leadership Group to hear very clearly from the bishops that there were no secret allegations/accusations against me.

The discussion then focused on whether or not Archbishop Chaput had shared his report with me. I stated definitively that I had never seen Chaput's report and that I was currently in correspondence with him, sending a list of questions from his own pursuit of what was said in interviews between the Apostolic Visitor, myself and his interviewees, seeking clarification about Chaput's comment to an Australian bishop in Madrid and his letter to the Archbishop of Melbourne. The Leadership Group expressed the belief that in the interest of justice and fairness the contents of the report should have been known at least to myself.

The Toowoomba Diocesan Leadership Group was greatly disturbed that the allegations in the unsigned document dated 28 June 2007, sent by the Congregation of Bishops, handed to me by the then Apostolic Nuncio, Archbishop Ambrose de Paoli in September 2007, had contained complaints and false assertions about myself and the diocese, and seemed to have been the official reasons for requesting my resignation.

The group then expressed surprise that the *unsigned* document— especially one so manifestly erroneous—could be considered authoritative. The bishops explained that because it was on the letterhead of a Vatican Congregation, it could be classed as a document and therefore would not need to be signed. It was supposed by the Toowoomba Diocesan Leadership Group that most of this document had been compiled from the false accusations originally made by a small number of people in the diocese who opposed my governance.

On the question of process, the bishops explained that Roman processes operate in a different manner from Western processes. It was stated by the bishops that Rome treats matters of conflict between a bishop and the Curia with what it sees as 'fraternal dialogue', not a 'canonical process', and would expect that a bishop would comply with requests immediately. My request that the meeting between myself and the cardinals be delayed from February to May when I would be in Rome for other reasons, would have been viewed by the Cardinals as a refusal to enter into dialogue and would have exacerbated the existing tension between myself and the cardinals.

The Queensland bishops expressed the view that a difference in cultural mindsets had been one of the root causes of the sad outcome of the whole process. It became a matter of quintessential Roman culture versus quintessential Australian culture. My directness, in place of possibly more obsequiousness, had sealed my fate. I would have been considered intransigent and therefore problematical. My position would have been seen as antithetical to the cardinals own, and so I was 'not of the mind of the Church'. However, the Toowoomba Diocesan Leadership Group maintained that whether a canonical or a fraternal process had been used, above all it was a matter of justice and morality and my treatment had been neither just nor moral.

The bishops from Queensland who were present reiterated that some of them had pleaded with Rome in correspondence and in person in support of myself but to no avail. It was also important to note, however, that not all bishops were of one mind on the matter. The Toowoomba Diocesan Leadership Group returned to the issue of the injustice done to myself: natural justice is about the victim; this man has been harmed; it is a moral issue that must be addressed.

The bishops replied, restating their endeavours on my behalf, but concluded that once the relationship between myself and Rome had soured, the outcome was inevitable.

Regarding my Advent Pastoral Letter of 2006, the bishops agreed that, when read carefully, it need not be construed as opposing Church teaching. It was noted that in the letter which dealt with the current staffing plan for the Diocese, I obliquely referred to ongoing worldwide discussion about ordaining women, but followed immediately by stating unequivocally that 'we remain committed to actively promoting vocations to the current celibate male priesthood and open to inviting priests from overseas'. In fact, the Toowoomba Diocesan Leadership Group reminded the bishops that after the publication of the letter, I very quickly stated on the Diocesan website and elsewhere that I definitely did not intend to oppose Church teaching. The Leadership Group were insistent that a fair reading of the letter in the broader context could not lead to a conclusion that I was opposing Church teaching.

Discussion then moved to an explanation of the issue of infallibility, explaining that the question of the non-ordination of women is part of the universal/ordinary Magisterium of the Church. The question then arose whether such a teaching has always been in place in the Church. At the same time it was emphasised by the Toowoomba Diocesan Leadership Group that I never taught that women should be ordained, neither did my 2006 Advent Letter promote such an idea. They argued that attempts to clarify any misunderstanding had not been heard or, if heard, had not satisfied Rome or others who were working with them.

The Leadership Group then requested that it be publicly and definitively stated to the rest of the diocese that there was no 'new' or 'hidden' reason for my forced retirement and that an explanation of Roman culture—how things work in Rome—should also be provided. This was agreed to, as well as that there should be a better process for resolving conflict between an individual bishop and Rome. The bishops agreed to recommend, through the Bishops Commission for Ministry, that the Australian Catholic Bishops Conference establish a group to work on devising a process to be used for matters pertaining to Canon 19.[1]

---

1. Canon 19: 'If on a particular matter there is not an express provision of either

The meeting concluded, thanking Bishop Brian Heenan who acted as Chair, and acknowledging and thanking me for my presence. It was agreed that there had been value in meeting and sharing openly. The members of the Leadership Group acknowledged that the description of the difference between Australian culture and the culture of Rome/ the Vatican did not take away the deep pain that they and many in the diocese were feeling, nor did it lessen their belief that I had suffered a grave injustice. However, the members of the group remained wholly committed to providing pastoral ministry with the same vitality as they had in the past, and they were looking forward to welcoming and working with a new bishop when he was appointed.

universal or particular law, nor a custom, then, provided it is not a penal matter, the question is to be decided by taking into account laws enacted in similar matters, the general principles of law observed with canonical equity, the jurisprudence and practice of the Roman Curia, and the common and constant opinion of learned authors.'

28

What Report?

Truth is stranger than fiction, but it is because Fiction is obliged to stick to possibilities; Truth isn't.

Mark Twain

The Apostolic Visitor's Report continues to be that black cloud that hangs over most discussions concerning my relationship with the Roman Dicasteries, but fails to bring any light to these discussions. Statements made by some, publicly reporting that I was shown Chaput's report, have not helped my integrity, but challenged my truthfulness and kept people in the dark.

Cardinal Levada, Prefect of the Congregation for the Doctrine of the Faith, at the meeting with the Australian Bishops on their *ad limina* visit in 2011, reported that he had read Archbishop Chaput's report and found it quite fair and reasonable. He went on to say that it was not Chaput's role to make any judgment but only to report what he had found. I believe it was the normal practice for the Visitor to inform the bishop concerned what the report would contain. Chaput discussed a number of issues with me from the material he brought from Rome and what he gleaned from his interviews. But never once said what the report would contain or gave any indication of the areas that would be covered.

There was talk that the four page unsigned memorandum handed to me by Archbishop Ambrose de Paoli was a four page summary of the report. As I have mentioned before this was never discussed with me in any forum and I find it extraordinary that if it was so, how could Chaput make so many errors concerning material which he had been given while conducting the visitation.

The question—whether or not Chaput discussed what he was going to put in the report with me—reached another levelat the World Youth Day in Spain when he sought out an Australian bishop to assure him that he had discussed the report. That bishop was surprised as he had made no approach to Chaput seeking information. This kept on adding fuel to the assumption that the report had been shared with me, which continually challenges my integrity and truthfulness and confuses the members of Christs' faithful, which would not have happened if there had been a due process. Then on 4 February 2012 in *The Age* the Archbishop of Melbourne, Denis Hart, claimed that Chaput 'said he discussed the contents of the report with Bishop Morris in Toowoomba'.

I am on record saying that I would like the report published because I think the people of the diocese deserve the right to know what Chaput, who wandered around the diocese for four days, had to say about the diocese and what judgements he may have made. While in Sydney, waiting to fly out of Australia, he sent me an email informing me that he was working on the report and he had sent an email to the Diocesan Chancellor, Father Brian Sparksman asking for clarification concerning the employment of two ex-priests. He finished off his email saying, 'you can see I am hard at work on the report'. If this information, which he was seeking from the Chancellor, was going to be in the report, then this is one area on record that was never discussed. The next communication I received was in the early part of May informing both the Chancellor and myself that he had sent an electronic copy as well as a hard copy to the Dicastery for Bishops. He then destroyed both his electronic and hard copy as ordered by Rome.

It was reported in the *National Catholic Reporter* that when asked whether or not the report would ever be made public, Chaput responded, 'any apostolic visitation is governed by strict confidentiality. This is for the benefit of all parties involved.' With uncertainty and confusion hanging in the air, I sent an email to Chaput on 12 March 2012, to try to clarify the rumours and statements that were being made about the Visitation and Report. The first concerned the Australian Bishop whom Chaput sought out at the World Youth Day in Spain, telling him that he had shared the Report with me. The second was Archbishop Hart who is on public record stating that

Chaput had discussed the report with me. I told him I found this quite perplexing as my notes and memory had no record of him ever saying to me, 'this is what I am going to put in the Report, these are the headings and the overall summary of the document'. I asked for clarification concerning these rumours as it is important for the truth to be told to the people of the Diocese. A few days later I received Chaput's response saying that he was quite surprised by emails he had received from people in Australia reporting that I have denied hearing from him about the Report when speaking publicly. He went on to say, 'you know full well that, at my request, we sat down together in your home at the end of the visitation and that I went through all the notes I had taken. I told you everything that I had heard—excluding the names of people—that would be in the report to the Holy See. Your public denials have been quite astonishing.'

The conversation raged on and towards the end of March I responded to Archbishop Hart's article in *The Age* and *The Sydney Morning Herald*. Once again I categorically denied that Chaput ever discussed or identified what he was going to put in the report, for his discussion was always focused on clarifying the questions he had brought with him from Rome, and those that had arisen in his inquisitorial examination of the Toowoomba Diocese. Hart's comments concerning the process by the Holy See were inaccurate but he was correct in stating that the Pope did not act against Canon Law because he is the Legislator and therefore decides what is canonical. However, he omitted to acknowledge that while the pope is the Vicar of Christ for the Universal Church, Vatican II clearly taught that each diocesan bishop is the Vicar of Christ in and for his diocese and his participation in the college of bishops came by virtue of his episcopal ordination, not through the authority of the pope. This highlights once again the need for due process, otherwise natural justice will be continually denied and misunderstanding and confusion will reign.

With this in mind I decided to ask Chaput for details of what he discussed with me, when and where. Were the matters listed in the unsigned document (memorandum) handed to me by the Nuncio, Archbishop Ambrose de Paoli, part of the report and if so how did he get the facts about ordinations and deacons so wrong?

I began by saying that it is on public record . . . as reported by Archbishop Hart in the *Melbourne Age* and the *Sydney Morning*

Herald, that you have said to others that you discussed the contents of your report with me before you left Toowoomba.

I went on to detail what I considered to be the huge discrepancies, gaps and errors in the negative picture reflected in the unsigned Document and in the concerns raised by the cardinals in their meeting with me. If the content of the unsigned Document and the cardinals' concerns did indeed reflect loosely the content of Archbishop Chaput's report, how did such a selective and limited picture result from the wealth of information provided to and shared with him by various people including myself? I finished the letter by saying:

> Charles, there is so much you never discussed with me. At no time did you make it clear to me what you were going to put into the report and what you were going to leave out from the matters discussed with the various groups and individuals in the diocese whom you interviewed. It is clear from the evidence and records that you never went through all your notes with me or told me everything you heard as you have stated. Since your report is never going to be seen by me or the diocese it is impossible to know what it contains and to see whether or not it gives a true picture of the life of the diocese—the unsigned Document certainly does not.
>
> It is because of this lack of transparency and due process that this question arises. If there had been transparency and due process I would have seen the major findings and recommendations of your Report and I would have been given a chance to respond to it. If what we discussed on the Friday afternoon was all that was in the Report it would have been very limited in its scope and certainly would not have given a complete picture of the diocese and my leadership. I believe you could only have shared what was in the Report with me when you had finished writing it.
>
> Given that I am denied access to your report, could I, in justice to me and the Diocese, now ask you to provide me with a summary of what you did discuss with me on the Friday before you left Toowoomba, what you

have described as the contents of your report. And I ask you to confirm which of these matters in the unsigned Document with the heading, *Congregatio pro Episopis* are consistent with the content of your report:

1. 'The local Church in Toowoomba is moving in a different direction than that of the Catholic Church';
2. The Diocese 'is going through a severe crisis that spreads its roots back over the last ten years';
3. The Bishop had failed 'to guide the faithful in fidelity to the doctrine and discipline of the Church; to work hard to promote priestly vocations; and to offer sound theological, spiritual and human formation to his Priests';
4. He has condoned 'liturgical abuses';
5. He continues to condone 'an unacceptable extension of the conditions required for "grave necessity" and that accordingly general absolution is still common';
6. Despite 'admonitions' the Bishop 'adamantly resists fulfilling his responsibility to apply Church norms properly';
7. 'The general theological climate of the Diocese and especially its priests fails 'to move towards an authentic Catholic identity';
8. That 'in the past seven years there has been no priestly ordinations';
9. The failure of the Diocese 'to have an effective and sufficiently dynamic program for promoting vocations or finding Priests from elsewhere';
10. The Bishop fails 'to offer the leadership necessary to reverse' the above situation;
11. Priests are being marginalised and retiring early because of their substitution by deacons and laity;
12. 'Bishop Morris' theological preparation and type of leadership are inadequate to confront the crisis of the Church in Toowoomba';
13. And accordingly, 'Toowoomba needs a Bishop who, with determination and courage, will tackle the

problems and rectify what is not in conformity with
the doctrine and discipline of the Catholic Church';
I hope you will agree that it would be worthwhile
for everyone's reputation, including your own, if you
were to ask the relevant Vatican Office to provide you
with a copy of your report so that you can provide
accurate answers to these queries.

On Tuesday 17 April 2012, I received Chaput's reply: 'Bishop Morris, your imagination is in 'over-drive'. I did share everything with you. I did not keep any notes after sending the report to Rome. How would I–or anyone–ever respond to your questions from memory? You are involved in an exercise of self-justification that is obscuring the truth and good reason.'

I leave it to the reader to draw their own conclusion.

29

Breathing Together

We must keep our ear on the heart of God and our hand on the pulse of time.

Martin Werlen, OSB

House by the Sea by Carol Bialock, rscj

I built my house by the sea.
Not on sand, mind you.
Not on the shifting sand.
And I built it of rock.
A strong house.
By a strong sea.
And we got well-acquainted, the sea and I.
Good neighbors.
Not that we spoke much.
We met in silences.
Respectful, keeping our distance,
but looking our thoughts across the fence
of sand.
Always, the fence of sand our barrier;
always the sand between.

And then one day
(I still don't know how it happened),
but the sea came.
Without warning.
Without welcome, even.
Not sudden and swift, but sifting across the
sand like wine.

Less like the flow of water than the flow
of blood.
Slow, but coming.
Slow, but flowing like an open wound.
And I thought of flight and I thought of drowning and I thought
of death.
And while I thought the sea crept higher,
till it reached my door.
I knew, then, there was neither flight nor

death nor drowning.
That when the sea comes calling you stop
being good neighbors,
Well-acquainted, friendly-from-a-distance
neighbors.
And you give your house for a coral castle,
And you learn to breathe under water.

I have been asked many times by many people in many places what am I doing now that I am 'retired' and by many how did you cope in all of this? Well, as the poem described, I learnt to breathe under water. I learnt that my life situation was not my life and the gift of being loved and living in the present was both life-giving and transforming. I learnt that it was for freedom, that Jesus set us free, a freedom that gave one the capacity to see that creation is a paradox, a both/and not an either/or, inviting us to find the balance between life and death, good and evil, the cross and resurrection.[1] In the words of Judy Cannato from her book, *Field of Compassion*:

> Freedom is the floor upon which all of these virtues and capacities dance. Love, service, community, justice, or peace cannot be if they are not rooted in freedom, for anything less than freedom will distort them and drain them of their power. I think that it is possible to describe the kind of freedom at the heart of the gospel as 'the capacity to choose to engage in the process of the evolution of consciousness'.

---

1. Galatians 5:1.

We are invited to be co-creators, to be surprised each day, to share our surprise in the dialogue of life which has its foundation in relationship. I learnt to breathe underwater by breathing together with my diocesan family.

A prophetic voice for me and for her time was Mary MacKillop who heard the voices crying in the wilderness of the Australian bush and responded by providing education for isolated country children. She heard the cries of the orphaned, the homeless, the prisoner, the prostitute and with great daring and faith encouraged them to dream of a better future and to trust in God who is faithful to all, who loves all and calls all to faithfulness, love and freedom. This was possible for her because she believed deeply in a God who was with her, a God whom she trusted completely and who would be faithful to her. That is why she was at peace in rejection, that is why she could breathe underwater. She knew she was in God, she knew her true self, she was true to herself. Mary's constant awareness of God's presence and love enabled her to remain open, to be surprised by her Beloved and to confess in prayer deep within her heart 'my desire for God must be none other than God's desire for me'. This was breath to me, this was my strength.

Jeremiah was another path-finder for me, showing how he could cope with rejection and remain totally faithful to God. When he came out of the shadows of Anathoth in answer to God's call he was accepted by a people who were experiencing freedom for the first time in many years with the collapse of the Assyrian Empire. After experiencing success in his preaching ministry for six years he started to feel the rejection by a people who did not want to be reminded of their responsibility in their relationship with each other and with their God. His love for God did not waver but he wanted to know that if he was doing what God wanted him to do why was he not being accepted? Why does not the way of the just flourish? Why does not my way flourish . . . the way I understand Your will? The answer comes through his prayer in Chapter 12 of his prophecy: 'You Yahweh know me and see me, you explore my heart with me, you explore walking with my footsteps as I plunge into the darkness of my life . . . You God are there with me.' This prayer makes my heart sing and I too, know that I am loved as I breathe together with my faith family and sing these lines under water.

It was very early in my ministry in the diocese that I realised we needed to be bold if we were going to identify the needs of the local Church and the widest representation would be vital to plan for the future which would help frame the pastoral strategies taking us into the twenty-first century. There is a richness that is unique to every individual in every community, and this has to be tapped into with an openness of heart and the guidance of the Holy Spirit. Our calling is to be prophets of hope, carrying and celebrating the message of a loving God for this generation to be passed on to the next in the freedom proclaimed by Jesus. I realised that we had no right to bind the Spirit in our own small worlds, thereby condemning the world around us to a life of mediocrity that is never surprised by the Spirit to take up new challenges and minister in new ways. It was dialogue that was important for opening up minds and hearts. John Paul II reminds us that it is, 'by dialogue we let God be present in our midst; as we open ourselves in dialogue to one another, we open ourselves to God'.[2]

We need to protect the limitlessness of God by refusing all definitions as final. It takes great courage to remain open under the controlling pressure to be certain. We must come to realise that there is always more. Rahner describes the idea of God as holy mystery in poetic, geographical terms:

> The horizon itself cannot be present within the horizon.
> The ultimate measure cannot be measured; the boundary
> which delimits all things cannot itself be bounded by
> still more distant limit. The infinite and immense which
> comprises all things: such an all-embracing immensity
> cannot itself be encompassed.[3]

As creation evolves we are invited to contemplate the reality of our present relationship with God, to discover what is new in that relationship and what is its future. We are to anticipate and prepare because within this relationship we realise we are caught up in the plan of God that directs us to the future. To help us see and hear

---

2. Elizabeth A Johnson, *Quest for the Living God* (New York/London: Contiuum, 2007), 163.

3. Johnson, *Quest*, 36.

the groaning of creation, to step out in hope and not to fear what is ahead of us, the paths we must follow are woven into the surface of creation by the lives of those who have gone before us, the living who challenge us and show us the way by the light and life of the man called Jesus.

Thomas Merton speaks of 'realised eschatology', the transformation of life and of human relations by Jesus now (rather than an eschatology focussed on future cosmic events). 'Realised Eschatology' is the heart of genuine Christian humanism and hence its tremendous importance for the Christian peace effort, for justice, by the very fact that we take our place in the Dialogue of Salvation, for we are co-creators with God, we are Agents of transformation and openness. The presence of the Spirit, the call to repentance, the call to see Christ in the human person, 'the presence of the Redeeming power of the Cross in the sacraments: These belong now to the age in which we live.'[4]

It is our responsibility, our duty and our call to find new ways in which the truth can be set free and celebrated. This was the challenge of Jesus to reveal to the world a liberating God where everyone shares. In every age the Spirit leads us to ask new questions, for God is found in the breath of life and the heartbeat of creation. If we are to discern how to evangelise our culture, the world of today, we need to be bold and have a listening heart. This boldness was spoken of by Cardinal Joseph Ratzinger in the challenge of Paul to Peter (Gal 2:11-14):

> yet, if it was a weakness in Peter to have compromised the freedom of the gospel for fear of James' supporters, it was his greatness which enabled him to accept the liberty of Paul, who 'rebuked him to his face'. And today the Church owes her life to this liberty and paved the way for her entry to the heathen world.

Ratzinger goes on to say:

> Perhaps we of today need to be reminded that boldness is one of the basic Christian attitudes referred to most frequently in the New Testament. Boldness it was that

---

4. Thomas Merton, *Daily Meditations from his Journals* (San Farncisco: HarperCollins, HarperOne, 2004), 71

made Peter step forward and preach to the Jews (Acts 2: 29; 4:13, 29, 31). What would it not mean for the Church in the world of today—in a century that thirsts after freedom, in an era which walked out of the Church for the sake of freedom, illusory though it may have been – if the words of Paul could ring with the force of old, could actually mature until veritably visible: those magnificent words into which Paul poured the full expression of his faith: 'but wherever the spirit of the Lord is, there is freedom' (2 Cor 3:17).[5]

'Dialogue, dialogue, dialogue' was the call of Pope Francis when speaking in Brazil on the occasion of World Youth Day 2013, calling it the cornerstone of all human progress. If this dialogue is to be creative and life-giving, truly embracing all relationships that form the life-blood of creation, there can be no unasked questions or the fear of punitive action. For where there is fear there is no dialogue and where there is no dialogue there is no relationship.[6] This dialogue will bear much fruit if it recognises the rights and responsibilities of all the baptised to participate in the deliberative decision making of the Church, linking church governance to baptism rather than ordination. In the words of Pope Francis, 'The Church is the people of God, pastors and people put together. The Church is the totality of God's people'.

In the words of Martin Werlen, 'we must keep our ear on the heart of God and our hand on the pulse of time', [7] so that breathing together is not a challenge but a way of life celebrated in the seamless whole of creation. It was this breathing together that affirmed me, giving the strength and courage to keep going in the search for truth and justice with the words of Thomas More's response to Cardinal Wolsey's retort ringing in my ears, 'if you could get away from that troublesome conscience of yours, you would be like the rest of us'. More responded, 'when a Statesman forsakes his private conscience

---

5. *The Ratzinger Reader*, edited by Lieven Boeve and Gerard Mannion (London: Continuum, 2010), 212.
6. C/f Chapter 3, Synod of Oceania.
7. Martin Werlen, OSB *Embers in the Ashes: New Life in the Church*. (New York: Paulist press, 2013), 10.

for the sake of his public duties he leads his country by a short route to chaos'. The same can be said of us as church leaders.

Let me finish this journey with the words from Vatican II:

> With a most profound wisdom and goodness,
> God created the whole world
> and from among all of creation
> God chose us humans to share in the divine life,
> to have an eternal walk with God
> arm in arm
> heart to heart.
> And although we have stumbled along
> and at times have even lost our way,
> God has not abandoned us.
> Instead, God remained radically present,
> eventually expressing the depth of parental love
> through Jesus Christ.
> Jesus Christ is the one around whom the Church Gathers.[8]

This makes breathing underwater possible!

Epilogue

Seventy years later the Tower of the City Hall is dwarfed by the towering structures of a modern city and the Brisbane Line is still a myth or a fact but lost in the shadows of time. My life, too, has changed but still embraced by a larger family who love and support me and continually call me to life. I celebrate this life with many communities, by being invited to give talks to Catholic organisations, to celebrate presence and to be part of the life of a number of religious orders; to journey with many individuals and families, to share in their joys and to be part of their sorrow and to hold them in their grief.

This large family encompasses schools where I have the privilege to be involved with principals, teaching staff, students and parents, sharing and breaking open the richness of our tradition seen with vision through the lens of the Word and Creation, always open

---

8. Vatican II in Plain English by Bill Heubsch (Thomas Moore, 1997) Chapter 1, Nos 2 & 3

to be surprised by the Holy Spirit. The story of Jesus is always the foundation to our celebration in the breaking of the bread and the sharing of the cup. This gift of celebration extends to parishes where I am given the honour to be part of their communities, and reflection days and seminars have become part of my life.

In response to the call of Jesus's prayer, 'that they may all be one', I participate in Ecumenical Pastoral Care formation programs and other areas of ecumenism, putting into practice the Lund Principle[9] which affirms that churches should act together in all matters except those in which deep differences of conviction compel them to act separately. Recently Pope Francis, in a homily, expressed confidence that the Holy Spirit would eventually unite Christians through 'reconciled diversity'.[10]

I have taken part in the anniversaries of parishes and jubilee celebrations in my home diocese of Toowoomba and am invited to participate in its sacramental life especially in the far west, as well as sharing the gift of play in flying kites in Outback skies.

In the future I hope to continue my work in formation and education programs as well as reflection days, retreat work and ecumenism. I will continue my involvement in schools and parishes and with religious orders, and will participate in my home diocese when invited. I will continue my relationship with the University of Southern Queensland in Toowoomba, being involved with the Multicultural Centre, focussing on Peace, Interreligious Dialogue and Culture, the Golden Key International Honour Society and other aspects of University life.

---

9. The Lund Principle was agreed by the 1952 Faith and Order Conference of the World Council of Churches held in Lund, Sweden.
10. Quoted in *The Tablet*, 1 February 2014, 30, Letter from Rome.

Appendix 1

Speech of Archbishop Francis Rush at the 1985 Extraordinary Synod of Bishops

[To review the work of Vatican II twenty years after it closed in December 1965, Pope John Paul II called a special meeting of the Bishops' Synod. On November 27, Archbishop Rush addressed the general assembly as President of the Australian Bishops' Conference]

Most Holy Father and my Brothers and Sisters in Christ, I speak for the Bishops of Australia when I thank God for the Second Vatican Council. I speak with gratitude for the considerable renewal the Council has already achieved, and with unbounded hope that the Holy Spirit will guide this Synod as He undoubtedly guided the Council. If there have been failures, they have not been the fault of the Council. They have emanated from neglect of the Council or from misinterpretation of its spirit and teachings. On behalf of the Bishops of Australia, I should like to underline two concerns. One has to do with the implementation of a major theme of *Lumen Gentium,* the other with the implementation of *Gaudium et Spes.*

Our first concern has to do with that aspect of *Lumen Gentium,* which is addressed by the third of our distinguished Relator's four *Argumenta Specialia.* [The church as Communion was the third in Cardinal Godfried Danneel's list of four special themes.] The question of Collegiality and the relationship of the Local Church to the Universal Church is a major internal question, which is causing sufficient anxiety and wasting enough energy to distract the Church from what should be its major concerns. From the first moment of his pontificate the Holy Father stressed the importance of Collegiality. His very first encyclical [*Redemptor Hominis 1979*] spoke of it at length [No 5]. Diversity among the Local Churches and the principle of subsidiarity argue that local solutions do not jeopardize the unity of the Local Churches with and under the Holy Father. Bishops and theologians sometimes get the impression that their orthodoxy is questioned lightly and that their difficulties and industry are not appreciated. This leads to a loss of trust which only damages the Church. We welcome the emphasis given by the esteemed Relator to the relationship between the Universal Church and the Particular Churches. We see the need for an even more refined theology [of] and more effective use of Episcopal Conferences.

Our second concern has to do with *Gaudium et Spes.* In *Catechesi Tradendae* [an apostolic exhortation of 1979] the Holy Father wrote of the secularization of our society. He described ours as a world which largely ignores God. It is a world in which too often there is 'indifferentism' or even contempt for religion as if it were incompatible with scientific progress (No 57). Secularisation, in the West and increasingly in every part of the world, is one significant phenomenon at the basis of most of the problems confronting the Church since the Second Vatican Council. Personal [salvation] and global salvation are being sought outside the Church, or along ways only loosely related to the Church, which rightly calls herself the 'sacrament of salvation'. *Gaudium et Spes* ushered in a transformation in our attitudes to the world. However, its message, or the best of our thinking based on it, has not succeeded in giving enough men and women a sufficiently clear and inspiring vision of the Church's role in the world of our time. Too many people, even among Catholics, find the Church peripheral to their concerns. It has been said but it cannot be exaggerated the task of translating the Council's theology of the Church into action has only begun. The great merit of the Synod will be the encouragement it gives to those who are anxious to complete the task. Our efforts will be strengthened enormously if they are linked with the preparation of our Local Churches for the 1987 Synod of the Laity.

The Conference of Australian Bishops will be glad to learn that *Quaenam est mission pro mundo huius temporis*? (What is the mission of the Church for the world today?) has been submitted to our consideration by the Relator as one of the four *Argumenta Specialis* [the fourth in Cardinal Danneels's list of special themes]. Page 12 of the *Relatio* describes vividly how the world's problems have worsened in the twenty years since the Council. It names three kinds of societies [rich countries, developing countries, and countries where the church is persecuted], each with its own special problems. For each the Church needs to search for and shape an answer to the only ultimate question: *Quis est Christus pro mundo huius temporis?* (Who is Christ for the world of today?)."

[For a full account of the 1985 Synod, see G Caprile, *II Sinodo dei Vescovi Seconda Assemblea Generale Straordinaria (24 novembre-8 decembre 1985)* (Rome: Civiltà Cattolica, 1986.]

Appendix 2

Statement of Conclusions

INTERDICASTERIAL MEETING
WITH A REPRESENTATION OF THE AUSTRALIAN BISHOPS
Statement of Conclusions

1. INTRODUCTION

1. Purpose of the Meeting.

Continuing the positive practice already established with other
Episcopal Conferences, at the wish of the Holy Father a meeting was
organized between some of the Dicasteries of the Roman Curia and a
significant representation of archbishops and bishops from Australia,
in connection with their *ad limina* visit, and on the occasion of the
Special Assembly of the Synod of Bishops for Oceania. The meeting was
conducted in the form of a dialogue aimed at better understanding the
situation of the Church in Australia, and at providing an opportunity
for a fraternal exchange of views and proposals.

It was recognized at the outset that, while the meeting may have
been occasioned by challenges facing the Church in Australia, many
of the issues discussed are problems that are found in other parts
of the Church throughout the world as well. Furthermore, these
deliberations covered only some areas of concern and were not
intended to deal with every aspect and dimension of the life of the
Church in Australia.

2. The Laity.

The role of the laity in the Church in Australia was regularly discussed
during this four-day meeting. Their vital commitment to the mission
of the Church in the world and their generous collaboration with
bishops, priests and religious in serving the needs of their parishes
and dioceses was often acknowledged with great gratitude. It is hoped
that the reflections in this document on the present situation of the
Church in Australia and on the ministry of bishops, priests and
religious will be of assistance to the laity themselves. The bishops of
Australia hope that any further renewal of the Church which these
deliberations bring about will support the laity in living their unique
role in the mission of the Church which flows from their consecration
in the sacraments of Baptism and Confirmation.

II. THE CURRENT SITUATION OF THE CHURCH IN AUSTRALIA

3. Positive Aspects

The discussion began by recognizing the path already travelled by the Church in Australia in response to the word of God and to the reforms initiated by the Second Vatican Council:

— the membership of the Catholic Church in Australia has increased numerically, making it the single largest Christian Church there. This has in turn created a great responsibility and duty for the Church with respect to the society in which she finds herself. The intense collaboration between the bishops, priests, religious and laity; the increase in active participation in liturgical celebrations; the network of Catholic schools; the presence of numerous centres of theological formation; and the extensive and comprehensive involvement of the Church in the corporal works of mercy, as well as its willingness to be a prophetic voice on social justice issues when needed, are all positive factors that enliven both the ecclesiastical community and society at large;

— from the beginning of its history, Australia, despite the tragic history of European interaction with the aboriginal people and the recent brief resurgence of racism, has succeeded with its spirit of tolerance and solidarity in amalgamating into one the diverse ethnic groups, cultures and traditions of the peoples who have immigrated to that continent;

— one finds among the faithful in Australia, and in society as a whole, a search for authenticity and spirituality which calls for pastoral dedication on the part of priests, consecrated persons and laity well-formed as collaborators with the ordained ministers. The assembly would here like to express its appreciation, esteem and support for their priestly brothers who carry the weight of the daily pastoral care of the faithful, and to express grateful appreciation for the men and women religious who have made such an important contribution throughout the history of Australia down to the present day by the example of their life of prayer in the midst of the People of God, and by their apostolic works, serving the mission of the Church in education, service of the poor and care for the sick and aged.

4. Weaknesses.

A Crisis in Faith. There is a crisis in faith which has as its basis, as the Encyclical Letter *Fides et Ratio* makes clear, a crisis concerning the ability to know the truth. The crisis of faith is world-wide. It is manifested in Australia by the rise in the number of people with no religion and the decline in church practice. The tolerance characteristic of Australian society naturally affects the Church also. While it has many positive elements, tolerance of and openness to all opinions and perspectives on the truth can lead to indifference, to the acceptance of any opinion or activity as long as it does not impact adversely on other people. It can also lead to a reluctance in claiming that any particular affirmation, belief or conviction is true. The loss of confidence in one's ability to know the truth inevitably involves a crisis of faith in God. All ideas about God, including the denial of his existence, become equally acceptable. This makes it very difficult to affirm that the God revealed in Sacred Scripture is indeed the one true God. There also appears to be a weakening of faith in eternal life, replaced by such things as social utopias and re-incarnation. This crisis of faith and truth provide the context for the following problems.

5. A Crisis in Christology

This crisis of truth is also a crisis in the profession of God as Person— the God of Abraham—and of Jesus as the true God, in such wise that one is able to say 'I know God'. It follows naturally then, that Christology is also in something of a crisis. Generally throughout the world, there is evidence of a weakening of faith in Christ, as well as a distortion of some doctrines based on the Scriptures and the early Councils of the Church. These modifications to Christology take two directions: in the first, a re-fashioning of Jesus into a great prophet of humanity, who, for example questions the rules of religion; in the other, substituting a pneumatological economy for the flesh and blood reality of Christ, true God and true man. Indeed, some aspects of feminist scholarship can lead to a rejection of the privileged place given to the scriptural language describing the Trinity and to Jesus' own teaching, and can even lead to rejection of the Trinity itself. The claims of other religions and non-religious movements can result in a blurring of the divinity or of the unique salvific role of Christ.

6. Challenges to Christian Anthropology.

Behind the above-mentioned elements is a profound paradigmatic change in anthropology that is opposed to classical anthropology. It is characterised, for example, by an extreme individualism, seen especially in a concept of conscience that elevates the individual conscience to the level of an absolute, thus raising the subjective criterion above all objective factors and having no point of reference beyond itself. Another example is a change in the relations between creation, nature, body and spirit, resulting in certain forms of feminism which express an anthropology profoundly different from classical anthropology.

7. Moral Problems.

From this paradigmatic change in anthropology, there follow great problems for Christian morality: indifference to the poor, racial prejudice and violence, abortion, euthanasia, the legitimation of homosexual relationships and other immoral forms of sexual activity. For example, in an anthropological perspective which ignores the "specifically human meaning of the body" (Encyclical Letter *Veritatis Splendor* 50), heterosexuality and homosexuality come to be seen simply as two morally equivalent variations.

8. Problems in Ecclesiology.

There are ecclesiological problems that flow from the uncertainties mentioned above concerning God and Jesus Christ. For example, if Christ is nothing more than a great figure in history, who defies the rules, who is anti-ecclesial and who did not create a hierarchy, then it follows that the Church is of merely human origin, and, along with the re-interpretation of Revelation, the Church needs to be re-organised to make it more suited to the present day. Truth is no longer discovered in a Revelation already given, but is based on the shifting sands of majority and consensus.

9. Response to These Challenges.

The bishops are confident that, in communion with the college of bishops throughout the world, and with the assistance of the Catholic theological community in Australia, they will be able to respond to these trends. God, in revealing himself, has revealed Truth, and the bishops remain determined to make the face of God visible to the people of today. Formation at all levels must continue and must rely on instruments offered by the Church: above all, the word of God, the documents of the Second Vatican Council, the Catechism of the Catholic Church and the teachings of the Magisterium of the Church which offer timely indications for dealing with the different challenges mentioned.

III. THE BISHOP

10. The Role and Responsibilities of the Bishop.

The bishop, in his role as chief pastor in his diocese, proclaims the "Good News" of salvation by his life and witness to the saving message of Jesus Christ: a message of truth, hope and joy for the world. Like a good shepherd, the bishop is close to his people, which has always been a mark of the Australian bishop, and in his episcopal ministry he is ever mindful that he is at the service of the People of God.

While every bishop is himself a witness to the truth and is the 'visible source and foundation of unity in the particular Church' (Dogmatic Const. *Lumen gentium* 23), each bishop is a member of the one episcopate, the single and undivided body of bishops. The unity of the episcopate is therefore one of the constitutive elements of the unity of the Church, and the visible source of the unity of bishops is the Roman Pontiff, head of the episcopal body. It is the authentic communion of the individual bishop with the Successor of Peter which, in a certain sense, guarantees and ensures that the voice of the bishop speaks the word of the Church and so witnesses to the same revealed truth. The bishop is entrusted with specific responsibilities and duties which are at times difficult and indeed burdensome. In our day we are only too aware of the multitude of influences in our society which work not only against the gospel message of truth, but are even directly hostile to the Catholic Faith. The People of God look to their shepherds for guidance and leadership now more than ever in these confusing and increasingly secularised times. The bishop, as servant of the Gospel, is a beacon of light, leading people to Christ, who is the way, the truth and the life.

The principal means by which bishops carry out this mandate from Christ to build up the unity of His Mystical Body, is through the three fold office of teaching, sanctifying and governing, which every bishop is called to exercise.

To Teach

11. The bishop teaches clearly and effectively in union with the Holy Father and the Magisterium of the Church: 'the teaching of each bishop, taken individually, is exercised in communion with the Roman Pontiff, pastor of the universal Church and with the other bishops dispersed throughout the world or gathered in ecumenical council. Such communion is a condition for its authenticity' (Congregation for the Doctrine of the Faith, Instruction *Donum veritatis* 19; cf *Lumen gentium* 25). The People of God who are entrusted to their care have a right to receive authentic and clear Catholic teaching from those who represent the Church in its various institutions.

The bishops in Australia are intensely conscious that they are authentic teachers 'endowed with the authority of Christ' and that it is their grave responsibility, clearly and unambiguously, to proclaim the Church's teaching and to do all that they can to preserve the faithful from error. As the 'visible source and foundation of unity' in his diocese, the bishop is committed to fostering unity among the faithful and to preventing factions and divisions from developing among the People of God. The bishop may not tolerate error in matters of doctrine and morals or Church discipline, and true unity must never be at the expense of truth. This delicate tension between truth and unity is experienced by most Australian bishops. When such cases of tension arise, the bishops intend to overcome it, trying to identify the truth by all appropriate and available means, especially consulting their brother bishops and the Holy See, and striving to correct errors, not by blunt use of authority, but through dialogue and persuasion. Making their voice heard by all Catholics (let alone non-Catholics) is a major problem for bishops today. They recognise the importance of a free press and legitimate criticism and, for their part, will endeavour to collaborate more effectively with all responsible forms of the media in order to find new ways for effectively communicating the Gospel in today's world.

The bishops of Australia, as *testes veritatis*, are committed to teach the Catholic Faith in Australia. They are assisted in this task by theologians. The Magisterium and theology are both, each in its own way, necessary for the building up of the People of God. In summary yet essential terms, one can say that the theologian has the task of reflecting on Revelation with the instruments of critical reason and of exploring the contents of the Faith with the arguments proper to the intellectual process, but always within the context of the Faith of the Church and in communion with its Pastors. The Magisterium, on the other hand, taking into consideration sound theology, has the task of safeguarding, expounding and teaching the deposit of the Faith in its integrity; that is, of interpreting, with an authority which comes from Christ, the word of God, whether written or transmitted in the living Tradition of the Church.

To Sanctify

12. The bishop is the guardian of the sacraments, the means of sanctification for the faithful, particularly the Holy Eucharist, which is 'the source and summit of the Christian life' (*Lumen gentium* 11). The bishop is called upon to exercise vigilance over the celebration and administration of the sacraments in his diocese. He ensures the sacraments are administered according to the proper liturgical norms set forth by the Church. If he discovers that these norms are not being followed properly, with integrity and reverence, he acts quickly to correct the error or abuse.

The Australian bishops realize that the sacred Liturgy is at the heart of their pastoral responsibilities. In promoting authentic sacred Liturgy, they have to provide against the introduction of spurious elements on the one hand, while, on the other, encouraging a Liturgy that is living and vibrant according to the prescribed norms and in the spirit of the liturgical reform. Most important is the bishop's own life of prayer which sustains his whole ministry, especially his central role in the Liturgy of his diocese. He must constantly return to the wellsprings of prayer in order to be strengthened by God in the grace of the Holy Spirit for his own personal sanctification for the good of the Church.

To Govern

13. Minister of Unity and Communion.

The bishop, in his pastoral governance, is entrusted with the important task of cultivating deep communion within the particular Church which, in turn, contributes to communion in the universal Church and for each and all members of his diocese: priests, members of institutes of consecrated life and societies of apostolic life, the lay faithful and other diocesan groups and associations. As the minister of unity in the diocese, the bishop exercises an authority in the service of truth and love. The bishop receives his responsibility and duty to govern as a mandate from Christ himself and therefore keeps watch 'over the whole flock of which the Holy Spirit has appointed you overseers, in which you tend the Church of God that he acquired with his own blood' (Acts 20: 28).

14. The Bishop in the College of Bishops.

The bishop's duty to teach, sanctify and govern is a personal one, received by virtue of his episcopal consecration and the laying on of hands. This duty is by divine right, and cannot be surrendered to others. The Australian Catholic Bishops Conference is a forum where a local bishop can seek the assistance of his fellow bishops in pursuing his mission to proclaim the Gospel message (cf *Motu Proprio, Apostolos suos* 5-7, 14-24). In collaboration with his brother bishops in his own country and throughout the world, and in communion with the Successor of Saint Peter, the local bishop can build up and strengthen the Body of Christ in his own diocese.

15. The Bishop and his Collaborators.

In choosing their collaborators in the diocesan administration, in the seminary and in parishes, bishops need to make these appointments with a careful eye and with great attention, always giving emphasis to sanctity of life, orthodoxy and pastoral competence. Continual vigilance is imperative in order to safeguard the integrity of the Faith and to ensure that it is clearly taught and explained at all levels of diocesan life. The bishop maintains contact with his people at many levels and in many different contexts. It is his special care to demonstrate gratitude and appreciation, and to encourage the faithful in their endeavours as members of the Church, both in their striving for holiness and their charitable service to others. He keeps close contact with the many different diocesan agencies and apostolates under his care.

16. The Bishop and His Special Relationship with His Priests.

The bishop nourishes a special relationship with his priests, treating them as friends and collaborators, encouraging them in their work, promoting a sense of fraternity in the presbyterate, organizing retreats and promoting opportunities for their on-going education. The bishop himself receives support and encouragement from his priests by their dedication, priestly example and friendship. On the human level, the bishop can foster the positive identity of the priest by being present to him in a caring, personal, direct way, affording him all possible attention and time. As the priest is the closest and most indispensable collaborator of the bishop, he has a primary call on the bishop as his spiritual father, thus no care expended on him can ever be seen to be excessive.

The bishop's care for priests extends to a special concern for the promotion of all vocations, especially to the priesthood, not only locally, but also nationally. One initiative already taken is the national network of vocation directors in Australia — 'Catholic Vocations Ministry Australia'—which provides support, ideas and materials.

As a personal responsibility enjoined upon him for the welfare of his seminarians, the bishop gives his assistance to the rector and staff of the seminary especially in the choice of candidates for admission. The bishop must have assurance of the candidates' proper motivation for entrance to the seminary and their preparation (doctrinal, moral, spiritual, human and pastoral) for ordination. The diocesan bishop must have moral certainty of the suitability of the candidate in terms of doctrine, spiritual life and human qualities, before he is ordained to the diaconate. The bishop should never ordain a candidate if there is any serious doubt as to his suitability for Holy Orders.

17. The Mystery of the Cross in the Life of the Bishop.

In the world in which we live today, for a bishop to be a true shepherd, he is called to teach doctrinal truth with gentle firmness and profound humility, to sanctify by word and example, and to govern with fidelity and genuine authority. This will necessarily lead to suffering and the Cross. We know well that when the bearers of apostolic office dare to exercise authority which is theirs in matters of doctrine and morals, they become a sign of contradiction to the world. While this is indeed a real challenge for the bishop today, it is at the same time his source of grace, strength and deep joy. The greatest sign of contradiction is also the greatest sign of hope. For in the mystery of the Cross we learn a wisdom which transcends our own weakness and limitations; we learn that in Christ truth and love are one, and in Him we find the meaning of our vocation.

IV. THE PRIEST

18. The Current Context.

In viewing the priestly landscape of the Church in Australia, it is difficult not to be struck by the dedication of priests, labouring faithfully under sometimes trying and varied conditions. They are to be lauded and encouraged as they give of themselves so generously for their flocks. The culture of secularism, which is pervasive today, is not of assistance to the priest as he attempts to carry out his sacred duties in a context that can be challenging, even hostile and apathetic at times to his vocational identity and to the ministry he exercises in the name of Christ and of His Church.

19. The Identity of the Priest.

It is not to be wondered at that in such an ethos the identity of the priest needs a strong affirmation and almost constant clarification. The priest acts in the person of Christ the Head and the Shepherd (Apostolic Exhortation *Pastores dabo vobis* 15; Catechism of the Catholic Church No 875; *Interdicasterial Instruction On Certain Questions Regarding the Collaboration of the Non-ordained Faithful in the Sacred Ministry of Priests*, p 13, No 1). To ensure this understanding it is fundamental that correct intellectual, ascetical and doctrinal formation, as well as dutiful and inspired discipline be assured in Seminaries. This should also be continued throughout priestly ministry and life.

20. The Spiritual Life of the Priest.

An integral component of true priestly identity is priestly spirituality. It is not a separate element but is at the heart of the identity of the priest. Being a man of God living in the culture of secularism, with all the contemporary pastoral demands and burdens, it is easy for a priest to lose zeal, energy and perspective unless he is firmly rooted in the Spirit of the Living God. Time spent in pursuing the spiritual life is not time taken from pastoral activity but is rather the means of sustaining and enriching pastoral charity in the most meaningful way possible.

Among the principal elements of the priest's prayer life are the daily Eucharistic celebration, frequent confession and spiritual direction, the Liturgy of the Hours, examination of conscience, mental prayer, *lectio divina*, retreats, Marian devotions, the Rosary, the *Via crucis* and other pious exercises, and the fruitful reading of the lives of the saints (cf *Directory on the Ministry and Life of Priests* 39). Attention to the annual Day of Sanctification for Priests can also be a rewarding and sustaining experience for those whose ministry is so essential to the Church.

Priestly associations which foster fraternal support, promote holiness in the exercise of the ministry and foster the unity of clergy with one another and with their bishop, are to be encouraged. On the other hand, associations which are pressure groups or are not in harmony with the mission of the Church and show division rather than unity, must be eschewed as unhelpful to priestly ministry and not constructive to the unitive mission of the Church.

21. Continuing Formation.

The pastoral demands of the age, as well as the priest's personal development require that his intellectual formation must not be seen as something pertaining to the seminary period of life only, but must be seen as a continuing, on-going and permanent aspect of his personal response to his vocation. The priest then must personally develop a systematic approach to on-going study as well as participate in the opportunities provided by his bishop, the diocese and the Episcopal Conference for in-service training.

In fact, permanent, on-going formation is essential in constructively dealing with the above-mentioned issues and situations. In this regard, prayerful, systematic study and assimilation of recent documents of the Holy See will provide practical guidance and assistance in the challenging areas of priestly ministry and life. Among those of particular relevance and strongly recommended for attention are: *Pastores dabo vobis, Directory on the Ministry and Life of Priests, On Certain Questions Regarding the Collaboration of the Non-Ordained Faithful in the Sacred Ministry of Priests,* and *Directory for the Ministry and Life of Permanent Deacons.*

22. Pastoral Charity.

The priest is the man in the front lines. His armament is spiritual, intellectual and pastoral. Despite the many attempts to remove the figure of the priest from the centre of the lives of believers, the faithful treasure their relationships with their spiritual fathers, despite the "earthen vessels" priests are. Because of his closeness to his people and their lives, and as he is constantly being bombarded by the easy pragmatic solutions to difficult pastoral problems proffered by the culture of secularism, it is not always easy for the priest to call his people to embrace the prophetic stance of the children of light, yet this is what he must do without fail. No pastoral solution can be so called that is not flowing from God's Revelation as this is interpreted by the Magisterium of the Church. Thus a practice in pastoral life which is contrary to the teachings of Christ and His Church, is not an act of compassion, but rather is one that radically disorders pastoral charity and has long term negative consequences for the faithful and for the unity and identity of the priesthood and the Faith. Thus, the priest acts truly in *persona Christi* when he brings the fullness of the truth of the High Priest to the People of God whom he serves. It is only that pastoral truth which can really set them free.

23. Collaboration of the Lay Faithful.

Despite the goodwill involved, in a sometimes functional approach to priesthood, the identity of the priest has been further clouded when tasks have been entrusted to laity that belong to the ministerial priesthood. There has, at times, been a concomitant excessive involvement of the priest in areas that should be attended to by a committed and well-formed laity. This situation has had the effect of blurring the lines between the baptismal priesthood and the ministerial priesthood with negative effects on both. Clarity in this area is essential for many reasons, not least of which are the preservation of the authentic identity of both priest and laity, good order within the Church and the promotion of vocations.

24. Responsibility for Catechesis.

As the preaching of the word of God and catechesis is such an important part of priestly ministry, and so necessary for the salvation of souls, priests must be aware of their responsibility in these areas. The matter of catechesis cannot be left solely in the hands of others, no matter how skilled they be. The transmission of the Faith is to be actively attended to by priests as this is an essential part of their ministry. Priests will find the Catechism of the Catholic Church and the Directory for Catechesis invaluable aids in carrying out their responsibilities in this area as well as a source of enrichment for their personal lives.

V. CONSECRATED PERSONS

25. Consecrated Life in Australia.

Consecrated life, as evidenced by its universal presence and evangelical witness, is not isolated and marginal but a reality which affects the whole Church. Because consecrated life manifests the inner nature of the Christian calling and has contributed significantly to the vitality of the Church in Australia, she is committed to supporting it. Elsewhere in this document, the great contributions of religious, oftentimes as pioneering innovators and at great personal and community sacrifice, have been recognised.

26. Vocations Decline.

The Church in Australia is undergoing a difficult period due to the decline of vocations to the consecrated life. In light of this challenge, the Church must pray for vocations. The Lord always heeds the prayer which issues from the Church and, in responding, always far exceeds our expectations. In addition to prayer (cf. Matt 9:37-38), and to heeding the invitation of Jesus to 'Come and see' (John 1:39), a primary responsibility of all consecrated men and women is to propose the ideal of the following of Christ, and then to support the response to the Spirit's action in the heart of those who are called.

27. Authenticity and Transparency of Life Attract the Young.

Consecrated persons need to show forth a life which is recognised for its transparency and authenticity, and this in regard to their spirituality, their ministry and their community living. All must be able to recognise in them the fact that they are distinguished by an intense spiritual life sustained by prayer, especially by the Eucharist, by fidelity to the evangelical counsels and by ascesis. Consecrated persons are to be 'experts in God', and in His ways. Their whole being ought to be suffused with the divine presence. When people approach religious, they should find men and women whose lives bespeak union with God, and whose lives invite others into that union.

Consecrated persons express the person of Christ—Christ saving and redeeming, Christ forgiving, Christ healing, Christ teaching, Christ in every gesture of compassion toward those in need, Christ loving his people. But there is still more to the apostolate. As the Apostolic Exhortation *Vita Consecrata* puts it: 'More than in any activity, the apostolate consists in the witness of one's own complete dedication to the Lord's saving will, a dedication nourished by the practice of prayer and of penance' (No 44). 'The very purpose of consecrated life is conformity to the Lord Jesus in his total self giving' (*Vita Consecrata,* No 65).

The authenticity and transparency of community life are a striking expression in our time of the fact that living together in grace, with one mind and one heart, is not merely a possibility, but a reality. The whole Church greatly depends on the witness of communities filled 'with joy and with the Holy Spirit" (Acts 13: 52). Such authentic common living, where each one supports and forgives the other, witnesses to the presence of Jesus and speaks directly to the deep yearnings of the heart. For members of Institutes of consecrated life, community life is of the essence of their vocation.

When consecrated persons live their vocation with authenticity and transparency, they are an example of total commitment to the Gospel lived in the spirit of their Founders. This example, joined with constant prayer, is a very effective vocational promotion program. As Pope Paul VI reminded us, people of our age, especially the young, have become sceptical of mere words, and are convinced by words only when these are accompanied by example (cf Apostolic Exhortation *Evangelii Nuntiandi*, No 41). The example of consecrated persons evidently rooted in Christ is the best way to convince and inspire young people, inviting them to follow Christ in religious Institutes.

28. Formation.

Formation, both initial and ongoing, is aimed at showing in the various moments of life that religious belong totally and joyfully to the Lord. Both formators and those being formed need clarity regarding the charism of the Institute. For this purpose, the establishment of structures to train those responsible for formation would be helpful. The whole person needs to be formed, in every aspect of one's being, human, cultural, spiritual, and pastoral. Ongoing formation for every member is an intrinsic requirement of consecrated life. Institutes have made great efforts in this area. As a result, religious are often found in solidarity with the most marginal elements of society and in new ministries. In some instances, however, problems have arisen because the selection of formators or of centres for ongoing formation was not made in view of full communion with the Magisterium of the Church.

29. Fragmentation.

Because of a changing world and changing expectations, of a desire to be closer to the people or to one's work, or because of the cost of maintaining large buildings, a number of religious have, with permission of their superiors, opted to leave communities in order to live in apartments or privately. Such an option, however, fragments the life and witness of an Institute. It is not enough that individual members of Institutes engage in employment in the secular sphere and find living accommodations singly. It is not enough that religious engage in any work whatsoever, even if they do this "in the spirit of the Founder." Such general dispersal of members and of energies prejudices the corporate witness of an Institute which was founded with a specific charism for a specific purpose. Such charisms are given by the Holy Spirit for the good of the entire Church, and religious need to be faithful to them.

30. Associate Members.

The fragmentation of Institutes is often accompanied by a practical redefinition of members. Various Institutes now have associate members or collaborators, who share for a period of time the Institute's community life and its dedication to prayer and the apostolate. This needs to be arranged in such a way, however, that the identity of the Institute in its internal life is not harmed. Though the collaboration of associates allows works conducted by the Institutes to continue, it needs to be recognised that lay associates are not members of the Institute in the way that professed members are. Associate members are not an alternative to the vocations decline.

31. Communion.

Vita Consecrata expresses a rich mystery in simple terms: 'The Church is essentially a mystery of communion, "a people made one with the unity of the Father, the Son and the Holy Spirit"' (No 41). This communion is expressed at every level of her life. It is communion that distinguishes her as a body from all other bodies, for communion is not mere regulation, but is an ordering of relationships, in charity, within the Body of Christ. Each member of the Body has a specific importance and role. The Church does not create her own ordering and structuring, but receives them from Christ himself.

32. Experts of Communion.

In light of the Council's strong teaching about communion, 'consecrated persons are asked to be true experts of communion and to practise the spirituality of communion . . . The sense of ecclesial communion, developing into a spirituality of communion, promotes a way of thinking, speaking and acting which enables the Church to grow in depth and extension' (*Vita Consecrata,* No 46). Indeed, 'the Church was not established to be an organization for activity, but rather to give witness as the living Body of Christ' (S. Congregation for Religious and Secular Institutes & S. Congregation for Bishops, Directive Note *Mutuae Relationes,* No 20). In the Founders and Foundresses we see a constant and lively sense of the Church, which they manifest by their full participation in all aspects of the Church's life and in their great cooperation with and ready obedience to the bishops, especially to the Roman Pontiff.

33. Consecrated Life in the Particular Church.

Consecrated persons must be in communion with their Pastors, and this at the level of both the particular Church and the universal Church. Consecrated persons are called to be mindful of the ancient dictum: *sentire cum Ecclesia*, to live and think and love with the Church. In this regard, *Vita Consecrata* is very explicit. 'A distinctive aspect of ecclesial communion is allegiance of mind and heart to the Magisterium of the bishops, an allegiance which must be lived honestly and clearly testified to before the People of God by all consecrated persons, especially those involved in theological research, teaching, publishing, catechesis and the use of the means of social communication. Because consecrated persons have a special place in the Church, their attitude in this regard is of immense importance for the whole People of God' (*Vita Consecrata,* No 46).

The special place of consecrated persons in the Body is recognised by the Church when she erects the Institutes, confirms their Constitutions, entrusts an apostolate to the community and recognises the profession of each member. Because the one Faith underlies the Church's life, all members must be in union with the teaching of the Church. In matters of the Faith, communion rules out such concepts as 'loyal opposition', or 'faithful subversion'. The faithful strive to deepen their understanding of the Faith, not to oppose it or to subvert it. Institutions, especially in the field of education, which are under the authority of consecrated persons should assure that lecturers, both those who are on staff and those who are invited, serve, in union with the Church, to deepen the understanding of Faith.

34. The Role of the Bishop.

Institutes, at the time of their founding, are notably in communion with the local bishop. When an Institute acquires the status of diocesan right, the bishop of the generalate house has particular responsibilities which are specified in common law; for Institutes of pontifical right, the Holy See has specific responsibilities (cf canon 589-96). All Institutes, however, are to integrate their pastoral activity within the overall pastoral plan of the diocese in which they are present and are to minister in communion with the bishop. He is responsible for discerning and respecting, promoting and coordinating all charisms in the diocese, including the charisms of the

Institutes of both pontifical and diocesan right. He needs to be willing to intervene when problems arise, and, according to circumstances, he may also seek the collaboration of other bishops involved, or of the Episcopal Conference, or of the appropriate Dicastery of the Holy See. Conferences of major superiors (cf canon 708-709) are formed to help each Institute achieve its purpose and to coordinate and cooperate with the Conference of Bishops and with individual bishops. These Conferences are not organs of parallel pastoral authority.

35. Public Status of Religious.

While relations between the bishops and the major superiors have been, generally, good, with most problems resolved by dialogue and understanding, still several difficulties have emerged with importance for the Church. Religious, by reason of their public state in the Church, are prominent in the eyes of the faithful and of the secular media. This prominence requires a more evident fidelity to the Magisterium than is required of ordinary faithful. What is true of all religious is even more true of major superiors, by reason of their office. What is true of major superiors is still more true of a conference of major superiors erected by the Holy See.

36. Some Concerns.

The Congregation for Institutes of Consecrated Life and for Societies of Apostolic Life has shared with the bishops several concerns about situations in Australia, and asks them to dialogue with the major superiors regarding such points as promoting prayer for ecclesial vocations, including those of consecrated life, and deepening both communion within the Church and assent to the Magisterium regarding such areas as the non-ordination of women to the priesthood, the theology of the Church and of the sacraments of faith, the theology of communion and moral problems.

VI. THE SACRED LITURGY AND THE SACRAMENTS

37. Gains and Future Prospects.

The work of renewal of the Church in Australia has made progress largely by means of the renewal of the Liturgy and the people's fuller participation in liturgical celebration.

In Australia, as elsewhere, experience bears out the Holy Father's observation that the vast majority of 'the pastors and the Christian people have accepted the liturgical reform in a spirit of obedience and indeed joyful fervour. For this we should give thanks to God for that passage of the Holy Spirit through the Church which the liturgical renewal has been' (Apostolic Letter *Vigesimus Quintus Annus*, No 12).

It is a pressing need that these positive results be built upon. The Australian Catholic Bishops Conference has already planned to set aside significant resources to produce educational materials on the Mass which can be used at a diocesan or parish level. Other concrete initiatives will also be devised to ensure the quality and authentic fidelity of liturgical celebration and sacramental practice as the third Christian millennium dawns.

38. The True Meaning of the Sacred Liturgy.

It is important that the sacred Liturgy as a whole be appreciated in all its profundity and mystery. The Liturgy is more than a recollection of past events, a means of imparting knowledge or a vehicle for expressing the faith and life of the celebrating community. It is fundamentally the manifestation of God's initiative and his loving will to save, expressed in the Paschal Mystery of our Lord Jesus Christ, made present and efficacious by the Holy Spirit. In the Liturgy, Christ's work is carried forward by the Church until the end of time.

The Council spoke therefore of the Liturgy as the summit or high-point toward which the activity of the Church tends and the fountainhead from which all her strength flows (cf. Constitution *Sacrosanctum Concilium* 10; cf. Apostolic Letter *Dies Domini*, No 32). By their participation in the earthly Liturgy all the faithful are formed in right conduct and prepared for that Liturgy in the heavenly city to which we journey as pilgrims (cf *Sacrosanctum Concilium*, No 8; *Dies Domini*, No 37).

39. The Liturgy: Act of Christ and of His Church.

The celebration of the Liturgy is therefore never a private action of the celebrant or of the community gathered in a particular place, but an act of the Church as such (cf. *Sacrosanctum Concilium*, No 26), in intimate union with Christ her Head. Accordingly, an insistence on 'good liturgy' is right and useful as long as the expression is not misunderstood as meaning a human virtuoso, external performance or 'choreography'. Rather, all participants should accommodate and subordinate themselves and their manner of thinking, acting and speaking to the great gift and mystery of God's Redemption, and to the person of Christ, our sole Saviour, with a special reverence for the Real Presence of Christ in the Holy Eucharist at the Mass and reserved in the tabernacle.

40. The Liturgy: Manifestation of the Nature of the Church.

Since it lies at the center of the Church's life, the Liturgy manifests the Church's very nature and directs it consciously and explicitly toward its ultimate goal. The Church is seen most perfectly in the celebration of the Eucharist, presided over by the bishop of the diocese, surrounded by his priests, deacons and the community of the faithful (cf. *Sacrosanctum Concilium*, No 26, 41; *Dies Domini*, No 34). This ideal phenomenon is realized in varying degrees in circumstances where the bishop is not able to be present and where he is represented ordinarily by a priest. Even in such circumstances, the bishop remains the essential point of reference and the celebration necessarily reflects the nature of the Church as a 'structured communion' whose nature is reflected in an 'ordered exercise of liturgical action' (*On Certain Questions Regarding the Collaboration of the Non-Ordained Faithful in the Sacred Ministry of Priests*, No 6 §§ 1-2; cf *Sacrosanctum Concilium*, No 26; *Lumen gentium*, Nos 10–11). It is when each takes part in the Liturgy according to his or her specific role in the Body of Christ that the whole Body is built up most effectively.

41. Authentic Promotion of the Liturgy.

In today's rapidly changing world it is all the more necessary to return constantly to the authentic teaching of the Church on the Liturgy, as found in the liturgical texts themselves and, among many other authoritative sources, as reaffirmed and explained in a lucid and accessible manner in the Catechism of the Catholic Church.

Many people today call for a more 'transcendental' Liturgy, and indeed liturgical celebrations must be permeated with a proper religious sense born of faith in unseen realities (cf *Dies Domini*, No 43). Care must be given to the beauty and elegance of the vestments, sacred vessels, surroundings, furnishings, and to the eloquence of the words and actions themselves, to factors which will encourage the participation of the faithful, and to catechesis concerning the meaning of the liturgical signs (cf. *Sacrosanctum Concilium* 11, 14; S. Congregation for the Sacraments and Divine Worship, *Inaestimabile Donum*, Nos 16-17; *Dies Domini*, Nos 35).

At the same time the Liturgy must be a living event, accessible to the people. There is a need in catechesis, in all pastoral care and in liturgical celebration itself to involve all Catholics, above all the young, more fully in the Liturgy and help them to understand and live out its meaning. The Church in Australia, as in other countries, faces a notable decline in recent years in the numbers of Catholics attending Sunday Mass, a situation which calls for a pastoral response (cf *Dies Domini*, Nos 36, 46-49).

42. Weaknesses and Correctives.

A weakness in parish liturgical celebrations in Australia is the tendency on the part of some priests and parishes to make their own changes to liturgical texts and structures, whether by omissions, by additions or by substitutions, occasionally even in central texts such as the Eucharistic Prayer. Practices foreign to the tradition of the Roman Rite are not to be introduced on the private initiative of priests, who are ministers and servants, rather than masters of the sacred Rites (*Sacrosanctum Concilium*, No 22 § 3; Instruction *Inaestimabile Donum*, No 5). Any unauthorized changes, while perhaps well-intentioned, are nevertheless seriously misguided. The bishops of Australia, then, will continue to put their energy above all into education, while correcting these abuses individually. Such education and corrective action are also the effective means for the pastoral care of those at the parish level who criticize and report the efforts of others, sometimes justly, but sometimes in a judgmental, selective, ill-informed and unproductive manner.

A return to a real sense of the Church and of Liturgy is the most effective path to overcoming obstinacy in personal tastes and to setting aside arbitrary action, fault-finding, conflict and division. Both in regard to the Liturgy and other questions in the life of the Church, there is a need for fidelity to the mind of the Church and willingness to dialogue with others, above all the pastors and bishops.

43. Liturgical Translations.

For authenticity in the Liturgy, it is essential that the translation of the texts not be so much a work of 'creativity' as of a faithful and exact vernacular rendering of the original text, which itself is the fruit of the liturgical renewal and draws upon centuries of cultural and ecclesial experience.

While fully respecting the genius of each language and avoiding a rigid literalism, an appropriate translation also carefully avoids paraphrase, gloss or interpretation. The explanation of the riches contained within the liturgical texts is the concern not of liturgical translation, but of the homily and of sustained catechesis. The substantial unity of the Roman Rite is an expression of the theological realities of communion and of ecclesial unity and contributes to the rich plurality of the Church. Within their respective historical and cultural contexts, of course, the same may be said for the other Catholic liturgical families of venerable antiquity. To this end, the practice of the recognitio of the Holy See as desired by the Second Vatican Council (cf. *Sacrosanctum Concilium* 36; cf. S. Congregration of Rites, Instruction *Inter Oecumenici*, No 20-31; canon 838) stands as a guarantee of the authenticity of the translations and their fidelity to the original texts. By means of this practice, a concrete sign of the bond of communion between the successor of Peter and the successors of the other Apostles, translations become truly the expression in the local Churches of the heritage of the universal Church. The Holy See may not divest itself of this responsibility, and the bishops, who bear the responsibility of overseeing and approving the translations, likewise regard their own role as a direct and solemn trust. In this delicate work, the Australian Catholic Bishops Conference will continue to cooperate in English-language questions in so far as possible with other English-speaking Episcopal Conferences.

44. The Sense of Sin.

Many bishops in Australia and elsewhere have noted a decline in the sense of sin, stemming from the deeper reality of a crisis of faith, and having grave repercussions for the sacrament of Penance. The situation calls for a renewed and energetic catechesis on the very nature of sin as opposed to salvation, and thus for a focus in sacramental praxis not only on the consolation and encouragement of the faithful, but also on instilling a true sense of contrition, of authentic sorrow for their own sins. Catholics should come to understand more deeply Jesus' death as a redeeming sacrifice and an act of perfect worship of the Father effecting the remission of sins. A failure to appreciate this supreme grace would undermine the whole of Christian life. They should be made fully aware, too, of the indispensable role in the reconciliation of sinners which Christ has entrusted to His Church.

45. The Sacrament of Penance or Reconciliation.

Individual confession and absolution remains the "sole ordinary means by which one of the faithful who is conscious of grave sin is reconciled with God and with the Church" (canon 960; cf *Rituale Romanum, Ordo Paenitentiae,* No 31; canon 960; *Catechism of the Catholic Church,* 1484). Energetic efforts are to be made to avoid any risk that this traditional practice of the sacrament of Penance fall into disuse.

The communal celebration of Penance with individual confessions and absolution should be encouraged especially in Advent and Lent, but it cannot be allowed to prevent regular, ready access to the traditional form for all who desire it. Unfortunately, communal celebrations have not infrequently occasioned an illegitimate use of general absolution. This illegitimate use, like other abuses in the administration of the sacrament of Penance, is to be eliminated. The teaching of the Church is reflected in precise terms in the requirements of the *Code of Canon Law* (cf. esp. canons 959-964). In particular it is clear that 'A sufficient necessity is not . . . considered to exist when confessors cannot be available merely because of a great gathering of penitents, such as can occur on some major feastday or pilgrimage' (canon 961 § 1).

The bishops will exercise renewed vigilance on these matters for the future, aware that departures from the authentic tradition do great wrong to the Church and to individual Catholics.

46. Appropriate Liturgical Formation.

So that the faithful may be sure to receive from their priests an authentic and informed ministry and teaching, insistence will continue to be placed upon the stipulation of the Council's Constitution

Sacrosanctum Concilium (No 16), that the sacred Liturgy be regarded as one of the principal subjects in major seminaries, a requirement that is the subject of further guidelines offered by the Sacred Congregation for Catholic Education's Instruction, *In ecclesiasticam* (3 June 1979).

Such liturgical formation needs to be followed through in all the different sections of the Catholic community and at the various levels in a consistent and permanent fashion. Only in this way will communities and individuals be brought to a deeper understanding of the Liturgy. Likewise, only by sustained programs of this kind can the Church in Australia be assured of a sufficient pool of resource persons to sustain the different areas of liturgical development.

VII. EDUCATION AND EVANGELIZATION

47. Evangelization.

While it is clear that education is not the only means of evangelization, it has been, and continues to be, in the Australian context, a very important one. Among other means, a competent use of the mass media figures as well in this area. We are mindful too of the words of Pope Paul VI: 'Techniques of evangelization are good, but even the most advanced ones could not replace the gentle action of the Spirit' (*Evangelii nuntiandi*, No 75).

Preparation for the Priesthood

48. Idea of the Priesthood.

Preparation for the priesthood takes place in the seminary which is 'an educational community, indeed a particular educating community' (*Pastores dabo vobis*, No 61). It is essential for the seminary to achieve its task, that the education imparted there be characterized by a clear and authentic idea of the ministerial priesthood, its specificity and its relationship to the priesthood of all the baptized (cf *Lumen gentium*, No 10). This idea, in turn, should be based on a sound Christology and ecclesiology, as transmitted by the Church. These ideas should be clear in the minds of both the teachers and the students.

49. Co-workers of the Bishop.

Candidates for the priesthood should be instilled with the idea that they will be the appreciated co-workers of their bishops and the bearers of the joy of the Gospel to the People of God. They are to be the bishops' collaborators in the work of evangelizing, sharing also, in virtue of their ordination and mission, in the three-fold task of teaching, sanctifying and shepherding.

50. Priesthood and Celibacy.

Seminarians should be helped spiritually, and in other appropriate ways, to nourish a conviction of the relationship of celibacy to their priestly vocation, and its fruitfulness in the priestly ministry, and to commit themselves to its observance.

51. Formation.

The Apostolic Exhortation *Pastores dabo vobis* proposes the essential aspects for a well-integrated formation of candidates for the priesthood in the context of today's world. These are: human formation as its basis; spiritual formation as the heart, to achieve union with God in Christ; intellectual formation containing a strong philosophical component, as an instrument for the understanding of the Faith; and pastoral formation, as its goal, to bring about in the priest a sharing in Christ's own pastoral charity.

Priestly formation requires not only formation of the candidates for the priesthood but also that of the educators in the seminary. The choice and preparation of the priests who will be rectors, spiritual directors and other members of the seminary's formation team require a special attention.

52. The Scrutinies.

For the good of individuals and of the whole Church, careful attention is to be given to the considerations set out by the recent circular of the Congregation for Divine Worship and the Discipline of the Sacraments regarding the *Scrutinies* to be held before each of the major steps in the advancement of candidates to Holy Orders. A candidate for the diaconate or the priesthood must be totally free before God and the Church to assume the responsibility of ordained ministry. For his part the diocesan Bishop must have a moral certainty of the suitability and worthiness of the candidate in terms of doctrine, spiritual life and human qualities, before the man is ordained to the diaconate.

53. Vocations.

Pastoral work, especially among the young, should have a vocation-promoting dimension to it. The 'soil' for welcoming the seed of vocations should also be cultivated among parents and within the family generally. The supernatural means of vocational promotion should underlie all such efforts, and the ecclesial sense of vocation should be clear. The idea of a continental congress for Australia on vocations, such as has been held for Latin America and for Europe merits consideration.

54. The Apostolic Visitation.

The Apostolic Visitation of the seminaries of Australia, interrupted in 1997, should resume as soon as is feasible.

Tertiary Education

55. The Ecclesiastical Faculty.

The curricula leading to ecclesiastical degrees at the Catholic Institute of Sydney, which was erected by the Holy See, should be utilized to the fullest extent possible. This is important because such a faculty, with its particular structure, has 'the aim of profoundly studying and systematically explaining, according to the scientific method proper to it, Catholic doctrine, derived with the greatest care from divine revelation. It has the further aim of carefully seeking the solution to human problems in the light of that same revelation' (Apostolic Constitution *Sapientia christiana*, No 66). Both the Chancellor and the Holy See have the right and the duty to safeguard the Catholic character of an ecclesiastical faculty.

56. Catholic Universities.

The recent establishment of two Catholic universities in Australia merits recognition, and they are deserving of the support of the whole Catholic population, particularly of those parts which are in the geographical areas where the Universities are located. The university itself and the bishops should be attentive to safeguarding the university's Catholic identity. The Catholic university 'makes an important contribution to the Church's work of evangelization. It is a living institutional witness to Christ and His message, in cultures marked by secularism' (Apostolic Constitution *Ex corde Ecclesiae,* No 49). The Catholic university performs this service in accordance with its nature as a university.

57. University Pastoral Ministry.

Of significant importance as well is the pastoral care offered to Catholic students, professors and staff in civil universities. Men and women should be carefully selected and suitably prepared for this work, which aims at a Catholic formation of persons in the university world that is congruent with their secular academic preparation.

58. Church Authority and Theological Formation.

The local ecclesiastical authority, who may seek the assistance of the Holy See in the matter, should follow with understanding and with active concern the question of the doctrinal soundness of the theological formation given either in departments of theology in Catholic universities or in other theological centres, called 'theological faculties' in Australia.

59. Formational Purpose.

While differing in some aspects of their functions and aims, all of these institutions and activities connected with tertiary education have precise formational intentions. They aim at an integral formation of persons, not just their preparation for a professional task. They aim as well at preparing leaders for the Church and for society at large who will be both competent in their respective fields and faithful in Catholic belief and behaviour. The fidelity to the Church's Magisterium in these institutions and in the publications by their professors will be an important gauge of the Catholic life of the nation today and an influence on it in the future.

Education in Catholic schools

60. Contribution of the Catholic Schools.

Catholic schools have made a tremendous contribution to the Church in Australia throughout its history, and continue to do so today. The Catholic school system is active and flourishing, well organized and generally of high quality, providing one of the foremost means of evangelization and of instructing young people in the Faith. Evangelization programs must take account of the increasing secularization of students, who no longer receive the basic faith formation at home as in the past and of the increasing number of non-Catholic students. Care is needed to ensure that a desire to be welcoming to all does not compromise the Catholic identity of the school.

61. Formation of Lay Teachers.

The rapid loss of religious men and women teaching in the schools has had an impact on the atmosphere and Catholic identity of the school. The lay teachers who have taken their places must be properly formed in the Faith, especially principals and those who teach religion. Much has already been achieved in this regard. Because Catholic school education involves interior education and formation in the Faith, a significant proportion of the staff should be practising Catholics, who look upon themselves as educators in the Faith as well as teachers of their specific subjects. All staff, both Catholic and non-Catholic, should support the religious formation of the students and the educational goals of the school.

62. The Place of the Catholic School in the Local Church.

The Catholic school does not exist in isolation, but is part of the wider faith community of the parish and the diocese. Students, teachers and parents should all be conscious of the school as a part of the ecclesial community, first in the parish, then in the diocese and the universal Church. For many children, the school rather than the parish represents their Church and is their only contact with the Church. Catholic education should lead to full participation and involvement in the Church—the Church which, at the local level, is centred in the parish. There need to be strong partnerships built between parish and educational programs; the parish should support the school as one of its most important apostolic works and the school should assist the parish in forming young people in their faith.

63. Atmosphere.

In a Catholic school, the educational climate should be permeated throughout by a Christian way of thought and life. Students should know as soon as they set foot in a Catholic school that they are in a different environment, one illuminated by the light of faith and having its own unique characteristics. Particular attention should be given in the school to prayer and the celebration of the sacraments.

VIII. CONCLUSION

The aim of the meeting between various Dicasteries of the Holy See and bishops representing the Australian Catholic Bishops Conference was to arrive at a deeper understanding of the situation of the Church in Australia in the area of doctrine and morals, the liturgy, the role of the bishop, evangelization and mission, the priesthood and religious life, and Catholic education. The vitality of the Church in this great continent was brought into full relief during the meeting, as were some of the challenges facing the Australian bishops, but most evident was the common desire to work together to overcome the problems. The meeting was therefore a great 'moment' of authentic *affectus collegialis* between the Church in Australia and the primary collaborators of the Roman Pontiff. To preserve and ever deepen this communion, the spirit of collaboration experienced in the meeting must continue into the future. The fraternal nature of this exchange of views will assist the regular cooperation between the Holy See and the Australian Catholic Bishops Conference, and the proposals will provide the context, at least in part, for their collaboration. By building on the good will and sustained efforts of many priests, deacons, religious and lay faithful, the Church in Australia will live out with ever greater fidelity the mystery of Christ in communion with the universal Church.

The bishops, as devoted shepherds of the Church in Australia, are well aware of its strengths and its weaknesses, and remain deeply committed to its service. They are confident that, with the assistance of the theological community and so many loyal priests, religious and lay faithful, along with the support and guidance of the Holy See, they will be well prepared to meet the challenges that confront them. This common labour is before all else a cooperation with the Grace of the Holy Spirit, each one praying for the wisdom always to give first consideration to the honour of God and the salvation of souls, and by begging for the strength needed for the task of building up the Body of Christ, so that all efforts may bear abundant fruit for the mission of the Church in Australia and beyond.

PARTICIPANTS

The participants from the Roman Curia were: His Eminence Cardinal Joseph Ratzinger, Prefect of the Congregation for the Doctrine of the Faith; His Eminence Cardinal Jorge Medina Estévez, Prefect of the Congregation for Divine Worship and the Discipline of the Sacraments; His Eminence Cardinal Lucas Moreira Neves, Prefect of the Congregation for Bishops; His Eminence Cardinal Darío Castrillón Hoyos, Prefect of the Congregation for Clergy; His Eminence Cardinal Eduardo Martínez Somalo, Prefect of the Congregation for Institutes of Consecrated Life and for Societies of Apostolic Life; His Eminence Cardinal Pio Laghi, Prefect of the Congregation for Catholic Education; His Excellency, the Most Reverend Tarcisio Bertone, Secretary of the Congregation for the Doctrine of the Faith; His Excellency, the Most Reverend Geraldo Majella Agnelo, Secretary of the Congregation for Divine Worship and the Discipline of the Sacraments; His Excellency, the Most Reverend Francesco Monterisi, Secretary of the Congregation for Bishops; His Excellency, the Most Reverend Csaba Ternyák, Secretary of the Congregation for Clergy; His Excellency, the Most Reverend Piergiorgio Nesti, Secretary of the Congregation for Institutes of Consecrated Life and for Societies of Apostolic Life; and His Excellency, the Most Reverend Giuseppe Pittau, Secretary of the Congregation for Catholic Education.

The participants from Australia were: His Eminence Cardinal Edward Clancy, Metropolitan Archbishop of Sydney, President of the Australian Catholic Bishops Conference; His Excellency, the Most Reverend Francis Carroll, Archbishop of Canberra and Goulburn; His Excellency, the Most Reverend George Pell, Metropolitan Archbishop of Melbourne; His Excellency, the Most Reverend Eric D'Arcy,

Archbishop of Hobart; His Excellency, the Most Reverend Leonard Faulkner, Metropolitan Archbishop of Adelaide; His Excellency, the Most Reverend Barry Hickey, Metropolitan Archbishop of Perth and Chairman of the Committee for Liturgy; His Excellency the Most Reverend John Bathersby, Metropolitan Archbishop of Brisbane; His Excellency, the Most Reverend Brian Heenan, Bishop of Rockhampton, Chairman of the Committee for Clergy and Religious; His Excellency, the Most Reverend Justin Bianchini, Bishop of Geraldton, Secretary of the Committee for Clergy and Religious; His Excellency, the Most Reverend Michael Putney, Auxiliary Bishop of Brisbane, Chairman of the Committee for Doctrine and Morals; His Excellency, the Most Reverend David Walker, Bishop of Broken Bay, Secretary of the Committee for Doctrine and Morals; His Excellency, the Most Reverend James Foley, Bishop of Cairns, Chairman of the Committee for Education and Secretary of the Committee for Liturgy; His Excellency, the Most Reverend Barry Collins, Bishop of Wilcannia-Forbes, Secretary of the Committee for Education; His Excellency, the Most Reverend Edmund Collins, Bishop of Darwin, Chairman of the Committee for Evangelization and Missions; and His Excellency, the Most Reverend William Morris, Bishop of Toowoomba, Secretary of the Committee for Evangelization and Missions.

Appendix 3

Pope John Paul II - Address to the Australian Bishops, 14 December 1998

Dear Cardinal Clancy,
Dear Brother Bishops,

1.

I warmly greet you, the Bishops of Australia, with the words of the
Apostle Peter: 'Peace to all of you who are in Christ' (1 Pt 5:14).
Your *ad limina* visit is taking place at the same time as the Special
Assembly for Oceania of the Synod of Bishops when, in the midst
of the joys and anxieties of your priestly service, you have entered
into the *colloquium fraternitatis* with your brother Bishops from New
Zealand, Papua New Guines and Solomon Islands and the whole
Pacific region on the centrality of Christ, the Way and the Truth, and
the Life of the peoples of your continent. Representatives of your
Conference have also met various heads of Dicasteries of the Holy
See to discuss aspects of your ministry in the particular situation of
the Church in your land. I wish to encourage you to look *the profound
strengths of the Catholic community in Australia, which in the midst of
often disconcerting change continues to listed to the word of God and to
bear abundant fruits of holiness and evangelical service.*

2.

Your meetings with some of the Congregations of the Roman Curia
have focused on questions of doctrine and morality, the liturgy, the
role of the Bishop, evangelisation and mission, the priesthood and
religious life, and Catholic education. In each of these areas, your
own personal responsibility as Bishops is absolutely vital, and so I
will make this the underlying theme of these brief reflections. From
the Second Vatican Council, *the figure of the diocesan Bishop* emerged
with new vigour and clarity. With your fellow Bishops and in union
with the Successor of Peter, you have by the power of the Holy Spirit
received the task of caring for the Church of God, the Bride purchased
at the cost of the blood of the only begotten Son, the Lord Jesus Christ
(cf. Acts 20:28).

The Bishops are "the visible source and foundation of unity in their own
particular Churches", just as the Successor of Peter is "the perpetual
and visible source and foundation of unity" of all the Bishops and with
them of the whole body of the faithful. Since the particular Churches

over which the individual Bishops preside represent a portion of the
People of God assigned to the Bishop's pastoral governance, they are
no complete in themselves but exist in and through communion with
the one, holy, catholic and apostolic Church. For this reason "all the
Bishops have the obligation of fostering and safeguarding the unity of
the faith and upholding the discipline which is common to the whole
Church" (cf. *Lemen Gentium, 23)*. Each individual Bishop, then, is
called to assume his full responsibility, setting his face resolutely
against all that might harm the faith and that has been handed down
(cf. 1 Cor.4:7). In order for his minister of sanctifying, teaching and
governing to be truly effective, it goes without saying that the manner
of a Bishop's life must be irreproachable: he must openly strive for
holiness, and give himself wholeheartedly and without hesitation to
the service of the Gospel.

3.
Until recently, the Catholic community in Australia knew nothing
but consistent growth. Yours is the remarkable story of a great
institution built quickly, despite limited resources. Dioceses, parishes,
religious communities, schools, seminaries, organisations of every
kind appeared, as testimony to the strength of the Catholic faith
in your land and the immense generosity of those who brought it
there. Now perhaps it appears that the momentum has slackened,
and the Church in Australia faces a complex situation which calls for
careful discernment on the part of the Bishops, and a confident and
committed response on the part of all Catholics.

The underlying question concerns the relationship between the
Church and the world. This questions was fundament to the Second
Vatican Council and it remains fundamental to the life of the Church
more than then thirty years later. The answer we give to this question
will determine the answer we give to a range of other important and
practical questions. The advanced secularization of society brings
with it a tendency to blur the boundaries between the Church and
the world. Certain aspects of the prevailing culture are allowed to
condition the Christian community in ways which the Gospel does
not permit. There is sometimes an unwillingness to challenge cultural
assumptions as the Gospel demands. This often goes hand in hand

with an uncritical approach to the problem of moral evil, and a reluctance to recognize the reality of sin and the need for forgiveness. This attitude embodies a too optimistic view of modernity, together with an uneasiness about the Cross and its implications for Christian living. The past is too easily dismissed and the horizontal is so stressed that the sense of the supernatural grows weak. A distorted respect for pluralism leads to a relativism which questions the truths taught by faith and accessible to human reason; and this in turn leads to confusion about what constitutes true freedom. All this causes uncertainty about the distinctive contribution which the Church is called to make in the world.

In speaking of the Church's dialogue with the world, Pope Paul VI used the phrase *colloquium salutis;* not just dialogue for its own sake, but a dialogue which has its source in the Truth and seeks to communicate the Truth that frees and saves. The *colloquium salutis* requires that the Church be different precisely for the sake of dialogue. The unfailing source of this difference is the power of the Paschal Mystery which we proclaim and communicate. It is in the Paschal Mystery that we discover the absolute and universal truth – the truth about God and about the human person which has been entrusted to the Church and which she offers to the men and women of every age. We Bishops must never lose confidence in the call we have received, the call to a humble and tenacious *diakonia* of that truth. The apostolic faith and the apostolic mission which we have received impose a solemn duty to speak that truth at every level of our ministry.

4.

As "the steward of the grace of the supreme priesthood" (*cf. Lumen Gentium, 26*) the Bishop's service to the truth has a specific and primary application in the liturgical life of his diocese. He must do everything necessary to ensure that the liturgy through which "the work of our redemption is exercised" (*Sacrosanctum Concilium, 2*) remains true to its most intimate nature: praise and worship of the Eternal Father (*cf ibid,7*). It is particularly important for the Bishop to provide for the sound teaching of liturgical theology and spirituality in seminaries and similar institutions. He must also see to the creation of the resources which his diocese needs, in the form of specially trained priests, deacons and lay people, properly functioning commissions and working groups for the promotion of the liturgy and of liturgical music and art, and for the construction and maintenance of churches which in their design and furnishings will be in close harmony with underlying values of the Catholic tradition. Again, among both clergy and laity, appropriate means must be available for permanent formation and for a constant catechesis regarding the deeper meaning of the various liturgical celebrations. In many cases, it will be helpful to pool resources with neighbouring dioceses or at a national level. Such arrangements should not, however, diminish the Bishop's task of ordering, promoting, and guarding the liturgical life of the particular Church (cf. *Vicesimus Quintus Annus, 21*).

Since the Sacrifice of the Mass is the "source and summit of the Christian life" (*Lumen Gentium, 11),* I encourage you to exhort priests and lay faithful alike to be willing to make substantial sacrifices in order to make available and to attend Sunday Mass. Earlier generations of Catholics in Australia showed the depth of their faith by their high regard for the Eucharist and the other sacraments. That spirit is an integral part of Catholic life, a part of our spiritual tradition which needs to be reaffirmed

5.

In preparing and celebrating the forthcoming Great Jubilee as a time of conversion and reconciliation, there is also ample room for a great catechizing effort in relation to the Sacrament of Penance. Today it is possible and necessary to overcome certain superficial applications of the human sciences. The Church in Australia should invite Catholics to encounter anew the saving mystery of the Father's love and mercy through that uniquely profound and transforming human experience that is individual, integral confession and absolution. As the *Catechism of the Catholic Church* points out, this remains the only ordinary way for the faithful to reconcile themselves with God and the Church (cf. No. 1484). The personal nature of sin, conversion, forgiveness and reconciliation is the reason why the Second Rite of Penance demands the personal confession of sins and individual absolution and appropriate only in cases of grave necessity, clearly determined by liturgical and canonical norms.

As those primarily responsible for Church life and discipline, you will know how to make clear to the faithful the theological, pastoral and anthropological reasons for the Church's practice of having children who have reached the age of reason receive the Sacrament of Penance before making their First Holy Communion (cf.Canon 914) At stake is respect for the integrity of their personal, individual relationship with God.

6. As has been repeatedly made clear in the present Synod, there is a direct link between the Ministry of the Bishop and the state of the priesthood in his diocese, with regard both to the recruitment of suitable candidates to the priesthood and to the exercise of priestly ministry. You have reported a decline in the numbers of those responding to God's call to the priesthood and religious life, a decline in the numbers of those in active ministry, and the increasing age of those presently serving the Church. You have rightly responded to this pastoral problem with prayer and various vocational promotion programmes. The fact that the shortage of vocations is not everywhere felt to the same degree would indicate that the ideal of commitment, service and unconditional self-giving for the sake of Jesus Christ still speaks to many hearts, especially where young people find priests who live out, as radically as possible, the love of the Good Shepherd who lays his life for the sheep (cf. Jn 10:11; *Pastores Dabo Vobis, 40)* Today the younger generation of Catholics shows a remarkable capacity to respond to the call to a self-giving and demanding spiritual life, precisely because they are quick to perceive that the prevailing self-centred culture is incapable of satisfying the deeper needs of the human heart. In this search they are looking for guidance; they need genuine witnesses to the Gospel message.

In many ways the decline in the number of priests in active ministry is offset by greater participation of the laity in the parish setting. Lay women and men often work closely with their parish priests in liturgical matters, in catechesis, in the material administration of the parish, and in efforts to draw others to the Church by their own works of the apostolate (cf. *Apostolicam Actuositatem, 10)*. It falls to the Bishop to order this collaboration properly, in particular by ensuring that the parish priest is not perceived as merely one minister among many, with particular responsibility for the sacraments, but whose teaching office and governance is limited by the will of the majority or of a vocal minority. The Australian sense of equality, must not be used as an excuse for stripping the parish priest of the authority and duties that pertain to his office, making it appear that the ministerial priesthood is less essential to the local Church community.

Every Bishop recognizes how important it is to be close to his priests, being a father to them, affirming them, and correcting them when necessary. In a cultural climate dominated by subjective thought and moral relativism, the transmission of the faith and the presentation of the Church's teaching and discipline has to be a matter of grave concern to the Successors of the Apostles. Unfortunately, the teaching of the Magisterium is sometimes met with reservation and questioning, a tendency, which is sometimes fuelled by media interest in dissent, or in some cases by the intention to use the media as a kind of stratagem to force the Church into changes she cannot make. The Bishops' task is not to win arguments but to win souls for Christ, to engage not in ideological bickering but in a spiritual struggle on behalf of truth, to be concerned not with vindicating or promoting themselves but with proclaiming and spreading the Gospel.

7. There is a great need to speak the truth clearly and with love, and to do so confidently, since the truth we proclaim belongs to Christ and is in fact the truth for which all people long, no matter how uninterested or resistant they may seem. Our *colloquium salutis* will produce good results only if the Holy Spirit breathes through our being and becomes our voice. Let us, then, at this moment of communion, invoke that same Holy spirit "whose coming is gentle", as St Cyril of Jerusalem says, "whose burden is light" . . . for he comes to save, to heal, to teach, to admonish, to strengthen, to exhort and to enlighten the mind" (*Catecheses, XVI 16).* I earnestly recommend to your prayer and reflection, to you responsibility and action, the document which summarizes your meetings with the various Dicasteries of the Holy See. We all well know that the Bishop's threefold ministry of teaching, sanctifying and governing is a difficult and often burdensome one, which involves suffering and the Cross. Yes, as the document itself states: "in the mystery of the Cross we learn a wisdom which transcends our own weakness and limitations: we learn that in Christ truth and love are one and in him we find the meaning of our vocation" (No, 17).

It is above all the Mother of the Redeemer who, in her Spirit-filled Magnificat, leads us in praise of God who has called us "out of darkness into his own wonderful light" (1 Pt 2:9). May Mary Help of Christians watch over your land and its people. As a pledge of grace and peace in him who is always "the Way, and the Truth and the Life" (Jn.14:6), I gladly impart my Apostolic Blessing to you and to the priests, religious and lay faithful who dwell in Australia.

From the Vatican, 14 December 1998

Signed: Joannes Paulus II

Appendix 4

The Faithful Have Charge
Of Their Sacramental Needs

Purpose

Sacramenta sunt propter homines [literally: the sacraments exist for people] is a phrase well-known to church lawyers and moral theologian:. Through sacramental celebrations worship is made to God; the Sabbath, for instance, was provided to us to do just that. See Mark 2:23 § 27.

Holiness

Second Vatican Council document on 'The church', No 41: 'Accordingly all Christians, in the conditions, duties and circumstances of their life and though all these, will sanctify themselves more and more if they receive all things with faith from the hand of the heavenly Father and cooperate with the divine will, thus showing forth in that temporal service the love with which God has loved the world.'

Holiness, and growth in holiness, cannot be other than both communal and personal. Therefore, Sacramental reconciliation embraces necessarily both the communal and the personal.

Good Order

God's GOOD ORDER does exist in the church as in the world. Right relationships with one another, God, and Church are re-establishing such is the substance of the penance sacrament; penance/reconciliation celebrations need to conform to the sacramental needs of the faithful penitentially-gathered.

Moral Matters Matter Most

- Charity as the principle in moral matters
- Compassion as God's part in our reconciliating
- The Primacy of conscience among moral authorities
- Moral Discrimination to gauge the gravity of one's direction in life and the accompanying failures.
- Intrinsic evil and its scope

All the above moral matters enter into consideration in responding to the sacramental needs of the faithful.

Physical or Moral Impossibility

CJC, Canon 960:

> Individual and integral confession and absolution constitute the sole ordinary means by which a member who is conscious of grave sin is reconciled with God and with the Church. Physical or moral impossibility alone excuses from such confession, in which case reconciliation may be attained by other means also.

Examples of *physical impossibility* that would be applicable in the Diocese of Toowoomba as indicating the use of a Communal Celebration of Reconciliation in the Third Rite:

- Large congregations in country areas where distance, age, infirmity or inability to travel make frequent recourse to a priest unlikely or difficult:
- The faithful have a right to receive Reconciliation in their own parish and from their own priests. Gathering priests for a communal rite is a matter of courtesy or opportunity not a requirement of Church law.

Examples of *moral impossibility* that would apply in the Diocese of Toowoomba as indicating the use of a Communal Celebration of reconciliation in the Third Rite:

- Where penitents are unable to use the First or Second Rites because of the following:
  - the necessity of anonymity for those in grave sin;
  - where a person or persons has had a bad experience in the past with individual confession;
  - if there would be scandal if the sin [grave] were revealed to the priest here present;
  - close friendship with the priest, which factor could well apply to most persons present at a celebration;
- where a community has been formed in the communal celebration of Reconciliation in the Third Rite, that particular Rite should not suddenly be removed.

Disadvantage

Odiosa sunt restringenda [literally: disadvantages ought to be limited] is a phrase well-known to church lawyers and moral theologians.

This dictum should be applied with God's customary largesse to all scenarios that celebrate the Rites of Reconciliation, so that the disadvantages to the Catholic faithful who wish to celebrate the Sacrament of Penance will be lessened.

Appendix 5

Congregation of Divine Worship and Discipline of the Sacraments

Congregatio Di Cultu Divino
Et Disciplina Sacramentorum

March 8, 2003

Your Excellency

Through the kind offices of the Congregation for Bishops, this Congregation for Divine Worship and the Discipline of the Sacraments has received a report of the Apostolic Nuncio in Australia, Archbishop Francesco Canalini, concerning continued recourse to 'general absolution' in the Diocese entrusted to your care.

Together with the aforementioned report this Dicastery has received copies of Your Excellency's letters to Archbishop Canalini dated July 5, 2001, January 11, 2002 and January 3, 2003, in which you have outlined certain guidelines for recourse to 'general absolution' in the Diocese of TOOWOOMBA.

This Congregation Divine Worship and the Discipline of the Sacraments is not a little surprised to be made aware that efforts at authorizing such recourse to 'general absolution' on the basis of *gravis necessitas* (that is, outside of cases of danger of death, as mentioned in canon 961§1,1⁰) should continue to be made, notwithstanding the Motu proprio *Misericordia Dei* of the Holy Father, which so clearly eliminated the unfortunate misinterpretations of law cited by Your Excellency in the aforementioned letters as motives for recourse to 'general absolution'. It is perhaps useful to remind Your Excellency of the further specification given to the norm of canon 961§1,2⁰ by the aforementioned *motu proprio, Misericordia Dei* (cf in particular, *Misericordia Dei*, No 4, attached to this letter for your convenience).

As Archbishop Canalini has indicated to Your Excellency, ready opportunities exist for the faithful to make individual and integral confessions in the Diocese of Toowoomba. This fact establishes conclusively that the faithful would *not* 'be deprived of sacramental grace or of holy communion for a lengthy period of time' (can. 961§1,2⁰) and, therefore, recourse may not be made to 'general absolution'. Indeed, the *motu proprio, Misericordia Dei* has specified that 'lengthy period of time" must be foreseen to be not less than one month (cf *Misericordia Dei*, No 4d). Not is it possible to describe the situation which arises in the Diocese of Toowoomba during each season of Advent and Lent as meeting the requirement of the same canon concerning *gravis necessitas,* as is likewise made quite clear in the same *motu poroprio.*

(Unsigned)

Appendix 6

Submission to the Dicastery for Divine Worship and Discipline of the Sacraments re Communal Rite
2004

PART A

THE USE OF GENERAL ABSOLUTION IN THE DIOCESE OF TOOWOOMBA

HISTORY

Norms

On 16 June 1972 the Sacred Congregation for the Doctrine of the Faith, with the approval of His Holiness Pope Paul VI, issued norms for the administration of general absolution of several penitents. In accord with the norms the Congregation for Divine Worship included a *Rite of Reconciliation of Several Penitents with General Confession and Absolution* in the Rite of Penance as revised in accord with the Instructions of the Second Vatican Council and promulgated on 2 December 1973. Vernacular translations of the new Rite of Penance came into force at various times after this as they were approved by Episcopal Conferences and confirmed by the Holy See. From this time on, many bishops in Australia, and in other places, authorised the use of the General Absolution in a liberal interpretation of the law.

Experience

It seems that in the experience of those places that approved the use of General Absolution in a more frequent way than the law envisaged was that there was an increase in the number of people who sought sacramental reconciliation. The number of people seeking Individual Reconciliation had been in decline for some time. In reply to a questionnaire we received replies from priests with experience of both rural and city parishes. They speak of a trend which began in the late 1960's. Some priests link the beginning of the decline with the publication of Humane Vitae.

Even through there were set times that priests went to the confessional for First Rite Reconciliation, it was obvious even then that only a minority was making use of the First Rite. Many of those who came were weekly regulars. Mention was also made of people bordering on scrupulosity who move from one church to another to seek absolution for "sins" which would be better treated by a psychologist. They do not want spiritual direction nor to discuss their situation. A quick absolution only is what is sought. At the same time there is some evidence of other people's dissatisfaction with habitual "quick" confessions with no alternatives. When a third rite became available they embraced it eagerly. The use of General Confession and Absolution seems almost always to awaken in people a sense of sin and the need for forgiveness and penance.

Widespread use

Since the widespread use of General Absolution there have been increasing calls from the Holy See to limit its use and hold to a strict interpretation of the law. This has happened despite the calls of bishops, collectively and individually, asking, pleading, and arguing for a more liberal use, based on the fact that pastoral experience has demonstrated the value of the sacrament celebrated in this form. At the sixth General

Assembly of the Synod of Bishops, 1983, a number of bishops called for the more widespread use of the rite of General Confession and Absolution, including the Most Rev Bernard Wallace, Bishop of Rockhampton, now deceased, a highly regarded Australian theologian.

The Code of Canon Law

The promulgation of the Code of Canon Law, 25 January 1983, saw a further tightening of the Law regarding the celebration of General Confession and absolution. The 1972 norms, no. 31, of the congregation said the conditions for use did not exist "when confessors were **able to be at hand,** merely because of a great recourse of penitents such as can for example occur on a great feast or pilgrimage." Canon 961, 2° says, 2° "A sufficient necessity is not, however, considered to exist when confessors **cannot be available** merely because of a great gathering of penitents, such as can occur on some major feast day or pilgrimage." It is noted that the Code of Canon Law abrogates the 1972 norms but the further restriction is noted. In the *motu proprio* *"Misericordia Dei"* of 7 April 2002 His Holiness Pope John Paul II restated and reinforced the Code of Canon Law on the matter.

I have continued to permit the use of General Absolution under guidelines promulgated by myself, believing them to be in full accordance with the Spirit and Letter of the Law, and in the best pastoral interest of this diocese. The Holy See now challenges my pastoral judgement in this area.

Custom

While not in full accord with the 1917 or 1983 Codes of Canon Law the experience of the people of the Diocese of Toowoomba, and other Dioceses around the world, have, at least elements in them that might be considered as establishing a custom. The use of General Confession and general Absolution has been accepted by "a community capable of receiving law" (c. 25), and its use has been approved by "a competent legislator" (c.26). I believe that the people see that a custom is already in existence.

SOME OF THE REASONS WHY THE THIRD RITE IS POPULARLY USED

Questionnaire

A questionnaire sent to priests and people involved in the past in the celebration of General Confession and Absolution has clearly shown to me that people have been regular participants in these celebrations. 100% of the people canvassed had attended a third rite ceremony and of those 90.7 % registered positive responses. People are, in fact, choosing this rite in favour of either the first or second rites. 18.6% choose the third rite against the second rite. I am happy to report that the survey clearly shows that people are not being denied the right to access the first rite they are simply choosing not to use it. According to the survey 100% of parishes make the first rite available. It is noted that there are "many," "plenty," or "weekly" opportunities given and also that the first rite is "regularly mentioned at Sunday Mass." At the same time it is noted that 58% of the people canvassed "seldom" or "never" use the first rite. Some parishes encourage people who use the First Rite to celebrate it in its entirety. It would seem that this happens more where an appointment has been made for First Rite Reconciliation and more time is given to sharing and pondering the Word of God. In most parishes few people use the first rite in its entirety.

Meaningful use of the Second Rite seems to be particularly applicable for children especially children preparing for their first celebration of Reconciliation. It is said that the Second Rite makes the social and familial dimension of sin and its effects obvious and that it resonates with the group nature of the preparation process, especially in cases where the children and their parents work in cluster groups as well as on their own at home.

On the other hand one priest highlighted indications that the people do not find satisfaction with the Second Rite. This priest wrote: "I tried it for adults the first Advent I was in this parish, about eighty or ninety attended and due to the lack of Confessors fifty left without receiving the sacrament. People indicate that they do not like the second Rite, as it is neither one thing nor the other." Country clergy, especially western clergy, refer to its limited success because of the scarcity of clergy and the distances. Lay peoples criticisms of the Second rite included the words, "impractical," "rushed and cumbersome," "waste of time for priests," "could hear what people said," "left feeling unfulfilled," "neither personal nor private," "still not fully with the community," and an unflattering "held like a bush Bar-b-que."

Positive responses to the Third Rite from the clergy include:

> "[It is] a deeply appreciated and valued celebration of the sacrament of Reconciliation and has become an integral part of the prayer life of our community."

> "When we come together as a community [we are] mindful of our personal and collective sinfulness."

> "These regular celebrations of the Third Rite over the years have helped to build up our community of faith."

> "Adults have a real sense of personal sin and that the third rite has enhanced/increased rather than decreased this sense and that for most it has been a most spiritual experience".

Numbers

In city parishes attendances at Third Rite ceremonies range between 250 and 300. In the country figures ranging between 100 and 120 were recorded

One priest reported that in Advent he asked those attending the third Rite to indicate their reasons for attending. He received eighty-four replies from a cross section of ages in which "Each commented on the prayerfulness of the celebration, the communal aspect, the sense of communal responsibility (and) that they would not have attended the Sacrament if it had not been a Third Rite."

Another priest wrote: "We celebrate the Communal Rite each Advent and Lent. During this time opportunity is given each day for ten days for people to attend the First Rite. Approx 30 people use the First Rite while 250 to 300 celebrate the third Rite.

One priest has commented that if people had lost the sense of sin they would not be interested in any Rite.

Anonymity

A matter of real import is that one of the chief reasons that people name for not using the First Rite is the fact that they know and are known to the priests available too well. The right to approach the sacrament of penance with anonymity is enshrined in the law itself, canon 964 §2 requires that prevision be made for a fixed grill in a confessional to facilitate this possibility. However, in small communities, such as ours invariably are, such a provision does not give a guarantee of anonymity as priest and people often are well known to each other. The only options left to people who cannot approach their own parish priest are to either go without the sacrament or to travel, often great distances, to another priest.

Size of Diocese and age of priests.

The total area of the Diocese of Toowoomba is 487, 456 square kilometres as is recorded in the *Annuario Pontificio*. This makes the diocese over 100, 000 square kilometres larger than the nation of Italy, according to the CIA World Fact book the total area of Italy, including Sardinia and Sicily, is 301, 230 square Kilometres. To cover this vast area the diocese currently has 35 parishes, with 28 active priests staffing them; three priests are in full-time special ministry in the curia or as a chaplain to an institution. In addition two parishes are served by priest who have retired but live in the community. There are eight other priests in retirement in the diocese only three of whom could be seriously be considered active to any real extent. The average age of the active clergy is currently 57.51.

Comparison

It is certain that the population of the Diocese is small compared to those of European, African, Asian and South American Dioceses, however the size the diocese more than compensates for the small numbers. Two parishes in the far west of the Diocese are both larger than for example the country of Belgium. Cunnamulla parish services the town of Cunnamulla itself and as well on a regular basis, Eulo, 75 kilometres away, Thargomindah 200 kilometre away on single lane sealed road and Hungerford, 200 kilometres away 125 kilometres of which are unsealed gravel and sand road. The nearest parish centre to Cunnamulla is Charleville, 200 kilometres to the north.

Natural hazards

The road to Charleville is sealed but often unfenced which means it is not unusual to encounter all manner of straying animals on the road. At night native and exotic wildlife make driving even more hazardous as Kangaroos, some times referred to as Roos, Emus (large flightless birds a little smaller than the ostrich), wild boar and wild goat can suddenly appear before the driver. An accident with any of these animals will severely damage a motor vehicle and not infrequently lead to injury to the driver and any passengers, on occasion such accidents have caused death.

Local considerations

Even in the more closely settled areas in the east of the Diocese, except for the City of Toowoomba itself, the minimum round trip is 40 Kilometres. In order to fulfil the requirements of the law to celebrate, within a reasonable time, the communal celebration of the sacrament of penance with individual confession of sin and absolution (second rite) the experience is that one is forced to ask priests to travel long distances and in many places it is simply impossible. The same factors are true for the people who, if they desire individual confession and absolution with at least a modicum of anonymity they must travel the same distances to another parish.

Australian Culture

Some attempts to address the shortage of clergy have been made. A number of priests have been accepted on loan to the diocese from India, with one exception these have been found to be failure, a result of cultural and language differences. Australia, now having experienced over 200 years of settlement from all nations has developed its own particular culture. There *is* a unique Australian culture that cannot be assessed or learnt overnight and which does affect the way in which Australian people more and more celebrate their spirituality.

Few Vocations

While vocations have and are still encouraged the response has been poor to nil. Some of the reasons for this may be found in the scandals that have wracked the Church in the first world. Young men just are not prepared to join the institution that is receiving such bad publicity. I believe that for the moment this is a state that will continue.

Sexual abuse image

Further adding to people's general unwillingness to approach the sacrament on the individual basis is the scandal caused by the sexual abuse of minors and vulnerable adults by clergy here in Australia and around the world. The abuse itself coupled with the general failure of the hierarchy, both local and universal, to address the scandal with full openness and pastoral care for the victims has left the priesthood with a very poor image in the minds of many people both Catholic and Non-Catholic. It will take many years of careful rebuilding of the image of the priesthood before it finds, if it ever does, its previous standing in the community. Anecdotal evidence suggests the lack of trust of the clergy because of the sexual abuse has been the cause of some people opting not to use the first rite of reconciliation. Actual abuse by clergy of some people has made it psychologically impossible for such people to approach the first rite out of fear of what has already been done to them by the clergy. This history of damage to people is mentioned privately to me by some priests as a significant reason why people no longer use the first rite of reconciliation. Small western communities have been and are still susceptible to such abuse and I have record of such problems in the past. It is this damage to people that I believe ultimately at this time imposes a moral responsibility on me and on all bishops to accede to request for the celebration of the third rite of reconciliation. Having said that I must add that the positive effects of the celebration of the third rite cannot of themselves be dismissed.

Loss of respect for hierarchy

Others still have lost nearly all faith in the hierarchy, both local and universal, because of what they perceive as the hierarchy's in action or inappropriate action over many years and the belief that such a response by the hierarchy had less to do with gospel values than it did with self-preservation of power and prestige. While such belief might be considered to over-state the matter it is nevertheless a factor in people rejecting the use of the first and second rites.

Past bad experience

Some people have ceased availing themselves of the first rite because of bad experience in the past where priests have treated them badly. Not necessarily in any way violent or sexual but rather where priests have mentally or verbally abused them. Many who still frequent the first rite, as evidenced by some of the clergy responses do so out of scruples that in some cases are the result of the same sort of abuse by priest in the confessional in the past.

Return to first rite.

I believe that one of the interesting facts that the survey of priests and people produced is that some people after a positive experience of the third rite have then found it both necessary and desirable to attend a first rite reconciliation. The use of the third rite has actually assisted people in returning to the first rite.

Not an emergency process but an emerging rite.

It must be noted that what is generally celebrated in the diocese, as a third rite of reconciliation is not exactly the emergency procedure envisioned by the rite itself and more closely resembles a second rite of reconciliation. The rite would usually follow the following plan: Opening hymn, greeting, prayer, Liturgy of the Word, homily, extended examination of conscience, general confession of sin, general absolution, hymn, penance, a prayer of thanksgiving, the sign of peace, the blessing and a final hymn. There is a reminder for people in grave sin that they need to attend the first rite before they may again avail themselves of a celebration of the Third Rite. There may be a ritual action included in the celebration, such as a sprinkling rite or the use of incense. It would be unusual for the celebration to take less than an hour, as it would be interspersed with periods of silence and reflection. I am sure that we are witnessing an emerging, meaningful and beautiful rite. When asked the direct question if they would return to use of the first rite only 7% said "Yes" against 51% who said "No" whereas 86% indicated that they believe the Third Rite to be an essential expression of the Sacrament of Reconciliation. It is popular with people because of its communal dimension and because of the prayerful way it is celebrated and because it gives them a real sense of being reconciled with God and with one another.

Civil Legal implications.

A further complication has been added in recent times to the problem. A bill was submitted to one of the State Parliaments of Australia, South Australia, that if passed would make it mandatory for a priest to report to state authorities any incident of the sexual abuse of a child, even if such a revelation were made in the confessional. While priests would generally ignore such legislation the mere possibility that they might be compelled to reveal confessional secrets is disturbing to some people and undermines their trust in the seal. Even though that bill failed to pass into law it is fair to presume that other states and territories will follow with similar legislation. I notice that this sort of public discussion undermines the people's confidence in the clergy and in the church.

SOME PRESUMPTIONS

In the overall debate about the use of the third rite as a regular means of reconciling the people of God rather than as something to be consider extra-ordinary there are certain presumptions being made but not necessarily voiced.

"An easy way out"

Some have suggested that the third rite is the easy way out but this view is erroneous. It takes a great deal more humility to stand before and in the midst of ones brothers and sisters and admit ones need for forgiveness and mercy in such a public fashion than slipping into the anonymous confessional box on Saturday morning. The people's responses themselves indicate that when celebrated properly the third rite is the exact opposite of "an easy way out."

Grave sin

Another presumption is that people are generally in grave or mortal sin. One can only come to this conclusion when one examines the requirements of canon law.

> *Can. 989 All the faithful who have reached the age of discretion are bound faithfully to confess their grave sins at least once a year.*

* Appendix 8,9,10

If only those in grave sin are required to confess their sins at least once a year and we are forbidding the use of the general confession of sin and general absolution then we must be of the mindset that sees most people in grave sin. Such a view necessarily holds that most people have sinned in grave matter with full knowledge and deliberate consent (Catechism of the Catholic Church, 1857). Such a view of the human person, I submit, does not match with Christian Anthropology, particularly as the Second Vatican Council enunciated it. Priests report to me that very few people have grave sin; that while subjectively people may believe they are in grave sin some priests say they can't remember when they last heard something which would be regarded as grave sin. Priests tell me that they often find themselves assuring penitents of the traditional teaching of the church of grave matter, full knowledge and full consent being needed for grave sin to be committed. They say that a number of these penitents would be struggling with an over scrupulous conscience and an entrenched fear of God.

Matter of conscience.

The use of the third rite requires that people be informed that if they are in serious or grave or mortal sin they must attend individual reconciliation as soon as possible and before receiving a further general absolution. It is wrong of us, or anyone, to presume to look into the conscience of an individual and judge, without any evidence, that he or she is in a state of mortal sin.

THE LAW

> Can. 375 §1 By divine institution, Bishops succeed the Apostles through the Holy Spirit who is given to them. They are constituted Pastors in the Church, to be the teachers of doctrine, the priests of sacred worship and the ministers of governance.
>
> §2 By their episcopal consecration, Bishops receive, together with the office of sanctifying, the offices also of teaching and of ruling, which however, by their nature, can be exercised only in hierarchical communion with the head of the College and its members.

All bishops through sacred ordination are endowed with the *tria munera: sanctificandi, docendi, regendi.* The *munera* are always exercised in communion with the Supreme Pontiff and the college of bishops.

> Can. 381 §1 In the diocese entrusted to his care, the diocesan Bishop has all the ordinary, proper and immediate power required for the exercise of his pastoral office, except in those matters which the law or a decree of the Supreme Pontiff reserves to the supreme or to some other ecclesiastical authority.

The Principle of Subsidiarity.

One of the central teachings of the Second Vatican Council concerning the exercise of authority in the Church was that of subsidiarity. This principle was adopted by the Synod of Bishops in 1967 as the fifth of the ten principles to guide the revision of the Code of Canon Law.

Careful attention is to be given to the greater application of the so-called principle of subsidiarity within the Church. It is a principle which is rooted in a higher one because the office of bishops with its attached powers is a reality of divine law. In virtue of this principle one may defend the appropriateness and even the necessity of providing for the welfare especially of individual institutes through particular laws and recognition of a healthy autonomy for particular executive power while legislative unity and universal and general law are observed. On the basis of the same principle, the new Code entrusts either to particular law or to executive power whatever is not necessary for the unity of the discipline of the universal Church so that appropriate provision is made for a healthy "decentralisation" while avoiding the danger of division into or the establishment of national churches.

The fact that no two particular churches are exactly alike, even within the boundaries of a single episcopal conference, requires individual bishops to act in different ways even under similar circumstances. The experience of a Diocese such as Toowoomba has called for a specific response. It is not the intention of the Diocese to harm the unity of the Church, fully aware, as we are, of the bonds of communion with the other particular Churches and especially with the mother Church of Rome. It does appear, however, by the reactions to the reasonable practice of the Diocese that this is what is perceived. It is argued that the guidelines established for the use of general confession and absolution fall well within the principle of subsidiarity as taught by the Council, established by the Synod as a principle for the revision of the Code and promulgated as the universal law by the Code.

Trust.

The way in which bishops, ordained as such with a mandate from the Holy See, which one would presume attested in itself to the orthodoxy and pastoral judgement of the one so ordained, are not trusted to exercise their office is disturbing.

*Can. 838 §1 The ordering and guidance of the sacred
liturgy depends solely upon the authority of the Church,
namely, that of the Apostolic See and, as provided by law,
that of the diocesan Bishop.*

*§2 It is the prerogative of the Apostolic See to regulate
the sacred liturgy of the universal Church, to publish
liturgical books and review their vernacular translations,
and to be watchful that liturgical regulations are
everywhere faithfully observed.*

*§3 It pertains to Episcopal Conferences to prepare
vernacular translations of liturgical books, with
appropriate adaptations as allowed by the books themselves
and, with the prior review of the Holy See, to publish these
translations.*

*§4 Within the limits of his competence, it belongs to the
diocesan Bishop to lay down for the Church entrusted to
his care, liturgical regulations which are binding on all.*

The primary regulator of the sacred liturgy is the Holy See; however,
certain areas of liturgical governance are the responsibility of the
Episcopal Conference and the Diocesan Bishop. The Diocesan
Bishop's responsibility for the *munus sanctificandi* is limited by:
Canon and Liturgical Law, and special legislative acts of the Supreme
Pontiff; and by decrees of the Episcopal Conference when it acts
within its competence. In the case of the use of general confession
and general absolution the Diocesan Bishop is the final arbiter of
whether the conditions for its use, as set down by Universal Law and
the Particular Law of the Episcopal Conference, are indeed met. This
would seem a sensible provision because no one else has the first-
hand knowledge of his diocese's circumstance that the bishop has. Lay
people and priests alike complain to me about people who "spy" and
distort information about celebrations of the Third Rite and the fact
that they seem to find a more ready ear in the Congregations than do
the bishops given the mandate to govern their diocese in communion
with the Supreme Pontiff and each other. It has been said to me that
such negative behaviour is destructive of the possibilities for grace for
a great number of the faithful.

Can. 961 §1 General absolution, without prior individual confession, cannot be given to a number of penitents together, unless:

1° danger of death threatens and there is not time for the priest or priests to hear the confessions of the individual penitents;

2° there exists a grave necessity, that is, given the number of penitents, there are not enough confessors available properly to hear the individual confessions within an appropriate time, so that without fault of their own the penitents are deprived of the sacramental grace or of holy communion for a lengthy period of time. A sufficient necessity is not, however, considered to exist when confessors cannot be available merely because of a great gathering of penitents, such as can occur on some major feast day or pilgrimage.

§2 It is for the diocesan Bishop to judge whether the conditions required in §1, n. 2 are present; mindful of the criteria agreed with the other members of the Episcopal Conference, he can determine the cases of such necessity.

Conditions

The conditions of the Diocese of Toowoomba are based not on the fact that there are large numbers of people at certain times but on the practicalities of the diocese as outlined above. People would be deprived of the sacramental grace of Penance for lengthy periods of time through no fault of their own if the use of the General Confession and Absolution were to be stopped in the Diocese.

Can. 989 All the faithful who have reached the age of discretion are bound faithfully to confess their grave sins at least once a year.

As it is only those who are conscious of grave sin who are bound to full integral confession of sin once a year then it would seem that the use of general confession and absolution for lesser sins is both perfectly reasonable and valid pastoral response to the need of people to ask and receive forgiveness for those minor infractions which inhibit their ongoing relationship with God and one another.

212 §2 Christ's faithful are at liberty to make known their needs, especially their spiritual needs, and their wishes to the Pastors of the Church.

The response of the laity both in the questionnaire and in their practice makes clearly known their desire for the continued celebration of the general confession and absolution. When asked whether they felt truly forgiven in such celebration 88.4% said "Yes" while others expressed some reservations. The Church has long held that the sense of the faithful is a valid interpreter of the faith of the Church and in the responses of the laity to the questionnaire has in some way pointed to the sense of the faithful on this matter. Likewise, Law to be effective must be received by the people; a law that is not so received must be questioned. Certainly, the law must be explained, which has been done, but a community capable of receiving law that objects to or rejects a law must be heard. It is possible that a community may seek to derogate from a specific universal law without wishing to disassociate from the universal Church. Such a desire to derogate may well be an expression of the cultural situation rather than an act of rebellion. The cultural situation is another element of the Council's teaching that must be taken into account. The inculturation of the liturgy, and thereby of the faith (Lex orandi, Lex credendi), must, at times, call for a reinterpretation of the law for the specific circumstances. I would submit that No universal law can take into account the diverse culture in which the Church works for the salvation of souls.

CONCLUSION

Fully aware of the law, both universal and particular, I have permitted the use of Rite of Penance with General Confession of Sin and Absolution. I have done so aware of my responsibility to provide for sacramental reconciliation for the people placed in my care. I have also done so aware of my responsibility to the communion of the Church. The motivations behind my decision are to be seen in the light of the particular nature of the Diocese of Toowoomba and the current climate of distrust created by the very public scandals caused by the behaviour of a very few priests and my observations of the faith in this diocese. I believe that the essence of my pastoral stance is well summed up in a recent letter of application for permission for the Third Rite from a country parish priest. I am including a copy of this letter. The reasons the priest submits could well be duplicated in many of the country parishes in this diocese. *

I have written in my quinquennial report that I inherited a diocese where the practice of the Third Rite of Reconciliation has been truly accepted into the minds and hearts of many of the people and that its continuation is a serious matter for many of them and moreover that I believe that many of our most devout and active Catholics are protagonists of the Third Rite.

Priests report to me both in the questionnaire and personally that the people comment on how meaningful and spiritually fulfilling the Third rite has been in their lives; that the people do exhibit a strong sense of sincere repentance and that the communal nature of the Rite reminds them of the need to ask forgiveness not only of God but of one another.

The First Rite of Reconciliation is in a period of transition in the minds and faith practice of many committed Catholics. In the past we did not always promote personal responsibility for sin and forgiveness; the repeated routine expression of sorrow for sins in an abbreviated form of the first rite encouraged the opposite. The responses of the laity to the questionnaire indicate that there is work to be done in catechising people in both the need and the usefulness of attending the first rite of penance. Such a task will be undertaken with the assistance of the Diocesan Catholic Education Office and the Diocesan Liturgical Commission.

However I submit that there are three legitimate ways to celebrate the sacrament of Reconciliation, each responsive to different pastoral needs of forgiveness.

Celebrating the sacrament of Reconciliation in all three Rites builds up and strengthens the faith life of our community and challenges us to be bearers of forgiveness, healing and reconciliation in the wider community beyond.

With due respect to the Law I submit that the current criteria for the celebration of the General Confession of Sin and Absolution of the Diocese of Toowoomba continue to be used. The result of the suppression of the celebration of this form of the sacrament of Penance would, in my opinion and the opinion of many of the priests and others lead to a further decline in attendance of the sacrament of Reconciliation in all its forms.

Yours in Christ
WILLIAM M MORRIS, DD
BISHOP OF TOOWOOMBA

Part B

Reconciliation Questionnaire - Clergy

Q1 Over time there has been a considerable fall in the use of the First Rite. In your experience when did this happen or begin to happen.

Q2 In general terms describe your experience of the celebration of the First Rite today.

   (a) In your parish do you have regular celebration of the First Rite of Reconciliation? How often?

   (b) Approximately how many would attend your regular celebrations of the First Rite?

   (c) How many people celebrate the First Rite in its entirety according to the Norms issued by the Congregation for Divine worship dated 2nd December 1973?

Q3 If you have celebrated the Second Rite in your parish, describe the success of that or those celebrations and the availability of clergy to assist in the hearing of individual confessions.

Q4 If you have used it in your parish, describe your experience of the celebration of the Third Rite of Reconciliation.

   (a) Do you believe that the people have a real sense of personal sin?

   (b) Do you believe that the people who attend sincerely repent?

   (c) Approximately how many people would attend such a celebration?

Q5 Do you believe that limiting the celebration of the Third Rite would see an increase in the First Rite? Please give reasons.

Q6 In your experience of individual reconciliation do you believe that many people are really in a state of grave sin?

Q7 Do you believe that the celebration of the Third Rite is an essential part of celebrating the Sacrament of Reconciliation in your parish?

Reconciliation Questionnaire – Laity

Q1 How frequently do you avail yourself of the First Rite of Reconciliation?

Q2 Are there sufficient times in your parish to do this?

Q3 If you choose NOT to use the First Rite of Reconciliation, please give your reasons?

Q4 Have you experienced the Second Rite of Reconciliation (communal celebration with individual confession and absolution)?

Q5 Describe the experience and what it meant for you?

Q6 Have you experienced the Third Rite of Reconciliation (general absolution still with the requirement of the later confession of grave sin)?

Q7 Describe the experience and what it meant for you?

Q8 Did you feel truly forgiven?

Q9 If the Third Rite of Reconciliation were no longer available would you see yourself returning to more frequent use of the First Rite?

Q10 Do you believe that the celebration of the Third Rite is an essential part of the overall celebration of the Sacrament of Reconciliation?

Q11 If so, what are your reasons?

Q12 Have you any further overall comment about the celebratio

Appendix 7

Advent Pastoral Letter 2006

ADVENT PASTORAL LETTER
2006

17 November 2006

Dear Priests, Pastoral Leaders, Pastoral Associates and Parish Pastoral
Councils
At the start of this year [23 January 2006] on the recommendation of
the Diocesan Pastoral Council and the Council of Priests, I wrote to
you about the new Policy and related Procedures for the appointment
of Priests and Pastoral Leaders in our diocese.

   With that letter I included a copy of the:

   a) Ministry Appointments Policy and Procedures
      document;
   b) Timeline covering the years 2005 to 2013 and
   c) Background Comments on the history of making
      appointments in our diocese and on the key elements
      in the new Appointments Policy.

I would encourage you to read this material again. It remains the
basis for implementing our Diocesan Pastoral Leadership Plan over
the nine year period that will draw to a close in Easter 2014.

   This letter invites you to look to the future with hope.

   Our new Diocesan Pastoral Leadership Plan with its associated
Staffing Plan and Appointment Policy for Priests and Pastoral Leaders
is a transitional measure covering nine years, beginning Easter 2005.
As with any interim measure, it calls into play uncertainties and
worries. We do face an uncertain future with regard to the number
of active priests in our diocese and we have yet to design what shape
priest staffing may take at Easter 2014 when this transitional period
draws to a close.

   But this in-between time is not all doom and gloom! Already we
have witnessed a flowering in lay-led ministry at a local level: Pastoral
Councils are being established or consolidated, Finance Councils are
being resourced and inserviced, Liturgy Committees and Baptism,
Marriage, Funeral, Confirmation and Eucharist, Social Justice and
Ecumenism ministry groups are being developed, St Vincent de Paul

Conferences and Care and Concern Groups continue their works of compassion, School Boards are in place in many schools. In several Parish communities Priests already work side by side with Pastoral Leaders, Pastoral Associates, Co-Workers and coordinators.

This interim period invites us into deeper faith in God's Spirit at work in our own time, trust in one another and hope for the future. We undertake this task together as best we can with the human and material resources we have to hand. We know this transitional time is neither ideal nor preferable but necessary: we accept the pastoral situation of our own day and work within it as people of faith and hope.

The **immediate task** before us is to develop the procedure for making appointments of priests in the diocese in the light of the discussion, discernment and appointment decisions made in these last twelve months. The new Ministry Appointment Policy and Procedures for Priests and Pastoral Leaders addresses this task.

The **long-term task** that remains as yet unaddressed is the development of a priest Staffing Plan for **Easter 2014**, once again within the wider context of a vision for Diocesan Pastoral Leadership. Current information on ages and numbers of priests currently working in the diocese presents a challenge.

In parish-based ministry in 2014, there will be:
- 65 years and younger: 6 priests with 3 in the 61-65 year group
- 66-70 years 8 priests (with the option to retire)

In diocesan ministry in 2014, there will be:
- 65 years and younger: 2 priests
- 66-70 years 2 priests (with the option to retire)
- 71-75 years 1 Bishop

We may well be moving towards a Staffing Plan that places two Priests in the larger towns or communities in each of the six regions, one priest 65 years or younger and the second priest from the older group (66–70), with the surrounding faith communities served by an increased number of Pastoral Leaders.

Given our deeply held belief in the primacy of Eucharist for the identity, continuity and life of each parish community, we may well need to be much more open towards other options for ensuring that Eucharist may be celebrated. As has been discussed internationally, nationally and locally the ideas of:

- ordaining married, single or widowed men who are chosen and endorsed by their local parish community;
- welcoming former priests, married or single, back to active ministry;
- ordaining women, married or single;
- recognising Anglican, Lutheran and Uniting Church Orders.

While we continue to reflect carefully on these options, we remain committed to actively promoting vocations to the current celibate male priesthood and open to inviting priests from overseas.

What is certain is that Easter 2014 is irrevocably approaching!

Please take some time to give these matters serious thought and reflection. In Advent this year, we begin preparing for the second three-year period of our Pastoral Leadership Plan by asking the priests two questions:

a) where are you willing and able to work for the next three years?
b) where would you prefer to work for the next three years?

Responses will be collated and used as the basis for discussion and discernment at our next Presbyteral Forum, to be held during Lent 2007. From the Presbyteral Forum will come advice on Priest Staffing for the period 2008 to 2010. As a pilgrim people who journey in hope we need to remain open to the Spirit so that we can be agents of change and respond wisely to the needs of all members of the local Church of Toowoomba.

I am aware of the pain of many of our brothers and sisters in the Diocese who are affected by drought. Let us hold each other in prayer knowing our God is with us. I would like to take this opportunity to wish you all the joy and peace of Christmas and every blessing for 2007.

Your Brother in Christ

WILLIAM M MORRIS, DD
BISHOP OF TOOWOOMBA

Appendix 8

Statement of Agreement with the Anglican Church

Statement of Agreement between Bishop William Morris of the Catholic Diocese of Toowoomba and Archbishop Peter Hollingworth of the Anglican Diocese of Brisbane

Preamble

This agreement follows discussion between Bishop William Morris and Bishop Raymond Smith, Regional Bishop, Western Region, Anglican Diocese of Brisbane.

The agreement is aimed at providing continued ministry in Catholic and Anglican parishes. It envisages that a priest of one denomination is absent for a period of time and the priest of the other denomination is still present in the community. This is often the case in the remote areas of both Dioceses.

Prayerful Support

It is hoped that the congregations of both denominations will support each other in prayer.

Sunday Worship

Where only one priest is present in the town arrangements will be made for combined Sunday worship. A service suitable to both denominations will be used on those occasions. Each denomination will make its own separate arrangements for Eucharistic worship.

Ministry to the Sick

This statement also concerns the extent to which priests of each denomination may minister sacraments of Eucharist Penance and Anointing of the Sick to members of the other church who may be extremely ill.

In cases where an Anglican person is extremely ill the Catholic priest may minister to them following specific guidelines issued by the Catholic Church for such instances. It is also agreed that where a Catholic person is extremely ill they may seek the prayerful support of an Anglican priest who may minister to them according to the guidelines of that Church.

Lay Leaders

Each denomination will appoint lay leaders to oversee other expressions of the full Christian life in their respective denominations.

Individual Conscience

This Statement of Agreement does not remove the right of conscience of individual members of either denomination to seek the ministry of the clergy of their own church.

The Most Reverend Dr Peter Hollingworth AC OBE
Archbishop of Brisbane

15 . 6 . 2001
Date

Most Reverend William Morris, DD
Bishop of Toowoomba

15 . 6 - 2001
Date

1. Both Anglican and Catholic signatories recommend that the Service used for combined Sunday worship follow "Guidelines for Ecumenical Worship in rural and remote areas" as produced by the Ecumenical Task Force on Collaborative Local Ministry. The Task Force was established by the Anglican Diocese of Brisbane, the Lutheran District Council, the Roman Catholic Archdiocese of Brisbane and the Uniting Church Synod of Queensland and published in Liturgy News March 1998.

    Otherwise recourse to sections 110-111 of the *Directory for the Application of Principles and Norms on Ecumenism* is recommended.

2. (a)   Catholic Priests will follow the direction of pars 130-132 of the *Directory for the Application of Principles and Norms on Ecumenism.*

    (b)   Add the note:
          While the Document acknowledges the local common usage of the title "priest" for both denominations, the very existence of the document acknowledges a difficulty regarding Orders. It is recognised that the Catholic Church does not accept Anglican Orders as valid.

The Most Reverend Dr Phillip Aspinall
BSc; Grad Dip RE; BD(Hons); PhD; MBA
Archbishop of Brisbane

The Most Reverend William Morris DD
Bishop of Toowoomba

18th February 2004

Date

23rd February 2004

Date

Appendix 9

Letters from 2006 – 2007

Letter A

CONGREGATIO DE CULTU DIVINO
ET DISCIPLINA SACRAMENTORUM

Prot. N. 817/00/L

December 21, 2006

Fax 07 463 922 51

Your Excellency,

The Holy Father has instructed the three Cardinals Prefect of the Congregations for the Doctrine of the Faith, for Bishops and for Divine Worship and the Discipline of the Sacraments, to hold a discussion with you on the practice of general absolution in the Diocese of Toowoomba.

We suggest two possible dates:
Tuesday 13th February or Friday 23rd February 2007, at 10 a.m. in the offices of the Congregation for Bishops.

I shall appreciate it if Your Excellency indicates to me soon which date you prefer, so that I can communicate that to the other two Cardinals.

With best wishes for Christmas, I express my religious esteem.

Devotedly Yours in Christ,

✠ Francis Card. Arinze

Copy to: His Eminence, Giovanni B. Card. RE
           His Eminence, William Card. LEVADA

For Information

His Excellency Most Rev
Msgr William M. **MORRIS**
Bishop of Toowoomba
73 Margaret Street
P.O. Box 756
Toowoomba, QLD 4350
AUSTRALIA

Letter B

BISHOP'S HOUSE

73 Margaret Street
P.O. Box 756
Toowoomba Qld. 4350
Australia

Tel.   (07) 4632 4277
Fax.   (07) 4639 2251

22 December 2006

His Eminence
+Francis Cardinal Arinze
Congregatio de Cultu Divino
Et Disciplina Sacramentorium
THE VATICAN

Your Excellency

I am in receipt of your fax of 21 December 2006. I will be in Rome in May 2007 during the week beginning 21st, for the Anglephone Meeting on Professional Standards. If it would be possible a meeting during that time with the three Cardinals Prefect of the Congregations for the Doctrine of the Faith, for Bishops and for Divine Worship and the Discipline of the Sacraments, would be more practical for me because of pastoral commitments, the provincial meeting of the Queensland Bishops, Easter, as well as the Australian Episcopal Conference.

It is my intention to be accompanied by at least one Canon Lawyer, possibly two.

I find this letter a little strange for since my meeting with yourself Cardinal Arinze, I have not given permission for the Celebration of the Communal Rite with general absolution. I have encouraged the Priests of the Diocese to make sure they always celebrate the Rites of Reconciliation according to the Canonical and Liturgical Norms of the Church's tradition. We have ongoing education concerning the sacraments and I have employed a Religious Priest from time to time to travel around the Diocese to spend time in all the communities especially in some of the most isolated areas giving our people the chance of a visiting confessor.

The Episcopal Conference is in the process of drawing up guidelines for the practice of the Communal Rite, with general absolution, for Australian conditions. After the Australian Episcopal Conference Meeting we should have a clearer guide as to what the particular regulations will be for Australia.

Our fax machine is not secure. I would appreciate any correspondence to be sent by Confidential Mail.

With every blessing for the Christmas Season and the New Year.

Your Brother in Christ

WILLIAM M MORRIS, DD
BISHOP OF TOOWOOMBA

Letter C

CONGREGATIO DE CULTU DIVINO
ET DISCIPLINA SACRAMENTORUM
—

Prot. N° 817/00/L

Vatican City, 4th January 2007

Your Excellency,

I thank you for your letter of Dec. 22, 2006, received yesterday.

The three Cardinals after due consideration of your letter, wish to say that the meeting with them to which you have been invited on February 13 or 23, 2007, is important enough to take precedence over the other possible schedules you mentioned. You are therefore requested to choose one of those two dates in February and communicate to us.

The meeting of its nature should be between Your Excellency and the three Cardinals, without the necessity for you to bring a Canon Lawyer into it. If you wish to bring a Brother Bishop it is all right. But if you insist on bringing in a Canon Lawyer, we can accept.

With best wishes for the New Year, I express my religious esteem.

Devotedly Yours in Christ,

+ Francis Card. Arinze
Prefect

Copy to: His Eminence **Giovanni Battista** Card. **RE**
              His Eminence **William** Card. **Levada**

                                            For Information

His Excellency
Most Rev. Msgr. **William M. MORRIS**
Bishop of Toowoomba
73 Margaret Street
P.O. Box 756
Toowoomba, QLD 4350
AUSTRALIA

Letter D

BISHOP'S HOUSE

73 Margaret Street
P.O. Box 756
Toowoomba Qld. 4350
Australia
Tel. (07) 4632 4277
Fax. (07) 4639 2251

17 January 2007

His Eminence
+Francis Cardinal Arinze
Congregatio de Cultu Divino
Et Disciplina Sacramentorium
THE VATICAN

Your Excellency

Thank you for your fax of 4 January 2007 forwarded to me by Monsignor Jude Thaddeus Okolo, Chargé d'Affairs a.i. from Apostolic Nunciature.

My prime responsibility, as I know you would appreciate, is to my Diocese and my pastoral responsibilities to the local Church do not allow me to be in Rome on 13th or 23rd February 2007.

I am happy to meet with the Cardinal Prefects when I am in Rome for the Anglophone Meeting on Professional Standards during the week of 21st till 28th May 2007. It is only at that time would I have the support of a Brother Bishop to accompany me to the Meeting.

Concerning a Canon Lawyer I will keep my options open as to whether or not I wish one to accompany me. In 2004 when I had a meeting with yourself, Cardinal Arinze, I was foolish enough to think that the meeting was between Brothers searching for the truth and reflecting together on the pastoral needs of the people of God. I will never place myself in that situation again and it is only in the company of a Brother Bishop and possibly a Canon Lawyer would I attend another meeting.

So that I can prepare myself I would like to receive an Agenda for the meeting with the questions that are going to be addressed.

Wishing you every blessing

Your Brother in Christ

WILLIAM M^cMORRIS, DD
BISHOP OF TOOWOOMBA

Cc's: His Eminence **Giovanni Battista** Card. **RE**
      His Eminence **William** Card. **Levada**

Appendix 10

Correspondence with Rome

<u>MEETING WITH CARDINAL RE, CARDINAL LEVADA AND CARDINAL ARINZE Saturday 19 January 2008 in Rome at 9am.</u>

May I begin by simply saying that if I have unintentionally offended any of you, in particular Cardinal Arinze, in past contact and correspondence, I apologise for any hurt caused.

A Diocesan Bishop is required to offer his resignation from Office for one of two reasons: reaching 75 years or ill-health [Canon 401; Christus Dominus Para 21]. Neither of which applies to me.

It appears that your Eminences are suggesting that the real causes for suggested resignation are contained in the unsigned Memorandum of 28 June 2007. The lack of truth in the unsigned memorandum leads to a lack of justice in the request for resignation.

I am unable to respond fully to issues raised against me because I have not been provided with a copy of the material carried by the Apostolic Visitor when he came to our diocese in April of this year nor have I seen the final Report.

Canon 220 guarantees my right to a good name and Canon 221 a right to defence.

I am exercising my right to defence as far as possible by responding to matters raised in the unsigned memorandum. I wish to respond to these six points, paragraph by paragraph.

1) A different direction......

Never once as a Bishop have I taught anything contrary to Catholic faith and morals. I wish to propose that the local Church of Toowoomba is quite in harmony with the Universal Church in spite of the comments in the unsigned Memorandum about the Advent 2006 Pastoral Letter. In my letter I referred to well known discussions throughout the world. However my letter stated " we remain committed to actively promoting vocations to the current celibate male priesthood and open to inviting priests from overseas.

[See Diocesan WebSite]

2) A severe crisis.....

Never once during my episcopate has there been official or sponsored discussion within the Diocese of Toowoomba of the ordination of married men. It is well known that such discussions occur throughout the world [e.g. Synod of Oceania 1998; Synod of Bishops on the Eucharist 2006]. The Diocese of Toowoomba is as normal and steady as anywhere else in spite of a small number of disaffected members. The Diocese is loyal to the Catholic Church and the Holy See. I as a Bishop have always professed fidelity to the Holy See. The challenges that we face in Toowoomba do not differ from other Dioceses in Australia and overseas.

3) Liturgical abuses....

It is my well publicised view that the authorized liturgical books must be used throughout the diocese. Liturgical abuses are in fact comparatively rare. Reports of aberrations have been addressed immediately, when referred to me.

4) General absolution....

I guarantee that every parish in the diocese has Individual Confession frequently and it is the ordinary form of celebration of the sacrament. In the past three years I have given permission only twice for general absolution by virtue of the provisions of Canon 961. Each of these permissions involved a situation in which the priest

2

was seriously ill. It has been my constant concern to maintain a keen appreciation of the value and importance of sacramental absolution.

5) Theological Climate.....

The Catechism of the Catholic Church is used as the basis for all catechesis in the Catholic schools of the Diocese. The Catechism has always provided and continues to provide the basis for in-service and formation of priests and pastoral leaders. The Catechism is at the centre of Adult Faith Education in parishes.

6) Ordinations...Vocations...Marginalisation of Priests...Alternative Sunday worship...

This is an unfortunate and inaccurate presentation of the facts. In fact, there have been four priests ordained in the last 8 years with the last ordained 4 years ago. Two priests are engaged in promoting vocations to the priesthood; they have been in this ministry for 7 years. Five priests are on loan to us from outside the diocese. As we have no deacons, I wonder if you are confusing us with another place. No priest under the age of 75 is retired except for serious health issues or at the priest's own request.
Sunday Celebration of the Word in the absence of a priest is provided only as an alternative in situations of necessity where a priest is not available and is celebrated in accordance with Vatican guidelines.
Programmes used.........
Parish Vocations Awareness Committee Guidelines – Fostering a 'Vocations Culture' across Australia.
A Pastoral Letter of the Bishops of Queensland on Vocations to the Priesthood.

When Archbishop Chaput made his Apostolic Visitation to the Diocese in April 2007, he was in possession of documentation of complaint of which I was not aware. I have

3

always responded immediately to matters not in conformity with the doctrine and the discipline of the Catholic Church that have been brought to my attention.

As a priest and Bishop, I have always encouraged people to be faithful to their vocation. This has been my practice with married people, Religious and Priests. In times of difficulty, I have encouraged people to stay committed to their particular vocation. It is now the same for me. The call to be a Bishop is a vocation. I cannot in conscience before God, resign.

After long and prayerful consideration and after taking counsel discreetly from trusted advisors, I do not intend to offer my resignation from the Office of Bishop of Toowoomba as suggested in the letters of **3 October 2007 and 30 November 2007.**

BISHOP'S HOUSE

73 Margaret Street
P.O. Box 756
Toowoomba Qld. 4350
Australia
Tel. (07) 4632 4277
Fax. (07) 4639 2251

24 January 2008

PRIVATE AND CONFIDENTIAL
His Eminence
Giovanni Battista Card. Re
Congregation for Bishops
THE VATICAN
ITALY

Your Eminence

I am very grateful for the meeting last Saturday and to discuss these matters face to face. At this initial stage, however, I reaffirm the position I made at the meeting itself that I am unable to resign.

However, I am giving consideration carefully in prayer to all the reasons surrounding your request for my resignation. As you realise I have many issues to reflect upon about my future and the future of the Priests and people of the Diocese of Toowoomba. My intention is to reply more fully before Easter.

With every blessing

Your Brother in Christ

William M Morris, DD
BISHOP OF TOOWOOMBA

CONGREGATIO
PRO EPISCOPIS

Prot. N. 387/1996

Vatican City, February 13, 2008
Strictly confidential

Your Excellency,

I have received your letter of January 24, 2008, in which you reaffirm your decision that you are "unable to resign" from leading the diocese of Toowoomba.

I am deeply surprised at your determination after the meeting with you on January 19th, together with Cardinal William Levada and Cardinal Francis Arinze.

I will attentively read your detailed reply which you have promised to send before Easter.

However, I cannot but repeat to Your Excellency, for the good of the diocese of Toowoomba, the invitation to find the courage to take the necessary step and submit your resignation as Bishop of the diocese. The reason for such an invitation is that your type of leadership of the diocese is seriously defective. I would be very sad for you if the Holy Father had to proceed toward your removal when confronted with your refusal.

I will be praying for you during the holy season of Lent. Wishing God's blessings on you and on the people of Toowoomba, I am

Sincerely yours in Christ,

+ G. Card. Re
Pref.

The Most Reverend William M. MORRIS, D.D.
Bishop of Toowoomba

BISHOP'S HOUSE

73 Margaret Street
P.O. Box 756
Toowoomba Qld. 4350
Australia
Tel: (07) 4632 4277
Fax: (07) 4639 2251
Email: bishsec@twb.catholic.org.au

24 December 2008

His Holiness Pope Benedict XVI
The Vatican
Rome
ITALY

Dear Holy Father

I write to you in extraordinary circumstances essentially concerning your own exercise of the Petrine ministry and my own position, before God, as a bishop of a particular local Church.

There have been serious protracted and disputed dealings between myself, as Bishop of Toowoomba and the Congregation for Bishops, Divine Worship and Doctrine of the Faith, the Cardinal Prefects of which are now requiring my resignation as bishop of the diocese.

Given that our differences have now reached such a polarised and inevitably personalised state, I am unable, in deepest conscience, to accede to their request, as I believe, and know to be true, that the processes leading to this have serious shortcomings and are based on actual errors of fact and misinformation.

Such demonstrable defects in processes and distortions of facts can not form a legitimate basis for a move of such gravity in the life of the Church.

Holy Father, I will be able to submit, with a clear conscience, to whatever you may decide and direct, if I know that you have received a comprehensive account either personally, or through some forum such as members of the Signatura which stands at some steps removed from the Cardinal Prefects who have, up-to-date, been so closely involved in the matter.

I have already for a number of years undertaken to comply with the discipline of the Third Rite of Reconciliation and to correct and clarify any ambiguity in my Advent 2006 Pastoral Letter.

Hence, the main key issues originally in contention in all of this have been resolved. Any further remedial measures in this regard, I am willing to initiate and see through to an appropriate pastoral conclusion in this diocese.

Letter from Bishop Morris   2
24 December 2008

However, it is now being asserted that, despite these undertakings, I am not suitable to be the ordinary of this diocese and that I have broken *communio* which I absolutely refute and reject.

Such a broad judgment surely needs to be objectively tested and further evidence is needed to substantiate this claim. Throughout this sad matter I believe I have been denied natural justice: I have not seen the report prepared by the Apostolic Visitor; the Apostolic Visitor did not discuss his findings with me; I have not been shown any of the "evidence" that was gathered, or even the list of the names of the "accusers". When I made the request to have an audience with you I was told this was not an option available to me until I had resigned.

There has been no canonical process to establish a "grave cause" for removal, such as a trial.

May I request that you review the report of the Apostolic Visitation undertaken by Archbishop Charles Chaput in 2007, my response to the unsigned memorandum handed to me in September 2006, my meeting with the Cardinal Prefects and my response, "Statement of Position", provided in March 2008.

I believe the views of the Bishops of the Province of Queensland and a selected group of Australian Bishops need to be canvassed as well. The assessment of my pastoral effectiveness or otherwise surely needs to be informed by the opinions of other bishops facing similar local issues.

Holy Father, again I assure you and undertake to conform to and abide by whatever is your determination in the Petrine Ministry you hold. What I request, what I need, in conscience before God, is the knowledge that my case has been fairly reviewed and that whatever your ultimate decision may be, that it has been adequately informed by the truth and my personal and respectful dialogue with you.

Assuring you of my prayerful support and that of the local Church and wishing you the peace and joy of the birth of Christ.

Your Brother in Christ

+ William M Morris, DD
BISHOP OF TOOWOOMBA

Appendix 11

Cardinals Re, Arinze, Levada's Statement at Meeting 19 January 2008 Rome

MEETING WITH BISHOP WILLIAM MORRIS, ORDINARY OF TOOWOOMBA

Welcome Bishop Morris and thank you Archbishop Wilson, as President of the Australian Catholic Bishops Conference, for accompanying Bishop Morris today.

1) Cardinal Arinze, Cardinal Levada and I will be happy to listen to Bishop Morris and we will offer our attention to what he wishes to say.

But first of all, I think it would be useful to explain the mind of the Holy See and then we will listen to what Bishop Morris and Archbishop Wilson want to say before discussing the matter together.

Secularization and other such problems exist in all dioceses throughout the world, but the reasons for worrying about the ecclesial situation in the diocese of Toowoomba have gone beyond acceptable limits.

Bishop Morris is well motivated by good will and he is generous and close to his priests and people, but **his leadership** does not correct nor rectify what is incompatible with the doctrine and the discipline of the Catholic Church. Consequently, the local Church in **Toowoomba is moving in a different direction than that of the Catholic Church.**

2) I will offer some concrete examples:
It was a surprise to read Bishop Morris's two thousand and six **Advent Pastoral Letter.** The letter touches on a serious and important problem: the ever-diminishing number of priests for the celebration of the Eucharist and pastoral work. This shortage of priests is of concern to all.

However, on reading Bishop Morris's letter, **not even a minimum of theological content** can be found as would seem logical to expect in a pastoral letter. The title says it is for "Advent", but then there is no reference to this liturgical season and to the coming of Christ.

There are, on the other hand, **pragmatic consideration** that invite one to be "more open towards options for ensuring that Eucharist may be celebrated", followed by an invitation to discuss as possible solutions:

- The recognition of **Anglican Orders.**
  But Anglican Orders were declared invalid by Pope
  Leo XIII. This Papal decision is *"definitive tenenda"*.
  What sense is there in discussing this "possibility" that
  is, in fact, impossible?
- In the same way, **Lutheran ordinations** are not
  sacraments. They are not valid ordinations because
  they are not ordinations at all!
- Similarly, you invite discussion about the **ordination
  of women.** There is a document written by Pope John
  Paul II in 1994 called *"Ordinatio Sacerdotalis"*, which
  states that "the Church has no authority whatsoever to
  confer priestly ordination of women" (N4). [1] This is a
  decision of the category *"definitive tenenda"*.
- To invite discussion on this topic as you did means
  not to accept the Pope's decision. A bishop cannot go
  against the decision of the Holy Father. A Bishop is not
  "an independent moderator of pragmatic solutions."
- To sum up briefly: to present these questions as topics
  for public discussion is to separate yourself from the
  teaching of the Catholic Church. An attentive reading
  of this pastoral letter reveals **a very poor theology and
  an ecclesiology that is not Catholic – and the Bishop
  must be the "Teacher of the Faith"**!

3) At least in the past eight years there have been no priestly
ordinations in Toowoomba. The Diocese does not seem to have an
effective and sufficiently dynamic pastoral programme for promoting
vocations or finding priests from elsewhere and the Bishop does not
offer the leadership necessary to reverse the situation.

Also, the early retirement of priests still in good health and their
substitution by deacons or laity in providing alternative Sunday
worship is not a valid solution in a situation where there is a shortage
of priests.

4) With regard to **"general absolution"**, we are glad to hear of Bishop
Morris's statement that "general absolution is no longer common."
For two years Bishop Morris was asked to give a clear indication to

the diocese to adhere to the regulation as stipulated in 2002 in Pope John Paul the seconds *"moto proprio"*, *"Misericordia Dei"*.

Bishop Morris had been asked to come to Rome to talk about this and other problems, and two possible dates were proposed to him. He replied by not accepting either date and postponing the encounter for a later time, as if it were something that was not important.

5) In the Diocese of Toowoomba there are some well-noted **liturgical abuses.**

A Bishop should ensure that the sacraments are administered according to proper liturgical norms established by the Church. In particular, the celebration of Mass by priests according to the liturgy of the Church is at the heart of the pastoral responsibility of the diocesan bishop.

Bishop Morris generally does not intervene to correct abuses, as if he considered them of little importance.

6) The general **theological climate** of the diocese, and especially of its priests, needs to move toward a more authentic Catholic identity, as found in the *"Catechism of the Catholic Church"*.

7) An **Apostolic Visitator** was sent to his diocese. He interviewed Bishop Morris and many priests and lay faithful.

8) **Conclusion**

The conditions in the diocese of Toowoomba are cause for deep concern to the Holy Father. The good of the Diocese requires a Bishop who will approach in a different way the challenges facing the Church today. Toowoomba needs a Bishop who, with determination and courage, will tackle the problems and rectify what is not in conformity with the doctrine and the discipline of the Catholic Church. Bishop Morris's theological preparation and type of leadership are inadequate to confront the crisis of the Church of Toowoomba, despite what may be his good intentions.

Bishop Morris is a person of integrity in morals, a man of good will and other gifts. He can continue to do much good, but the right role for him is not that of Diocesan Bishop of Toowoomba.

He should be given another assignment, with special duties. With this in mind, the Holy Father asks the Metropolitan Archbishop of Brisbane and the President of the Australian Catholic Bishops' Conference to help find the most appropriate responsibility in which Bishop Morris can continue to effectively serve the Church elsewhere in Australia, while obviously being assured of financial security for a suitable living.

1. "Ut igitur omne dubiom auferatur circa rem magni momenti, quae ad ipsam Ecclesiae divinam constitutionem pertinent, virtute ministerii Nostri confimandi fratres (cf. Lc 22,32), declaramus Ecclesiam facultatem nullatenus habere ordinationem sacerdotalem mulieribus conferendi, hancque sententiam ab omnibus Ecclesiaw fidelibus definitive tenendam"

Appendix 12

Corrections on Diocesan Website

Correction on Diocesan Website

In my Advent Pastoral Letter of 2006 I outlined some of the challenges facing the diocese into the future. In that letter I made reference to various options about ordination that were and are being talked about in various places, as part of an exercise in the further investigation of truth in these matters. Unfortunately some people seem to have interpreted that reference as suggesting that I was personally initiating options that are contrary to the doctrine and discipline of the Church. As a bishop I cannot and would not do that and I indicated this in the local media at the time. I and all the bishops of the Catholic Church form a college with the Holy Father and cannot act contrary to the teaching and practice of the Universal Church. Encouraging vocation to the priesthood must remain a priority for our local Church and we pray this Christmas and as we begin the New Year that more young men will consider deeply their response to God's call."

Appendix 13

Diocesan Pastoral Statement

Vision

Pilgrim people living God's dream...

'To bring good news to the poor to proclaim release to captives and recovery of sight to the bling, to let the oppressed go free, to proclaim the year of the Lord's favour.'

Lk 4:18–19

Mission

We are Christian faith communities called to work together in a spirit of trust and openness to bring about hope, love, justice and peace in our world.

Key Pastoral Directions

Through baptism we are called to live out God's dream by . . .

> Embracing action for social justice
> Evangelizing life and culture
> Respecting and honouring faith traditions
> Promoting and celebrating life-giving liturgy
> Developing and updating faith education and spirituality
> Exploring and implementing various pastoral leadership models

Through baptism we are called to live out God's dream by... Embracing Action for Social Justice:

Action on behalf of justice and participation in the transformation of the world fully appears to us a constitutive dimension of preaching the gospel. (Justice in the World: Synod of Bishops, 1971)

Priority Actions:

- Support the Diocesan Social Justice Commission
- Address the issues in justice impacting on:
  Indigenous Peoples
  Refugees and Migrants
  The environment

Developing and Updating Faith Education and Spirituality

The faith of adults . . . . . . must be continually enlightened, developed and protected, so that it may acquire that Christian wisdom which gives sense, unity and hope to the many experiences of personal, social and spiritual life. (General Directory for Catechesis 173)

> Priority Actions:
> - Provide training and formation for ministry roles in the church
> - Tell the 'new story': a theology/spirituality for 21st Century Australians
> - Promote relevant programs already operating (e.g. Beginning Theology)

Respecting and Honouring Faith Traditions:

"it is absolutely clear that ecumenism, the movement promoting Christian Unity, is not just some sort of 'appendix' which is added to the Church's traditional activity. Rather ecumenism is an organic part of her life and work, and consequently must pervade all that she is and does." (That All May Be One, 20 John Paul II)

Priority Actions:

> - Promoting ecumenical dialogue and education including education about Eucharistic Hospitality
> - Encourage and support ecumenical liaison

Promoting and Celebrating Life-giving Liturgy:

The Church earnestly desires that all the faithful be lead to that full, conscious and active participation in liturgical celebrations called for by the very nature of liturgy. Such participation by the Christian people as a chosen race, a royal priesthood, a holy nation, God's own people is their right and duty by reason of their baptism. In the reform and promotion of the liturgy, the full and active participation by all the people is the aim to be considered before all else. (Constitution on Sacred Liturgy 14)

Priority Actions:

- Promote and enable life-giving liturgy and ritual, with the main emphasis being on Sunday worship and/or Liturgy of the Word
- Form and educate in all areas of liturgy and sacraments
- Promote the use of diocesan and other liturgical documents
- Revitalize the RCIA in the diocese

Evangelizing Life and Culture

"Evangelizing is in fact the grace and vocation proper to the Church, her deepest identity. She exists in order to evangelize." (Evangelii Nuntiandi 14)

Priority Actions:

- Provide education and formation in evangelization
- Encourage and support study groups around the diocese
- Outreach to those who struggle in our church and society

Exploring and Implementing Various Pastoral Leadership Models:

"All the faithful enjoy a true equality with regard to the dignity and the activity which they share in the building up of the Body of Christ". (Constitution on Church 32)

Priority Actions for Parish Pastoral Councils and Leadership Teams:

- Support the development and facilitation of a relevant structure in each parish that enables two-way communication between the appointed pastoral leadership team and the people of the parish
- Support and facilitate the development of models for Pastoral Leadership across parish and deaneries
- Provide training and on-going in-service for people undertaking pastoral leadership roles in the diocese

Appendix 14

May All Be One: Pastoral Guidelines for Eucharistic Hospitality

DIOCESE OF TOOWOOMBA
MAY ALL BE ONE

FOREWORD

My dear People,

An existing dimension of Church in our area is its commitment to Ecumenism. One of the challenging issues to be faced is that of Eucharistic Hospitality. This statement addresses the matter.

At Easter 1995, Archbishop John Bathersby issued a document called "Blessed and Broken" – Pastoral Guidelines for Eucharistic Hospitality. He acknowledged the work of the Archdiocesan Commission for Ecumenism in the preparation of that document. That document is the basis of this statement, which has been adapted by our Diocesan Ecumenical Commission.

I would ask you, the clergy and laity of the Diocese, to use the statement to promote the movement for unity.

With every best wish,

Yours in Christ,

William M Morris, DD
BISHOP OF TOOWOOMBA
November 1996

The 1993 Directory
Issued by the
Pontifical Council for promoting Christian Unity
strongly recommends
episcopal conferences or diocesan bishops
so establish local norms
for the application of the general norms
given in the Directory

No. 130

PASTORAL GUIDELINES FOR EUCHARISTIC HOSPITALITY

Pastoral Guidelines for Providing Access to Holy Communion for Christians of Other Churches

• INTRODUCTION

A strong desire to see the unity of all God's people is a concern of many Christians today. The Second Vatican Council clearly committed the Catholic Church to the ecumenical movement. The Council invited all Catholics to cultivate a positive ecumenical attitude, the starting point being the sacrament of baptism. The Directory for the Application of the Principles and Norms of Ecumenism (1993) elaborates on this fact.

> By the sacrament of baptism a person is truly incorporated into Christ and into the Church and us reborn to a sharing of the divine life. Baptism, therefore, constitutes the sacramental bond of unity existing among all who through it are reborn. Baptism, of itself, is the beginning, for it is directed toward the acquiring of fullness of life in Christ.

Catholics are encouraged to take every opportunity to pray with Christians whose Churches, like our own, are members of Queensland Churches Together. Pastors are called to do all that they can to make such opportunities available to their parishioners. Not only is it highly desirable that Catholics participate in ecumenical services, they are encouraged from time to time to attend services of other Churches to show friendship and interest, and in order to understand how other Christians express themselves in worship. Other Christian should be made welcome at Catholic Masses.

Many Catholics have a desire to share holy communion with other Christians. They recognise that incorporation into Christ through baptism should find expression at a shared Eucharistic table. Though the exact nature of the unity desired for all Christians is still unclear, it is generally agreed that it must ultimately involve the ability of Christians to celebrate the Eucharist together.

• CENTRALITY OF THE EUCHARIST

Ours is essentially a Eucharistic church. Catholic identity can be seen most clearly when the parish gathers for the celebration of the Eucharist. It is then that we show to one another, to other Christians, and to society in general that Catholics are united in faith and worship and life. Without the Eucharist and the other sacraments, we could not maintain our Catholic identity. *For Catholics Eucharist, sharing is inseparably linked to, and is the visible expression of full church membership.* The members of any local Catholic community are primarily bonded through baptism. In the Eucharist they celebrate their unity with one another and that openness to all Christian which baptism demands. Such communities are also united to every other Catholic Eucharistic community. It is made clear in the words of every Mass that the local community, through its bishop, is united to the pope who is the centre of catholic unity, and through the pope to every other Catholic Eucharistic community.

• UNITY IN FAITH

Sadly, Christians do not always agree as to what constitutes the Christian faith. There are some elements of that faith which Catholics consider to be essential but other Christians do not. Some examples are the necessity of the divinely appointed leadership of the papacy, the role of the Virgin Mary in the life of the church, and the manner in which Christ is present in the Eucharist. Official dialogue between the Catholic Church and other Churches is clarifying what we each believe about these and other matters, but agreement about all the essentials of faith has not yet been reached.

Because the Eucharistic celebration is by its very nature a profession of faith of the church, it is impossible for the Catholic Church presently to engage in general Eucharistic sharing.

The Catholic Church does not permit her members to receive holy communion in Anglican, Lutheran and Protestant Churches, and she offers Eucharistic hospitality to Christians from these Churches only in situations of serous and pressing spiritual need.

Between the Catholic Church and the Orthodox Churches there is a very close relationship in matters of faith. When necessity requires, ir a genuine spiritual need exists, it is lawful for a Catholic to receive holy communion in an Orthodox Church. Some Orthodox Churches, however, restrict holy communion to their own members. Although Catholic priests may lawfully administer holy communion to members of Orthodox Churches, in Australia these Churches generally prefer that their members do not receive holy communion at Catholic Masses.

• EUCHARISTIC HOSPITALITY

There are significant events in the lives of individual Christians and their families when requests to receive holy communion at a Catholic Mass will be made. If we consider the high frequency of marriage between Catholics and other Christians in Australia, the extensive sacramental preparation programs for children which require the participation of parents, many of who are not Catholic, and the increasingly favourable ecumenical climate in our Diocese, it is very likely that such requests will be forthcoming on a variety of occasions. This will be more so once our Church's openness to responding to the spiritual needs of other Christians is better known. The following are some examples of spiritual need: for the partner at a marriage celebrated with a nuptial Mass; for the parent of a child baptised at a Catholic Mass; for the parent of a child receiving confirmation and first holy communion; for the family of the deceased at a funeral Mass. Similarly, requests may come from Christians who are denied easy access to a minister of their own Church because they are confined to a health care facility, or are subject to some form of institutional confinement.

There should not be a general invitation from the presiding priest for Christians from other churches to receive holy communion at a Catholic Mass. Pastoral discretion and respect for those present would urge against an explicit statement of exclusion from receiving communion. Each case must be considered on its merit. The person must make a request without any kind of pressure, must manifest the Catholic belief in the Eucharist, and must have appropriate dispositions. *In the Diocese of Toowoomba it is sufficient for the presiding priest to establish by means of a few simple questions, whether or not these conditions are met.*

When a Christian from another Church makes frequent requests to receive holy communion, different circumstances prevail. In such a case joint pastoral care by the clergy of both Churches should be offered to help the person understand the significance of such requests.

• INTERCHUCH MARRIAGES

The Directory on Ecumenism states that Eucharistic sharing for a spouse in a mixed marriage can only be exceptional. The Directory, however, recognises a category of mixed marriages where each partner lives devotedly within the tradition of his and her Church. It sees such couples making a significant contribution to the ecumenical movement. A spouse in such a marriage now commonly called an interchurch marriage, could well experience a serious spiritual need to receive holy communion each time he or she accompanies the family to a Catholic Mass. *Requests for this kind of Eucharistic hospitality should be referred by the parish priest to the Bishop.*

• OTHER SACRAMENTS

Similar principles to the above would apply to the sacraments of penance and the anointing of the sick.

• CONCLUSION

These Pastoral Guidelines are offered as part of the ongoing conversations taking place between the churches in our region. Effective ecumenism is built on candid sharing of positions, to be taken up by all in the conversation. We acknowledge our position on Eucharistic hospitality. It is not without its difficulties both for ourselves and for the people of other faiths with a tradition of Eucharistic hospitality.

> To believe in Christ means to desire unity; to desire unity means to desire the Church; to desire the Church means to desire the communion of grace which corresponds to the Father's plan from all eternity. Such is the meaning of Christ's prayer: "That They May All Be One".

(Pope Paul II – Encyclical Letter *UT UNUM SINT*)

Appendix 15

The Law

THE LAW

Can. 1629 No appeal is possible against:

1° a judgement of the Supreme Pontiff himself, or a judgement of the Apostolic Signatura;

Can. 220 No one may unlawfully harm the good reputation which a person enjoys, or violate the right of every person to protect his or her privacy.

Can. 221 §1 Christ's faithful may lawfully vindicate and defend the rights they enjoy in the Church, before the competent ecclesiastical forum in accordance with the law.

§2 If any members of Christ's faithful are summoned to trial by the competent authority, they have the right to be judged according to the provisions of the law, to be applied with equity.

§3 Christ's faithful have the right that no canonical penalties be inflicted upon them except in accordance with the law.

Can. 375 §1 By divine institution, Bishops succeed the Apostles through the Holy Spirit who is given to them. They are constituted Pastors in the Church, to be the teachers of doctrine, the priests of sacred worship and the ministers of governance.

§2 By their episcopal consecration, Bishops receive, together with the office of sanctifying, the offices also of teaching and of ruling, which however, by their nature, can be exercised only in hierarchical communion with the head of the College and its members.

Can. 401 §1 A diocesan Bishop who has completed his seventy-fifth year of age is requested to offer his resignation from office to the Supreme Pontiff, who, taking all the circumstances into account, will make provision accordingly.

§2 A diocesan Bishop who, because of illness or some other grave reason, has become unsuited for the fulfilment of his office, is earnestly requested to offer his resignation from office.

Can. 188 A resignation which is made as a result of grave fear unjustly inflicted, or of deceit, or of substantial error, or of simony, is invalid by virtue of the law itself.

Can. 189 §1 For a resignation to be valid, whether it requires acceptance or not, it must be made to the authority which is competent to provide for the office in question, and it must be made either in writing, or orally before two witnesses.

§2 The authority is not to accept a resignation which is not based on a just and proportionate reason.

Can. 1717 §1 Whenever the Ordinary receives information, which has at least the semblance of truth, about an offence, he is to enquire carefully, either personally or through some suitable person, about the facts and circumstances, and about the imputability of the offence, unless this enquiry would appear to be entirely superfluous.

§2 Care is to be taken that this investigation does not call into question anyone's good name.

§3 The one who performs this investigation has the same powers and obligations as an auditor in a process. If, later, a judicial process is initiated, this person may not take part in it as a judge.

Can. 1718 §1 When the facts have been assembled, the Ordinary is to decide:

1° whether a process to impose or declare a penalty can be initiated;

2° whether this would be expedient, bearing in mind Can. 1341;

3° whether a judicial process is to be used or, unless the law forbids it, whether the matter is to proceed by means of an extra-judicial decree.

§2 The Ordinary is to revoke or change the decree mentioned in §1 whenever new facts indicate to him that a different decision should be made.

§3 In making the decrees referred to in §§1 and 2, the Ordinary, if he considers it prudent, is to consult two judges or other legal experts.

§4 Before making a decision in accordance with §1, the Ordinary is to consider whether, to avoid useless trials, it would be expedient, with the parties' consent, for himself or the investigator to make a decision, according to what is good and equitable, about the question of harm.

Can. 1719 The acts of the investigation, the decrees of the Ordinary by which the investigation was opened and closed, and all those matters which preceded the investigation, are to be kept in the secret curial archive, unless they are necessary for the penal process.

Can. 1734 §1 Before having recourse, the person must seek in writing from its author the revocation or amendment of the decree. Once this petition has been lodged, it is by that very fact understood that the suspension of the execution of the decree is also being sought.

§2 The petition must be made within the peremptory time-limit of ten canonical days from the time the decree was lawfully notified.

§3 The norms in §§1 and 2 do not apply:

1° in having recourse to the Bishop against decrees given by authorities who are subject to him;

2° in having recourse against the decree by which a hierarchical recourse is decided, unless the decision was given by the Bishop himself ;

3° in having recourse in accordance with cann. 57 and 1735.

Can. 1445 §1 The supreme Tribunal of the Apostolic Signatura hears:

1° plaints of nullity, petitions for total reinstatement and other recourses against rotal judgements;

2° recourses in cases affecting the status of persons, which the Roman Rota has refused to admit to a new examination;

3° exceptions of suspicion and other cases against Auditors of the Roman Rota by reason of things done in the exercise of their office;

4° the conflicts of competence mentioned in can. 1416.

§2 This same Tribunal deals with controversies which arise from an act of ecclesiastical administrative power, and which are lawfully referred to it. It also deals with other administrative controversies referred to it by the Roman Pontiff or by departments of the Roman Curia, and with conflicts of competence among these departments.

§3 This Supreme Tribunal is also competent:

1° to oversee the proper administration of justice and, should the need arise, to take notice of advocates and procurators;

2° to extend the competence of tribunals;

3° to promote and approve the establishment of the tribunals mentioned in cann. 1423 and 1439.

Can. 1598 §1 When the evidence has been assembled, the judge must, under pain of nullity, by a decree permit the parties and their advocates to inspect at the tribunal office those acts which are not yet known to them. Indeed, if the advocates so request, a copy of the acts can be given to them. In cases which concern the public good, however, the judge can decide that, in order to avoid very serious dangers, some part or parts of the acts are not to be shown to anyone; he must take care, however, that the right of defence always remains intact.

§2 To complete the evidence, the parties can propose other items of proof to the judge. When these have been assembled the judge can, if he deems it appropriate, again issue a decree as in §1.

PASTOR BONUS

Art. 79 — Furthermore, the Congregation applies itself to matters relating to the correct exercise of the pastoral function of the bishops, by offering them every kind of assistance. For it is part of its duty to initiate general apostolic visitations where needed, in agreement with the dicasteries concerned and, in the same manner, to evaluate their results and to propose to the Supreme Pontiff the appropriate actions to be taken.

Art. 121 — The Apostolic Signatura functions as the supreme tribunal and also ensures that justice in the Church is correctly administered.

Art. 122 — This Tribunal adjudicates:

1. complaints of nullity and petitions for total reinstatement against sentences of the Roman Rota;
2. in cases concerning the status of persons, recourses when the Roman Rota has denied a new examination of the case;
3. exceptions of suspicion and other proceedings against judges of the Roman Rota arising from the exercise of their functions;
4. conflicts of competence between tribunals which are not subject to the same appellate tribunal.

Art. 123 — § 1. The Signatura adjudicates recourses lodged within the peremptory limit of thirty canonical days against singular administrative acts whether issued by the dicasteries of the Roman Curia or approved by them, whenever it is contended that the impugned act violated some law either in the decision-making process or in the procedure used.

§ 2. In these cases, in addition to the judgement regarding illegality of the act, it can also adjudicate, at the request of the plaintiff, the reparation of damages incurred through the unlawful act.

§ 3. The Signatura also adjudicates other administrative controversies referred to it by the Roman Pontiff or by dicasteries of the Roman Curia, as well as conflicts of competence between these dicasteries.
Art. 124 — The Signatura also has the responsibility:

1. to exercise vigilance over the correct administration of justice, and, if need be, to censure advocates and procurators;
2. to deal with petitions presented to the Apostolic See for obtaining the commission of a case to the Roman Rota or some other favour relative to the administration of justice;
3. to extend the competence of lower tribunals;
4. to grant its approval to tribunals for appeals reserved to the Holy See, and to promote and approve the erection of interdiocesan tribunals.

Art. 125 — The Apostolic Signatura is governed by its own law.

Appendix 16

Correspondence between Pope Benedict XVI and Bishosp Morris in 2009

To the Venerable Brother
William Morrris
Bishop of Toowoomba

I wish to acknowledge your letter of 24 December 2008 in which you informed me of your difficulties in presenting your resignation as Bishop of Toowoomba.

I have read your letter attentively and I have noted your openness with which you wrote to me.

With equal clarity and fraternal love, I would like to tell you that your guidance of the diocese seems to be weak and insufficient for the challenges and the circumstances of Toowoomba. The pastoral demands of the good of the diocese require a bishop who will be able to rectify the course and give fresh vitality to the diocese in steadfast fidelity to the Magisterium of the Church.

I read in your letter the expressions of respect which you have towards me, and I know that I can fully rely on your obedience to the Successor of Peter.

Soon after this coming Easter, I would be willing to receive you in Audience and talk with you. Please contact Archbishop James M. Harvey, Prefect of the Pontifical Household, to arrange a suitable date.

With deep affection I assure you of my prayers and I invoke God's blessing on you and on the diocese of Toowoomba.

Vatican City, 31 January, 2009.

Benedictus II m.

BISHOP'S HOUSE

73 Margaret Street
P.O. Box 756
Toowoomba Qld. 4350
Australia
Tel. (07) 4632 4277
Fax. (07) 4639 2251

12 November 2009

His Holiness Pope Benedict XVI
The Vatican
Rome
ITALY

Dear Holy Father

It is just over five months since you favoured Archbishop Philip Wilson and I with a meeting. For that opportunity I thank you.

On the 9 July 2009 I received a letter from Cardinal Re (in response to my letter to you of 19 June 2009) requiring my resignation "as promised to you" at our meeting. On the return of Archbishop Wilson from overseas I checked his recollection of our meeting and conversation. Archbishop Wilson concurred with me that nothing I said to you could be taken or construed as a promise to resign, in fact Archbishop Wilson reminded me that I said to him as we left the meeting that "I would not be resigning".

This accords with my letters to you dated 24 December 2008 and 19 June 2009 in which I put to you, that for me, this is a deeply held matter of conscience.

Cardinal Re's claim that "I promised my resignation" is but further troubling evidence of a lack of care for the truth which has characterised this whole process to which I have been subjected. It cannot be "of God" when the truth is not respected and exactness is not preserved.

My dilemma remains intense for I cannot see how such evident defects in process and distortions of facts can form a legitimate basis for a move of such gravity in the life of the Diocese for which I was ordained, and have been committed to for the past sixteen and a half years. I fear for the consequences for the people of this Local Church and indeed the damage and scandal this would cause to the whole Church's authority generally.

Searching my own motivation, I discern no personal preferences, practical convenience or human ambition. Quite the contrary! This detachment and my reluctance "to play politics" may have caused or contributed to the situation in which I now find myself.

I do not want – let alone seek – any notoriety which would only damage the Church, locally and generally, as I have stated above.

2

Letter to Pope Benedict XVI
From: Most Rev William M Morris, DD
Bishop of the Toowoomba Diocese, Queensland, Australia

In conscience I am unable to offer my resignation for that would imply an acceptance or at least a compliance with the procedures and processes which have been lacking in natural justice, transparency and truthfulness. My "unsuitability to be a Diocesan Bishop" is a most broad general assertion which has not been adequately substantiated or demonstrated to me. Those areas in which I have been at fault I have done my best to correct. The matters raised in my Pastoral Letter, which I acknowledge could have been worded better, are those which are in ferment generally across the Church.

Our respective cultural and linguistic backgrounds may influence the manner and the words chosen in which we try either to conceal or to confront the problems facing the Church.

I admit that the tone of some of my correspondence may have seemed too direct or too blunt for curial diplomacy. Surely though this is more a matter of style rather than of substance – a case of cultural difference rather than broken Communion.

Holy Father, I regret that my situation has added to the weight of your concern for all the churches. Yet as the allegations remain unspecific, my best efforts at restorative justice and a genuine reconciliation are severely hampered.

My words, actions and intentions have always been to preserve rather than pervert ecclesial communion. This is supported by my brother bishops here in Queensland and other parts of Australia who would testify to the worth of my ministry and they are aware of my fidelity to the Magisterium.

What I still ask is precisely where, when and exactly how have I failed? As I have pointed out before, I have been denied natural justice and due process; I have never seen the Report prepared by the Apostolic Visitor. The Apostolic Visitor rather indicated to me and to others that the conditions in the Toowoomba Diocese are not so very different from those across the English speaking Church. I have not been shown any of the "evidence" that was gathered, or even names of my "accusers". This seems "contra Scripture" (Mt.5/23-26, 10/26-27, 18/15-18.etc.) There has not been a canonical process to establish a "grave cause" for removal and the conditions of Canon 401 §§ 1,2 have not been met.

As I have been denied natural justice and due process, I could not accept in conscience some artificially created, extra-diocesan position. In Australian culture this would be seen and ridiculed for what it is – a sinecure, and would only further damage the Church's standing in this country. I do realise that there are marked differences between the adversarial and inquisitorial legal traditions from which we respectively come. It is, though, the vague generality and the evident factual inaccuracies in the very limited information, of which I have been made aware, which leave me unconvinced and unconvicted in my own conscience.

Holy Father, I have had to express this as forthrightly as possible to capture the moral dilemma in which we are embroiled. For me it is a matter of conscience. My resignation would mean that I accept the assessment of myself as breaking *communio*. I absolutely refute and reject this assessment so it is out of my love for the Church

3

Letter to Pope Benedict XVI
From: Most Rev William M Morris, DD
Bishop of the Toowoomba Diocese, Queensland, Australia

that I cannot do so. We are both aware that any discernment based on false premises cannot lead to the truth.

Assuring you of my prayerful support and fidelity and that of this Local Church and I respectfully remain in need of your guidance and wisdom.

With every blessing

Your Brother in Christ

+ William M Morris, DD
BISHOP OF TOOWOOMBA

To my Venerable Brother
WILLIAM M. MORRIS
Bishop of Toowoomba

I wish to acknowledge receipt of your letter of 12 November 2009, in which you explain your reluctance to present your resignation as Bishop of the Diocese of Toowoomba.

The closing lines of your letter, "I respectfully remain in need of your guidance and wisdom," inspire me to write to you frankly and fraternally.

In your letter you refer to "defects in process." We have been engaged instead in a fraternal dialogue, in which we appeal to your conscience and ask you to renounce freely the office of diocesan bishop. Some of your doctrinal utterances cause grave concern in view of the responsibility of the bishop to teach the entirety of the doctrine of the faith authentically, and it was our intention to explain to you our firm conviction in this matter. Canon Law does not make provision for a process regarding bishops, whom the Successor of Peter nominates and may remove from office.

You write that there has been a "lack of care for the truth" on the part of the Holy See. Clearly there has been a misunderstanding. In our meeting I tried to show you why your resignation was necessary, and it was my understanding that you had expressed your openness to comply and to resign as Bishop of Toowoomba. From your letter, however, I see that you had no such intention. I realize this now, but I must say decidedly that there has not been "a lack of care for the truth."

You also allude to your situation as a case of "cultural difference" that does not affect ecclesial communion. However, in your Advent Pastoral Letter 2006 – besides containing some very questionable pastoral choices – there are at least two options presented that are incompatible with the Catholic faith:

a)   ordaining women in order to overcome the priest shortage. Yet, the late Pope John Paul II has decided infallibly and irrevocably that the Church has not the right to ordain women to the priesthood;

b) "recognizing Anglican, Lutheran and Uniting Church Orders". But according to the doctrine of the Catholic faith, ministers from these communities are not validly ordained and therefore do not share in the Sacrament of Holy Orders; and as such their actions are not joined to the ministerial priesthood.

There is no doubt that your pastoral intentions are good, but clearly your doctrinal teaching contains errors. Furthermore, as was made clear to you during the meeting on 19 January 2008 with the Prefects of three Roman Dicasteries, your leadership of the priests and faithful of your diocese raises serious questions. Furthermore, the diocesan bishop must above all be an authentic teacher of the faith, which is the foundation of all pastoral ministry.

Before Christ who will one day judge me and you, I renew my request to you to tender your resignation as Bishop of Toowoomba and to accept another responsibility, in which you can continue to serve the Church in Australia in another ministry more in keeping with your gifts and talents.

Assuring you of my prayers, I invoke God's blessing on you and on the Diocese of Toowoomba.

From the Vatican, 22 December 2009

Benedictus PP. XVI

Appendix 17

Correspondence with Cardinal Re of 2010

CONGREGATIO
PRO EPISCOPIS
___

Prot. N. 536/2009

Vatican City, February 6, 2010
Strictly confidential

Your Excellency,

At a recent Audience with the Holy Father, His Excellency Most Reverend Philip Wilson, Archbishop of Adelaide and President of the Australian Conference of Catholic Bishops, presented your proposal of resigning as Bishop of Toowoomba in May of 2011.

The Holy Father instructed me to tell you that he has decided to meet your desire which you forcefully expressed, and thus he accepts that the notice of your retirement as Bishop of Toowoomba will be published in May of 2011.

Assuring you of the support of my prayers and imploring God's blessings on you and on the people of Toowoomba, I am

Sincerely yours in Christ,

+ B. Card. Re
Pref.

The Most Reverend William M. MORRIS, D.D.
Bishop of Toowoomba

BISHOP'S HOUSE

73 Margaret Street
P.O. Box 756
Toowoomba Qld. 4350
Australia
Tel. (07) 4632 4277
Fax. (07) 4639 2251

8 December 2010

His Holiness Pope Benedict XVI
The Vatican
Rome
ITALY

Dear Holy Father

In February I received a letter from the Congregation of Bishops informing me that they would be announcing my retirement in May 2011. In July I wrote to the Apostolic Nuncio Archbishop Guiseppe Lazzarotto informing him that May would not be the most appropriate time for me to retire because of the sexual abuse cases that we are dealing with here in the Diocese, due to the actions of a teacher in one of our Catholic Schools. Archbishop Lazzarotto has informed me that the Congregation has decided not to extend my retirement date to later in the year so that I can pastorally care for the victims and their families while mediation is carried out.

There were thirteen young girls who were sexually abused, and as you can appreciate they and their families are devastated, suffering from stress and anxiety and looking for support and healing so that they can get on with their lives. I have just spent this week in mediation with five of the victim's families and we have been able to bring about a certain degree of healing and they have expressed for the first time their deep appreciation of the compassionate way the Church has handled their cases.

In 2011 we are preparing to carry out this mediation with the rest of the families. It is our hope that this can be finalised as early as possible in the new year. Unfortunately these things cannot be rushed and our Solicitors have advised that all these cases because of the legal proceedings will not be settled until later in the year.

I am not the only one that can mediate and help bring about healing to the victims and their families but I am the constant Church Authority for them at this moment in time. They have started to develop a trust in the way we are handling this horrific incident in their lives and they feel supported by the Church for the first time since this sexual abuse happened. I believe it would be another abuse of their growing trust in the Church if I retired in May before the mediation was carried out with the rest of the victims and their families.

Holy Father, I am not asking for myself but for the children and their families that I be able to walk with them during the final stages of mediation. The Church at last is starting to be seen to care for the victims, to take the appropriate steps to help them, and to make sure that they

2

are looked after appropriately. I have spoken to Archbishop Wilson, President of the Australian Catholic Bishops Conference and he supports me in my request to you for an extension of a few months so that the victims and their families can be looked after and this sad episode in the life of the Toowoomba Church can be handled with dignity and respect.

I had to dismiss the Principal and two Education Officers for not following the appropriate protocols with regards to child protection, which put more young girls at risk of being sexually abused and unfortunately some were. One of the Education Officers is suing the Diocese of Toowoomba and myself for defamation. This case will come before the Courts in mid-2011, if the Education Officer decides to proceed. I will be needed to represent the Diocese in these Court proceedings and defend my actions. It is the firm belief of those who know the facts of the case and our legal representatives that we have very solid grounds for the actions that were taken and it will be very difficult for the Education Officer to disprove the evidence.

I know that you have placed the abuse crisis at the heart of your Pontificate and how sad you are for the victims and their families and wish to do all in your power to bring about healing in their lives and for the Church to do the right thing in looking after the victims. Like you, I have the Local Church and especially the victims and their families at heart when I ask you to allow me to represent the victims in the mediation and court proceedings.

Holy Father, I would keep Archbishop Guiseppe Lazzarotto informed of the mediation and court proceedings. When they have been finalised I would write to you according to Canon 401 §§ 1,2 requesting retirement.

Thank you for considering my request and I take this opportunity to wish you every blessing for Christmas and the New Year with the assurance that you are carried in the hearts and the prayers of the Diocese of Toowoomba.

Your Brother in Christ

✝ *[signature]*

William M Morris, DD
BISHOP OF TOOWOOMBA

Appendix 18

Correspondence with Papal Nuncio 2010 -2011

BISHOP'S HOUSE

73 Margaret Street
P.O. Box 756
Toowoomba Qld. 4350
Australia
Tel. (07) 4632 4277
Fax. (07) 4639 2251

21 July 2010

Most Rev Guiseppe Lazzarotto, DD
Apostolic Nuncio, Apostolic Nunciature
PO Box 3633
MANUKA ACT 2603

Your Excellency

By now you would be aware of the child sexual abuse cases we are dealing with here
in the Diocese. A teacher in one of our schools sexually abused thirteen, 10 year old
girls. We first became aware of this abuse in late 2008 when he was arrested at the
school.

Since then the Principal was charged for not reporting this to the police and
subsequently through the courts was found not guilty, on a technicality of this charge,
even though he admitted to being aware of possible sexual abuse by this teacher.

Through our own internal investigations we found that the Principal and two
Executive Officers failed in their duty of care and were subsequently dismissed in
December 2009.

Five of the thirteen children who were abused have brought claims against the
Diocese, the other eight are still to do so. As you can appreciate, my first and highest
priority is to look after the children and their families affected by the former teacher's
actions. Recognizing that the process to settle these claims can be both stressful and
worrying for the claimants and their families, it is my hope that these matters can be
resolved as considerately and expeditiously for them as soon as possible. To do this I
have acquired the services of a former Justice of the High Court of Australia, the
Hon. Ian Callinan, AC to mediate the civil claims by the victims.

The families of the children who have not yet pursued formal claims will also be
invited to participate in the proposed mediation process.

As you can appreciate the most important people here are the victims and their
families, and I am doing everything in my power to respect their dignity, and needs,
by putting in the processes that I have described. I have no control over the length of
time these negotiations will take, especially if they go to court. My hope would be
that they would be completed before May 2011 and if not, within a short time
afterwards.

In writing this letter I am asking for your assistance concerning my retirement. The proposed dated for the announcement is in May next year but now may need to be delayed to deal with this matter.

I have spoken with Archbishop Philip Wilson and he agrees with me that it would be distressing for the victims and their families if I retired while ministering to them, as they deal with this very tragic event in the lives of their children.

It would be my proposal to keep you informed of these negotiations so that together we could choose the most appropriate time for the announcement of my retirement once these matters have been dealt with.

I look forward to your guidance in this matter.

Wishing you every blessing

Your Brother in Christ

William M Morris, DD
BISHOP OF TOOWOOMBA

APOSTOLIC NUNCIATURE
AUSTRALIA

PO Box 3633
Manuka A C T 2603

21 February 2011

Prot. N° 1282/11

His Lordship
The Most Rev. William M. Morris
Bishop of Toowoomba
73 Margaret Street
PO Box 756
Toowoomba QLD 4350

My Lord,

   I am instructed to convey to you the reply to the letter that you have recently addressed to the Holy Father through the Secretariat of State. After attentively considering what you have outlined in your correspondence to him, Pope Benedict XVI has confirmed his previous decision and asks you to submit, as from now, your resignation as Bishop of Toowoomba which, as already indicated, will be made public on 2 May 2011.

   I understand that this is a painful step for you to take particularly in the present circumstances of the Diocese. However, I am sure that you will accept this definitive decision of the Holy Father in a spirit of ecclesial communion with the Supreme Pastor of the Universal Church. For the governance of the Diocese, and until otherwise provided, an Apostolic Administrator will be appointed. I have no doubt that you will do your best to facilitate, in any possible way, the transition of duties and responsibilities. In due time, I will inform you of what will be decided in this regard. I have also been asked to inform you that your resignation does not affect your present position as Chairman of the National Committee for Professional Standards and that, even after relinquishing the governance of the Diocese, you may retain your responsibilities in the said office.

   Assuring you that this Apostolic Nunciature will offer any assistance you may require and with every good wish, I am

Sincerely yours in Christ,

Archbishop Giuseppe Lazzarotto
Apostolic Nuncio

BISHOP'S HOUSE

73 Margaret Street
P.O. Box 756
TOOWOOMBA Qld. 4350
Australia
Tel. (07) 4632 4277
Fax. (07) 4639 2251
Email. bishsec@twb.catholic.org.au

15 March 2011

PRIVATE AND CONFIDENTIAL
Most Rev Guiseppe Lazzarotto, DD
Apostolic Nuncio, Apostolic Nunciature
PO Box 3633
MANUKA ACT 2603

Your Excellency

I have never wavered in my conviction that for me to resign is a matter of conscience and my resignation would mean that I accept the assessment of myself as breaking *communio*. This accords with my letters to the Holy Father dated 24 December 2008, 19 June 2009 and 12 November 2009. The Holy Father in a letter to me dated 22 December 2009 pointed out that '*Canon Law does not make provision for a process regarding bishops, whom the Successor of Peter nominates and may remove from office*'.

Archbishop Philip Wilson, President of the Australian Catholic Bishops Conference met with the Holy Father in January 2010 affirming my position and putting forward the proposal that I was prepared to negotiate an early retirement. My proposal was that I would retire at seventy but this was found to be unacceptable. The other possibility was to retire in eighteen months depending on whether or not the sexual abuse cases I was dealing with here in the Diocese were finalised. This was accepted and ratified in a letter to me dated 6 February 2010.

It became evident that more time would be needed to finalise these cases and to pastorally care for the victims and their families. I wrote to you on 21 July 2010 requesting further time and you responded to me in the negative at the November ACBC Meeting. I wrote to the Holy Father on 8 December 2010 with the same request which in your letter of 21 February 2011 has also been denied.

As my request to postpone my early retirement for these pastoral reasons has been denied and to resign is a deeply held matter of conscience for me, I accept that on 2 May 2011 my proposal presented to the Holy Father and accepted by him for an early retirement will be announced.

With every blessing

Yours in Christ

William M Morris, DD
BISHOP OF TOOWOOMBA

PERSONAL AND CONFIDENTIAL

APOSTOLIC NUNCIATURE
AUSTRALIA

PO Box 3633
Manuka A C T 2603

18 April 2011

Prot. N° 1914/11

His Lordship
The Most Rev. William M. Morris
Bishop of Toowoomba
73 Margaret Street
PO Box 756
Toowoomba QLD 4350

My Lord,

I am writing to confirm that on Monday 2 May, 2011 your resignation as Bishop of Toowoomba will be made public at 8:00 p.m. EST. At the same time it will also be announced that Most Rev. Brian Finnigan, Auxiliary Bishop of Brisbane, has been appointed as Apostolic Administrator *ad nutum Sanctae Sedis* of the diocese of Toowoomba. You may consider contacting Bishop Finnigan in order to work out with him a suitable way for the transfer of governance.

While assuring you of my prayers at this moment in your life, I wish you a very happy Easter celebration and I am,

Sincerely yours in Christ,

Archbishop Giuseppe Lazzarotto
Apostolic Nuncio

21 April 2011

PRIVATE AND CONFIDENTIAL
Most Rev Guiseppe Lazzarotto, DD
Apostolic Nuncio, Apostolic Nunciature
PO Box 3633
MANUKA ACT 2603

Your Excellency

Thank you for informing me that Bishop Brian Finnigan has been appointed as the Apostolic Administrator of the diocese of Toowoomba on the announcement of my retirement on Monday 2 May 2011. As I indicated to you in my letter of 15 March 2011 I have never wavered in my conviction that for me to resign is a matter of conscience and my resignation would mean that I accept the assessment of myself as breaking *communio*. I absolutely refute and reject this assessment and it is out of my love for the Church that I cannot do so.

As you are aware Archbishop Philip Wilson affirmed this position to the Holy Father and that I was prepared to negotiate an early retirement as a way through this moral dilemma. The Holy Father agreed to this. Your letter stating that my resignation will be announced is but further troubling evidence of a lack of care for the truth which has characterised this whole process to which I have been subjected. As I mentioned to Pope Benedict it cannot be 'of God' when the truth is not respected and exactness is not preserved.

At the appropriate time I will be informing the Priests and people of the Diocese of Toowoomba and the Bishops of Australia that I have not resigned, that I have never written a letter of resignation, but have negotiated early retirement.

I thank you for your prayers and I too wish you a very happy Easter.

Sincerely yours in Christ

William M Morris, DD
BISHOP OF TOOWOOMBA

APOSTOLIC NUNCIATURE
AUSTRALIA

PO Box 3633
Manuka A C T 2603

27 April 2011

Prot. N° 1914/11

His Lordship
The Most Rev. William M. Morris
Bishop of Toowoomba
73 Margaret Street
PO Box 756
Toowoomba, QLD 4350

My Lord,

Thank you very much for your letter of 21 April last. I would like to assure you that I have attentively read what you have shared with me concerning your early retirement and I understand perfectly that the step that you are taking is not an easy one, neither for you nor for the diocese that you have served all these years.

As customary here in Australia, the Communications Office of the Episcopal Conference will circulate a short press release to be made public on Monday 2 May 2011 at 8:00 pm EST. In it there will be no reference to a "resignation" on your behalf; but it will read that "the Holy Father has released you from the governance of the diocese of Toowoomba" and that Bishop Brian Finnegan has been appointed Apostolic Administrator of the same diocese. It would be appreciated if no public announcement be made prior to the date and the time indicated above.

I renew my cordial best wishes and I remain,

Sincerely yours in Christ,

Archbishop Giuseppe Lazzarotto
Apostolic Nuncio

Email dated 29 April 2011

Josephine Rice

To:	nuntius@cyberone com.au
Subject:	Message from Bishop Morris

Your Excellency

I received your letter this morning outlining the wording of the Press Release to be made public on Monday 2 May at 8pm EST.

The Statement: "the Holy Father has released you from the governance of the diocese of Toowoomba" can only be of the Truth if it contains the words ...."the Holy Father has accepted the **retirement** of Bishop William Morris and has released him from the governance of the diocese of Toowoomba".

That statement would respect in part the truth of the negotiations.

With every blessing

Yours in Christ

William M Morris, DD

William M Morris, DD
Bishop of Toowoomba
PO Box 756
TOOWOOMBA QLD 4350
Phone: 07 4632 4277
Fax: 07 4639 2251
bishsec@twb.catholic.org.au

1

APOSTOLIC NUNCIATURE
AUSTRALIA

PO Box 3633
Manuka A C T 2603

DIOCESE OF TOOWOOMBA

+++

Under Embargo until 2 May 2011
12:00 Noon local time in Rome - 8:00 p.m. AEST

———————————

His Holiness Pope Benedict XVI
has accepted the retirement of **Most Rev. William M. Morris**
and has released him from the governance of the Diocese of
Toowomba.

The Holy Father has appointed Apostolic Administrator of the
Diocese of Toowoomba *ad nutum Sanctae Sedis*
Most Rev. Brian V. Finnigan, Titular Bishop of Rapido and
currently Auxiliary Bishop of Brisbane.

Canberra, 2 May 2011

Appendix 19

Hon WJ Carter QC
Memorandum to Toowoomba Diocesan
Leadership Group

The forced retirement of Bishop William Morris as the Ordinary of the Diocese of Toowoomba on 2nd May 2011 and its antecedent processes raise serious questions for the Church and generally.

In his final appeal to Pope Benedict XVI on 24th December 2008, after the three Cardinal Prefects of the Congregation for Bishops, Divine Worship and Doctrine of the Faith had repeatedly required his resignation as Bishop of Toowoomba Diocese, he wrote to the Holy Father:

'. . .the processes leading to this have serious shortcomings and are based on actual errors of fact and misinformation.'

and

'Throughout this sad matter I believe I have been denied natural justice.'

In support of the latter the Bishop briefly summarised some of his relevant concerns:

> 'I have not seen the report prepared by the Apostolic Visitor; the Apostolic Visitor did not discuss his findings with me; I have not been shown any of the "evidence" that was gathered or even the list of the 'accusers'. When I made the request to have an audience with you I was told that this was not an option available to me until I had resigned.'

The factual bases for these concerns and others require further analysis.

However, before attempting that, it is necessary to deal firstly with the 'natural justice' issue and its relevance to the facts of this case. It needs to be said at the outset, that despite the depth of the Bishop's concern, it is idle to suggest that the issue now has any justicable potential or that specific relief might be sought by means of any canonical or civil process.

Although robustly rejecting the Cardinal Prefects' persistent requests for his resignation, which requests the Bishop rejected with equal persistence because—'I cannot in conscience before God, resign'—he finally assured Pope Benedict that 'I . . . undertake to conform and abide by whatever is your determination . . .'

That determination, clearly influenced by the Cardinal Prefects' intervention was an unfavourable one but was 'prayerfully' accepted by Bishop Morris. Notwithstanding, he remains firm in his belief that the process which led to his 'resignation' as the Bishop of Toowoomba was procedurally unfair and breached the principles of natural justice.

Natural Justice, a product of the Natural law, imposes the need for, and recognises a general duty of fairness. This will be more compelling in the case of any decision making process which may adversely affect the rights and interests of the person, the subject of the decision. And similarly when that person has a legitimate expectation that he/she will be treated fairly by those with the apparent capacity to make decisions concerning him/her which affect adversely his/her rights or interests.

One example will suffice. If evidentiary material, relevant to the decision is not only false but not disclosed to the person who is prejudicially affected by it there is, prima face, unfairness.

The Administrative Law in this country is replete with cases involving the use of undisclosed reports by decision makers. But if a decision maker received a prejudicial report or other evidentiary material concerning another ex parte, and which is not disclosed to the person affected, this is a compelling case for judicial intervention. It represents the high water mark of unfairness.

The principles of natural justice and fairness lie at the heart of the maxim: 'Not only must justice be done, it must manifestly be seen to be done.'

Nor should this principle in its application be restricted only to the Civil Law. In that other branch of human, as distinct from Divine Law, namely, the Canon Law, the requirement for fairness and equity should apply a fortiori, certainly, with equal force. Canons 220 and 221 of the Code recognise this:

> Canon 220—'No one may unlawfully harm the good reputation which a person enjoys or violate the right of every good person to protect his or her privacy.'
> and
> Canon 221—'Christ's faithful may lawfully vindicate and defend the rights they enjoy in the Church before the competent ecclesiastical forum in accordance with the law.'

It would be a contradiction in terms for anyone to suggest that the fundamental principles of fairness and equity and natural justice have no place in the Canon Law. It is noted that in *Gaudium Et Spes* (N 79) Natural Law is identified as 'that permanent and universal binding force with all embracing principles'.

Natural Law and legal concepts of fairness and justice therefore possess a moral content. Here morality and legality coincide.

Given the nature and extent of the allegations made against Bishop Morris by the Cardinal Prefects and relied upon by them to require his resignation, it is not open to doubt that he was, as a matter of legal and canonical principle, entitled to and legitimately expected that he would be treated fairly and with equity and in accordance with the principles of natural justice.

THE RELEVANT FACTS

Events Prior to 3rd October 2007

The first relevant document to be noted is a letter dated 21st December 2006 to the Bishop from Cardinal Arinze, the Cardinal Prefect for Divine Worship. By way of background, one knows that in the Australian Church, the practice of general or communal absolution had become controversial for some years prior to December 2006. An apparent relaxation of the canonical requirements in respect of communal absolution in Australia had come to the notice of Church authorities in Rome and appropriate intervention resulted in the rite of reconciliation being henceforth celebrated 'according to the Canonical Liturgical Norms of the Church's tradition'.

In 2004, at a time when the issue was a live one, Bishop Morris, on the occasion of a visit to Rome, was invited to a meeting with Cardinal Arinze to discuss the use of the communal rite in his Diocese. One notes that Toowoomba is a 'very sparsely settled and diverse Diocese' extending west from the dividing range to the Northern Territory/ South Australian border. Its area is 487,000 square kms. It has a Catholic population of 66,000—about 30% of the total population. On the relatively rare occasions when a Priest had travelled long distances and had access to a sizeable congregation, the communal rite had been celebrated, but otherwise the canonical and liturgical norms were followed. Bishop Morris went to the meeting with Cardinal Arinze unconcerned expecting a meeting 'between Brothers searching for the truth and reflecting together on the pastoral needs of the people of God'. To his surprise Cardinal Arinze was accompanied by an Archbishop and two Monsignors—apparently Canon Lawyers. He felt compromised by the tone of the meeting which at times was exceedingly robust. He later wrote to Cardinal Arinze (17th January 2007) in response to the letter dated 21st December 2006, with reference to the 2004 meeting, that 'I will never place myself in that situation again' and would attend any further meeting only if accompanied by 'a Brother Bishop and possibly a Canon Lawyer'.

Cardinal Arinze's Letter dated 21st December 2006

Bishop Morris, upon receipt of this letter was not unduly concerned although it asserted that:

> 'The Holy Father has instructed the three Cardinal Prefects of the Congregation for the Doctrine of the Faith for Bishops and the discipline of the Sacraments, to hold a discussion with you on the practice of general absolution in the Diocese of Toowoomba.'

His lack of concern is apparent in his reply dated 22nd December 2006. While commenting that he found the cardinal's letter 'a little strange' because he had 'not given permission for the celebration of the communal rite with general absolution' since his prior meeting with the cardinal in 2004, he emphasised that the Priests of the Diocese were encouraged to act in accordance with the canonical and liturgical norms and that the Diocese had employed a Religious Priest to travel the Diocese to give people a chance of a visiting confessor in more isolated communities and to provide 'ongoing education' concerning the sacraments.

He concluded with advice that the Australian Episcopal Conference was in the course of drawing guidelines for the use of the communal rite with general absolution for Australian conditions. Accordingly the need for a meeting with the three Cardinals in Rome on the same subject matter at short notice was therefore not readily apparent to Bishop Morris.

The cardinal's letter suggested two possible dates—Tuesday 13th February 2007 or Friday 23rd February 2007 at 10am in the office of the Congregation for Bishops—about six weeks hence from his receipt of the letter. Nor was the need for such urgency for such a meeting readily apparent to him. In his prompt reply to the Cardinal's letter Bishop Morris advised his unavailability for the February dates 'because of pastoral commitments, the provincial meeting of the Queensland Bishops as well as the Australian Episcopal Conference'. He advised that he had to be in Rome in the week commencing 21st May 2007 and requested that the meeting take place at that time.

I have referred to this initiating correspondence and the surrounding circumstances in some detail because of what follows.

On 4th January 2007 Cardinal Arinze advised in peremptory terms that the proposed meeting 'is important enough to take precedence over the other possible schedules you mentioned'. His letter concluded:

'You are therefore requested to choose one of the two dates in February and communicate to us . . .'

and

'If you wish to bring a Brother Bishop it is all right. (sic). But if you insist on bringing in a Canon Lawyer we can accept. (sic)."

Bishop Morris now had good reason to be concerned as within a matter of days (21st December 2006 – 4th January 2007) the mind and intention of Cardinal Arinze and his Cardinal colleagues had shifted from the apparent need to hold a discussion with the Bishop concerning the practice of general absolution in his Diocese to one which implicitly rejected his informative response, asserting that the proposed meeting at short notice 'is important enough to take precedence over other possible schedules . . .'

In his response dated 17th January Bishop Morris, perhaps unwisely, stood firm. Over and above the matters referred to earlier his 'pastoral responsibilities' then also included his care and support for a terminally ill young Diocesan Priest as well as significant issues arising in the national committee for professional standards of which Bishop Morris was co-chair.

The Bishop again sought a May meeting and added that at that time he would have 'the support of a Brother Bishop'. Wisely he sought 'an agenda' for the meeting with the questions that are going to be addressed.

One can only question the integrity of the earlier stated proposal for "a discussion "concerning general absolution. Later correspondence and meetings with the Cardinals disclose that a discussion on this issue was never a priority. It was later mentioned, if at all, only in passing.

The Bishop received no reply to his letter of 17th January 2007. Two months later, Cardinal Re, Prefect of the Congregation of Bishops, by letter dated 16th march 2007 advised Bishop Morris that Pope Benedict after consultation with 'the three Cardinal Prefects' had decided to send an Apostolic Visitor 'to the Diocese', namely Archbishop Charles Chaput of Denver, USA, and that he would arrive in Toowoomba on 23rd April 2007.

The stated 'reason for the visit' in Cardinal Re's letter makes no mention of the prior concern about the practice of general absolution in the Toowoomba Diocese. This was the matter said by Cardinal Arinze to be 'important enough' to require Bishop Morris to attend a meeting in Rome at short notice and as such to 'take precedence' over the Bishop's then heavy demanding and time consuming pastoral commitments. This was the matter which the Bishop was expecting he would discuss with the three Cardinals in the course of his May visit to Rome. His request for an agenda of the matters to be discussed received no reply. It was Cardinal Re's letter of 16th March 2007 however which revealed at last the real issue. The 'reason' for the apostolic visit by Archbishop Chaput was:

> 'That the doctrinal and disciplinary line you are following seems not in accordance with the Magisterium of the Church.'

One could hardly imagine a more serious allegation that could be made against a Diocesan Bishop. It was later to be repeated and broadened with added vigour.

By way of an addendum Cardinal Re added:

> 'An expression of this is also found in some phrases of your Advent Pastoral Letter 2006.'

Yet Bishop Morris' Advent Pastoral letter had been issued to the Diocese on 17th November 2006—several weeks prior to Cardinal Arinze's original letter of 21st December when the alleged concern was the communal rite. The events and correspondence in the period dealt with above, 2nd December 2006 – 17th March 2007, provided the relevant background to what follows.

The present enquiry has only to focus on Bishop Morris' concern that he suffered a denial of natural justice and unfairness in the course of the administrative processes adopted by Church authorities in Rome in requiring his resignation as the Bishop of Toowoomba. Whilst the above catalogue of events prior to the Apostolic Visit are not in any way decisive of the issue, they do provide a useful backdrop in any attempt to validly assess the character of later events.

The Apostolic Visit

The Visitor spend the night of Monday 23rd April 2007 with Archbishop Bathersby in Brisbane and arrived in Toowoomba on Tuesday 24th April 2007. He met informally with Bishop Morris and then with the Council of Priests, various Diocesan bodies, officials, Priests, Directors of Church agencies and the people of the Diocese. Prior to his arrival had had named various people, clergy, officials and groups with whom he wished to meet. Others were nominated by the Bishop. Accordingly, the Apostolic Visitor was provided with a cross section of people and clergy of the Diocese representing all levels of support and opposition to the Bishop. On Wednesday 25 April and Thursday 26 April, with Bishop Morris, he travelled to parts of the Diocese and met with people and clergy at Miles, St George and Dalby. On Friday 27 April and Saturday 28 April interviews were resumed in Toowoomba. He departed Toowoomba for Brisbane at midday on Saturday 28 April 2007.

Bishop Morris' expectation was that the Visitor's report would be prepared for the Congregation of Bishops in time for his proposed visit to Rome in May 2007. Immediately after the Apostolic Visitor's departure, unknown to the Bishop, the majority of Diocesan Clergy (except three), Pastoral Leaders in the Diocese, members of the Diocesan Pastoral Council and others signed letters of support for the Bishop which were forwarded to the Congregation of Bishops. Receipt of these letters has never been acknowledged.

Bishop Morris had for many years been aware of a small group of Priests and people in his Diocese who reflect a particular view of Church life and in his 'Statement of Position' dated 14 March 2008 written shortly after his meeting in Rome with the three Cardinal Prefects on 19 January 2008 he said with reference to the former:

'They see me as exemplifying all that they think is wrong with the "post Vatican II". The *Lepanto Journal*, which I am aware has been sent to the Congregation of Bishops, has little credibility and its promoters are obsessed with finding instances of lack of orthodoxy. Their reports are exaggerated and lack context. *I have not had the opportunity to deal with any specific complaints they have made.*' (My emphasis)

When the Visitor first met with the Bishop of Toowoomba he expressed a measure of surprise that the Visitor was being asked to investigate the Bishop because as far as he could see, from the material provided to him, things 'that I had reportedly said and done were happening in other places as well.'

In a later conversation with Archbishop Bathersby, the Visitor also questioned the need for him to investigate Bishop Morris. Again when being driven to Brisbane by Father Brian Sparksman (Diocesan Chancellor and Canon Lawyer) at the conclusion of his visit, the Apostolic Visitor remarked that he would be astounded if the Diocese was to lose its Bishop. Not only was Bishop Morris, at all material times, totally ignorant of the material in the Visitor's possession when he arrived in Toowoomba, nor was he told anything to identify his accusers or the real reason for the visit, nor was he given a copy of the Visitor's report or any information concerning its contents. As of now he still has never seen it.

Accordingly, it is of considerable importance to hypothesise that the Apostolic Visitor's report concerning the Bishop and his leadership of the Diocese may have been unfavourable. Equally, it may have been favourable or even neutral. I will return to this point below when dealing with the unsigned document dated 28 July 2007, which emanated from the Congregation for Bishops led by Cardinal Re and which is a document of prime importance in any assessment of the relevant processes.

After the Visitor's departure Bishop Morris anticipating his planned May visit to Rome expected that he would be advised by Cardinals Arinze or Re concerning the time and location of the meeting with them which had been proposed earlier. However, he heard nothing before he left Toowoomba and when in Rome completed his business there and returned to his Diocese at the end of May without having met any of the relevant Cardinals; nor had he been invited to any such meeting.

The Unsigned Document dated 28 June 2007/The Congregation for Bishops

On or about 17 September 2007 while attending a conference of Australian Bishops, he was handed an unsigned document by the Apostolic Nuncio, Archbishop de Paoli. The authorship of this document has never been identified nor has any relationship between its contents and any report of the Apostolic Visitor been revealed. The document carried the heading: 'Congregatio pro Episcopis' (the Congregation for Bishops)

In summary this four page document is a scathing presentation of Bishop Morris' alleged failings and failures on account of which he was considered by the author of the document to be unfit to continue as the Bishop of Toowoomba. It contains these allegations:-

1. 'The local Church in Toowoomba is moving in a different direction than that of the Catholic Church';
2. The Diocese 'is going through a severe crisis that spreads its roots back over the last ten years';
3. The Bishop had failed 'to guide the faithful in fidelity to the doctrine and discipline of the Church: to work hard to promote priestly vocations; and to offer solid theological, spiritual and human formation to his Priests';
4. He had condoned 'liturgical abuses';
5. He continues to condone 'an unacceptable extension of the conditions required for "grave necessity" and that accordingly general absolution is still common';
6. Despite 'admonitions' the Bishop 'adamantly resists fulfilling his responsibility to apply Church norms properly';
7. 'The general theological climate of the Diocese and especially its Priests' fails 'to move towards an authentic Catholic identity';
8. That 'in the past seven years there has been no priestly ordinations';
9. The failure of the Diocese 'to have an effective and sufficiently dynamic program for promoting vocations or finding Priests from elsewhere';

10. The Bishop fails 'to offer the leadership necessary to reverse' the above situation;
11. Priests are being marginalised and retiring early because of their substitution by deacons or laity;
12. 'Bishop Morris' theological preparation and type of leadership are inadequate to confront the crisis of the Church of Toowoomba';
13. And accordingly, 'Toowoomba needs a Bishop who, with determination and courage, will tackle the problems and rectify what is not in conformity with the doctrine and discipline of the Catholic Church'.

n December 2006/January 2007, according to Cardinal Arinze, there was the need for a discussion on the practice of general absolution in the Diocese. By 28 June 2007 the concerns of the Congregation for Bishops had widened remarkably. As pointed out the authorship of these serious allegations is obscure. The chronology suggests that they were reproduced in the unsigned document. Whether they were or not required some analysis.

If what the Visitor had said to Bishop Morris, Archbishop Bathersby and Father Sparksman in late April 2007 truly reflected his state of mind both before and at the conclusion of his short visit and the same was contained in his report to the Congregations in Rome, then it is inconceivable that in a report dated 28 June 2007 he could catalogue such a list of damaging allegations against Bishop Morris. Further, the nature and extent of certain of the more scandalous allegations:

- That over the last ten years Toowoomba Diocese had gone through 'a severe crisis' of faith;
- That the 'general theological climate of the Diocese' had failed to reflect an authentic Catholic identity;
- That the Bishop had failed to promote vocations and to offer 'solid theological spiritual and human formation to his Priests';

Could only be validly asserted after a lengthy and detailed assessment of all aspects of Catholic life in this large far flung Diocese and more particularly after the collection and assessment of a large body of cogent factual evidence to support such generalities. These general assertions in the 28 June 2007 document are just some of the alleged findings relied upon by some unknown and unidentified decision make that 'Toowoomba needs a Bishop who with determination and courage will tackle (these) problems', and 'rectify what is not in conformity with the doctrine and discipline of the Catholic Church'. And finally it is because of these very damaging and sweeping failures that 'Bishop Morris' theological preparation and type of leadership are inadequate to confront the crisis of the Church in Toowoomba'. Not only does the document display an appalling lack of evidence and particularity, it certainly contains demonstrable errors of fact. It is stated that there have been 'no priestly ordinations' in the Diocese for seven years. In fact there have been four new Priests ordained in the previous eight years. It also states that Priests had been "marginalised" and 'deacons and laity' substituted. In fact the Toowoomba Diocese has never engaged any deacons to serve in this Diocese.

These simple factual errors are typical of a substandard fact finding process, if one was ever undertaken. Rather they reflect a process of decision making by high ranking Church officials, more likely based on gossip and hearsay.

The relevant circumstantial evidence tends to suggest that, consistent with what he had said to others, the Apostolic Visitor and his report were not the basis for the 28 June 2007 document. That would mean that it was authored by someone else whose identity is and remains unknown as is the evidence upon which these damaging finding were made. The same unidentified person also concluded that the Bishop had to be removed from leadership of the Toowoomba Diocese.

When Bishop Morris first saw and read the document in September 2007, it is clear from the text that decisions as to his future had already been made. More importantly it is strongly arguable that the decision of the Congregation of Bishops or of its Prefect had been made without evidence or on the basis of evidence which was factually untrue; he the Bishop was denied knowledge of the authorship of this document; he was not made aware of any of the evidence made to support what can only be regarded as seriously damaging affects upon his reputation as a Bishop of the Church. Nor had he been asked to respond to, comment upon or explain the core of these allegations.

In short he has been denied the right to be heard; he has been treated unfairly. He had not been provided with any evidence to support the case against him nor was he given any opportunity to respond to and correct known errors of fact and generalised assertions.

One could not imagine a more striking case of a denial of natural justice inherent in the preparation and publication of the unsigned document.

This conclusion is somewhat aggravated by the fact that much later on 12th November 2009 when the Bishop complained to Pope Benedict about 'defects in process' and 'a lack of care for the truth', the Pope himself in his response dated 22nd December 2009 dismissed these complaints as 'a misunderstanding'.[1]

The above analysis has so far proceeded on the basis that the document of 26th June 2007 was not based on the report of the Apostolic Visitor.

If on the contrary it was, the same conclusion is ever more compelling.

Immediately the visit was concluded, all the Priests of the Diocese (except three), the Diocesan Pastoral Council and other Church agencies wrote letters to Rome strongly supporting the leadership of Bishop Morris in his many years as the Ordinary of the Diocese. Bishop Morris was then unaware of all this. Therefore by the time the 28th June 2007 document was written the Congregation of Bishops not only would have had an 'unfavourable' report of the Apostolic Visitor but strongly favourable reports from respected clergy and lay pastoral leadership in the Diocese. The fact that the receipt of the latter was not even acknowledged suggests they were ignored. In any event any unfavourable report by the Visitor after his short visit would have needed to be evaluated in the light of the supportive reports from those representatives of the Catholic Church in the Diocese. In the light of any such competitive assessments, those, those with the capacity for decision making could not avoid a finding of procedural unfairness and denial of natural justice without providing to Bishop Morris particulars of the adverse findings in the report and the evidence upon which the report was based so as to provide the Bishop with the opportunity to be heard and to provide evidence based material to challenge what was alleged against him in such a report.

---

1. C/F Chapter Twenty-One Page 113 – Apology to Galileo: 'a tragic mutual incomprehension' equals 'a misunderstanding' in Vatican speak.

Further, if on his departure from Toowoomba the Visitor proposed to report unfavourably it was his primary duty to inform the Bishop, with particularity, of his findings and the supporting evidence, so as to thereby give the Bishops the opportunity to respond. He was denied that opportunity. Such an unfair process was seriously aggravated by a failure and/or refusal of the Congregation of Bishops and the three Cardinal Prefects to do likewise if it was intended to act on this unfavourable report for the purpose of decision making concerning Bishop Morris' future.

Therefore, irrespective of whether the visitors report was favourable or otherwise the subsequent process engaged upon by Church leaders in Rome was seriously flawed. There can be no doubt that the decision to have Bishop Morris removed from position of leadership of the Toowoomba Diocese was made, at the latest, by the time of the compilation of the unsigned document dated 28th June 2007. Nor in my view can that process be considered to be other than unfair and characterised as a serious denial of natural justice.

Letter from Cardinal Re dated 3rd October 2007

When Bishop Morris received the unsigned document from the Apostolic Nuncio on or about 17th September 2007 its contents both surprised and concerned him. He was about to go on annual leave. He wrote to Cardinal Re on the same day:

> 'My annual leave is due on October and during that time I will take the opportunity to pray and think about my response so that my letter can form a basis for future dialogue.'

Cardinal Re's response to this letter dated 3rd October 2007 is a defining document. It persuasively demonstrates that by that date the relevant decision to oust Bishop Morris had been made—not to be resiled from. Bishop Morris' future had been decided unequivocally at the latest by Cardinal Re by 3rd October 2007. Later correspondence reveals that Cardinal Re had been in close collaboration with his Cardinal colleagues, Arinze and Levada. They who had invited him to Rome to discuss the communal rite of reconciliation in December 2006/January 2007 had by now decided upon his removal as Bishop of Toowoomba perhaps by 28th June 2007 and certainly by 3rd October 2007 and the basis for his decision was the unsigned document which had been given to the Bishop only three weeks before Cardinal Re's letter of 3rd October. He had had no practical opportunity to respond.

In spite of the Bishop's concern about the contents of the unsigned document and the tainted processes surrounding its origins and in spite of the Bishop's courteous response that he proposed to reply to it so that that response 'can form the basis for future dialogue' he was presented in Cardinal Re's letter of 3rd October 2007 with an unequivocal and decisive decision requiring his removal as Bishop of Toowoomba, before any opportunity could arise for the Bishop's response to what were obviously scathing allegations which damaged Bishop Morris' personal and vocational reputation nor had the evidence to support these damaging accusations been identified.

In the 3rd October 2007 letter Cardinal Re wrote to the Bishop:

> 'I trust that during these days (whilst the Bishop was on leave) the Lord will enlighten you and so give you courage in order to take this step which I know will be for you painful, but also essential. I ask you, first and foremost, to consider the good of the Diocese of Toowoomba which should have a solid Bishop who is in accord with the Pope and the universal Church.
>
> In the name of the Holy Father I ask (you) to submit your resignation…
>
> I expect to receive your letter of resignation by the end of this October for the good of the local Church in Toowoomba.'

Bishop Morris' future had already been determined. He had never been offered nor given the opportunity to respond to this catalogue of alleged failures set out in the unsigned document.

In the light of what had occurred between the Bishop and the Cardinals prior to 3rd October 2007 and the circumstances relating to the unsigned memorandum which he had received only shortly prior to that date. Bishop Morris' response was entirely predictable. He wrote on 6th November 2007:

'I would like to present a detailed reply to the comments in the memorandum but I find this difficult in view of the general nature of some of them. For example, I am not sure how one assesses "the general theological climate of the Diocese' or what would be a 'sufficiently dynamic pastoral program for promoting vocations'. Nor do I believe that general absolution 'is still common'.

The memorandum, I must assume, has been drafted in the light of information which the congregation has to hand. I am not aware of that information, nor have I had any opportunity to respond to it. I would welcome receiving more specific details of the material that has formed the basis for the conclusions which are set out in the memorandum.

I respectfully suggest that my detailed reply to that material which I will undertake to deliver within 14 days of its receipt should form the basis for a discussion face to face.

By letter dated 30th November 2007 Cardinal Re wrote in reply that it was only after 'prayerful reflection' that he (Cardinal Re) accepted Bishop Morris' request to meet with him in January 2008. He advised that Cardinals Arinze and Levada 'will be with me'. His letter continued:

> 'The Holy Father however will receive you only after the publication of your resignation.'

And finally:-

> 'Regarding your request for more detailed information that was used in drawing up the memorandum, I would invite you to re-read your own 2006 Advent Pastoral Letter. It is a Pastoral Letter (that is, a document written by you as Bishop of Toowoomba) which presents a vision and a pastoral approach that does not conform with the doctrine and discipline of the Church.'

This letter confirms two things: firstly, that the Bishop's resignation was insisted upon; indeed it was a condition president for a papal audience; and secondly, the Bishop's request to respond to the allegations in a meeting with Cardinal Re was accepted but only as a matter of grace and again only after 'prayerfully reflection'. Yet Bishop Morris had not so far had the opportunity to respond nor had he been provided with any evidentiary material; only an oblique reference to his Advent Pastoral Letter.

The Advent Pastoral Letter dated 17th November 2006

Cardinal Re's letter dated 30th November 2007 can only be interpreted to mean that the Bishop's Advent Pastoral Letter dated 17th November 2006 provided the substance of the basis for the several damaging allegations catalogued above and referred to in the unsigned memorandum. In his 30th November 2007 letter to the Bishop he advised that he (Cardinal Re) and the other Cardinals would meet Bishop Morris in Rome on 19th January 2008 at 9am and that Archbishop Wilson, the President of the Australian Catholic Bishops Conference would also attend. It needs to be emphasized that when the Bishop replied on 22nd December 2006 to Cardinal Arinze's original letter of 21st December 2006 requiring an urgent meeting on the practice of general absolution, the Bishop had replied, without qualification:

> '... since my meeting with yourself Cardinal Arinze (in 2004), I have not given permission for the celebration of the communal rite with general absolution.'

Yet in the unsigned document its author claimed that 'general absolution is still common' and further 'there is a tendency to abandon or to reduce individual confession with consequential serious harm to the spiritual life of the faithful . . .' And yet in his letter six months earlier the Bishop had told Cardinal Arinze:

> 'I have encouraged the Priests of the Diocese to make sure they always celebrate the right of reconciliation according to the canonical and liturgical norms of the Church's tradition.'

These statements had been ignored or gratuitously rejected. Only in his letter of 30th November 2007 did Cardinal Re accept 'that general absolution is no longer a common practice in Toowoomba' yet it had been positively and wrongly asserted as a fact in the unsigned memorandum months before.

One then turns to the Bishop's Advent Pastoral Letter of November 2006. The Bishop first learnt of Rome's concerns when he read the unsigned document on or about 17th September 2007. That document had alleged:

> 'The local Church in Toowoomba is moving in a different direction from that of the Catholic Church. One expression of this is seen in Bishop Morris' 2006 Advent Pastoral Letter . . .'

and

> 'An attentive reading of this Pastoral Letter reveals a flawed ecclesiology resembling that of a Protestant Church.'

One can only question whether the author of these declarations had read the Pastoral Letter 'attentively', or indeed, at all.

> The main thrust of the Pastoral Letter is obvious. It's focus is the Diocesan Pastoral Leadership Plan with its associated Staffing Plan and Appointments Policy for Priests and Pastoral Leaders which was a transitional measure adopted by the Diocese for the nine years commencing Easter 2005 to Easter 2014. Against that background the Bishop identified 'the immediate task' and 'the long term task'. He then wrote:-
> 'The immediate task before us is to develop the procedure for making appointments of Priests in the Diocese in the lights of the discussion, discernment and appointment decisions made in these last twelve months. The new Ministry Appointments Policy and Procedures for Priests and Pastoral Leader addresses these tasks'.

He then went on to refer to the long term task as follows:-

> 'The long term task that remains as yet unaddressed is the development of a Priests Staffing Plan for Easter 2014, once again within the wider context of a vision for Diocesan Pastoral Leadership.'

Having detailed the number and age of the Priests who will be engaged in Parish based and Diocesan based Ministry in 2014 the Bishop when on:

> 'We may well be moving towards a Staffing Plan that places two Priests in the larger towns or communities in each of the six regions, one Priest 65 years or younger and the second Priest from the older group (66/70), with the surrounding faith communities served by an increased number of Pastoral Leaders.'

In short in the context of discussing a major and important pastoral issue for the Diocese in 2014 and beyond the Bishop in his letter was proposing a possible future planning initiative whereby two Priests would be placed in the larger towns and communities, with the surrounding faith communities being served by an increased number of lay Pastoral Leaders. He went on to outline this then Advent 2006 plan for the second three year period of the nine year Pastoral Leadership Plan and the consultation which he proposed to undertake so that the responses could be used as a basis for discussion at the 'next Diocesan Presbyteral Forum' to be held during Lent 2007.

It was in this context that the Bishop, as an aside, referred to the 'other options' which had been discussed internationally, nationally and locally including the ordaining of married men, and welcoming former Priests back to active Ministry, ordaining women and recognizing Anglican and other orders. He then continued in his letter immediately:

> 'We remain committed to actively promoting vocations to the current celibate male priesthood and open to inviting Priests from overseas.'

It was only in this broader context when discussing Pastoral Planning in the Diocese that Bishop Morris made reference to 'other options' but then immediately concluded that he and the Diocese were committed to the current celibate male priesthood.

It seems however that it was his brief reference to the matters mentioned in the broader context of developing pastoral leadership for the Diocese and at the same time confirming his commitment to the current celibate male priesthood that led to his removal as the Bishop of Toowoomba. Whilst the Bishop in later documents conceded that his presentation may have been 'clumsy' and 'could have been worded better' he reaffirmed that:

> 'My invitation to the Diocese that we reflect on all of these matters does not mean that we, or I, reject the current teaching of the Church. On the contrary, once I became aware of some level of misconstrued reading of my Letter, I responded through the local media immediately and later through our Diocesan website, to correct this misunderstanding and misinterpretation of my words.'

Again he stated:-

> 'The statement of Cardinal Re at our meeting (19th January 2008) and related comments from Cardinals Arinze and Levada allege that my Advent Letter amounted to a rejection of the teaching of the Catholic Church on the ordination of women and the validity of Anglican orders. May I assert clearly in response that I have never rejected the teaching of the Church on either of these matters.'

Yet in the face of such denials by Bishop Morris during 2008, rather than retract, the Cardinal Prefects persisted in reaffirming their long held view (at least since 28th June 2007) that Bishop Morris was unfit to continue as the Bishop of Toowoomba.

Bishop Morris's first opportunity to respond was not given until his meeting with the Cardinal Prefects on 19th January 2008. By that time Cardinal Re had thrice already (28th June 2007, 3rd October 2007 & 30th November 2007) determined that the Bishop must resign.

Immediately subsequent to the 19th January meeting Bishop Morris on 24th January 2008 reaffirmed in his letter to Cardinal Re 'that I am unable to resign'. In response Cardinal Re again on 13th February 2008 insisted upon the receipt of the Bishop's resignation because 'your type of leadership of the Diocese is seriously defective'.

Canon 401, clause 2 states that 'a Diocesan Bishop who because of illness or some other grave reason has become unsuited for the fulfilment of his office, is earnestly requested to offer his resignation from office'. It can be assumed that the Cardinal Prefects were seeking the Bishop's resignation pursuant to Canon 401 for 'grave reasons'. In terms of Canon 401, Clause 1 'age' and 'grave cause' are said to provide the basis for such a request.

The gravity of the 'reason' or 'cause' connotes the need for some serious canonical disqualifying or disabling reason or cause before such a request can be validly made. But whether validly made or not, bearing in mind his strong factual evidence based response, the canonical process implicit in Canon 401 must be procedurally fair and one which accords with the principles of natural justice.

Appendix 20

Letter from the Australian Bishops Conference to the Toowoomba Diocesan Apostolic Administrator 2011

Dear Bishop Brian

On behalf of the Australian Bishops, I write to you—and through you especially to the priests, religious and faithful of the Diocese of Toowoomba—to express our sadness at the retirement of Bishop Bill Morris. The decision came at the end of a complex process which began thirteen years ago and which ended in deadlock. It was then that the Holy Father found it necessary to exercise his Petrine care for the whole Church. This has been difficult and distressing for all concerned, and it is not surprising that the decision has caused varied and intense reactions.

Much of our time at the recent meeting of the Australian Bishops was given to discussion of what has happened—a discussion which at one point included hearing the concerns of forty leaders of Religious Congregations, many of whom have members working in the Diocese of Toowoomba. We sought to understand the events and agree on the best way to respond.

We reflected on our responsibility as bishops and on what it means for us to serve the communion of the Church and to exercise our ministry collegially as pastors of Christ's flock, as teachers of the apostolic faith and as moderators of the sacred liturgy.

We also reflected upon the unique role of the pope as head of the College of Bishops. It is his task to guard and promote the communion of the Church and the integrity of the Church's faith. We reaffirm our faith in this mission which the Successor of Peter has received from Christ himself, and we gratefully acknowledge Pope Benedict's faithfulness to the Petrine ministry, even when it involves very difficult decisions. We commit ourselves anew to teaching faithfully what Christ taught as the Church has handed it down.

Discussion of the process and the decision which it produced will continue during our *ad limina* visit to Rome later this year. There we will have the opportunity to share with the Holy Father and members of the Roman Curia the fruits of our discussion and to share our questions and concerns with an eye to the future. We will also have the opportunity to pray at the Tombs of the Apostles Peter and Paul, to whose intercession we will entrust our own ministry, the Diocese of Toowoomba and the Church in Australia.

We appreciate that Bishop Morris' human qualities were never in question: nor is there any doubt about the contribution he has made to the life of the Church in Toowoomba and beyond. The pope's decision was not a denial of the personal and pastoral gifts that Bishop Morris has brought to the episcopal ministry. Rather, it was judged that there were problems of doctrine and discipline, and we regret that these could not be resolved. We are hopeful that Bishop Morris will continue to serve the Church in other ways in the years ahead.

Our prayers are very much with you as Apostolic Administrator, with Bishop Morris and with the priests, religious and faithful of the Diocese of Toowoomba at this difficult time. We especially encourage the priests to reassure their people and to strengthen them in faith. The Diocese of Toowoomba has a great history of faith, and that faith has never failed in the face of many hardships. It will surely not fail now as the Diocese looks to the future.

We express our support for you personally as you assume the challenging task of Apostolic Administrator, and we are confident that you will help to bring peace and unity to the Diocese. May the prayers of Mary of the Southern Cross and of St Mary MacKillop guide us all safely on the journey that lies before us.

Yours fraternally in Christ,
Archbishop Philip Wilson – 12 May 2011

The response to Archbishop Philip Wilson from the Toowoomba Diocesan Leadership Group is as follows:

We received the letter from the Bishops' Conference through Bishop Brian Finnigan (dated 12 May 2011) and we wish to respond. These are our concerns.

The Conference did not respond to our motion concerning an independent inquiry into the removal of Bishop Morris (the text of the motion is provided at the end of our letter). It chose not to respond to us and still has not responded. That is what disappoints us.

The Conference letter to Bishop Finnigan does not acknowledge that Bishop Morris' retirement was a forced one. This recognition is important in assessing the whole situation.

> There is no recognition of any injustice meted out to Bishop Morris at all. Why?

Of particular concern to us is the disparity between the alleged doctrinal and disciplinary offences and the penalty imposed. The Conference recognised the tension in the dispute but did not acknowledge any injustice in the way the dispute was handled.

The Conference letter to Bishop Finnigan said that the bishops pondered and reaffirmed their own call and the unique call of the Pope. The Conference affirmed that it was the Pope's Petrine care for the whole Church that led him to ask Bishop Morris to stand down. The Conference then contrasted the Pope's Petrine care with Bishop Morris' abundant human qualities.

The Conference didn't have to resort to acknowledging his human qualities. Theologically, his care for his local Church was on sound theological grounds. Vatican II made it clear that each local Church (diocese) is not just a branch of the universal Church. The Diocesan Bishops are not branch managers. The local Church IS the universal church in this particular place. As the pope does, bishops receive their call from the Risen Christ. As such they are Christ's vicars. Together with and under the Pope (*cum et sub* of the Second Vatican Council) they bring Christ's care to the People of God.

Acknowledging Bishop Morris' personal qualities may have been courteous but hardly relevant to the appropriateness of this removal.

The Conference said that they discussed Bishop Morris' situation with forty Leaders of Religious Congregations. They were silent about what these Leaders said. Why? Surely their views would carry much weight.

The Conference made an effort at appeasement by saying that there will be ongoing discussion of this issue during their *ad limina* visit in October 2011. Those who remember the Oceania Conference (1998) and the subsequent Statement of Conclusions will be forgiven for being a shade down on enthusiasm, excitement and hope about the outcome of the forthcoming *ad limina* visit.

The Conference encouraged the priests to keep leading their people in faith. The Bishop Finnigan Letter acknowledged that our diocese has a "great history of faith…in the face of hardship". However, in the context of the Conference letter, this would suggest that the majority of us, priests and people, disagree with the pastoral leadership of Bishop Morris. That is patently an unfounded assumption.

The Conference said nothing of the injustice of the Apostolic Visitation of Archbishop Chaput in April 2007. How many of you would appreciate having your diocese evaluated in four days? This has not only been unjust but seriously flawed especially when after eighteen years of dedicated service, the results of the investigation have not been made available to Bishop Morris. Then or now.

In conclusion. One sadness of this whole sorry situation is that Bishop Morris was dismissed by a small group of men who knew him only marginally. But the Australian Bishops, most of whom have known him for eighteen years or longer, have no such excuse. Bishop Morris could have expected something better from his own Episcopal colleagues.

The Vatican's removal of Bishop Morris isolated the people of the Toowoomba Diocese. The Conference letter to Bishop Finnigan did nothing to relieve this isolation.

May St Mary MacKillop understand us and pray for us.

We trust this letter will be fully considered and responded to by the Permanent Committee of the Australian Catholic Bishops Conference at the meeting scheduled for 2 August 2011.

Appendix 21

Letter from Hans Küng

Hans Küng email dated 10 May 2011
Dear Bishop William Morris,

I would like to express most warmly my solidarity and support for you in your conflict with the Vatican. My former colleague at Tübingen University Joseph Ratzinger, now Pope Benedict XVI, and myself are the last still fully active 'Periti' of the Second Vatican Council.

This may give me some authority to say: Your removal from you episcopal chair of the Diocese of Toowoomba is a clear betrayal of the Second Vatican Council, which solemnly declared the collegiality of the Pope with the bishops. Your removal has been achieved in the medieval authoritarian way without consulting the Australian bishops, your own clergy, and your own community. The 'visitation' by an ultraconservative US Archbishop is nothing more than the usual Roman inquisition procedure. It violates also the human right to a fair trial.

I have not to give you advice, but I would be happy if you strongly resist against this act that our Lord Jesus Christ would never approve, but seriously condemn. You should also resist in favour of your fellow bishops whom the Vatican tried to intimidate, while facing more and more opposition from ordinary believers and clergy all over the world against his pre-conciliar authoritarian policy.

This way of proceeding of the hierarchy was completely unknown in the first millennium of Christianity, it arose only in the High Middle Ages through the Gregorian Reform of the 11th century. In my recent book *Ist die Kirche noch zu retten? (Can the Church be saved?)* I offer an extensive diagnosis and propose therapies for our church which is really sick and suffering under this Roman system. I hope this book which sold already 50,000 copies in German language will be published very soon by Continuum in London and New York.

As a sign of solidarity I am sending you a German copy by airmail. Maybe you have friends who can read it in German.

Despite everything keep your confidence and your courage.

Sincerely yours,
Professor Hans Küng
University of Tübingen/Germany

Appendix 22

Images from the Eucharist in Celebration of the Ministry of Bishop William Morris, DD Sunday 28 August 2011

31 August 2011

We were more graced and deeply blessed than any of us could have expected, taking part in the Mass of Thanks for Bishop Bill Morris's ministry at St Patrick's Cathedral, Toowoomba, last Sunday.

There was neither bitterness nor recrimination. Rather there was good humour and loving tears quietly shed.

When Bill himself began to speak and to thank, he was momentarily overcome. He then uttered unprepared words, which are so characteristic of him: "I don't get upset like this – when people are so not nice to me!"

Bill has been consistently so throughout this tragedy in which there are no winners.

The reasons, the causes and the motivations for what has occurred may be known only unto God, Who alone may judge.

Consistently and officially it has been stated that neither Bill's own integrity nor his pastoral effectiveness are questioned. The fruits – the proof - of this were palpably evident in Sunday's celebration.

Now, after almost two decades attending episcopal testimonials and funerals, I have never witnessed so simple yet profound an out-pouring of appreciation and love. As one of the other bishops there observed afterwards: The best way to go may be to get sacked!

Bishops have to attend all sorts of civic and religious events – from Deb Balls to Papal Ceremonies. So you develop some sort of sixth sense in assessing the real worth of events.

Never have I been more struck than by the sincerity and depth of Faith at this recent Mass of Thanksgiving. The solid no-nonsense Catholic Faith of the people of the Toowoomba Diocese was un-self-consciously and un-pretentiously on display.

Distributing Communion to a congregation of a 1,500 which took 25 minutes, gave a privileged perspective: entire family groupings; well and warmly dressed people; farmers with strong working hands; some with obvious disabilities. Though there were some faces showing that rich cultural diversity now so striking among Catholic Mass goers, in Toowoomba, faces and names of Irish origins still predominate.

For all of us graced to participate in this Mass of Thanksgiving, it was as powerfully as ever that simultaneous experience of Death and Resurrection, of degradation and glorification, which in the tradition of the Gospel of John are either sides of Christ's Saving Event, which is made present again in every Eucharist.

+James Foley
BISHOP OF CAIRNS

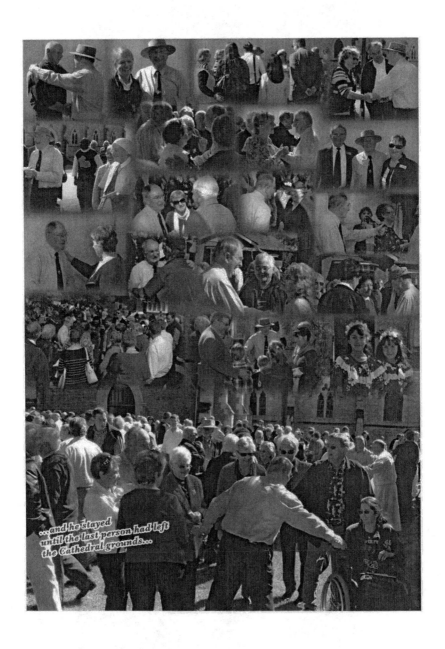

Index

Index of Names

CPSIA information can be obtained at www.ICGtesting.com
Printed in the USA
BVOW03s1915231114

376127BV00002B/7/P